Portraits of Pioneers
in Psychology

Portraits of Pioneers in Psychology

VOLUME VI

Edited by

Donald A. Dewsbury

Ludy T. Benjamin Jr.

Michael Wertheimer

AMERICAN PSYCHOLOGICAL ASSOCIATION
Washington, DC

LAWRENCE ERLBAUM ASSOCIATES, PUBLISHERS
Mahwah, New Jersey   London

Second Printing 2006, October 2006

Published by
American Psychological Association
750 First Street, NE
Washington, DC 20002
http://www.apa.org/

Lawrence Erlbaum Associates, Inc., Publishers
10 Industrial Avenue
Mahwah, NJ 07430

Typeset in Times by World Composition Services, Inc., Sterling, VA

Printer: Edward Brothers, Inc., Ann Arbor, MI
Cover designer: Berg Design, Albany, NY
Project Manager: Debbie Hardin, Carlsbad, CA

The opinions and statements published are the responsibility of the authors, and such opinions and statements do not necessarily represent the policies of the American Psychological Association or Lawrence Erlbaum Associates, Inc.

Library of Congress Cataloging-in-Publication Data
Portraits of pioneers in psychology / edited by Gregory A. Kimble, Michael Wertheimer, Charlotte White
     p.   cm.
  "Sponsored by the Division of General Psychology, American Psychological Association."
  Includes bibliographical references and index.
  ISBN 0-8058-0620-2 (alk. paper)—ISBN 0-8058-1136-2 (pbk.)
  1. Psychologists—Biography. 2. Psychology—History. I. Kimble, Gregory A. II. Wertheimer, Michael. III. White, Charlotte. IV. American Psychological Association. Division of General Psychology.
BF109.A1P67   1991
150′.92′2—dc20

[B]   91-7226
                                                       CIP

Portraits of Pioneers in Psychology: Volume VI has been published under the following ISBNs:
  APA: 1-59147-417-5
  LEA: 0-8058-5930-6

British Library Cataloguing-in-Publication Data
A CIP record is available from the British Library.

Printed in the United States of America
First Edition

In memory of Gregory A. Kimble.

Contents

Preface

The goal in the *Portraits of Pioneers in Psychology* series is to provide a set of chapters about both the scholarly and the personal lives of psychologists who have made significant contributions to the development of the field. The chapters have been constructed to be authoritative yet accessible. The objective is to make the chapters of interest to undergraduate students, graduate students, and faculty members in psychology. They should be of interest not only to psychologists but also to scholars in many related fields. The chapters should be especially valuable in the field of the history of psychology. However, we hope that they may also be useful in courses and scholarly research in many of the diverse subfields of psychology.

This is the sixth volume of the series. For this volume, Michael Wertheimer continues to serve as a coeditor, as he has from the beginning of the series. In addition, two new coeditors, Ludy T. Benjamin Jr. and Donald A. Dewsbury, have joined the team and taken substantial responsibility for the volume.

In selecting subjects for this volume, we tried to preserve the diversity that has characterized earlier volumes. Each of the subjects covered made significant contributions to the development of psychology and thus are legitimately regarded as pioneers. Kenneth B. Clark was involved in the landmark *Brown v. Board of Education* litigation that helped end segregation in public schools. James McKeen Cattell was the great entrepreneur in publishing and pioneer in the mental testing movement. Coleman Griffith is regarded as the founder of the dynamic field of sport psychology. Edmund Clark Sanford, Karl M. Dallenbach, and Robert S. Woodworth were important in laying the foundations for experimental psychology. Calvin Perry Stone, Charles Henry Turner, and Nikolaas Tinbergen, among other things, contributed to comparative psychology; in addition, Tinbergen won a Nobel prize. Turner was a Black American who contributed to science in spite of significant barriers. Frieda Fromm-Reichmann, Henry A. Murray, David Shakow, and Abraham H. Maslow were important in the development of various clinical approaches. Marion Almira Bills is best known in industrial psychology; Donald G. Patterson, in counseling psychology; Magda B. Arnold in the field of emotion; and Mary Cover Jones, in developmental psychology. Psychology is a marvelously rich and diverse field. We hope that these chapters reveal the growth, diversity, and excitement of psychology as it developed.

To bring these psychologists to life, we chose the best authors we could find. This volume is a bit of a departure from previous ones in that we have concentrated more on authors who have made substantial contributions to the field of the history of psychology. They are people who not only have worked in the area but also have a reputation for their ability to write in such a way as to convey the material consistently with the goals stated earlier. We hope that with this volume we have been able to continue the standards of excellence set by the previous editors.

With six volumes and 121 chapters, it seemed appropriate to provide a complete list of subjects and authors. That information appears in the table that follows. In addition, we have provided two descriptor terms for each of the subjects. We hope that this information will enable instructors who wish to supplement their courses in substantive areas of psychology to locate relevant chapters with ease. Assigning such descriptors is a difficult task, and one can surely quibble with some of the choices. Nevertheless, we hope that this will help to make the chapters both accessible and useful for instructors in psychology.

The book owes its existence to the contributions of many people. We especially want to acknowledge the efforts of the chapter authors, as well as the personnel at the American Psychological Association.

Subjects and Authors in Volumes I through VI of *Portraits of Pioneers in History*

Volume	Subject of Chapter	Author of Chapter	Fields of Interest	
			Primary	Secondary
5	Ainsworth, M.	Bretherton, I.	Developmental	Personality
3	Allport, F. H.	Katz, D., et al.	Social	Personality
5	Anastasi, A.	Hogan, J. D.	Testing	Applied
5	Angell, J. R.	Dewsbury, D. A.	Systems	Administration
6	Arnold, M.	Shields, S. A.	Emotion	Personality
5	Asch, S.	McCauley, C., & Rozin, P.	Gestalt	Social
4	Bartlett, F. C.	Roediger, H. L., III	Memory	Cognitive
5	Bayley, N.	Rosenblith, J.	Developmental	Testing
4	Beach, F. A.	Dewsbury, D. A.	Comparative	Physiological
6	Bills, M.	Koppes, L., & Bauer, A. M.	Applied	Testing
3	Binet, A.	Fancher, R. E.	Testing	Personality
5	Bingham, W.-V.	Benjamin, L. T., Jr., & Baker, D. B.	I/O Psychology	Testing
2	Blatz, W. E.	Wright, M. J.	Developmental	Learning
5	Brunswik, E.	Kurz-Milcke, E., & Innis, N. K.	Perception	Systems
2	Burks, B. S.	King, D. B., et al.	Developmental	Genetics
1	Calkins, M. W.	Furumoto, L.	Gender	Self
1	Carr, H.	Hilgard, E. R.	Systems	Experimental
6	Cattell, J. McK.	Sokal, M.	Testing	Administration
6	Clark, K. B.	Jackson, J. P.	Race	Social
4	Cook, S. W.	Brigham, J. C.	Social	Personality
6	Dallenbach, K.	Evans, R. B.	Experimental	Sensory
3	Darwin, C.	Masterton, R. B.	Evolution	Comparative
2	Dewey, J.	Barone, D. F.	Systems	Philosophy
2	Dix, D.	Viney, W.	Clinical	Gender
2	Doll, E. A.	Doll, E. E.	Applied	Social
5	Downey, J. E.	Hogan, J. D., & Thompson, D. N.	Testing	Personality

(continued)

Volume	Subject of Chapter	Author of Chapter	Fields of Interest	
			Primary	Secondary
3	Duncker, K.	King, D. B., et al.	Gestalt	Cognition
3	Ebbinghaus, H.	Boneau, C. A.	Memory	Experimental
3	Erickson, M.	Schiffman, H.	Hypnosis	Clinical
4	Eysenck, H.	Jensen, A. R.	Testing	Personality
2	Fechner, G. T.	Adler, H. E.	Perception	Experimental
3	Festinger, L.	Brehm, J. W.	Social	Cognition
1	Freud, S.	Beier, E. G.	Psychoanalysis	Personality
6	Fromm-Reichman, F.	Hornstein, G.	Psychoanalysis	Clinical
1	Galton, F.	McClearn, G.	Genetics	Testing
2	Gibson, J. J.	Reed, E. S.	Perception	Ecological
2	Gilbreth, L.	Perloff, R., & Naman, J. L.	Applied	Gender
5	Goldstein, K.	Pickren, W. E.	Physiological	Clinical
2	Graham, C.	Brown, J. L.	Perception	Learning
6	Griffith, C.	Green, C.	Sport	Education
2	Guthrie, E. R.	Prenzel-Guthrie, P.	Learning	Social
5	Hall, G. S.	Hogan, J. D.	Administration	Developmental
5	Harlow, H. F.	LeRoy, H. M., & Kimble, G. A.	Comparative	Physiological
4	Hathaway, S. R.	Butcher, J. N.	Testing	Personality
2	Hebb, D. O.	Glickman, S. E.	Physiological	Comparative
1	Heidbreder, E.	Henle, M.	Systems	Cognition
4	Heider, F.	Malle, B. F., & Ickes, W.	Social	Gestalt
4	Helmholtz, H.	Adler, H. E.	Perception	Physiological
3	Hickock, L. P.	Bare, J. K.	Philosophy	Religion
2	Hollingworth, H.	Benjamin, L. T., Jr.	Applied	Clinical
1	Hollingworth, L. S.	Shields, S. A.	Gender	Testing
4	Hooker, E.	Kimmel, D. C., & Garnets, L. D.	Gender	Personality

Volume	Subject of Chapter	Author of Chapter	Fields of Interest	
			Primary	*Secondary*
4	Horney, K.	Paris, B.	Psychoanalysis	Gender
4	Hovland, C. I.	Shepard, R. N.	Learning	Social
1	Hull, C. L.	Kimble, G. A.	Learning	Hypnosis
1	Hunter, W. S.	Cofer, C. N.	Experimental	Learning
1	James, W.	Ross, B.	Systems	Philosophy
1	Jastrow, J.	Blumenthal, A.	Experimental	Aesthetics
6	Jones, M. C.	Rutherford, A.	Developmental	Personality
1	Jung, C. G.	Alexander, I. E.	Psychoanalysis	Personality
4	Koch, S.	Finkelman, D., & Kessel, F.	Systems	Cognition
1	Köhler, W.	Sherrill, R.	Gestalt	Cognition
3	Krech, D.	Innis, N. K.	Learning	Social
3	Kuo, Z.-Y.	Gottlieb, G.	Comparative	Developmental
1	Lashley, K. S.	Bruce, D.	Physiological	Comparative
5	Leibniz, G. W.	Fancher, R. E., & Schmidt, H.	Philosophical	Perceptual
3	Lewin, K.	Lewin, M. A.	Gestalt	Social
5	Lord, F. M.	Green, B. F.	Testing	Statistics
6	Maslow, A.	Coon, D.	Humanistic	Personality
5	McDougall, W.	Innis, N. K.	Systems	Learning
3	McGraw, M.	Dalton, T. C., & Bergenn, V. W.	Developmental	Physiological
5	Metzger, W.	Götzl, H.	Perception	Gestalt
5	Michotte, A.	Gavin, E. A.	Perception	Phenomenology
2	Milgram, S.	Blass, T.	Social	Personality
4	Müller, G. E.	Sprung, L., & Sprung, H.	Experimental	Learning
4	Münsterberg, H.	Benjamin, L. T., Jr.	Applied	Forensics
2	Murchison, C.	Thompson, D.	Administration	Social
6	Murray, H. A.	Barenbaum, N.	Personality	Clinical

(continued)

Volume	Subject of Chapter	Author of Chapter	Fields of Interest Primary	Secondary
3	Nissen, H. W.	Dewsbury, D. A.	Comparative	Evolution
6	Paterson, D. G.	Baker, D. B.	Counseling	Personality
1	Pavlov, I. P.	Kimble, G. A.	Learning	Physiological
3	Piaget, J.	Zigler, E., & Gilman, E.	Developmental	Cognition
1	Puffer, E.	Scarborough, E.	Gender	Aesthetics
5	Ratliff, F.	Werner, J. S., & Spillmann, L.	Perception	Experimental
2	Rhine, J. B.	Feather, S.	Parapsychology	Perception
4	Robertson, G. C.	King, D. B.	Philosophy	Physiological
3	Rogers, C. R.	Lakin, M.	Clinical	Humanistic
6	Sanford, E. C.	Goodwin, C. J.	Experimental	Administration
2	Schiller, P. H.	Dewsbury, D. A.	Comparative	Learning
4	Schneirla, T. C.	Tobach, E.	Comparative	Learning
2	Sechenov, I. M.	Kimble, G. A.	Learning	Physiological
6	Shakow, D.	Cautin, R.	Clinical	Education
3	Skinner, B. F.	Bjork, D. W.	Learning	Applied
4	Spearman, C. E.	Jensen, A. R.	Testing	Cognition
3	Spence, K. W.	Kimble, G. A.	Learning	Systems
4	Sperry, R. W.	Puente, A. R.	Physiological	Comparative
2	Stern, W.	Lamiell, J. T.	Personality	Testing
6	Stone, C. P.	Pickren, W. E.	Comparative	Physiological
4	Stumpf, C.	Sprung, H., & Sprung, L.	Perception	Aesthetics
1	Sullivan, H. S.	Chatelaine, K. L.	Psychoanalysis	Clinical
4	Sumner, F. C.	Guthrie, R. V.	Race	Education
4	Terman, L.	Crosby, J. R., & Hastorf, A. H.	Testing	Developmental
1	Thorndike, E. L.	Thorndike, R. I.	Learning	Testing
3	Thurstone, L. L.	Jones, L. V.	Testing	Personality

Volume	Subject of Chapter	Author of Chapter	Fields of Interest	
			Primary	Secondary
6	Tinbergen, N.	Dewsbury, D. A.	Comparative	Ethology
1	Titchener, E. B.	Evans, R. B.	Experimental	Systems
1	Tolman, E. C.	Gleitman, H.	Learning	Systems
2	Tomkins, S. S.	Alexander, I. E.	Personality	Emotion
1	Tyron, R. C.	Schlesinger, K.	Genetics	Learning
6	Turner, C. H.	Abramson, C.	Comparative	Sensory
5	Tyler, L.	Fassinger, R. E.	Testing	Counseling
3	Underwood, B. J.	Freund, J. S.	Experimental	Learning
4	Upham, T.	Fuchs, A. H.	Systems	Philosophy
5	Washburn, M. F.	Viney, W., & Burlingame-Lee, L.	Comparative	Systems
1	Watson, J. B.	Brewer, C. L.	Systems	Learning
1	Wertheimer, M.	Wertheimer, M.	Gestalt	Cognition
2	Witmer, L.	McReynolds, P.	Clinical	Comparative
5	Wolfe, H. K.	Benjamin, L. T., Jr.	Experimental	Education
6	Woodworth, R. S.	Winston, A. S.	Experimental	Systems
3	Wundt, W. M.	Blumenthal, A. L.	Experimental	Cultural
2	Yerkes, R. M.	Dewsbury, D. A.	Comparative	Testing

Portraits of the Authors and Editors

Charles I. Abramson, author of the chapter on Charles Henry Turner, is professor of psychology at Oklahoma State University, Stillwater, Oklahoma. Born in Brooklyn, New York, Abramson received his doctorate in experimental–physiological psychology from Boston University, where his dissertation research was supervised by M. E. Bitterman, now at the University of Hawaii. Abramson is the author of more than 100 published articles and chapters and author or editor of 10 books. His primary research area is in the field of comparative psychology, where he studies the behavior of animals, ranging from ants, bees, earthworms, and planarians to elephants and humans. He has earned several teaching awards, including the 2003 Robert S. Daniel Award from the Society for the Teaching of Psychology of the American Psychological Association. Abramson first became interested in Professor Turner while an undergraduate at Boston University. This chapter and his other work on Professor Turner were greatly assisted by his interactions with the Turner family.

 David B. Baker, author of the portrait of Donald G. Paterson, is director of the Archives of the History of American Psychology and professor of psychology at The University of Akron, Akron, Ohio. He received his PhD in psychology from Texas A&M University in 1988. He has taught the history of psychology at the undergraduate and graduate levels for the past 15 years, and in 1995 was named Professor of the Year by the Texas Psychological Association Division of Students in Psychology. Baker became the director of the Archives of the History of American Psychology in 1999. Recognized as the largest archival collection of its kind, its mission is to acquire, preserve, and make available primary source material in the history of psychology. In addition to his administrative and teaching duties, Baker maintains an active program of research and writing on the rise of professional psychology in 20th-century America. His most recent publications include *From Séance to Science: A History of the Profession of Psychology in America* (coauthored with Ludy T. Benjamin Jr.; 2004) and the edited volume *Thick Description and Fine Texture: Archival Research in the History of Psychology* (2003). Baker is a fellow of the American Psychological Association.

Nicole B. Barenbaum, author of the portrait of Henry A. Murray, is a professor of psychology at the University of the South, Sewanee, Tennessee, where she joined the faculty in 1990. She received her AB degree from Cornell University and her MA and PhD degrees in personality psychology from Boston University. She has served on the History Oversight Committee of the American Psychological Association (APA) and as president of the Society for the History of Psychology (APA Division 26). She is a member of Cheiron (the International Society for the History of the Social and Behavioral Sciences) and of the Society for Personology. Barenbaum's work has examined the history of case studies and biographical methods in personality psychology, focusing on the work of Murray and Gordon W. Allport. She has published several papers on Allport and has coauthored chapters with David G. Winter on the history of personality psychology. Her recent research focuses on the careers of A. A. Roback and other Jewish psychologists who sought academic positions in psychology early in the 20th century.

Adrienne M. Bauer, coauthor of the portrait of Marion Almira Bills, is an organizational effectiveness consultant for the Office of Institutional Effectiveness at Eastern Kentucky University, Richmond. She earned her MS in industrial–organizational psychology at Eastern Kentucky University in 2003. Bauer's master's thesis focused on variables (life satisfaction, personality, and just-world beliefs) predicting academic citizenship behaviors. In 2004, she conducted research on cultural differences relating to citizenship behaviors between American and Czech Republic college-level students. Bauer is a member of the Society for Industrial and Organizational Psychology (SIOP) and the American Psychological Association; she currently serves on the editorial board of *The Industrial–Organizational Psychologist.* Her interests include job satisfaction, cross-cultural psychology, and organizational effectiveness, including organizational citizenship behaviors and organizational communication.

Ludy T. Benjamin Jr., coeditor, is the Glasscock Professor of Teaching Excellence, Presidential Professor of Teaching Excellence, and Professor of Psychology and Educational Psychology at Texas A&M University, College Station, where he has been on the faculty since 1980. He received his doctorate in experimental psychology from Texas Christian University in 1971. His initial academic appointment was at Nebraska Wesleyan University, where he served for 8 years. He then served for 2 years as director of education for the American Psychological Association before going to Texas A&M. Much of Benjamin's work as a historian of psychology has focused on applied psychology, including a recent book with David B. Baker, *From Séance to Science: A History of the Profession of Psychology in America* (2004). Benjamin contributed four chapters to earlier volumes in this series—on Harry Hollingworth, Hugo Münsterberg, and Walter Van Dyke Bingham, all of whom were important pioneers in industrial psychology, and Harry Kirke Wolfe, arguably the most inspirational teacher of psychology of his generation. His most recent book is a second edition of *A History of Psychology in Letters* (2006).

Robin L. Cautin, author of the chapter on David Shakow, is assistant professor of psychology at Manhattanville College, Purchase, New York, where she teaches courses in the history of psychology and psychopathology. Her current interests include the history of clinical psychology and the philosophy of psychology. She earned her BA degree in psychology and philosophy from the University of Delaware and her PhD in clinical psychology from Case Western Reserve University in Cleveland, Ohio. Her training included a clinical internship at the University of Virginia, Charlottesville, and a postdoctoral fellowship at Columbia University. She was the 2003 recipient of the J. R. Kantor Fellowship awarded by the Archives of the History of American Psychology, where the bulk of the original materials used in her chapter in this volume were obtained.

Deborah J. Coon, author of the chapter on Abraham H. Maslow, received a bachelor's degree in psychology and philosophy from Bucknell University, a master's degree in experimental psychology from the University of Colorado, and a master's and doctoral degree in history of science from Harvard University. Her research interests include William James, psychology's boundaries with other sciences and "pseudosciences," and the histories of behaviorism and humanistic psychology. She has taught at Harvard University, Rensselaer Polytechnic Institute, the University of New Hampshire, the University of San Diego, Claremont Graduate University, and California State University, San Marcos. Coon's articles appear in the *Journal of American History, Technology and Culture,* the *American Psychologist, Journal of the History of the Behavioral Sciences, History of Psychology,* and *Science.* She won the 2002 Eisenstein Prize for Excellence in Scholarship from the National Coalition of Independent Scholars for her article, "Salvaging the Self in a World Without Soul: William James's *The Principles of Psychology.*"

Donald A. Dewsbury, coeditor and author of the chapter on Nikolaas Tinbergen, is professor of psychology at the University of Florida, Gainesville, Florida. Born in Brooklyn, New York, he attended Bucknell University. His PhD is from the University of Michigan and was followed by postdoctoral work with Frank Beach at the University of California, Berkeley. Through much of his career he has worked as a comparative psychologist, with an emphasis on social and reproductive behavior, but in recent years his work has shifted to a primary focus on the history of psychology, with work in comparative psychology remaining as a secondary interest. He has served as president of two American Psychological Association divisions and the Animal Behavior Society. He is the author or editor of 15 volumes, including *Comparative Animal Behavior, Comparative*

Psychology in the Twentieth Century, Evolving Perspectives on the History of Psychology, and *Monkey Farm: A History of the Yerkes Laboratories of Primate Biology, 1930–1965.* He has also published more than 350 articles and chapters.

Rand B. Evans, author of the chapter on Karl M. Dallenbach, is a historian of psychology and professor of psychology at East Carolina University, Greenville, North Carolina. Born in Texas in 1942, he received his doctorate in 1967 from the University of Texas, Austin, where he conducted research under Dallenbach. He has been associate director of the history of psychology program at the University of New Hampshire, department chair at Texas A&M University and East Carolina University, and dean of liberal arts at the University of Baltimore. He has been visiting scholar in the history of science department at Harvard University and at the Max Planck Institute for the History of Science in Berlin. He has written widely on the history of experimental psychology, early American psychology, and scientific instruments. He is editor of the history and obituary section of the *American Journal of Psychology.* He is in the final stages of completing his biography of Edward Bradford Titchener and also a history of psychological instruments.

C. James Goodwin, author of the chapter on Edmund Clark Sanford, is an emeritus professor at Wheeling Jesuit University, Wheeling, West Virginia, where he taught for 30 years before retirement. He is currently a visiting professor at Western Carolina University, Callowhee, North Carolina, and living in the mountains at the western edge of North Carolina. He earned a bachelor's degree from the College of the Holy Cross and a master's and doctorate in experimental psychology from Florida State University, specializing in memory and cognition. He is a fellow of the American Psychological Association in Divisions 2 (Society for the Teaching of Psychology) and 26 (Society for the History of Psychology). His research interests on the empirical side are in the area of cognitive mapping and wayfinding, but his prime interest is in the early history of experimental psychology in the United States. He is the author of two undergraduate textbooks, one on research methods (*Research in Psychology: Methods and Design*) and one on the history of psychology (*A History of Modern Psychology*).

Christopher D. Green, author of the chapter on Coleman Roberts Griffith, is a professor in the History and Theory of Psychology program at York University, Toronto, Canada. He has PhDs in both psychology (1992) and philosophy (2004) from the University of Toronto. His recent publications include "Psychology Strikes Out: Coleman Griffith and the Chicago Cubs" (*History of Psychology,* 2003), "Where Did the Ventricular Localization of Mental Faculties Come From?" (*Journal of the History of the Behavioral Sciences,* 2003), and (with Philip R. Groff) *Early Psychological Thought: Ancient Accounts of Mind and Soul* (2003). He has founded a number of electronic resources, including *Classics in the History of Psychology* (http://psychclassics.yorku.ca) and *The History and Theory of Psychology Eprint Archive* (http://htpprints.yorku.ca), and has produced a video documentary on the public controversy that surrounded the hiring of James

Mark Baldwin at the University of Toronto in 1889 (freely available for viewing online at http://www.yorku.ca/christo/papers/pubs.htm#video). He is now producing a new documentary on the prehistory of American functionalism. In January 2006 he became the editor of the *Journal of the History of the Behavioral Sciences*.

Gail A. Hornstein, author of the portrait of Frieda Fromm-Reichmann, is professor of psychology at Mount Holyoke College, South Hadley, Massachusetts, and was founding director of the Five College Women's Studies Research Center for its first 10 years. She has published widely in personality and social psychology, and her recent work focuses broadly on the history of 20th-century psychology, psychiatry, and psychoanalysis. She is the author of *To Redeem One Person Is to Redeem the World: The Life of Frieda Fromm-Reichmann* (2000), the first full-length biography of the pioneering psychoanalyst. Hornstein's research has been supported by grants from the National Library of Medicine, the American Council of Learned Societies, the National Science Foundation, and the National Endowment for the Humanities, and by fellowships from the Bunting Institute, Radcliffe College; Clare Hall, Cambridge University; Magdalen College, Oxford University; the School of Advanced Study, University of London; and the Centre for Research in the Arts, Social Sciences, and Humanities, Cambridge University. Her current project, "Hearing Voices: Conversations With 'the Mad,'" seeks to reconceive fundamental assumptions about madness and its treatment from the perspective of those who have experienced it.

John P. Jackson Jr., author of the portrait on Kenneth B. Clark, received his PhD in the history of science and technology from the University of Minnesota, Twin Cities. His broad interests are in the history of the scientific study of race. He has written two books on how scientific ideas about race influenced American debates about segregation and desegregation in the 20th century: *Social Scientists for Social Justice: Making the Case Against Segregation* (2001) and *Science and Segregation: Race, Law and the Case Against* Brown v. Board of Education (2005). He is the editor of *Science, Race, and Ethnicity: Readings From Isis and Osiris* (2002) and coauthor, with Nadine W. Weidman, of *Race, Racism and Science: Social Impact and Interaction* (2004). He was the recipient of the 2004 Early Career Award for Scholarship in the History of Psychology from the Society for the History of Psychology. He is an assistant professor in the Department of Communication at the University of Colorado, Boulder.

Laura L. Koppes, coauthor of the portrait of Marion Almira Bills, is associate professor of industrial and organizational psychology and associate vice president of institutional effectiveness at Eastern Kentucky University, Lexington. She is a U.S. Fulbright Scholar, and she recently completed her work in the Czech Republic, teaching, developing curricula, and researching human resource management and organizational psychology. Koppes established the position of historian for the Society for Industrial–Organizational Psychology (SIOP; Division 14 of the American Psychological Association [APA]) and has contributed to the preservation of the history of SIOP and industrial–organizational psychology through international and national presentations, publications, and other documents. She was an executive committee member of APA Division 26 (Society for the History of Psychology) as membership chair. Koppes was the chair of SIOP's education and training committee, and is now the editor of *The Industrial–Organizational Psychologist*. Her interests include cross-cultural differences, leadership, organizational citizenship behaviors, and history of industrial psychology. Currently, Koppes, as editor, is completing a book on the history of industrial–organizational psychology.

Wade E. Pickren, author of the chapter on Calvin Perry Stone, earned his PhD in the history of psychology with a minor in the history of science under the direction of Donald A. Dewsbury. Pickren now serves as historian and director of archives and library services for the American Psychological Association. He is also the editor of the history of psychology and obituaries section of the *American Psychologist*. Wade's scholarly interests include the history of post–World War II American psychology, the history of medicine and psychology, and psychology and the public imagination. His most recent book is *Psychology and the National Institute of Mental Health: A Historical Analysis of Science, Practice, and Policy* (2005), coedited with the late Stan Schneider.

Alexandra Rutherford, author of the portrait of Mary Cover Jones, is an assistant professor of psychology in the History and Theory of Psychology Graduate Program at York University in Toronto, Ontario, Canada. Her historical research interests include the work and cultural influence of B. F. Skinner, the history of behavior modification, and the history of women and feminism in psychology. She serves as assistant editor of the *Journal of the History of the Behavioral Sciences* and as editor of the Heritage Column for the Society for the Psychology of Women newsletter, *Feminist Psychologist*. In 2001, she received the early career award for scholarship in the history of psychology from the Society for the History of Psychology (Division 26 of the American Psychological Association). She is currently working on a book-length manuscript that examines the intra- and extradisciplinary growth of Skinnerian psychology in the 1950s, 1960s, and 1970s. In addition to her historical training and scholarship, she is also a practicing clinical psychologist.

Stephanie A. Shields, author of the portrait of Magda B. Arnold, is professor of psychology and women's studies at Pennsylvania State University, University Park. Her research focuses on the social meaning of emotion (e.g., emotion stereotypes; "appropriate" emotion), especially its connections to gender and the micropolitics of emotion. She also studies the history of the psychology of women and gender and women's participation in American psychology. She received her MS and PhD in psychology from Pennsylvania State University. For a number of years she served on the faculty of the University of California, Davis, where she was founding director of the UC Davis Consortium for Research on Women. She has served as director of women's studies at both UC Davis and Pennsylvania State. Her work has been supported by the 4-H Center for

Youth Development, the National Science Foundation, and the Rockefeller Foundation. Her book, *Speaking From the Heart: Gender and the Social Meaning of Emotion* (2002) received the Association for Women in Psychology's 2003 Distinguished Publication Award.

Michael M. Sokal, author of the portrait of James McKeen Cattell, is professor of history in the Department of Humanities and Arts at Worcester Polytechnic Institute, in Worcester, Massachusetts. He studied engineering at The Cooper Union in New York City (BE, 1966), and history of science and technology at Case Western Reserve University in Cleveland, Ohio (MA, 1968; PhD, 1972). He spent a postdoctoral year (1973–1974) at the National Museum of American History of the Smithsonian Institution. Sokal has taught at Worcester Polytechnic Institute since 1970 and has been honored with the Trustees' Award for Outstanding Creative Scholarship, the President's Award for Outstanding Undergraduate Project Advising, and a 2-year term as Paris Fletcher Distinguished Professor in the Humanities. Since 1997 he has also served as founding editor of *History of Psychology*, a scholarly journal published quarterly by the American Psychological Association for the Society for the History of Psychology. In January 2004, he began a 2-year term as president of the History of Science Society. In writing about Cattell, an important American scientific editor and organizer, Sokal has sought to practice "applied history of science."

Michael Wertheimer, coeditor, was educated at Swarthmore College (BA), Johns Hopkins University (MA), and Harvard University (PhD). He taught for 3 years at Wesleyan University before coming in 1955 to the University of Colorado at Boulder, where he became full professor in 1961 and professor emeritus in 1993. He has been president of Psi Chi (the national honor society in psychology), the Rocky Mountain Psychological Association (RMPA), and four divisions of the American Psychological Association (APA): 1, Society for General Psychology; 2, Society for the Teaching of Psychology; 24, Society for Theoretical and Philosophical Psychology (twice); and 26, Society for the History of Psychology. Director of the undergraduate honors program in psychology at the University of Colorado at Boulder for almost 4 decades, he also directed doctoral programs there in experimental and sociocultural psychology. Among his awards are one for Distinguished Teaching in Psychology from the American Psychological Foundation, one for Distinguished Career Contributions to Education and Training in Psychology from the APA, awards for distinguished service from the RMPA and from APA Divisions 1 and 24, and a Lifetime Achievement Award for Sustained, Outstanding, and Unusual Scholarly Contributions from Division 26. Among several hundred articles and dozens of books (most about the history of psychology) are an oral history of Psi Chi (2000), coauthored with Stephen F. Davis, the fourth edition of his *Brief History of Psychology* (2000), and *Max Wertheimer and Gestalt Theory* (2005), coauthored with D. Brett King.

Andrew S. Winston, author of the portrait of Robert S. Woodworth, is a professor of psychology at the University of Guelph in Guelph, Ontario, Canada.

Born in Elizabeth, New Jersey, he received his BA at Northwestern University and his PhD in developmental psychology at the University of Illinois at Urbana–Champaign. His publications have focused on the history of antisemitism and racism in psychology, the history of "experiment" and "cause" as central concepts, and the influence of Woodworth. He has also published on psychological aesthetics, art, and child behavior. He is currently studying the use of psychological research on race by extreme political groups and the careers of psychologists who assisted these groups. He serves as executive officer of Cheiron, The International Society for the History of Behavioral and Social Sciences. He edited *Defining Difference: Race and Racism in the History of Psychology* (American Psychological Association, 2004).

Portraits of Pioneers
in Psychology

Edmund Clark Sanford (Photo courtesy of the Clark University Archives)

Chapter 1

Edmund Clark Sanford and the Consequences of Loyalty

C. James Goodwin

When G. Stanley Hall became the first president of Clark University in 1888, one of his initial tasks was to hire faculty. Clark had been created as a graduate-school-only institution, with a strong emphasis on science, and one of the five original departments (besides mathematics, physics, chemistry, and biology) was going to be Hall's discipline—psychology. Hall began hiring by turning to a former student: In September 1888, Edmund Clark Sanford (1859–1924) became the first faculty member to be hired at Clark University (Goodwin, 1987). Sanford never left the university, remaining loyal to Clark and to Hall for the next 36 years. This loyalty earned the respect of his peers and the admiration of his students over the years, but it ultimately cost him a chance at a more prominent career as a psychological scientist. Despite his many notable accomplishments— director of a major laboratory, writer of American psychology's first laboratory training manual, creative apparatus inventor, journal editor, president of the American Psychological Association (APA), and a ranking as the 11th most important psychologist in America in Cattell's 1903 *American Men of Science* (cited in Visher, 1947, p. 143)—Sanford is little known to students of psychology today and only vaguely recalled (at best) by professors of psychology.

A BIOGRAPHICAL SKETCH

Although Sanford grew up in Oakland, California, his family had deep roots in New England. Sanford was raised in a home that shaped in him the traditional

3

values of hard work, devotion to duty, loyalty, and individual responsibility. He taught high school briefly after graduating from the University of California at Berkeley, and then enrolled in graduate school at Johns Hopkins University in 1885. Hopkins at the time was just 9 years old, but it had already established a strong reputation. It was noted for being created deliberately to reflect the *Wissenschaft* trend in higher education in Germany, with its emphasis on creating new knowledge through a focus on original research. Hopkins's innovative president, Daniel Coit Gilman, encouraged the development of laboratory training and the use of the seminar model of instruction at the university, and attracted strong graduate students by creating the idea of a university "fellowship" that paid a generous stipend ($500) and waived tuition (Hawkins, 1960). Gilman also recognized that rapidly expanding enrollments in higher education would create a need for university instructors, so under his leadership, Hopkins became a "place for the training of professors and teachers for the highest academic posts" (Ryan, 1939, p. 31). According to Ryan, during Johns Hopkins' first 10 years, 56 of its doctoral graduates became employed as professors in 32 different colleges and universities. The goal of training university professors was evidently attractive to young Sanford—in response to a request on the application form to state his reason for applying to Hopkins, Stanford wrote that he wished to undertake the "[s]tudy of social science, with a view to teaching biology, political economy, and psychology" (E. C. Sanford, 1885, p. 1).

It was at Johns Hopkins that Sanford first encountered one of American psychology's most recognizable pioneers, G. Stanley Hall, and began an affiliation that endured until they both died in 1924. From the beginning, Hall was the mentor and Sanford was the student. This fundamental relationship never changed, and Sanford acknowledged it. As he later wrote to a former student, ". . . though he was fifteen years my senior and the relation of pupil to teacher was never wholly lost, I received many kindnesses at his hands and we worked together at the University for more than thirty years" (M. L. Sanford, 1925, pp. 6–7). Sanford learned much from Hall, but ultimately the connection with Hall and the loyalty to him might have cost Sanford as much as it benefited him.

While a student at Hopkins from the fall of 1885 to the spring of 1888, Sanford took no fewer than 14 courses from Hall, ranging from philosophy to physiological psychology to education (Goodwin, 1987). In his third year, he earned one of Gilman's prestigious fellowships, and he completed his dissertation, an experimental study (with a pragmatic twist) on the readability of the lower-case letters, in the spring of 1888 (E. C. Sanford, 1888). His observers had to name printed letters that were presented briefly from varying distances. He found the kinds of confusions you might expect (e.g., calling an "e" a "c" by mistake, and vice versa) and he made recommendations based on his findings (e.g., use a print type that exaggerates the top part of the letter "e").

As a newly minted PhD, Sanford spent a fourth academic year as an instructor at Hopkins, while Hall toured Europe in preparation for the start of his presidency at Clark University. Sanford joined Hall for Clark's opening year in the fall of 1889 as director of the psychology laboratory (although he was not given the official title of director until 1892), and he remained in the department until 1909, when he was named second president of Clark College, the university's undergraduate branch that opened in 1902. In 1920, the college and university merged following Hall's retirement and, after a sabbatical year, Sanford returned to the psychology department, where he remained until his sudden death from a heart attack in 1924, just a few months shy of retirement (Goodwin, 1987).

SANFORD AND EXPERIMENTAL PSYCHOLOGY'S FIRST LABORATORY MANUAL

Hall was determined to make Clark a world-class research university as quickly as possible, so he was generous with laboratory budgets, and Sanford was able to develop an outstanding research facility. In the first 3 years of the laboratory's existence, Sanford had a total budget of just under $3,000,[1] enabling him to buy a wide range of equipment. The *Account Book* for 1889 through 1890 alone covers 10 pages and documents the purchase of more than 150 items, ranging from tools and simple office supplies to such well-known apparatus pieces as a set of tuning forks ($63.60), an ophthalmoscope ($30), an eye model ($45), a stand perimeter ($30), and the well-known (and expensive) Hipp chronoscope ($280.50; *Account Book,* 1889–1890). Sanford's new laboratory also included virtually all of the apparatus from the psychology laboratory at Johns Hopkins. When he left Baltimore, Hall took most of the apparatus with him, claiming ownership. Thus stripped, the laboratory at Johns Hopkins closed soon after Hall's departure and did not reopen until 1903 (Ross, 1972).

With a nicely equipped laboratory, Sanford turned to the question of how to train his students to be experimental psychologists. In the university's first year, according to the *Clark University Register,* Sanford directed research and gave two courses—"The Physiological Psychology of Vision" in the fall and "The Application of Time-Measurements to Psychology" in the spring (*Clark University Register,* 1889, p. 12). In both courses, the aim was to "demonstrate all the important experiments mentioned in the course, with suitable apparatus" (p. 12). These courses eventually became simplified and evolved into what came to be known as the "drill course," in which psychology students learned the fundamentals of how to do research and operate the apparatus by repeating the classic experiments in such areas as psychophysics and reaction time. Once they knew the basics and could replicate standard findings, students were ready for advanced courses or to develop their own research projects.

---

[1]This amount would be worth approximately $58,600 in 2003 (for an inflation calculator, see http://www.westegg.com/inflation).

The need for a textbook or manual to accompany the drill course soon became apparent to Sanford, and he began working on one in the early 1890s. His was not the first attempt—James McKeen Cattell started to write a laboratory manual in the late 1880s, but did not complete it and did not publish any of it (Sokal, 1981, p. 300). Sanford's effort began as a series of long articles in the *American Journal of Psychology (AJP)*, which had been founded by Hall in 1887 and, in the early 1890s, was little more than a vehicle for publishing work from Clark. Sanford published six articles between 1891 and 1896. The first four pieces were reorganized and published as a separate volume in 1894 by D. C. Heath. The final product, incorporating all the journal articles, appeared in 1898, with the title *A Course in Experimental Psychology I: Sensation and Perception* (E. C. Sanford, 1898a). Sanford planned a second volume, to cover such topics as reaction time, memory, and attention, but the book never got past the planning stage. With a modesty that typified him, Sanford apologized in the preface for including far more experiments than could be completed in a year-long laboratory course, but noted that "[w]hat a good laboratory course ought to include is not yet wholly clear, and can only be settled by trial; [un]till this has been done a superfluous liberty of selection may not be wholly a disadvantage" (1898a, p. iii).

The 449-page manual included 239 experiments, most of them simple demonstrations of sensory and perceptual phenomena, some of which still find their way into modern introductory textbooks (e.g., examining and interpreting visual illusions, identifying monocular depth cues, finding the blind spot). Although experiments on vision occupied most of the book (three of the nine chapters and 130 of the 239 experiments), there were also experiments on hearing (43), the skin senses (32), kineasthesis (19), and taste/smell (9). Many of the experiments were psychophysical in nature. A separate chapter was devoted to evaluating Weber's law through six separate studies that served the purpose of teaching students how to use standard psychophysical methods. Most of the experiments included fairly detailed instructions about how to proceed, descriptions of the outcomes to expect, and, in some cases, brief summaries of existing research on the particular topic.

Recognizing that most psychology laboratories would not be as well equipped as his, Sanford included demonstrational experiments that for the most part required a bare minimum of apparatus. And to aid the instructor in acquiring (e.g., color wheels) or building the necessary apparatus (e.g., a binocular stereoscope), Sanford included a 57-page closing chapter called "Suggestions on Apparatus." The chapter included numerous drawings and diagrams, as well as lists of materials needed to complete the experiments in the earlier chapters.

Although Sanford's laboratory manual would soon be eclipsed by E. B. Titchener's monumental effort (1901, 1905), and joined by three other contemporary manuals (Judd, 1907; Seashore, 1908; Witmer, 1902), it was a landmark book, the first laboratory guide for completing a course in experimental psychology. As such, it helped standardize instruction in experimental psychology during the 1890s, as it "guided the uninformed and steadied the unstable," as Titchener later put it (1924, p. 162). That Sanford's effort was valued by his peers is evident from the reviews that soon appeared:

> [I]t would be hard to overestimate the labor, care, and skill that show themselves in every line of Professor Sanford's book; as an elementary laboratory course it is not only a pioneer—it is at the same time a brilliant success. (Scripture, 1898, p. 25)

> [T]he psychological laboratory is now recognized as worthy of equal consideration with those connected with the other sciences . . . [but the] same can hardly be said regarding . . . a highly desirable consensus as to what is fundamental in content or method. . . . It is as the most distinctive contribution to such effort . . . that Sanford's "Course in Experimental Psychology" merits widespread recognition. . . . Viewed in its entirety the volume must unhesitatingly be pronounced to be a highly successful achievement of a highly difficult task. (Jastrow, 1898, pp. 414–416)

It appears that the manual was used on campuses other than at Clark.[2] Sales figures have been lost, but it was reprinted three times in the 10 years after the full version appeared in 1898 (*National Union Catalog,* 1968). Its use and its value are mentioned in at least five chapters in Murchison's *History of Psychology in Autobiography* series; it was also mentioned in several journal articles, newspaper accounts, and contemporary course descriptions; and as late as 1932, Robert Woodworth still had it listed as recommended reading on the syllabus for his advanced experimental psychology course (Woodworth, 1932). If the manual had a flaw, it was that Sanford could have been more complete in some of his instructions about how to run the experiments. This difficulty was noted in an early review by Titchener (1894), whose later effort was marked by considerable attention to detail—his famous sets of manuals (one set for qualitative experiments and one for quantitative) included separate student and instructor volumes, and the latter were twice the length of the former. Titchener considered Sanford his best friend in America (Goodwin, 1985) and, despite the criticism of Sanford's occasional cursory instructions, Titchener heaped lavish praise on Sanford's landmark effort, writing that the work had

> high historical importance, as the first manual of experimental psychology; it has exerted, and still exerts, a wide influence, as the gateway through which American students are introduced to laboratory work; and it is a monument of accurate erudition. (Titchener, 1901, Vol. 1, Part 2, p. xxxii)

---

[2] Apparently uneasy at the prospect of profiting at the expense of his own students, Sanford gave back his royalty payments to Clark students who had to buy the book (Wilson, 1898).

SANFORD AS A TEACHER, A GENERALIST,
AND AN APPARATUS CREATOR

Sanford's bibliography is not a long one. The 77 items mingle psychology-related pieces with commencement addresses, obituaries, reports of meetings, and even poems. Of relevance for psychology, there is the laboratory manual, about half a dozen articles on apparatus (e.g., E. C. Sanford, 1890), another half dozen research articles (e.g., E. C. Sanford, 1893b), and several fine narrative pieces that summarized fields of study. These latter articles include a comprehensive three-part series on the history of reaction time (E. C. Sanford, 1888–1889). In his classic history text, E. G. Boring (1950, p. 150) specifically referred to Sanford's articles as a major source of reliable information on the history of the "personal equation." Sanford's generalist writings also include articles on the alleged mathematical abilities of horses, including the celebrated Clever Hans (E. C. Sanford, 1914); the development and decline of mental ability across the life span (E. C. Sanford, 1902); sensory processes in fish (E. C. Sanford, 1903a); research methods in educational psychology (E. C. Sanford, 1912); and how best to teach psychology's introductory course (E. C. Sanford, 1906). Concerning the latter, Sanford outlined two general approaches to the course, a focus on hard science or a focus on application, and opted for the latter. He pointed out that few students taking the course would become professional psychologists. Rather, the typical student would be "very likely to become a teacher, still more likely to have a hand in the begetting and bringing up of children, and is certain to need to deal rationally with a . . . number of his fellow men" (p. 118). He also argued strongly that a major benefit of the course would be to instill in students the general attitudes and values of the psychologist–scientist—objectivity, rationality, and a reliance on conclusions based on empirical evidence.

In an obituary for Sanford, and perhaps with a touch of kind rationalization for his friend, Titchener (1924) attributed Sanford's meager published output to fragile health (a string of childhood illness including typhoid, rheumatic fever in his early years at Clark, and the heart disease that eventually killed him). But a second reason for the relative lack of productivity was Sanford's devotion and loyalty to his students; he seemed more interested in training productive scholars than being one himself. Mary Calkins of Wellesley College made special note of this commitment in an obituary, writing that Sanford would have produced more if not for his "unparalleled generosity to his students" (Calkins, 1924, p. 12). It was a generosity extended to Calkins as well—Sanford collaborated with her on a study of dreams (Calkins, 1893), and Calkins attributed the development and success of her laboratory at Wellesley to Sanford, who provided her with a constant source of advice and counsel. She went as far as to write that it was Sanford, not she, who deserved credit for the creation of the Wellesley lab (Calkins, 1930). On the day he died, Sanford was en route to give a talk at Wellesley and to visit Calkins.

One indication of Sanford's student-centered orientation can be found in a series of "minor studies" that were published from the Clark laboratory, most of them appearing during the 1890s. These were projects that Sanford developed in collaboration with graduate students, much more elaborate than their modest-sounding label, for which his contributions easily merited the status of coauthor or, in some cases, senior author. Yet on the 21 minor studies (five authored by women, including the Calkins dream study) in which he was involved, Sanford's name appears as coauthor just twice.[3] Sanford seemed to be more concerned with his students' vitae than his own. It is also worth noting that although the topics of the minor studies stay generally within the range of sensation/perception/ attention, they range widely, a result of Sanford's allowing students to develop projects reflecting their own interests, rather than his.

Aside from generally supervising his students' research, Sanford also participated in many of the studies (common practice at the time), but his main contribution typically involved creating or adapting the research apparatus used in the project. Like other experimentalists in experimental psychology's formative years, and out of necessity, Sanford was a talented and creative apparatus builder. The minor studies are full of brief notes of appreciation for Sanford's help with the apparatus. Bolton (1894), for instance, wrote that without Sanford's apparatus skills, "the work could not have been carried on" (p. 238).

Sanford's contribution to the history of research apparatus goes beyond his specific help to students developing their projects, however. He is also known for creating a simple chronoscope that made it possible for instructors to teach students about reaction time without having to invest in expensive timing devices (e.g., the Hipp chronoscope). He called it the Vernier chronoscope, and it combined in one easily built device the means for conducting a simple reaction-time experiment using telegraph keys and the means for recording the reaction times with acceptable accuracy (to .01 second) for instructional purposes. Sanford (1898d) shared the design with the readership of the *AJP* and had duplicates of the chronoscope made in the Clark shop and shipped to colleagues. The device was also a commercial success, appearing as late as 1940 in the catalog of C. H. Stoelting and also sold by the Marietta Apparatus Company (R. Evans, personal communication, September 2004). Additional indication of its popularity and longevity is that several articles in the *AJP* in the late 1920s suggested improvements on the design (Dimmick, 1929; Fernberger, 1926; Ruckmick, 1927).

Sanford's second contribution to general-purpose apparatus is a major one: His idea for an animal learning task led directly to psychology's first maze-learning experiments with rats. The discipline of comparative psychology, in its infancy in the mid-1890s, found a home at Clark, primarily the result of Hall's interest in evolution (Dewsbury, 1992). Two Clark students who made an early

---

[3] This total excludes two articles that Sanford published that concerned apparatus (1893a, 1895b), but are listed with the minor studies.

impact on the field, Linus Kline and Willard Small, came under Sanford's influence in his role as laboratory director.[4] They studied several species, examining natural behavior, but were also interested in learning. As Kline later reported to Walter Miles, while discussing with Sanford the best way to study "home-finding" behavior in rats, he

> described to [Sanford] runways which I had observed . . . made by large feral rats to their nests under the porch of an old cabin on my father's farm in Virginia. These runways were from three to six inches below the surface of the ground and when exposed during excavation presented a veritable maze. Sanford at once suggested the possibility of using the pattern of the Hampton Court maze for purposes of constructing a "home-finding" apparatus. (Miles, 1930, p. 331)

It is not clear why Sanford thought of the Hampton Court maze, but the maze at the royal palace outside of London is famous, and Sanford had just been in England on sabbatical, so it is possible that he had recently visited the maze. Whatever the origin of Sanford's suggestion, it was quickly put into effect, not by Kline, who was immersed in other projects, but by his fellow graduate student and friend Willard Small. Under Sanford's direction, Small adjusted the Hampton maze's trapezoidal shape to rectangular, but kept the basic design the same while building two 6′ × 8′ mazes (with wire mesh rather than solid walls). Small then examined the home-finding tendencies of several white rats, and he also made a comparison between blind and sighted rats. With a conclusion essentially the same as John Watson's (Carr & Watson, 1908; Watson, 1907), whose subsequent maze studies surpassed Small's in methodological rigor, Small argued that kinaesthesis was the key sense underlying the maze learning (one piece of evidence: no difference in performance between blind and sighted rats). It is also worth noting that although in later years the maze sometimes came to be seen as an "artificial" laboratory apparatus, Small saw the matter differently. He believed that the maze was an excellent simulation of the rat's real world of tunnels and labyrinths, and that his studies had created "as little difference as possible between the conditions of experiment and of ordinary experience" (Small, 1901, p. 209).

Sanford reported on Small's work at the 1899 annual meeting of the APA, and Small (1901) published in the following year. As was his style, Sanford contributed mightily to Small's pioneering research but did not attach his name to Small's publication. Small nonetheless acknowledged his "indebtedness to Dr. E. C. Sanford for the initial suggestion, for ample laboratory facilities, and for continued interest and helpful criticism" (1901, p. 239).

---

[4] Also, to establish the status of comparative psychology at Clark, Hall named Sanford Professor of Experimental and Comparative Psychology in 1900 (Goodwin, 1987).

One final point about Sanford and apparatus was that he was always more than willing to share his knowledge. This is clear from (a) Sanford's direct contributions to students in the minor studies, (b) in the closing chapter in his laboratory manual on apparatus, and (c) in the generous help he gave to Calkins when she was setting up her Wellesley laboratory. One last example is an article that he wrote for the *AJP* in 1893: "Some Practical Suggestions on the Equipment of a Psychological Laboratory" (E. C. Sanford, 1893c). He considered topics ranging from the ideal room configuration (a large main laboratory with several smaller rooms for individual projects), to furniture (comfortable chairs— "physical discomfort is a serious hindrance to successful work for both the subject and the operator" [p. 431]), to apparatus construction (the instructor should have some basic skills, but the ideal arrangement is to have access to university carpenters and machinists). As for which apparatus was essential for a working laboratory, Sanford recognized that budgets would vary considerably, so in addition to a general recommendation that a fully equipped laboratory would cost between $4,000 and $5,000 to start and several hundred dollars a year to maintain, he also pointed out that much money could be saved if the instructor had some mechanical aptitude, and he even made a recommendation for a bare minimum laboratory for the director with severe budget limits:

> If a starvation appropriation is all that is to be had, the most satisfactory pieces would probably be: a sonometer and a few tuning forks for audition, a color-mixer and a Wheatstone stereoscope for vision (the latter home made), and a stop watch for time measurements. (1893c, p. 436)

SANFORD AND THE PROFESSIONALIZATION OF PSYCHOLOGY

A new discipline becomes recognized as a profession when training programs develop, journals are created, and professional organizations are founded and grow. We have already seen how Sanford contributed to the training of experimental psychologists; he was also quite active in the other two indicators that a profession was developing its identity. He was a key figure in the publication of the *AJP* for many years and he was highly visible as a contributing member of the APA.

Sanford's editorial work for Hall's *AJP* began in the second year of its existence (1888). Shortly after defending his dissertation, Sanford was made acting editor while Hall spent a year touring universities in Europe. After Hall's return, Sanford was heavily involved in the routine detail of producing the journal. It was an arrangement that was convenient for Hall, who had no interest in or capacity for attention to detail, but costly to the loyal Sanford, who could have made more productive use of his time. In 1895, in response to competition from the brand new *Psychological Review*, Hall reorganized the *AJP*, naming Sanford and Titchener as coeditors with himself. Sanford remained affiliated with the journal for the rest of his life, and the work occupied a tremendous amount of his time and energy. Because the journal was produced at Clark, and Hall would not bother himself with the details, Sanford bore the brunt of the effort to produce the journal from issue to issue. Aware of the effect the work would have, especially after the 1895 reorganization, Sanford wrote to Titchener that "[as] all of the seeing of the *Journal* through the press is going to fall to [me], I shall not have much time for writing myself" (E. C. Sanford, 1895a).

If the burden of this routine and tedious work was not enough, Sanford also found himself in the position of mediator between the equally strong-willed Hall and Titchener over a long series of disagreements between the two. A major point of contention was Hall's insistence that the arrangement making Sanford and Titchener editors had to be renewed, annually for the first few years, and then every three years. The sensitive Titchener believed that Hall was showing a lack of respect, and frequently threatened to leave the *AJP* (the threats would increase just before the times when the arrangement was to be renewed). Sanford was often called on to mediate the inevitable disputes, "pouring oil on troubled waters," in Titchener's (1907) words. The issues involved were occasionally important (e.g., whether reviews should be signed or anonymous), but often trivial beyond measure (e.g., books would arrive for review free of charge to the *AJP*, to be distributed among the editors and other reviewers; Titchener apparently believed that Hall hoarded all the good ones).[5]

Sanford's unselfish work for the *AJP* was seldom rewarding for him personally, but the journal was an important one, and some of his editorial decisions undoubtedly advanced the field. He derived greater satisfaction from his long involvement with the APA. He was in the room at the founding meeting hosted by Hall in his study on July 8, 1892 (Dennis & Boring, 1952), and he became a charter member. Sanford seldom missed a meeting, and he quickly became one of the new organization's leaders—elected to the position of secretary–treasurer for 1895 and to the ruling three-person APA Council for 1896–1898, and named to several important task forces. In 1902, the APA chose Sanford to be its 11th president. In his presidential address—"Psychology and Physics"—Sanford (1903b) gently chided his colleagues for their "at times . . . embarrassing" (p. 105) infatuation with the physical sciences as the ideal model for psychology as a science. Turning the tables on the traditional sciences, he pointed out that one could take an "ultrapsychological" point of view, and argue that psychology, the study of conscious experience, is more fundamental because scientists ultimately rely on their senses and consciousness to evaluate physical data and formulate theory in their disciplines. Sanford also argued for an interactionist model of mind and body over a parallelist one, urged research to explore the nature of the interaction, and suggested that an evolutionary model might be an appropriate framework

---

[5] Remarkably, there is correspondence between Sanford and Titchener concerning this issue of who gets the new books that stretches over a 10-year period, 1896–1905 (Goodwin, 1987).

for the development of psychological theory. Unfortunately, he also proved to be a poor prophet, believing that psychologists would be unlikely to embrace a purely objective approach, one that would focus on overt behavior rather than on the introspective life of the mind.

IN THE LONG SHADOW OF HALL

Sanford clearly belongs among the important early pioneers in American experimental psychology. His first-of-its-kind laboratory manual, his creativity with apparatus, his direction of a major laboratory, and his contributions to the *AJP* and the APA combine to produce a significant contribution. He might have accomplished even more had he not stood in the long shadow of Hall. I have indicated in a few places that Sanford's relationship with Hall was a mixed blessing. Sanford certainly benefited from the association to a degree—an excellent education from one of early psychology's leading figures, the directorship of a well-financed laboratory, being a part of the origins and development of both the *AJP* and the APA. He responded with a life-long loyalty to Hall and to Clark University. This part of Sanford's nature, loyalty mixed with a strong devotion to duty, traces to the values he learned as a young man and to the fact that when Sanford was a graduate student, Hall was his first real mentor and the teacher–student relationship never quite changed. Although Sanford's allegiance was manifested most obviously in his connection with Hall, it also extended to his relationships with close colleagues (e.g., Titchener, Calkins) and to his students at Clark. Sanford's consistent loyalty was an admirable trait, but one that almost certainly cost him a larger place in psychology's history.

Sanford's allegiance to Hall was put to a strong test in 1892. Clark University opened with great hopes in 1889, and in its first few years, it approached Hall's ideal of a true research university built on the German model. But Hall has been described as arbitrary, capricious, and dissembling as a leader (Ross, 1972), and he soon began alienating faculty. Problems came to a head in 1892, when a national economic depression magnified financial problems that had been growing at the university. Jonas Clark, the university's founder, had always envisioned Clark as a place for the youths of Worcester, Massachusetts, to receive a world-class education, but Hall had convinced Clark that the new university would earn an international reputation as a graduate school. Clark believed that Hall had promised the eventual development of an undergraduate college, and Hall apparently led Clark to think just that, without ever intending to follow through on the alleged promise (Koelsch, 1987). By 1892, the founder was frustrated enough to begin withdrawing financial support. In the middle of this financial crisis, the University of Chicago, just created and richly endowed with Rockefeller money, began recruiting faculty, and Clark's faculty was an especially inviting target. The temptation was too great for many, who were otherwise faced with an uncertain future at Clark and attracted to the much larger salaries at Chicago. The result of Hall's failed leadership and the lure of Chicago was mass defection: Roughly two thirds of the faculty and three quarters of the graduate students left Clark at the end of 1892, with at least half of them finding their way to Chicago (Ross, 1972). Of the original five departments at Clark, only psychology remained as a viable one, with instruction in the other departments severely limited and the total university faculty numbering about 10 (Koelsch, 1987). Hall's university limped through the remainder of the nineteenth century.

Through all of these troubles, Sanford remained steadfast, at one point assuring Hall that "[w]hatever may be the outcome of the present trouble I propose to stand by the university and yourself" (E. C. Sanford, 1892). Sanford's declaration put him firmly on Hall's "side," and Hall did not hesitate to take advantage of his former student's choice. We have already seen that Hall used Sanford's skillful attention to detail to ensure the continued production of the *AJP*. A poignant example of Hall's domineering style and Sanford's reluctant submission to it can be seen in a pair of letters that Sanford sent to Titchener in 1898, during one of those times when the editorial agreement for the *AJP* was to be renewed. In the morning of June 14, 1898, Sanford had written to his friend that he would be "glad to get rid of the drudgery of the [*AJP*]" and "be free to accomplish something" (E. C. Sanford, 1898d). But after sending the letter, Sanford met with Hall and quickly acquiesced to Hall's demand that he stay on. As he wrote later that same day to Titchener, "Of my letting go of the thing entirely, he is not willing to hear. My desire to be rid of it is not less, but ... for the present at least, disregard my [earlier] letter of this date" (E. C. Sanford, 1898c). It is no wonder that Titchener later lamented to Clark's librarian, L. N. Wilson, that Sanford would be more productive if he could stick to a focused program of research (between the lines—Titchener wanted Sanford to be more like Titchener), because he was "a most original, careful, and judicious researcher"; instead, however, "he will wander off with random suggestions from Hall, and give way, and compromise, and take up a thing and let it down—instead of sticking to work in his own line" (Titchener, 1906, n.p.).

Although his letters to Titchener make it clear that he often chafed under the influence of Hall, Sanford nonetheless remained loyal, and late in his life he wrote a remarkable letter to Titchener in which he showed that he had completely rationalized his secondary status to Hall:

> Once in conversation you suggested that I might have had more of a career if I had not all these years stood in [Hall's] shadow. I have thought of that a good many times, but have reached the deliberate conclusion that you were wrong. My mental and temperamental outfit has marked me, as I look at it, even from high school days for a "second" rather than a "first" position. The situation [with Hall] gave me ideal conditions. (E. C. Sanford, 1924)

Ironically, Sanford remained in Hall's shadow even when he died in 1924. Hall also died that year, and the APA held a special program on Hall's passing. One might think that Sanford's loyal service to the APA would have produced some official notice, but Sanford was largely ignored, mentioned just briefly in two papers (Burnham, 1925; Starbuck, 1925) that celebrated Hall's life and work.

CONCLUSION

The 1890s was a time of excitement and great promise for the fledgling discipline of academic psychology in America. Laboratories of experimental psychology were being created with an ever-increasing frequency, new journals were being established to report the outcomes of this laboratory work, and a professional organization to legitimize the discipline, the APA, was created. Sanford was in the middle of all these developments, director of a major laboratory, coeditor of a major journal, and quickly rising to a leadership position in the fledgling APA. In addition, his laboratory manual made a substantial contribution to the training of experimentalists in the 1890s, and his apparatus creations led to the production of new knowledge about psychological phenomena. His contributions to the discipline faded with the new century, and a strong sense of loyalty to his mentor, G. Stanley Hall—combined with Halls's willingness to exploit this loyalty— cost Sanford a greater place in psychology's history. Yet his work, especially in the key decade of the 1890s, makes him a worthy and important pioneer in psychology.

REFERENCES

Account book. (1889–1890). Financial records, October 10, 1889 through March 29, 1890. Worcester, MA: Clark University Archives, L. N. Wilson papers.

Bolton, T. L. (1894). Rhythm. American Journal of Psychology, 6, 145–238.

Boring, E. G. (1950). A history of experimental psychology (2nd ed.). Englewood Cliffs, NJ: Prentice-Hall.

Burnham, W. H. (1925). The man: G. Stanley Hall. Psychological Review, 32, 89–102.

Calkins, M. W. (1893). Statistics of dreams. American Journal of Psychology, 5, 311–343.

Calkins, M. W. (1924). Edmund Clark Sanford. In L. N. Wilson (Ed.), Edmund Clark Sanford: In memoriam (pp. 11–17). Worcester, MA: Clark University Press.

Calkins, M. W. (1930). Mary Whiton Calkins. In C. Murchison (Ed.), A history of psychology in autobiography. Vol. 1 (pp. 31–62). Worcester, MA: Clark University Press.

Carr, H. A., & Watson, J. B. (1908). Orientation in the white rat. Journal of Comparative Neurology and Psychology, 18, 27–44.

Clark University Register. (1889). Registrar records. Worcester, MA: Clark University Archives, G. Stanley Hall Papers.

Dennis, W., & Boring, E. G. (1952). The founding of the APA. American Psychologist, 7, 95–97.

Dewsbury, D. A. (1992). Triumph and tribulation in the history of American comparative psychology. *Journal of Comparative Psychology, 106,* 3–19.

Dimmick, F. L. (1929). A further modification of the Sanford chronoscope. *American Journal of Psychology, 41,* 475–476.

Fernberger, S. W. (1926). Improvements on the Sanford Vernier chronoscope. *American Journal of Psychology, 37,* 154–155.

Goodwin, C. J. (1985). On the origins of Titchener's Experimentalists. *Journal of the History of the Behavioral Sciences, 21,* 383–389.

Goodwin, C. J. (1987). In Hall's shadow: Edmund Clark Sanford (1859–1924). *Journal of the History of the Behavioral Sciences, 23,* 153–168.

Hawkins, H. (1960). *Pioneer: A history of the Johns Hopkins University, 1874–1899.* Ithaca, NY: Cornell University Press.

Jastrow, J. (1898). Psychological literature. *Psychological Review, 5,* 414–416.

Judd, C. H. (1907). *Laboratory manual of psychology.* New York: Scribner's.

Koelsch, W. A. (1987). *Clark University: A narrative history.* Worcester, MA: Clark University Press.

Miles, W. R. (1930). On the history of research with rats and mazes: A collection of notes. *Journal of General Psychology, 3,* 324–337.

National Union Catalog. (1968). London: Mensell.

Ross, D. (1972). *G. Stanley Hall: The psychologist as prophet.* Chicago: University of Chicago Press.

Ruckmick, C. (1927). Some suggestions on laboratory apparatus. *American Journal of Psychology, 38,* 647–648.

Ryan, W. C. (1939). *Studies in early graduate education.* New York: Carnegie Foundation.

Sanford, E. C. (1885). Application form. Ferdinand Hamburger Jr. Archives, Johns Hopkins University, Baltimore.

Sanford, E. C. (1888). Relative legibility of the small letters. *American Journal of Psychology, 1,* 402–435.

Sanford, E. C. (1888–1889). Personal equation. *American Journal of Psychology, 2,* 1–38, 271–298, 401–430.

Sanford, E. C. (1890). A simple and inexpensive chronoscope. *American Journal of Psychology, 3,* 174–181.

Sanford, E. C. (1892). Letter to G. S. Hall, January 23, 1892. Hall Papers, Clark University Archives, Worcester, MA.

Sanford, E. C. (1893a). A new pendulum chronograph. *American Journal of Psychology, 5,* 385–389.

Sanford, E. C. (1893b). On reaction times when the stimulus is applied to the reacting hand. *American Journal of Psychology, 5,* 351–355.

Sanford, E. C. (1893c). Some practical suggestions on the equipment of a psychological laboratory. *American Journal of Psychology, 5,* 429–438.

Sanford, E. C. (1894). *A course in experimental psychology.* Boston: D. C. Heath.

Sanford, E. C. (1895a). Letter to E. B. Titchener, March 19, 1895. Titchener Papers, Cornell University Archives, Ithaca, NY.

Sanford, E. C. (1895b). Notes on new apparatus. *American Journal of Psychology, 6,* 575–584.

Sanford, E. C. (1898a). *A course in experimental psychology I: Sensation and perception.* Boston: D. C. Heath.

Sanford, E. C. (1898b). Letter to E. B. Titchener, June 14, 1898 (1st). Titchener Papers, Cornell University, Ithaca, NY.

Sanford, E. C. (1898c). Letter to E. B. Titchener, June 14, 1898 (2nd). Titchener Papers, Cornell University, Ithaca, NY.

Sanford, E. C. (1898d). The Vernier chronoscope. *American Journal of Psychology, 9,* 191–197.

Sanford, E. C. (1902). Mental growth and decay. *American Journal of Psychology, 13,* 426–449.

Sanford, E. C. (1903a). The psychic life of fishes. *International Quarterly, 7,* 316–333.

Sanford, E. C. (1903b). Psychology and physics. *Psychological Review, 10,* 105–119.

Sanford, E. C. (1906). Sketch of a beginner's course in psychology. *Pedagogical Seminary, 13,* 118–134.

Sanford, E. C. (1912). Methods of research in education. *Journal of Educational Psychology, 3,* 303–315.

Sanford, E. C. (1914). Psychic research in the animal field: Der Kluge Hans and the Elberfeld horses. *American Journal of Psychology, 25,* 1–31.

Sanford, E. C. (1924). Letter to E. B. Titchener, April 25, 1924. Titchener Papers, Cornell University Archives, Ithaca, NY.

Sanford, M. L. (1925). Biographical sketch. In L. N. Wilson (Ed.), *Edmund Clark Sanford: In memoriam* (pp. 3–10). Worcester, MA: Clark University Library.

Scripture, E. W. (1898, July 1). Review. *Science, 8* (New Series), 24–25.

Seashore, C. E. (1908). *Elementary experiments in psychology.* New York: Henry Holt.

Small, W. S. (1901). An experimental study of the mental processes of the rat. II. *American Journal of Psychology, 12,* 206–239.

Sokal, M. M. (Ed.). (1981). *An education in psychology: James McKeen Cattell's journal and letters, from Germany and England, 1880–1888.* Cambridge, MA: MIT Press.

Starbuck, E. D. (1925). G. Stanley Hall as a psychologist. *Psychological Review, 32,* 102–120.

Titchener, E. B. (1894). Notices of new books. *Philosophical Review, 3,* 759–762.

Titchener, E. B. (1901). *Experimental psychology: A manual of laboratory practice. Vol. 1. Qualitative experiments. Part 1, Student's manual. Part 2, Instructor's manual.* New York: Macmillan.

Titchener, E. B. (1905). *Experimental psychology: A manual of laboratory practice. Vol. 2. Quantitative experiments. Part 1, Student's manual. Part 2, Instructor's manual.* New York: Macmillan.

Titchener, E. B. (1906). Letter to L. N. Wilson, June 6, 1906. L. N. Wilson Papers, Clark University Archives, Worcester, MA.

Titchener, E. B. (1907). Letter to L. N. Wilson, May 9, 1907. L. N. Wilson Papers, Clark University Archives, Worcester, MA.

Titchener, E. B. (1924). Edmund Clark Sanford (1859–1924). *American Journal of Psychology, 36,* 156–170.

Visher, S. S. (1947). *Scientists starred 1903–1943 in "American Men of Science": A study of collegiate and doctoral training, birthplace, distribution, and developmental influences.* Baltimore: Johns Hopkins University Press.

Watson, J. B. (1907). Kineasthetic and organic sensation: Their role in the reactions of the white rat to the maze. *Psychological Review Monograph Supplement, 8* (Whole no. 33).

Wilson, L. N. (1898, October 28). Letter to E. B. Titchener. Titchener Papers, Cornell University Archives, Ithaca, NY.

Witmer, L. (1902). *Analytical psychology: A practical manual for colleges and normal schools.* Boston: Ginn.

Woodworth, R. S. (1932). Course syllabus. Gillette Papers, Archives of the History of American Psychology, Akron, OH.

James McKeen Cattell (Photo courtesy of Lafayette College)

Chapter 2

James McKeen Cattell:
Achievement and Alienation

Michael M. Sokal

Early 21st-century psychologists know James McKeen Cattell (1860–1944) best as their predecessor who, late in the 19th century pioneered in the study of individual differences through his program of mental tests; who early in the 20th century effectively promoted the goal of an applicable psychology; and who—through his efforts as an editor and organizer—provided their science and discipline with the institutional infrastructure that enabled it to grow and prosper as it did throughout the 20th century. These accomplishments emerged from a complex personal history that involved as much failure as success and that often saw Cattell alienate his colleagues in psychology. Indeed, Cattell's life and achievement in psychology provide a fine example of just how an individual's character and temperament, and the specific circumstances of his or her early life and upbringing, can help shape (and perhaps determine) the course of that person's career and, quite possibly, even the content of his or her scientific ideas. To be sure, some philosophically aware historians of science argue that such claims derive from a focus on the "accidentals" of the past and that they downplay the real significance of an individual's scientific work. But biographers and psychologists interested in life histories know better, and this realization well justifies careful attention to the details of Cattell's early years. If this chapter illustrates the value for the history of science of an intense focus on an individual's character and temperament, and on the circumstances of his or her life—even as it traces and explicates the origins and import of Cattell's achievements as a pioneering psychologist—it will have served its purpose.

The contents of this chapter reflect and derive from my research on Cattell since the late 1960s and the many publications that these studies led to (for example, Sokal, 1971, 1973, 1980a, 1980b, 1981a, 1981b, 1982, 1984, 1990, 1992, 1994, 1995, 1997, 2003). Additional documentation for the details and interpretations presented—beyond that given in this chapter—may be found in each of these publications.

CATTELL'S EDUCATION

James McKeen Cattell was born in 1860 in Easton, Pennsylvania, where his father William C. Cattell was professor at Lafayette College and his wealthy maternal grandfather (whose name he bore) was the college's most generous benefactor. In 1863, the elder Cattell became president of Lafayette, which held most of its classes in McKeen Hall, and Cattell grew up in the insular community of Easton almost as scion of the lord of the manor. He began formal studies at the college in 1876 and thrived academically, even as—much like Anson Hunter, the protagonist of F. Scott Fitzgerald's (1926) story, "The Rich Boy"— he noticed "the half-grudging American deference that was paid to him" (p. 28) even by his professors. Like Fitzgerald's character, Cattell "accepted this as the natural state of affairs" and thus developed "a sort of impatience with all groups of which he was not the center . . . which remained with him for the rest of his life" (p. 28). And at times this attitude played a significant role in shaping Cattell's career.

At Lafayette three strands of study converged to shape Cattell's later scientific views. Two derived from the teachings of Francis A. March, an eminent Anglo Saxon philologist and Lafayette's most distinguished scholar. March taught the college's required senior course in mental philosophy—a course that most American college seniors in the 1870s had to complete—and like most such courses March's focused on the faculty psychology of 18th-century Scottish common-sense realism. This psychology supported the notion that appropriate mental discipline could develop each of the mental faculties, and it thus meshed well with the goals of many contemporaneous American colleges. But in America in the second half of the 19th century it had deteriorated into scholastic disputation with overly precise terminologies applied to trivial points—for example, the classification of human desires within the categories of hunger, thirst, and sex. No wonder these ideas faced serious challenges at several leading universities from such competing approaches as German idealism and Herbert Spencer's evolutionary psychology.

Faculty psychology never satisfied Cattell, no more than it did other well-read Americans who had begun to turn elsewhere. Despite March's fine teaching and the well respected text by Joseph Haven (1876) that March taught from, Cattell continually disparaged this philosophy. March, for example, had his students analyze such questions as, "Is consciousness ever wholly interrupted?" and "Is it possible to recall by direct effort of the will?" and "Is there any such thing as immediate perception?" Cattell's response (1879) to this third question— "I do not know, and I doubt if anyone else knows"—reveals his impatience with, and willingness to challenge, views he could not accept.

Cattell responded more positively to the philosophy of Francis Bacon (1561– 1626), the other major thrust of March's teachings. With its emphasis on the utility of knowledge and the collection of masses of empirical details, it always shaped March's own academic views. For example, the 1869 compendium that made his scholarly reputation (*A Comparative Grammar of the Anglo-Saxon Language: In Which Its Forms Are Illustrated by Those of the Sanskrit, Greek, Latin, Gothic, Old Friesic, Old Saxon, Old Norse, and Old High German*) derived from thousands of interrelated details he had gathered for years. And each year at Lafayette he took the junior class through Bacon's *Essays* and his commentary stressed this view of science. Few active scholars have made their epistemologies as clear as March did.

Despite this clarity, late-19th-century American Baconianism shared little with the subtle empiricism then emerging in Europe, often in connection with insightful exegeses of Scottish–realist ideas. Instead, Americans often reduced Bacon's work to a "vulgar empiricism" that stressed the simple collection of large amounts of elemental data and that avoided or even denigrated hypothesis and interpretation. To be sure, the impact of these views had begun to ebb by the 1870s, especially at major American centers of higher education. But they remained influential at Lafayette, where March's presence kept them strong. Even as Cattell disparaged the Scottish realism of March's formal classes, he seemed impressed that his professor actually used Baconianism in his scholarship. Throughout his scientific career, Cattell retained much of March's kind of Baconianism, always taking an empirical approach to the world around him, collecting bits of data wherever he could, avoiding hypotheses and interpretations, and usually stressing the utility of his work.

The third strand of study at Lafayette that helped shaped Cattell's scientific views derived directly from the circumstances of his personal life. His father— like most other effective college presidents of his generation—was also an ordained minister (in his case, a Presbyterian) to whom students and colleagues often looked for personal guidance. But in all others aspects of his life William Cattell exhibited an extreme genteel neurasthenia that often left him nervous and edgy, and that at times forced him to withdraw entirely from the practicalities of life. Such complaints remain common today, of course, and early 21st-century psychologists use other terms to explain them. But 130 years ago neurasthenia was the diagnosis of choice for those upper-middle-class Americans who exhibited these symptoms, and the condition seemed fairly common among those who, like William Cattell, saw themselves as learned.

In his suffering William Cattell found himself emotionally dependent on his wife, Elizabeth McKeen Cattell, and only her devoted care and attention could calm his nervousness. Cattell's parents thus became the center of each other's emotional world, and after her husband's death, Elizabeth Cattell wrote often about how much she missed the chance to dote on her husband. Throughout his childhood, then, Cattell lived in a family in which his mother provided emotional sustenance, and through her altruistic devotion to her husband and their sons (James and his younger brother Henry) enabled them all to achieve all that they did. For the rest of his life Cattell carried with him the ideal of the close-knit family with the mother at its emotional center, but deferring always to the father's interests.

Cattell's science felt the impact of this vision almost immediately. In graduating from Lafayette in 1880, Cattell was scheduled to give his class's valedictory address on "The Ethics of Positivism." Auguste Comte, the founder of Positivism as a formal philosophical system, denied Christian teachings, and he sought the basis of ethical living in the concept of altruism, which stressed the good that individuals do for others. Comte even identified as his model of altruistic (and hence ethical) behavior the sacrifice of mothers in childbirth, and practitioners of his "Religion of Humanity" revered images of mothers and infants that resembled the Madonna and Child portrayed by Renaissance artists. Although many contemporaneous critics called this practice "Catholicism without Christianity," it emphasized the importance of family and, for many, the centrality of the mother in the family setting. No wonder Cattell resonated with these views. Only a few years later, as a 20-year-old student in Germany, he spent a large sum of money—even for somebody with access to his grandfather's wealth—for a copy of Raphael's *Sistine Madonna*. And no wonder he devoted the time he must have to preparing his address.

No copy of Cattell's address seems now to exist. But anyone who spoke on Comtean Positivism in 1880 must have immersed himself in a philosophy that equated "positive knowledge" with science, and that stressed—with its law of three stages and the hierarchy of knowledge—the authority of a quantitative understanding of nature. Comte's disciples developed quantitative methods in their study of nature, and although Positivism never stressed empiricism, the focus of Comte's writings often carried an empiricist bias. This empiricism meshed well with Baconianism, which might have helped lead Cattell to Positivism in the first place. By 1880, when Cattell graduated from Lafayette College, he had developed a scientific ideology that disparaged speculation and combined a Comtean emphasis on quantification with a Baconian appreciation for the hypothesis-free collection of empirical "facts" and the usefulness of knowledge. And throughout his later career in psychology he adopted methods that produced quantitative data about (potentially applicable) psychological phenomena, even if he often could not explain them.

EARLY POSTGRADUATE STUDY

After Lafayette, Cattell spent 2 years in Germany, studying first in Göttingen with Herman Lotze and then moving on to Leipzig, where he attended Wilhelm Wundt's philosophical lectures. In doing so, he did not seek advanced training in psychology but—like 10,000 other American students between 1865 and 1914—simply sought an acquaintance with the world of research and scholarship then not commonly available in America. In 1882, his father's connections helped him beat John Dewey in a competition for a fellowship in philosophy at the Johns Hopkins University—one of the few American institutions that then promoted scholarship—and he soon began a series of informal experiments that embodied his first real experience with the kind of empirical studies that Bacon had called for. During his first months in Baltimore, his classmates introduced him to such psychedelic and narcotic drugs as hashish, opium, and morphine and, like other Americans of the period, he began using them regularly. Contemporaneous medical researchers and philosophers formally investigated their effects, and although Cattell first took them for recreation, his interest soon included a real Baconian component. Even during his first experience with hashish, for example, he noted that, "I seemed to be two persons one of which could observe and even experiment on the other" (cited in Sokal, 1981a, pp. 50–51). He recorded his observations, including data on his pulse rate and temperature, and through his year at Baltimore tried many different drugs. Like others of his time and place, he inhaled ether and chloroform, smoked tobacco, took caffeine, and drank an extract of tea— "equal to 10–20 cups of ordinary tea" (cited in Sokal, 1981a, p. 61)—to study their effects. One evening he "drank fifteen glasses of beer or there abouts— then three whiskeys," but abandoned his observations soon after he had begun. The next day, he noted that, "I drank that alcohol partly for experiment, partly for the emotional affects, not intending to carry either as far when I began" (cited in Sokal, 1981a, p. 69).

He also studied in George S. Morris's philosophy seminar and, after January 1883, when G. Stanley Hall joined the Hopkins faculty, in Hall's "Psychology: Advanced Course." More important, Cattell went to work in Hall's "new physio-logico–psychological laboratory" (cited in Sokal, 1981a, p. 64), and within a month he had performed some original experimental studies of reading, precisely measuring reaction times to the millisecond, in accordance with his Baconian and Comtean scientific ideology. Cattell also claimed utility for his results by arguing that they showed that readers recognize words at least as quickly as they recognize individual letters, and for years others cited these experiments in promoting whole-word (as opposed to phonic-based) reading instruction. Even in 1883 Cattell's successes impressed Hall, who tried to appropriate his student's data as his own, and in the ensuing conflict Cattell alienated the entire Hopkins faculty. The episode led to Cattell's expulsion from Johns Hopkins, to the transfer of his fellowship to Dewey, and to his decisions to study with Wundt in Leipzig and to look explicitly to a scientific career in the new psychology based on the precise laboratory study of psychological questions. Cattell's career as a psychologist had begun.

At Leipzig in the fall of 1883, Cattell began the series of reaction-time experiments that established his reputation as perhaps the leading American experimental psychologist of his generation. At first he followed Wundt's procedures, which called for experimenters (in measuring simple reaction times) to react as soon as possible to any stimulus presented and (in measuring more complicated processes, such as *Unterscheidungszeit,* the time required to perceive the difference between two possible sense impressions) to react only after they had consciously realized that they had perceived the distinction. (Wundt called this method *Selbstbeobachtung,* or self-observation. Many previous writers have mistranslated this term as "introspection" and, in doing so, have confused this technique with the more precisely defined introspective methods later practiced by Edward B. Titchener.)

But just as Cattell could not answer March's questions about the reality of immediate perception, he found it impossible to observe his mental activity as closely as Wundt wanted. As he later noted, "I apparently either distinguished the impression and made the motion simultaneously, or if I tried to avoid this by waiting until I had formed a distinct impression before I made the motion, I added to the simple reaction, not only a perception, but also a volition" (Cattell, 1886, p. 378). Cattell thus declared his experimental results using Wundt's methods as "worthless" (Sokal, 1981a, p. 99) and during the next 2 years developed his own approach to reaction-time studies.

In doing so, he sought (as his scientific ideology expected) to measure these phenomena as precisely as possible. To reach this goal, he modified instruments that Wundt and his colleagues had long used (such as the Hipp Chronoscope) and designed new apparatus (such as the lip key and the gravity chronometer) that soon became staples of German and American psychological laboratories (Sokal, Davis, & Merzbach, 1976). More important, he separated the roles of the experimental subject (and he was apparently the first to use this term)—who reacted in specified ways to a range of sense impressions—and the experimenter, who presented the stimuli to the subject. In addition, he arranged his experiments to eliminate *Selbstbeobachtung* entirely. That is, even after he determined his subjects' simple reaction times he designed all of his later experiments to again call for them to react as quickly as possible. For example, in measuring *Unterscheidungszeit* he had his subjects respond only when a particular stimulus (perhaps a colored light) appeared. This reaction time was longer than a simple reaction time and, for Wundt and Cattell, the extra time was the time required to discriminate between a colored and an uncolored light. Similarly, in measuring *Wahlzeit,* or choice time, Cattell had his subjects vary their reactions in response to the different stimuli presented. For example, he asked them to react as quickly as possible to red lights with their right hands and to green lights with their left hands. In this way, Cattell refocused psychological research away from experimenters' self-observation of their mental activity and toward subjects' behavior in a laboratory setting precisely defined by experimenters. Cattell did not highlight this shift in his experimental reports, and first noted them publicly almost 20 years later. By then other psychologists had implicitly adopted Cattell's perspective.

In the same way, Cattell at first never highlighted one aspect of these experiments that others later explicitly saw as revolutionary. But once he realized just how original this feature was he joined with others in emphasizing their path-breaking nature. In his first experimental reports—published both in English and German—Cattell did note that his subjects' reaction times under similar conditions differed from one another. But he did so only as an aside, and it was not until the 1910s that Cattell and others began asserting that these experiments represented the origins of his—and organized psychology's—formal interest in individual differences. Many years later Cattell (1921, p. 158) even admitted that he mentioned such differences only as epiphenomena. Instead, in initially reporting his results, Cattell strongly emphasized their experimental precision and that he had consistently measured all sorts of reaction times in milliseconds. To be sure, in his English reports he tried to interpret these results within a physicalistic framework, and argued that his experiments had not measured mental activity but rather "the time taken up by cerebral operations" (see Cattell, 1886, p. 277). This concern may have reinforced his decision not to address the precise psychological import of these measurements. But his Baconian–Comtean scientific ideology also denigrated any attempts at hypothesis formation. Indeed, since this ideology required the collection of large numbers of highly precise quantitative observations of the world, he rarely if ever felt the need to go further.

CAMBRIDGE, PENNSYLVANIA, AND COLUMBIA

Despite these successes and his Leipzig PhD, Cattell could not find an American position he and his father considered suitable, and in the fall of 1886 he enrolled in St. John's College, Cambridge, as a fellow–commoner, an honorary position with perquisites that included the formal deference that he always enjoyed. Fortunately for him, Cattell's family that year had an income of $12,000, which enabled him both to afford Cambridge's high costs and to defer assuming an instructorship at the University of Pennsylvania that his father arranged soon thereafter. He enjoyed his celebrity status at Cambridge as the English speaker best acquainted with the new psychology. Of more intellectual importance, he grew to know Francis Galton, Darwin's cousin, who introduced him to his own strong interests in the differences between individuals; that is, the variation that makes natural selection possible. Specifically, Cattell visited Galton's Anthropometric Laboratory in London, which used standard methods that previous observers had used to characterize the average physical traits of a given population—height, weight, length of limbs, strength of squeeze, breathing capacity, keenness of eyesight, and so forth—to gather precise quantitative data on the variation of these traits among the British public. This highly quantified exercise in data gathering reinforced whatever latent interests Cattell might earlier have had in studying individual differences, and these interests dominated the rest of Cattell's scientific career. Indeed, Cattell apparently later claimed that three men named Francis—Bacon, March, and Galton—determined the course of his scientific career.

In 1889, Cattell returned to America and a professorship at the University of Pennsylvania that his father had arranged, and there began with collaborators two highly significant experimental studies: an extension of his reaction-time studies through an investigation of the velocity of the nervous impulse (with Charles S. Dolley) and a careful review of traditional psychophysical methods. In both cases his reports presented the phenomena he studied physicalistically; for example, where earlier psychologists had used psychophysical methods to study "just noticeable differences" of (mental) sensation, Cattell and his colleague George S. Fullerton argued that these methods really measured errors of observation. Two years later, as American universities finally began to bid against each other for psychologists, he doubled his salary by moving to Columbia College in New York. There he developed an active psychological laboratory and built fruitful teaching collaborations with Columbia's philosophers and anthropologists. Columbia formally evolved into a university in 1895, and by the time Cattell left the institution in 1917 he had directed (or played a significant role in) the doctoral dissertations of more than 40 students, many of whom became leaders of American psychology and its profession. At least seven—Edward L. Thorndike, Robert S. Woodworth, Shepherd I. Franz, Harry L. Hollingworth, John F. Dashiell, Albert T. Poffenberger, and Herbert Woodrow—later served as presidents of the American Psychological Association (APA), and others also had distinguished careers. Cattell also importantly played a leading role in bringing to Columbia anthropologist Franz Boas in 1896 and philosopher John Dewey, his Johns Hopkins classmate, in 1904.

In 1892, as G. Stanley Hall founded the APA, Cattell became active in the new association's affairs. As its second secretary, he argued that "we psychologists ought not to draw the sex-line" (Cattell, 1893, n.p.), and the APA became one of the first national scientific societies to admit women as full members. He also edited (without published credit) the APA's first proceedings, played an active role in its earliest committee on psychological testing, and established himself as a leader of the American psychological community. In 1895, he served as APA's fourth president.

A year earlier, Cattell founded (with James Mark Baldwin of Princeton) *The Psychological Review*—largely to lessen the dominance of G. Stanley Hall's *American Journal of Psychology*—and during the 10 years they jointly edited the journal it became the outlet of choice for American psychologists doing functional research. The following year he entered into the larger American scientific community by assuming the ownership and editorship of *Science,* the weekly journal whose fortunes had declined despite support successively from Thomas A. Edison and Alexander Graham Bell. But Cattell succeeded where Edison and Bell had failed. *Science* thrived under his editorship, and he retained its ownership and editorship even after it became the official journal of the American Association for the Advancement of Science (AAAS) in 1900. In that year, too, he took over another failing journal, *The Popular Science Monthly,* which (similar to the early-21st-century's *Scientific American*) brought thoughtful reports on current science before the educated public. Cattell's publishing empire continued to grow so that, by 1915, he owned and edited two weekly journals (*Science* and *School and Society*) and two monthly journals (*The American Naturalist* and *The Scientific Monthly*). And appropriately for one who had been drawn to science by a philosophy that emphasized altruism in women, his editorial success derived largely from the role of his wife—Josephine Owen Cattell, a Welshwoman whom he had met as she studied music in Leipzig in the mid-1880s—who served as managing editor for all of his journals.

ANTHROPOMETRIC TESTING

Most important, with his junior colleague Livingston Farrand at Columbia Cattell extended Galton's program to carry out a series of anthropometric tests, designed to measure the individual attributes of each freshman enrolled at the all-male Columbia College in the mid-1890s. This series included some of the physiological measurements that Galton had made—such as an individual's strength of squeeze—and added others, such as his rate of movement and the pressure that caused him pain. But Cattell's series also included measurements of a variety of psychological traits of each student, such as his reaction time for sound, the least-noticeable difference of weight he could perceive, his ability to bisect a 50-centimeter line, his judgment of a 10-second time, the number of letters he could repeat from a list after one hearing, and the time he took in marking each of 10 As embedded in a 10 by 10 array of letters. Many of these individual tests simply involved the procedures that Cattell had previously used in his experiments, and all were relatively easy to perform. Most notably (for his scientific ideology, at least), all could yield highly precise results that he could readily quantify. In reporting the initial results of these tests (Cattell & Farrand, 1896, p. 648), he thus characterized them as "mere facts" and emphasized that he did not "wish to draw any definite conclusions" from them. After all, his scientific ideology never required any such "definite conclusions."

To be sure, other American psychologists in the mid-1890s—such as Cattell's coeditor Baldwin—maintained that the Columbia anthropometric testing program focused too heavily on the elemental and the physiological and argued that, in any such program, "the tests [should have as] psychological a character as possible" (Baldwin, 1898, p. 175). For their part, as the program began, Cattell and Farrand noted that they could not spell out any functional relationships among the traits they measured. Instead, they sketched a series of questions that they hoped the tests would answer.

> To what extent are the several traits of body, of the senses and of mind interdependent? How far can we predict one thing from our knowledge of another? What can we learn from tests of elementary traits regarding the higher intellectual and emotional life? (1896, p. 648)

Within a few years, Cattell's testing program provided answers to these questions, but the answers proved disappointing. That is, even as other psychologists followed Cattell and proposed or actually performed similar series of anthropometric tests at their own university, among such groups as inmates in prisons, and, as they were called, "schools for the feebleminded," others followed Baldwin by criticizing the narrowness of Cattell's focus, and even by comparing his tests with those being developed in France by Alfred Binet and his collaborators. Cattell and Farrand (1896) themselves noted that they "fully appreciate[d] the arguments urged by MM. Binet and Henri in favor of making tests of a strictly psychological character," but stressed that "measurements of the body and of the senses come as completely within our scope as the higher mental processes" (p. 623). They went further, noting that "if we undertake to study attention or suggestibility"—traits of functional significance—"we find it difficult to measure a definite thing" (p. 623). Cattell's scientific ideology thus led him and Farrand to avoid investigating that which they could not easily quantify and to focus instead on what they knew they could measure. They thus avoided what they knew was more significant—according to their colleagues, at least—to address what they could work with easily. Years later, Alfred North Whitehead developed the notion of the fallacy of misplaced concreteness, and although he apparently never applied it to Cattell's work, he well could have.

By the late 1890s, as Cattell collected sets of data of about 1,000 Columbia students, he learned that Galton and Karl Pearson had developed statistical methods to determine how closely two sets of measurements of any group of individuals were related to each other, or correlated. He soon recognized that these techniques could help him and his students interpret his data, and he tried to learn them. But almost immediately he realized that, despite his constant stress on the importance of quantification, "the mathematics are too much for me" (Cattell, 1901), and his graduate students had to go directly to his colleague Boas to learn how to calculate coefficients of correlation.

One who did study with Boas was Clark Wissler, an 1897 graduate of Indiana University who had come to New York to work on Cattell's testing program.

At Columbia, Wissler's interests evolved toward anthropology, and he worked especially closely with Boas. In 1901, Cattell had Wissler calculate the correlation between the results of several pairs of his tests, between tests results and grades earned in any one class, and between grades earned in different classes. Wissler's calculations showed almost no correlation between the results of any two tests, even those concerned with closely related skills such as what he called "quickness and accuracy." For example, 252 students took both the reaction-times test and the marking-As test, and Wissler found a -0.05 correlation between the results of the two tests. As he explained this result for those unfamiliar with statistical analysis, "an individual with a quick reaction-time is no more likely to be quick in marking out the A's than one with a slow reaction-time" (1901, p. 27). More striking, Wissler's analysis showed no correlation between the result of any of Cattell's tests and the college standing of any of the students tested; the correlation of +0.08 between college standing and the results of Cattell's association tests was about typical. Finally, Wissler found that academic performance in most subjects correlated well with that in most other subjects, as he calculated correlations of +0.75 between grades in Latin and Greek, and even +0.30 between grades in French and rhetoric. As he concluded, even "the gymnasium grade, which is based chiefly upon faithfulness in attendance, correlates with average class standing [+0.53] to about the same degree as one course with another" (Wissler, 1901, p. 36). In all, this analysis struck most psychologists as definitive, and many soon cited it to discredit anthropometric testing.

ORDER-OF-MERIT STUDIES

Cattell gradually withdrew from Columbia's psychological laboratory after Wissler published these results, and some of his later students noted his disengagement from their experimental work. But he did not leave psychology. For example, late in the 1890s he extended Galton's techniques of "statistics by intercomparison." That is, in 1875 Galton noted that individual differences need not be measured precisely to be treated statistically. Instead, observers could rank-order differences in an ascending scale, and as a person's height need not be measured to determine his or her place in a size-ordered line, a teacher could rank a schoolchild's ability at the top—or in the middle, or at the bottom—of a class. Cattell tried to apply this technique to study perceptual abilities and reaction times by creating 211 gray-colored cards—which passed imperceptibly from the darkest black to the brightest white—and asking his observers to judge which of two cards presented simultaneously for 3 milliseconds was brighter. He found that reaction times and errors increased as the grays grew closer in hue, and this result encouraged him to extend this work. However, he soon abandoned these studies because he realized that, by collecting relatively large numbers of sets of judgments of the rank order of just about anything—much as Galton's observers had rank-ordered individuals by height—he could establish an "order of merit" of whatever trait he was studying. Furthermore, by comparing individuals' placements in this order of merit he could extend his studies of individual differences. He also came to realize that such a set of judgments need not be made in the laboratory and, indeed, that many already existed, at least in an implicit form. After about 1901, then, Cattell moved most of his psychological research out of the laboratory and into the library.

In 1903, for example, Cattell published a study that presented a rank-ordering of the 1,000 "most eminent" individuals in history. He determined the place of each person in this order of merit by counting the number of lines he or she received in six standard biographical dictionaries. Cattell's first papers on this topic emphasized his methods and admitted their limitations. But he claimed that, even if the precise order of merit of each individual was questionable, the entire set, taken as a whole, gave him the data needed for a study of the individual differences that contributed to the trait of eminence. But after providing some demographic and other statistics about his 1,000 subjects, Cattell presented little analysis of these data.

Instead, Cattell soon identified another set of 1,000 individuals who he claimed deserved attention. In 1902, he offered to create for the newly founded Carnegie Institution of Washington a roster of all active American scientists. The institution awarded Cattell its second grant, and he expected to have the list ready within 3 months. But not until 1906 could Cattell publish the first edition of *American Men of Science,* which included brief biographical entries on about 4,000 American scientific workers. Over the next 38 years Cattell and his colleagues issued six more editions of this directory, continued today as *American Men and Women of Science.* But as early as 1903—when he began to collect data for this project— Cattell viewed it as a source of data for his studies of individual differences. He started by artificially dividing all scientific activity into 12 categories— mathematics, physics, chemistry, and so forth—that is, just those Comte had recognized in his hierarchy of the sciences, presented in Comte's order. He then identified 10 judges for each science, and he asked each judge to rank-order those who worked in his or her field. He used the resulting rankings to create orders of merit for each science. He did not—at least in 1906—publish the precise order of merit for any one science. Instead, he performed for each science—and for the 1,000 most highly rated scientists across all fields (whose entries he starred in the published volumes)—the kind of statistical analyses he had for the 1,000 most eminent individuals in history. In later years he repeated these analyses using data from the later *American Men of Science* editions, and in 1910, for example, he argued that his data had shown that the faculties of certain universities (such as Harvard and Wisconsin) had gained in stature, whereas others (like his own Columbia) had declined. Late-20th-century observers described these studies as providing the first quality rankings of American universities.

FURTHER INSTITUTION BUILDING

Through the 20th century's first decade, as Cattell's growing involvement with publishing, the AAAS, and the national scientific community gradually dominated his attention (Kohlstedt, Sokal, & Lewenstein, 1999), he devoted even less of his time to psychological research, even out of the laboratory. In 1901, for example, he became the first psychologist elected to the National Academy of Sciences, and although his membership citation noted his earlier experimental achievements, the larger community's familiarity with his editorships clearly helped his election. His psychological colleagues continued to call on his expertise, however, and before the decade ended he had worked with more than one APA committee seeking to promote the association's publications program. They also drew on his stature in the American scientific community at large.

Most notably, as Harvard psychologist Hugo Münsterberg organized the International Congress of Arts and Sciences in St. Louis in 1904 that accompanied (with the Olympic Games) the Louisiana Purchase Exposition, he called on Cattell to speak on "The Conceptions and Methods of Psychology." In this address Cattell (1904) emphasized the behavioral nature of his earlier research and noted that "it is usually no more necessary for the subject to be a psychologist than is for the vivisected frog to be a physiologist" (p. 181). Many who heard Cattell speak in St. Louis resonated strongly with this remarks. One of his own students, Robert S. Woodworth (1931, p. 47), later emphasized how they made "articulate in the way of definition" many commonly held assumptions, and the presentation led another auditor—John B. Watson, who later claimed great originality for his behaviorist viewpoint—to dedicate his 1914 book, *Psychology From the Standpoint of a Behaviorist,* to Cattell.

Most important, Cattell's Baconianism led him to stress the practical applications of his field and to call for the creation of "a profession of psychology." He explicitly stated that "if I did not believe that psychology . . . could be applied in useful ways, I should regard my occupation as nearer to that of the professional chessplayer or sword swallower than to that of the engineer or scientific physician" and saw no reason why "the application of systematized knowledge to control human nature may not in the course of the current century accomplish results commensurate with the nineteenth century applications of physical science to the natural world" (Woodworth, 1931, p. 185). Cattell was not, of course, the first psychologist to practice or even to argue for an applicable psychology. But many of Cattell's younger colleagues who were especially active in the emerging "profession of psychology"—including James R. Angell, Lewis M. Terman, J. B. Watson himself, and Robert M. Yerkes—later cited Cattell's St. Louis address as a particularly powerful stimulus that had a major impact on the courses of their individual careers.

Even as Cattell continued to shift the focus of his attention from psychology to the scientific community at large he remained eager to work with his psychological colleagues in institutional settings. For example, he actively participated in talks about an International Congress of Psychology projected for 1913 in the United States (Evans & Down Scott, 1978). Nothing positive came of these discussions, because the extremely nasty backbiting of all involved undermined American psychology's ability to develop effective plans. Through the rest of the 1910s, Cattell focused his attention on publishing and other institutional matters. In 1917, he faced a serious personal crisis when Columbia University dismissed him from the professorship he had held since 1891 (Sokal, 2001). In taking this action the university cited Cattell's antimilitarist statements as the nation entered World War I. But all who knew Cattell also knew that his continued expectation of deference to his views on all issues had long since grown obnoxious, that he had brought unfavorable press attention to Columbia, and that he had alienated just about all of his Columbia colleagues. Indeed, few within the academic world tried to defend Cattell, and he soon attacked those few who did for not supporting every statement he had ever made. Even as he continued to edit his journals—which after all he owned—it seemed to some that Cattell's influence in psychology, and in the larger American scientific community, had ended.

Early in the 1920s, however, Cattell used the almost $25,000 financial settlement he received from Columbia to establish The Psychological Corporation, a commercial firm designed to implement his 1904 call for an applied psychology (Sokal, 1981b). In his planning of the corporation, however, Cattell devoted more attention to its organization—which he saw as a series of coops of psychologists in cities where many of them taught at local universities—than to how his colleagues would actually apply their science. By this time, of course, many psychologists had established successful consulting practices in industrial and other areas of applied psychology. But Cattell ignored them—or was perhaps even ignorant of them—and instead sketched how the corporation would use its income to fund his colleagues' research. Many psychologists found Cattell's promise of research funding attractive and devoted time to the venture. But most of them had no experience in practical settings and most had no idea of how to apply their theoretical or experimental work; thus, the corporation floundered. Finally, in 1926, Cattell left the everyday direction of the firm to Walter Van Dyke Bingham, a psychologist with significant experience in industrial and advertising psychology. He soon employed well-trained psychologists with appropriate applied experience, and the firm gradually emerged as a significant publisher of psychological tests and supplier of applied psychological services.

CONCLUSION

By this time, Cattell was 66 years old, and even as he took on oversight of a printing business for his journals and became chair of the AAAS board, he still tried to remain active in psychology. He involved himself heavily in planning for the 1929 International Congress of Psychology that met at Yale in September 1929, less than a month before the stock market crash and the start of the Great Depression. He served as the Congress's president and devoted days to writing a presidential address, which presented his view of the history of psychology in America and which he distributed to all attendees as a pamphlet well illustrated with portraits of many leading psychologists of his generation and the one before it. Many appreciated the details that Cattell had gathered, but just as many thought the entire exercise pretentious. No matter how they responded to this address, all attendees found shocking Cattell's personal attack of William McDougall, then at Duke University, who reported on a series of long-term experiments designed to demonstrate the Lamarckian claim for the inheritance of acquired characteristics. Other psychologists shared Cattell's doubts about McDougall's results. But only he stood up after McDougall spoke to say the following:

> These experiments are interesting but of course they are wrong. . . . I must be permitted to say that your methods are not valid. . . . There is not sufficiently correlation . . . that can be demonstrated. . . . Dr. McDougall, do you know why they were a failure (No.) I do, and I will tell you later. (Miles, 1929, n.p.)

Before Cattell died in 1944, those attending APA annual conventions regularly pointed him out to their students, as he rarely missed a meeting. But unlike those who revered such other "pioneers of psychology" as William James in their old age, Cattell's younger colleagues often saw him as a fossil who represented psychology's "bad old days." This attitude dismissed all of Cattell's significant achievements, largely in demonstrating the value of experimental precision, in focusing psychologists' attention on behavior, in stimulating their interests in testing and individual differences, in promoting an applicable psychology, and in building an institutional infrastructure for psychology. These accomplishments emerged directly out of Cattell's scientific ideology, which in turn derived from boyhood experiences. To be sure, these experiences also led to and reinforced the character traits that later helped limit the impact of all that Cattell did and that alienated him from many of his colleagues in psychology, and that led them to denigrate his successes. As presented in this chapter, Cattell's life and career as a pioneering psychologist thus illustrate the value for the history of science of an intense focus on the circumstances of an individual's life, even as it traces and explicates the origins and import of Cattell's achievements. And as noted, if this chapter has done so successfully, it will have served its purpose.

REFERENCES

Baldwin, J. M. (1898). Physical and mental tests. *Psychological Review, 5,* 172–179.

Cattell, J. M. (1879). Unpublished undergraduate essays. James McKeen Cattell papers, Manuscript Division, Library of Congress, Washington, DC.

Cattell, J. M. (1886). The time taken up by cerebral operations. III. The perception–time. *Mind,* *11,* 277–392.

Cattell, J. M. (1893). Undated draft letters to G. S. Fullerton, W. James, and G. T. Ladd, Unpublished letterbook. James McKeen Cattell papers, Manuscript Division, Library of Congress, Washington, DC.

Cattell, J. M. (1901, October 15). Letter to Simon Newcomb. Simon Newcomb papers, Manuscript Division, Library of Congress, Washington, DC.

Cattell, J. M. (1904). The conceptions and methods of psychology. *Popular Science Monthly, 66,* 176–186.

Cattell, J. M. (1921). In memory of Wilhelm Wundt. *Psychological Review, 28,* 155–159.

Cattell, J. M., & Farrand L. (1896). Physical and mental measurements of the students of Columbia University. *Psychological Review, 3,* 618–648.

Evans, R. B., & Down Scott, F. J. (1978). The 1913 International Congress of Psychology: The American congress that wasn't. *American Psychologist, 33,* 711–723.

Fitzgerald, F. S. (1926, January and February). The rich boy. *Redbook, 46,* 2–32, 144, 146; 75–79, 122, 124–126.

Haven, J. (1876). *Mental philosophy: Including the intellect, sensibilities, and will.* New York: Sheldon.

Kohlstedt, S. G., Sokal, M. M., & Lewenstein, B. V. (1999). *The establishment of science in America: 150 years of the American Association for the Advancement of Science.* New Brunswick, NJ: Rutgers University Press.

March, F. A. (1869). *Comparative grammar of the Anglo-Saxon language: In which its forms are illustrated by those of the Sanskrit, Greek, Latin, Gothic, Old Saxon, Old Friesic, Old Norse, and Old High-German.* New York: Harper & Brothers.

Miles, W. R. (1929, September 5). Entry in personal diary. Walter R. Miles papers, Archives of the History of American Psychology, University of Akron, OH.

Sokal, M. M. (1971). The unpublished autobiography of James McKeen Cattell. *American Psychologist, 26,* 626–635.

Sokal, M. M. (Ed.). (1973). APA's first publication: Proceedings of the American Psychological Association, 1892–1893. *American Psychologist, 28,* 277–292.

Sokal, M. M. (1980a). Graduate study with Wundt: Two eyewitness accounts. In W. G. Bringmann & R. D. Tweney (Eds.), *Wundt studies: A centennial collection* (pp. 210–225). Toronto, Canada: C. J. Hogrefe.

Sokal, M. M. (1980b, 4 July). Science and James McKeen Cattell. *Science, 209,* 43–52.

Sokal, M. M. (Ed.). (1981a). *An education in psychology: James McKeen Cattell's journal and letters from Germany and England, 1880–1888.* Cambridge, MA: MIT Press.

Sokal, M. M. (1981b). The origins of The Psychological Corporation. *Journal of the History of the Behavioral Sciences, 17,* 54–67.

Sokal, M. M. (1982). James McKeen Cattell and the failure of anthropometric mental testing, 1890–1901. In W. R. Woodward & M. G. Ash (Eds.), *The problematic science: Psychology in nineteenth-century thought* (pp. 322–345). New York: Praeger.

Sokal, M. M. (1984). James McKeen Cattell and American psychology in the 1920s. In J. Brozek (Ed.), *Explorations in the history of psychology in the United States* (pp. 273–323). Lewisburg, PA: Bucknell University Press.

Sokal, M. M. (1990). Life-span developmental psychology and the history of science. In E. W. Garber (Ed.), *Beyond history of science: Essays in honor of Robert E. Schofield* (pp. 67–80). Bethlehem, PA: Lehigh University Press.

Sokal, M. M. (1992). Origins and early years of the American Psychological Association. *American Psychologist, 47,* 111–122.

Sokal, M. M. (1994). James McKeen Cattell, the New York Academy of Sciences, and the American Psychological Association, 1891–1902. In H. E. Adler & R. W. Rieber (Eds.), *Aspects of the history of psychology in America: 1892–1992* (pp. 13–35). New York: Annals of the New York Academy of Sciences.

Sokal, M. M. (1995). Stargazing: James McKeen Cattell, American Men of Science, and the reward structure of the American scientific community, 1906–1944. In F. Kessel (Ed.), *Psychology, science, and human affairs: Essays in honor of William Bevan* (pp. 65–86). Boulder, CO: Westview Press.

Sokal, M. M. (1997). Baldwin, Cattell, and the *Psychological Review*: A collaboration and its discontents. *History of the Human Sciences, 10,* 57–89.

Sokal, M. M. (2001, August). *James McKeen Cattell in 1917.* Wallace A. Russell Lecture, Meeting of the Division of the History of Psychology, American Psychological Association, San Francisco.

Sokal, M. M. (2003). "Micro-history" and the history of psychology: "Thick description" and "The fine texture of the past." In D. B. Baker (Ed.), *Thick description and fine texture: Studies in the history of psychology* (pp. 1–18, 181–183). Akron, OH: University of Akron Press.

Sokal, M. M., Davis, A. B., & Merzbach, U. C. (1976). Laboratory instruments in the history of psychology. *Journal of the History of the Behavioral Sciences, 12,* 59–64.

Wissler, C. (1901). The correlation of mental and physical tests. *Psychological Review Monograph Supplements, 16.*

Woodworth, R. S. (1931). *Contemporary schools of psychology.* New York: Ronald Press.

Charles Henry Turner (Photo courtesy of Ms. Terri Small-Turner and
Charles Henry Turner II)

Chapter 3

Charles Henry Turner: Pioneer of Comparative Psychology

Charles I. Abramson

Charles Henry Turner (1867–1923) is a name with which most readers may not be familiar. He was a pioneer of the comparative animal behavior movement from the last decade of the 1800s to the first quarter of the 20th century. I became aware of Turner while studying ant learning as part of an undergraduate research project during the mid-1970s (Abramson, Collier, & Marcucella, 1977). As my reading of Turner's work continued, I became fascinated by a psychology that searches for general principles by studying the behavior of a wide range of organisms and uses animals as natural research preparations. Turner's work encouraged me to make comparative psychology my vocation. Indeed, as will become evident, one of the characteristics of Turner was his ability to inspire.

As a graduate student I continued my investigation of insect learning with the expectation of advancing lines of research begun by Turner. One of my early attempts was to replicate his experiments on the ability of cockroaches to modify their preferences by punishment (Turner, 1912). The technique used in these experiments is still used today to investigate, for instance, learned helplessness in the cockroach (Brown, Davis, & Johnson, 1999). My experiments did not progress far because the cockroaches escaped as soon as I opened the shipment

This chapter was adapted from *Selected Papers and Biography of Charles Henry Turner (1867–1923), Pioneer of Comparative Animal Behavior Studies,* by C.I. Abramson, L. D. Jackson, and C. L. Fuller (Eds.), 2003, Lewiston, NY: Edwin Mellen Press. Copyright 2003 Edwin Mellen Press. Adapted with permission. A Web site containing many photographs related to Professor Turner is available at http://psychology.okstate.edu/museum/turner/turnermain.html.

The book, this chapter, and the Web site would not have been possible without the continued collaboration of Terri Small-Turner and Charles Henry Turner II.

and subsequently infested the Boston University experimental psychology laboratories. Given a choice between living with ants or three-inch-long cockroaches, I opted for the former. This experience only increased my growing admiration for Turner, because here was an individual who mastered a wide variety of rearing techniques that could be used to study not only cockroaches but various species of ants, bees, wasps, moths, spiders, crustaceans, pigeons, snakes, and plants. Such mastery is not as easy as it sounds.

This chapter provides a brief biography of Turner, followed by a discussion of some of his contributions. These contributions include studies and experiments in the areas of morphology, tropisms, learning, death feigning—and civil rights. The chapter closes with some of the recognition he has received since his death.

BIOGRAPHY

There are several excellent biographies about Turner. These include Hayden (1970), Cadwallader (1984), and Ross (1997), and the reader is encouraged to consult these biographies to learn more.

Charles Henry Turner was born 2 years after the end of the Civil War on February 3, 1867, in Cincinnati, Ohio. His father was a church custodian who had emigrated from Alberta, Canada, and his mother was a practical nurse from Lexington, Kentucky. His family settled in Cincinnati because Cincinnati had a reputation of being a haven for African Americans (Woodson, 1916).

Turner received the majority of his formal education in Cincinnati. He attended Woodard High School and graduated valedictorian of his class. After graduation he enrolled in the University of Cincinnati in 1886 and, following his marriage to Leontine Troy in 1887, earned his BS degree in biology under the direction of his mentor, Clarence. L. Herrick, in 1891. That same year he published his first paper, a lengthy three-part morphological study of the avian brain, which was undertaken as a degree requirement (Turner, 1891). Graduate school soon followed, and in 1892 Turner earned his MS degree from the University of Cincinnati, again under the direction of Herrick.

By all accounts Turner was an exceptional student. Charles Judson Herrick, a classmate of Turner and younger brother of Clarence Herrick, characterized Turner's personality as reserved and pleasing, and portrayed the young Turner as both a tireless worker and perhaps the brightest of his class. Such an impression is supported by the fact that several of his early publications were the direct result of data gathered while he was an undergraduate. In the same account Charles Herrick described the relationship between Turner and his fellow students as one of mutual respect and civility; for example, they all participated in the social events of the laboratory. Herrick described these social events as "a beautiful demonstration of the cardinal principle that science recognizes no distinction of sex, creed, or race" (C. J. Herrick, 1955).

The year 1892 was busy for Turner. In addition to receiving his MS, he published his first paper on a psychological topic. The paper described the web-making habits of the gallery spider (Turner, 1892d). He also published a summary of his undergraduate thesis in the journal *Science* (Turner, 1892a). The appearance of this article marks Turner as probably the first African American to publish in that journal. Turner soon followed up the first *Science* paper with another that described the growth of grape-vine leaves (Turner, 1892b). As if these accomplishments were not enough, Turner also published a paper on the aquatic invertebrates of Cincinnati in which several new species were described (Turner, 1892c); he found time to volunteer at the Cincinnati Observatory; and he celebrated the birth of his first son, Henry Owen Turner (1892–1956). Turner also had a daughter named Louisa Mae (birth date unknown). A second son was born in 1894 and was named Darwin Romanes Turner (1894–1983). Darwin graduated from the University of Chicago School of Pharmacy, and with his brother Owen operated a pharmacy in Chicago for many years.

After completing his MS, Turner was employed from 1892 to 1893 as an assistant instructor in the biological laboratory at the University of Cincinnati. But on leaving this position, he was frustrated in looking for an academic position at a research university. During the years 1893 to 1908 he applied, unsuccessfully, for a position at Tuskegee Institute (1893); became a professor of biology and chair of the science department at Clark University in Atlanta, Georgia (1893–1905; his length of service is unclear); left that position to become a high school principal at College Hill High School in Cleveland, Tennessee (1906); and then left Tennessee for a position as professor of biology and chemistry at Haynes Normal and Industrial Institute in Augusta, Georgia (1907). In 1907 he applied for a position at the University of Chicago, but was rejected. In 1908 Turner finally settled down as a teacher at Sumner High School in St. Louis; the school, founded in 1875, was the first African American high school west of the Mississippi. Turner remained at Sumner until his retirement in 1922.

Despite his changing positions during the years between his MS degree and the Sumner appointment, Turner remained productive. Not only did he publish 21 papers and a book, but he also pursued a PhD degree in absentia from Denison University in Granville, Ohio (1893–1894). The program was started by his mentor Clarence L. Herrick, but it did not last long. Turner spent the summer of 1906 and the 1906–1907 academic year at the University of Chicago, where he eventually earned his PhD in zoology (magna cum laude) in 1907.

His productivity during these years is even more remarkable when one considers that in 1895 his wife of 8 years died while they were in Atlanta. It is suggested that Leontine Troy Turner suffered from mental illness during the latter stages of her life (Ross, 1997). If this is true, such an illness could only have contributed to an already arduous burden characterized by changing positions, low pay, heavy teaching loads, and sparse research facilities. In 1907–1908,[1] he married for a second time. His second wife, Lillian Porter Turner, remained at his side until Turner's death in 1923. Lillian died in Chicago on January 13, 1948.

Turner continued to be productive at Sumner. From 1908 until his death in 1923 he published 41 papers, with an average publication rate of three articles a year. This publication rate was accomplished while he was teaching classes in biology, chemistry, and psychology (Gray, 1979). If the latter can be confirmed, it represents an early attempt to put psychology into the high school classroom.

While he was at Sumner, Turner's work continued to be noticed by his peers in the animal behavior community both in the United States and abroad. From 1907 until 1914 he contributed book and literature reviews of invertebrate behavior to the *Psychological Bulletin* and produced similar reviews from 1911 to 1917 for the *Journal of Animal Behavior*. Turner was elected to membership in the Academy of Sciences of St. Louis in 1910 (some sources list 1912 as the date of his election). Also in 1910 the French naturalist V. Cornetz named the exploratory circling movements of ants returning to their nest "tournoiement de Turner" in honor of its discoverer, and he was honored in 1912 by *The Crisis* magazine as one of its "Men of the Month" (Du Bois, 1912).

In 1922 Turner retired from Sumner High School because of ill health and moved to Chicago to live with his son Darwin Romanes Turner. Charles Henry Turner died of acute myocarditis in Chicago on February 14, 1923, 11 days after his 55th birthday, and is interred in Lincoln Cemetery in Chicago. The death certificate incorrectly lists Turner's occupation as "druggist." The site is also the resting place for Lillian Porter Turner, Darwin Romanes Turner, and Henry Owen Turner.

When considering the academic career of Turner, one is struck by his inability to secure a professorship at a major university. In reviewing the biographical literature on Turner I believe there are at least three reasons why such an appointment was not forthcoming: (a) his race, (b) his interest in securing an academic appointment, and (c) lack of available jobs. I will comment briefly on all three.

The first and most obvious barrier to obtaining an academic appointment was racism. In discussing the issue, W. E. B. Du Bois (1929) recounted a story in which Turner was going to be offered an appointment at a large midwestern research university. Unfortunately, the department head who had supported Turner's appointment died, and his successor would not have a person of color in the department.

In contrast to the view of Du Bois, some Turner biographers have suggested that he actually was offered the job at this midwestern university but declined.

---

[1] The exact date is not known.

McKissack and McKissack (1994) argued that the responsibilities of earning tenure, serving on committees, and teaching duties associated with a large university did not appeal to Turner. Turner preferred to teach at a high school where he believed he could better serve the African American community.

The suggestion of the McKissacks that Turner did not want to work under a tenure system is not supported. The tenure system was not yet in place at the time he was seeking a university appointment. The American Association of University Professors (AAUP), which developed the tenure system, was founded in 1915, 7 years after Turner accepted the job at Sumner High School (AAUP, 1990). Moreover, if we accept Du Bois's account, Turner was close to accepting a position but was denied because of the untimely death of a supportive department head and the racism of his successor. It should also be recalled that Turner attempted to secure a position at Tuskegee Institute in 1893 but could not be hired because of funding constraints (Abramson, Jackson, & Fuller, 2003).

Racial bias certainly made it difficult for Turner to secure an academic appointment—and there is some suggestion that he did not want one. Job availability must also be considered. Issues of race aside, there were few professorships available in the United States for the study of animal behavior in the early 1900s (Cadwallader, 1987; Warden & Warner, 1927). Clearly, the competition for the few available faculty positions was intense and Turner's race may have been an issue in at least one instance during his search for positions.

TURNER'S CONTRIBUTIONS

In a review of Turner's work, four themes emerge. First, there is the comparative perspective. Many of his papers included investigations of several species within the same manuscript. In his undergraduate thesis (Turner, 1891, p. 39), he studied "over one hundred and fifty birds belonging to nine orders, twenty families, more than forty genera, and above fifty species." His comparative emphasis is also nicely illustrated in his dissertation (Turner, 1907b), in which he studied 12 species of ant, and in an earlier paper where he compared the brains of arthropods and annelids (Turner, 1899).

A reading of his papers makes clear that Turner's comparative approach led him to reject the "mechanical" view of behavior offered by Edward L. Thorndike, Jacques Loeb, and John B. Watson. He went beyond the behaviorist view by allowing for cognitive processes in his invertebrate subjects. One can only imagine how comparative psychology and the behaviorist school might have evolved if Turner had had access to students and facilities at a research-level university.

Second is the wide range of problems he investigated. His published papers concern morphological studies of vertebrates and invertebrates, apparatus design, naturalistic observations, death feigning, and explorations of basic problems in invertebrate learning. In conducting his experiments he paid attention to the use of controls and to such subject variables as sex and age. He also was aware of the importance of training variables such as intertrial and intersession intervals.

Third is productivity. During a 33-year career Turner published at least 70 papers, for an overall rate of 2.1 articles per year. His publication record compares favorably with that of the first generation of women psychologists, who on average published 16 papers over the course of their careers ($N = 25$, range 0 to 83) and to a random selection of White male professors of the same time period who published an average of 26 papers in their careers ($N = 25$, range 0 to 100; Scarborough & Furumoto, 1987, p. 169).

Fourth is Turner's dedication to research. Reading his papers makes it obvious that he enjoyed his vocation. The literature reviews are thorough, and he does not belittle the contributions of others even though he may disagree with their conclusions. One can argue that his perseverance and dedication to the field of comparative-behavior analysis was nothing less than inspiring. It is worth emphasizing that in conducting his research Turner had to confront challenges on an almost daily basis. These challenges included few formal laboratory facilities, no easy access to research libraries, no opportunity to train research students at the undergraduate or graduate level, heavy teaching loads, low pay, and restricted research time. In regard to the latter, many of his experiments were run in the summer or after his high school duties were completed. Equally remarkable is that for his 70 or so papers, Turner had coauthors on only two (Clarence Herrick in 1895 and Ernst Schwarz in 1914).

Morphology and Anatomy

Turner began his career by continuing a line of research begun by his mentor C. L. Herrick (Cadwallader, 1984). Turner contributed original articles on the comparative anatomy of the pigeon brain, directly compared the brains of arthropods and annelids, and studied the mushroom bodies of crayfish. His pigeon work is more than 100 pages in length and is a fine example of the skills in dissection, histology, observation, drawing, and analysis that were to characterize his career (Turner, 1891). It is remarkable that this paper was done to fulfill the requirements for his undergraduate degree. In addition to the morphological contributions, this paper contains several novel contributions, including the description of a tool to handle delicate tissue, development of a new stain, and a suggestion that the compactness of the avian brain can be used as a taxonomic indicator. He published a total of seven morphological–anatomical papers, with the last appearing in 1901 (Turner, 1901).

Experiments on Tropisms

A second line of research initiated by Turner concerned the area of tropisms. The central question of this research was how insects navigate. There were several competing theories that suggested that insects navigate either by a homing instinct, tropism, limited learning ability, or higher intelligence (Turner, 1907b).

Turner constructed an elaborate maze with pupae as the reward and tested 12 species. The experiments were begun at Clark University (Atlanta) and concluded at the University of Chicago. The project took 5 years to complete. His results showed that the movements of ants are not the results of tropisms or a homing instinct. Although ants are influenced by olfactory, visual, kinesthetic, and tactile stimuli, they also possess variability in their behavior, have memory, and exhibit a form of associative learning. In summarizing the results he noted, "Ants are much more than mere reflex machines; they are self-acting creatures guided by memories of past individual (ontogenetic) experience" (Turner, 1907b, p. 424). Turner also confirmed previous observations that the direction of light influences the behavior of ants. The experiment also contained observations on the influence of caste membership and sex differences on performance. Turner noted (Turner, 1907b, p. 424) "the males seem unable to solve even the simplest problems."

This experiment is noteworthy not only because of the method and the research design but because he instituted controls that were not deemed necessary at the time. For example, he ran many replicates of his observations and used heat filters when using light as a stimulus. He was also concerned with such contemporary factors as sex and age differences on performance. Turner continued this line of research by extending it to other species, including honey bees, wasps, and caterpillars (e.g., Turner, 1918).

Experiments on Learning

The study of navigation suggested that associative learning plays a large role in the ability of an insect to return to its nest. Invertebrate learning was a main research interest. Turner conducted experiments on learning in a wide variety of insects, including honey bees, ants, and cockroaches. In some cases he used learning procedures to investigate other processes, such as determining the existence of color and pattern vision in honey bees.

His earliest paper on learning was based on observations of the gallery spider, although it also contained reports on the results of some experimental manipulations (Turner, 1892d). In this study Turner presented a classification of web design and intentionally changed the environment to assess how the spider would modify its web. The results suggested to Turner that some type of instinct stimulates the spider to construct a web, but that the form a web takes is the result of learning.

Another example in which Turner introduced modifications into a natural situation is found in the paper "Do Ants Form Practical Judgments?" (Turner, 1907a). This paper appeared before his 1907 dissertation, and the experiment was conducted entirely at the University of Chicago. He intentionally introduced modifications in the nest, such as making a crack in the brood chamber and removing "trash." Following these manipulations he observed the behavior of the workers. The rationale behind the experiment was to determine whether ants could use "instinctive" behavior patterns in novel ways. The answer for Turner was yes.

In addition to his 1907 dissertation paper on the homing of ants, perhaps the best examples of his use of learning procedures to investigate problems in insect behavior are his papers on color vision and pattern vision of honey bees. For both papers elaborate apparatus was constructed and controls were implemented that conclusively showed that honey bees perceive both color and pattern (Turner, 1910, 1911).

The color-vision paper provided data under controlled conditions (Turner, 1910). Such experiments were theoretically important because of the perceived interactions between honey bees and flowers. Turner began the paper with a scholarly review of the literature in which various theories of why bees should see colors were summarized, followed by a discussion of the limitations of the existing literature.

To investigate the problem, he studied honey bees in O'Fallon Park in St. Louis. He designed various colored disks, colored boxes, and cornucopias into which the bees were trained to fly. Thirty-two experiments were designed, and controls for the influence of odor and brightness were instituted. The results of his experiments showed that bees see colors and discriminate among them. It is interesting that in considering the results of his experiments, he believed that bees might be creating, in his words, "true percepts" of the environment. The idea of percepts certainly sounds contemporary (Turner, 1910, p. 279).

The final papers to be considered in this section report Turner's work with cockroaches. The rationale for his first experiment was to determine whether the reaction of roaches to light can be modified by experience (Turner, 1912). Turner was intrigued by the punishment method developed by Robert Yerkes for his studies of the Japanese dancing mouse and adopted the technique for the study of roaches. Consistent with his previous work, he used a wide range of subjects, including adult males and females and larval females. In some cases he studied roaches with amputated antennae.

At first he tried to develop a new apparatus; after several designs he decided to use the dark-avoidance paradigm developed earlier by Szymanski (1912). Turner interpreted the avoidance of a previously preferred place not as a reversal of a phototropic response but as a result of learning to associate darkness with punishment. In some cases memory of the task lasted 21 days. Additional results suggested that male roaches learn faster than female roaches, that there are large individual differences in performance, and that avoidance of a dark chamber survives molting. Of particular interest is a variation of the paradigm in which roaches trained to avoid darkness in one apparatus retained the behavior when transferred to a differently shaped apparatus.

Turner extended this line of investigation in a second paper (Turner, 1913). Here, a new type of maze was constructed and the reward was a return to the home container. The results indicated that the roaches could benefit from experience. Interesting aspects of the results included discussions of "jumping activities," "acrobatic feats," and "toilet-making habits." This paper also contained a discussion of the tactile, olfactory, auditory, and visual senses of the roach and how they related to learning the maze. Anticipating some modern animal cognitivists, Turner suggested (Turner, 1913, p. 381) that roaches "act as though experiencing the emotion the psychologists call will." The roach experiments are also an excellent example of the types of variables of interest to Turner. These included intertrial and intersession intervals, individual differences, and age- and sex-related changes in performance. Investigating such variables is now a standard part of animal behavior literature.

Experiments on "Playing Possum"

One of the more interesting lines of research conducted by Turner is in the area of death feigning. Turner's first study on the issue used the ant-lion (Turner, 1915). Ant-lions get their name from the vivacious appetite of the larvae of ants and other insects. The larvae are popularly known as doodlebugs. This study reported the results of five experiments and investigated such parameters as (a) relative duration of successive death feints, (b) the influence of temperature, (c) stimulus intensity, and (d) hunger. In discussing his results Turner concluded that the behavior is an example of "terror paralysis" that is not based on experience.

The experiments on ant-lions were unique because they provided one of the earliest descriptions of ant-lion behavior, including descriptions of the pits constructed to capture its prey; the methods of excavation; the posture of the ant-lion; its feeding behavior, locomotion, and growth cycle; and the types of stimulation needed to elicit death-feigning. Such naturalistic observations of invertebrate behavior are common in Turner's work and form the basis of many of his contributions.

NATURALISTIC OBSERVATIONS

Throughout his career Turner engaged in the observation and classification of invertebrates. Most of his papers, whether or not they were specifically designed as observational studies, contain behavioral descriptions. The descriptions are often in such detail that one is left with the impression that his descriptive skills were acquired from his earlier morphological work. Many of these papers also contained results of preliminary experiments.

Turner, for example, provided a description of micro-organisms of Cincinnati (Turner, 1892c). This paper was unique in that it contained observations of a new species that he discovered. He extended this work by providing descriptions of, for instance, the *Cladocera* of Georgia (Turner, 1894). Descriptions of various aspects of invertebrate behavior are also available, including feeding and sexual reproduction (e.g., Turner, 1916).

Acoustic Experiments

One of Turner's major contributions to the insect behavior literature was providing the first experimental evidence that insects can hear airborne sounds (Turner & Schwarz, 1914). Consistent with his comparative approach, five species of moth were tested. The procedure involved sounding a Galton whistle at various distances from the moth and observing its reactions. Sir Francis Galton invented the Galton whistle in 1876; it is a variable-pitch whistle that can produce pure tones reaching into the ultrasonic range. Controls were implemented to ensure that the animals were not responding to the sight of the whistle or to its air puffs. The results indicated that *Catocala* moths respond to high-pitched notes by either flying away or by making quivering movements, but do not respond to low frequency sounds.

In a companion paper Turner conducted a laboratory test of the ability of four species of moth to hear sounds (Turner, 1914). Individual animals were confined beneath "wire dish covers" in such a way that the wings could move but not provide lift. Sounds were produced by an adjustable organ pipe, an adjustable pitch pipe, and a Galton whistle. The dependent variable was wing movement. Psychophysical experiments were performed to determine thresholds. Of the moths tested only *Telea polyphemus* showed little responsiveness to auditory stimuli. Following up on a suggestion in the Turner and Schwarz paper that a sound might need to be made "significant," he performed a classical conditioning experiment in which a tone was paired with "rough handling." The results indicated that the moth learned to associate the sound with the noxious stimulus. This paper may be the first published descriptions of classical conditioning in insects, although controls now known to be important were not implemented (Abramson, 1994).

Civil Rights Papers

Of the 70 or so papers Turner published, four were concerned with civil rights issues. The first of these papers appeared in 1897 (Turner, 1897). In this and his other papers on race relations, the emphasis was always on education. In reading these papers one is struck by how contemporary they sound.

Perhaps his most comprehensive comments on race relations and the importance of education are contained in an article written for an encyclopedia (Turner,

1902). In this article Turner stressed that only through education can problems between races be resolved and argued that prejudice can be examined through comparative psychology. He proposed that eight "virtues" could change the behavior of racists: (a) manners of a gentleman, (b) cultured homes, (c) business honesty, (d) thrift, (e) Christian morality, (f) the ability to do something well, (g) the ability to lead, and (h) love for justice and contempt for lawlessness.

CONCLUSION

Several leaders of the animal behavior movement in the early 20th century recognized the importance of Turner's work. For example, John B. Watson, in commenting on a study on ant behavior, called Turner's method "ingenious" (Watson, 1907). Turner's work was also discussed favorably in various books and articles written by such well-known psychologists as Margaret F. Washburn, T. C. Schneirla, Carl J. Warden, and E. L. Thorndike.

Turner's achievements as a scientist, educator, and humanitarian were formally recognized after his death. In 1925 the Charles Henry Turner Open Air School for Crippled Children was established in St. Louis, near Turner's last career position as a high school principal. This school is now known as the Charles Henry Turner Middle Branch (founded 1954) and has become part of the new Charles Henry Turner MEGA Magnet Middle School (founded 1999). In 1962, Turner–Tanner Hall (now known as Tanner–Turner Hall) at Clark College in Atlanta was named in his honor. More recently, in 2002 the Animal Behavior Society created an annual Charles H. Turner Poster Session and Travel Award for undergraduate presentations.

Another estimate of the impact of Turner is provided by a citation search. From 1974 to 2001, Turner was cited 67 times for a wide variety of contributions, including studies of honey bee, wasp, spider and cockroach learning and of anatomical studies of crayfish and pigeon brains (Abramson et al., 2003).

It is hoped that this chapter will encourage readers to explore further the many contributions of this remarkable scientist. In addition, acquainting a new generation of students with Turner's work may inspire more people of color to enter careers in the comparative analysis of behavior and other natural sciences. His story continues to be inspiring more than 80 years after his death.

REFERENCES

Abramson, C. I. (1994). *A primer of invertebrate learning: The behavioral perspective.* Washington, DC: American Psychological Association.

Abramson, C. I., Collier, D. M., & Marcucella, H. (1977). An aversive conditioning unit for ants. *Behavior Research Methods and Instrumentation, 9,* 505–507.

Abramson, C. I., Jackson, L. D., & Fuller, C. L. (2003). Charles Henry Turner: Significant events and unanswered questions. In C. I. Abramson, C. L. Fuller, & L. D. Jackson (Eds.), *Selected papers and biography of Charles Henry Turner (1867–1923), pioneer of comparative animal behavior studies* (pp. 19–69). Lewiston, NY: Edwin Mellen.

American Association of University Professors. (1990). *AAUP policy documents and reports.* Washington, DC: Author.

Brown, G. E., Davis, E., & Johnson, A. (1999). Forced exercise blocks learned helplessness in the cockroach (*Periplaneta americana*). *Psychological Reports, 84,* 155–156.

Cadwallader, T. C. (1984). Neglected aspects of the evolution of American comparative and animal psychology. In G. Greenberg & E. Tobach (Eds.), *Behavioral evolution and integrative levels: The T. C. Schneirla conference series* (pp. 15–48). Hillsdale, NJ: Erlbaum.

Cadwallader, T. C. (1987). Origins and accomplishments of Joseph Jastrow's 1888-founded chair of comparative psychology and the University of Wisconsin. *Journal of Comparative Psychology, 101,* 231–236.

Du Bois, W. E. B. (1912, January). Men of the month. *The Crisis,* 102–103.

Du Bois, W. E. B. (1929, June). Postscript. *The Crisis,* 203–204, 212.

Gray, B. (1979, February). Charles Henry Turner: Scientist, teacher, author, humanitarian. In *Dignity of humanity.* Washington, DC: U.S. Department of Commerce.

Hayden, R. C. (1970). *Seven black American scientists.* Reading, MA: Addison-Wesley.

Herrick, C. J. (1955). Clarence Luther Herrick: Pioneer naturalist, teacher, and psychobiologist. *Transactions of the American Philosophical Society, 45,* 1–85.

Herrick, C. L., & Turner, C. H. (1895). Synopsis of the Entomostraca of Minnesota with descriptions of related species, comprising all known forms from the United States included in the orders Copepoda, Cladocera, Ostracoda. *Geological and Natural History Survey of Minnesota, Zoological Series, 2,* 1–552.

McKissack, P., & McKissack, F. (1994). *African-American scientists.* Brookfield, CT: Millbrook.

Ross, M. E. (1997). *Bug watching with Charles Henry Turner.* Minneapolis, MN: Carolrhoda Books.

Scarborough, E., & Furumoto, L. (1987). *Untold lives: The first generation of American women psychologists.* New York: Columbia University Press.

Szymanski, J. S. (1912). Modification of the innate behavior of cockroaches. *Journal of Animal Behavior, 2,* 81–90.

Turner, C. H. (1891). Morphology of the avian brain. *Journal of Comparative Neurology, 1,* 39–93, 107–133, 265–286.

Turner, C. H. (1892a). A few characteristics of the avian brain. *Science, 19,* 16–17.

Turner, C. H. (1892b). A grape vine produces two sets of leaves during the same season. *Science, 20,* 39.

Turner, C. H. (1892c). Notes upon Cladocera, Copepoda, Ostracoda and Rotifera of Cincinnati with description of new species. *Bulletin of the Scientific Laboratories of Denison University, 6,* 57–74.

Turner, C. H. (1892d). Psychological notes upon the gallery spider: Illustrations of intelligent variations in the construction of the web. *Journal of Comparative Neurology, 2,* 95–110.

Turner, C. H. (1894). Notes on the Cladocera of Georgia. *Bulletin of the Scientific Laboratories of Denison University, 8,* 22–25.

Turner, C. H. (1897). Reason for teaching biology in Negro schools. *Southwestern Christian Advocate, 32,* 2.

Turner, C. H. (1899). A preliminary paper on the comparative study of the arthropod and annelid brain. *Zoological Bulletin, 2,* 155–160.

Turner, C. H. (1901). Mushroom bodies of the crayfish and their historical environment: A study in comparative neurology. *Journal of Comparative Neurology, 11,* 321–368.

Turner, C. H. (1902). Will the education of the Negro solve the race problem? In W. Culp (Ed.), *Twentieth century Negro literature or: A cyclopedia of thought on the vital topics relating to the American Negro* (pp. 162–166). Naperville, IL: J. L. Nichols.

Turner, C. H. (1907a). Do ants form practical judgments? *Biological Bulletin, 13*, 333–342.

Turner, C. H. (1907b). The homing of ants: An experimental study of ant behavior. *Journal of Comparative Neurology and Psychology, 17*, 367–434.

Turner, C. H. (1910). Experiments on color vision of the honey bee. *Biological Bulletin, 19*, 257–279.

Turner, C. H. (1911). Experiments on pattern vision of the honey bee. *Biological Bulletin, 21*, 249–264.

Turner, C. H. (1912). An experimental investigation of an apparent reversal of the responses to light of the roach *Periplaneta orientalis* L. *Biological Bulletin, 23*, 371–386.

Turner, C. H. (1913). Behavior of the common roach (*Periplaneta orientalis* L.) on an open maze. *Biological Bulletin, 25*, 380–397.

Turner, C. H. (1914). An experimental study of the auditory powers of the giant silkworm moths, *Saturniidae*. *Biological Bulletin, 27*, 325–332.

Turner, C. H. (1915). Notes on the behavior of the ant-lion with emphasis on the feeding activities and letisimulation. *Biological Bulletin, 29*, 277–307.

Turner, C. H. (1916). Notes on the feeding behavior and oviposition of a captive American false spider (*Eremobates formicaria* Koch). *Journal of Animal Behavior, 7*, 405–419.

Turner, C. H. (1918). The locomotions of surface-feeding caterpillars are not tropisms. *Psychological Bulletin, 35*, 137–148.

Turner, C. H., & Schwarz, E. (1914). Auditory powers of the catocala moths: An experimental field study. *Biological Bulletin, 27*, 275–293.

Warden, C. J., & Warner, L. H. (1927). The development of animal psychology in the United States during the past three decades. *Psychological Review, 34*, 196–205.

Watson, J. B. (1907). Review of: Turner, C. H., A preliminary note on ant behavior. *Psychological Bulletin, 4*, 300–301.

Woodson, C. G. (1916). The Negroes of Cincinnati prior to the Civil War. *Journal of Negro History, 1*, 1–22.

Robert S. Woodworth (Photo courtesy of the American Psychological Association Archives)

Chapter 4

Robert S. Woodworth and the Creation of an Eclectic Psychology

Andrew S. Winston

In 1956, the American Psychological Foundation awarded its first Gold Medal to Robert Sessions Woodworth (1869–1962) for "unequaled contributions to shaping the destiny of scientific psychology" (Shaffer, 1956, p. 587). Woodworth did not receive this honor for his specific empirical or theoretical contributions. He was honored for his creation of a general framework for psychological inquiry, for his nurturing of many students who became influential psychologists, and perhaps most of all for his textbooks. These were far from ordinary textbooks in scope, depth, and clarity, and they were used around the world. Through these texts, Woodworth articulated an inclusive, eclectic vision for 20th-century psychology: diverse in its problems, but unified by the faith that careful empirical work would produce steady scientific progress.

EARLY LIFE AND EDUCATION

Born to a New England family with farming roots, Woodworth was the son of a "sternly religious" Congregationalist minister.[1] His mother was a founder and the first principal of a women's seminary, now Lake Erie College in Painesville, Ohio, where she taught mathematics and botany, an extraordinary accomplishment

---

[1]Except where noted, all biographical information is taken from Woodworth's (1930) autobiographical sketch, Poffenberger (1962), Seward (1958), and material in the Robert S. Woodworth Papers, Columbia University Archives.

for a woman of the mid-1800s. She also taught "mental philosophy," making Woodworth perhaps the only early psychologist to have a *mother* who was something akin to a psychology professor. Because of his father's assignment to different churches, the family moved frequently: Woodworth was born in Belchertown, Massachusetts, spent his first 6 years in Iowa, the next 6 in Connecticut, and his teenage years in Newton, Massachusetts, a suburb of Boston. His mother was his father's third wife, and the extended family of siblings, stepsiblings, aunts, uncles, and cousins was large and apparently amiable. The young Woodworth aspired in turn to be an astronomer, farmer, musician, and finally a teacher. His parents would have preferred that he chose the ministry, which he considered, but they supported his plans for a scholarly career. His early aspirations never entirely disappeared: He was devoted to singing, playing the piano, and even composing music throughout his life. In the 1920s, he took a break from academic life by working as an anonymous farm hand during the summer.

Woodworth selected Amherst College rather than Harvard, which was preferred by many of his classmates at Newton High School. At Amherst, he was influenced by the philosophy course taught by Charles Garman, who included much material on psychology. Woodworth won a prize in mathematics, and after graduating in 1891, he taught high school science and mathematics for 2 years, and then became the chair of mathematics at Washburn College in Topeka, Kansas. He read the recently published *Principles of Psychology* by William James (1890), and was also inspired by G. Stanley Hall's conception of research and the university. Woodworth decided to quit mathematics, and entered Harvard in 1895 to study psychology and philosophy, which were not yet clearly distinct to Woodworth or to Harvard. Here he made a lifelong friend: Edward L. Thorndike, later known for his work on learning and measurement.

Woodworth studied primarily with Josiah Royce and William James, who set him to work on the perception of time, language and thought, dreams, motivation, and mind–body relations. He became convinced that "no positive system of philosophy could claim any absolute validity" (Woodworth, 1930, pp. 366–367). Thus Woodworth's interest in a broad and nondoctrinaire approach to philosophical and psychological problems was developed early on, and showed the influence of William James. But when James arranged for Woodworth to study physiology with the eminent Henry Bowditch, as background for further work in psychology, Woodworth chose to emphasize psychology over philosophy, and he studied physiology intensively for the next 6 years. After receiving a master's degree at Harvard in 1897, Woodworth accepted a fellowship under James McKeen Cattell at Columbia University. Woodworth credited Cattell as a powerful influence, and Cattell's emphasis on both experimentation *and* individual differences is apparent throughout Woodworth's writings. The anthropologist Franz Boas had just joined the

Columbia University faculty, and Woodworth studied statistical methods and "anthropometry" under Boas.

Unlike many other laboratory "heads," Cattell allowed his students substantial latitude in choosing research topics, a practice Woodworth later followed with his own students. For his dissertation, Woodworth chose to study the accuracy of voluntary hand movements under varied conditions of speed, practice, and fatigue. After receiving his doctorate degree in 1899, Woodworth taught physiology at Columbia and at Bellevue Hospital Medical College. Ever eager to know more, he continued his studies of physiology by traveling to Europe, and served as assistant to the noted English physiologist Charles Sherrington at the University of Liverpool in 1902 to 1903. Woodworth met and married his wife, Gabrielle Schjöth, during his studies in England.

RETURN TO COLUMBIA

When Cattell invited him back to Columbia as an instructor in 1903, Woodworth accepted and remained at Columbia, except for brief absences, for his entire career. He was pleased to join the Columbia faculty, and his department became the most important source of new PhDs in psychology during the first three decades of the 20th century. He was made a full professor in 1909, and succeeded Cattell as the executive officer of the Psychology Department. The duties were heavy, and undoubtedly had a negative effect on the development of Woodworth's research career. Cattell spent little time at Columbia and handed over most of the responsibilities to Woodworth years before Woodworth formally took over the running of the department. Woodworth did not think much of his own abilities as an administrator. He did not make decisions easily, and tended to ruminate and delay (Poffenberger, 1962).

By 1900, Woodworth had already published his dissertation in the *Psychological Review Monograph Supplements*, and he continued to publish on movement and the development of motor skills. In *Le Mouvement* (Woodworth, 1903), written while he was abroad and published in France, Woodworth showed the premier skill that would mark his career: the ability to comprehensively summarize and synthesize large and diverse literatures. In these early publications, he also showed that he could approach a topic such as muscular movements both as a basic problem of physiology and as a problem of applied psychology. For example, in "The Best Movement for Handwriting," Woodworth (1899) argued that handwriting strategies using the thumb and forefinger were inefficient and led to cramps, whereas a change in position and the use of the wrist produced more rapid and uniform writing. In this and later works, Woodworth moved easily back and forth between basic and applied concerns, and never placed these in opposition. This comfortable relationship between basic and applied work became a general feature of psychological research at Columbia University and of Columbia "functionalism."[2]

From the beginning of his career, Woodworth's interests were wide-ranging and included the control of muscular movement, reflexes, transfer of training, imageless thought, psychophysics, time perception, and psychological testing. In 1899 to 1900 he conducted studies of transfer of training with his close friend Edward L. Thorndike, who had just begun his appointment at Teachers College, Columbia University. They hoped to test an old and popular idea known as "formal discipline," which maintained that the study of Latin or geometry would produce general intellectual "strengthening" in a manner analogous to muscular exercise. Formal discipline had been an influential idea in education, although it was much disputed in the late 1800s. In their experiments, Thorndike and Woodworth trained their subjects to estimate the size of rectangles, and tested for transfer to estimating the size of triangles and other shapes. They also tested for transfer on various letter and word cancellation tasks. They found little or no evidence of transfer, and concluded that transfer was unlikely except when the two tasks contained identical elements (Thorndike & Woodworth, 1901a, 1901b, 1901c; Woodworth & Thorndike, 1901). Their work helped inspire a large literature and long debate over transfer of training.

WOODWORTH AND PSYCHOLOGICAL TESTS

Problems of individual differences were not central to Woodworth's work on physiology, movement, or transfer. But Cattell had enthusiastically promoted the study of individual differences and the development of what he called "mental tests," although the tests ultimately failed to predict academic performance (see Sokal, 1988). Testing became an important feature of work at Columbia, and with the influence of Boas, there was an interest in both psychological testing and the measurement of physical characteristics. Woodworth was asked to head the Anthropology Department of the 1904 St. Louis Purchase Exposition, also known as the St. Louis World's Fair. The Exposition featured outdoor exhibits of people from the Philippines, Ainu from Japan, "Pigmies" from the Congo, and a variety of Native American groups. Assisted by Frank G. Bruner, Woodworth compared the groups on exhibit with groups of White visitors to the Fair. They conducted anthropometric and psychometric assessments on 1,100 individuals,

---

[2]Boring (1950) identified Woodworth as a functionalist, although Woodworth did not generally describe his dynamic psychology as a kind of functionalism. Klein (1958), a Woodworth student, described his mentor's position as "dynamic functionalism," and maintained that all dynamic psychology was based on a functionalist outlook. Woodworth (1938) grudgingly acknowledged that "It may be true, as has been said, that the present author represents the functional school of psychology in the broadest sense of the word" (p. v).

testing muscular strength, speed, accuracy, vision, and hearing. They also attempted to assess intelligence by using a "form board" where geometric forms must be placed in the appropriate positions on the board as quickly as possible.

The results of this work were never fully analyzed or published, but Woodworth (1910) discussed the findings in general terms. Although many White visitors to the fair looked on the exhibits as evidence of the inferiority of "primitive" peoples and many White psychologists believed that scientific data would provide evidence of White superiority, Woodworth was cautious about racial comparisons, and dubious of the claims commonly made. He noted that the comparisons of "Negro" and "White" brain weights "partakes not a little of the ludicrous" (p. 172). Woodworth criticized the popular notion that innate differences between groups could be inferred from current differences in their degree of cultural or industrial development. He cautioned psychologists against overreliance on group averages, and urged the proper recognition of group overlap, within-group variation, and the role of culture. He also warned of the dangers of assuming a hereditary source for differences and of using average group differences for selecting immigrants. Unfortunately, his warnings were rarely heeded. During the 1930s, he argued that individual characteristics were always a joint product of heredity and environment, rather than so much of one plus so much of the other (e.g., Woodworth, 1934). His thoughtfulness in matters of heredity and environment was known and respected in subsequent decades, and the Social Science Research Council asked him to survey this topic for a widely read monograph (Woodworth, 1941). However, he never adopted a critical stance on the concept of "race" itself. He left open the possibility that future research might reveal a genetic basis to racial differences on IQ tests (Winston, Butzer, & Ferris, 2004).[3]

In 1906, just before Henry Goddard introduced Binet's new tests to America, interest in tests and measurement was intense. The American Psychological Association (APA) appointed Woodworth and Frederick Wells to develop "association tests" with tasks such as color naming, geometric form naming, or giving the opposite of a word printed on a card. These tests were used in later work on many topics, including Leta Hollingworth's (1914) doctoral research on the relationship between the menstrual period and test performance, which showed no effect.

Although at age 47 Woodworth was too old to enter the army during World War I, he was commissioned by the APA to create a test of emotional stability for army recruits. This test, known as the Woodworth Personal Data Sheet, was

---

[3] Despite his cautionary stance, Woodworth encouraged research on racial differences during the 1920s and 1930s. As editor of the *Psychological Archives*, he allowed A. L. Crane (1923) to describe the sample in his Columbia University dissertation research as "one hundred Southern darkies" who could only be gotten into the laboratory with "threats, cajolery, flattery, bribery, and every other conceivable ruse within the bounds of reason and the law" (p. v), language that was unscholarly even in those times. Woodworth was not an anti-racist activist.

his most important contribution to psychological measurement. He gathered a list of neurotic symptoms from case histories and discussions with clinicians, and eliminated those that a "normal" sample showed with high frequency. The test consisted of a set of simple yes–no questions and was designed to substitute for a psychiatric interview. It was not used in the war but was later used for civilians and was clearly the forerunner of modern personality tests. As was typical of Woodworth, he neither copyrighted nor aggressively promoted the use of his test, and let others develop it further while he moved on to other problems. Thus Woodworth's own personality and lack of driving ambition may have contributed to his eclectic outlook and career. He remained interested in testing; in 1929 he served as president of the Psychological Corporation, a company created by Cattell to promote the application of psychology, and Woodworth remained on the Board of Directors until 1960.

WOODWORTH'S BOOKS

Woodworth was productive despite the heavy demands of administering the Psychology Department at Columbia, and over his career he authored at least 246 books, articles, and reviews. His greatest influence on the direction of American psychology was undoubtedly through his books. George T. Ladd invited Woodworth to help him revise Ladd's widely used *Elements of Physiological Psychology*, first published in 1887, one of the most important texts of its time. Woodworth rewrote the sections on the nervous system, and expanded the book considerably. Thorough and clearly written, the revised edition (Ladd & Woodworth, 1911) became known as "Woodworth's Physiological Psychology," and was the standard text in the field for many years.

In his *Dynamic Psychology* (1918), Woodworth had the opportunity to articulate his own general position for psychology. Based on a series of eight lectures at the American Museum of Natural History in 1916–1917, he laid the groundwork for the study of motivation. The problem of motivation had been of interest to Woodworth since his student days at Harvard, and he and his friend Edward Thorndike discussed it often. By 1916, he saw a "dynamic approach" as the solution to the conflict between consciousness and behavior as the basic objects of study. In his second lecture, he outlined the advantages and deficiencies of both "behavioristic" and "introspectionist" (in E. B. Titchener's sense of the term) approaches, and argued that in their extreme and exclusionary versions, "neither party has rightly envisaged the real problem for psychology" (Woodworth, 1918, p. 34). Instead, he proposed an emphasis on "cause and effect" or "dynamics," which required the study of consciousness, behavior, *and* physiology to provide a coherent account of human feelings and actions. The basic questions of a dynamic approach were "how we do something," the mechanism, and "why we do something," the drive. For Woodworth, drives were not to be limited to a fixed set of native or inherited instincts, as argued by William McDougall. Instead, a mechanism for skill at numbers or music could in turn become a drive or motive for engaging in those activities. In general, any mechanism could furnish drive or lend drive to other mechanisms, and motivation can arise from any system of the body, Woodworth maintained. He then used this general position to analyze problems of learning and originality and of abnormal and social behavior. Woodworth retained this emphasis on dynamics throughout his career, and titled his last book *Dynamics of Behavior* (Woodworth, 1958). Motivation, conceived in Woodworth's general way, became a standard topic in psychology, and his phrase "dynamics of behavior" became part of course descriptions and, at my own university, the title of an introductory psychology course. However, the influence of Woodworth's own introductory text, *Psychology,* and his 1938 *Experimental Psychology*, was far greater than that of his *Dynamic Psychology.*

WOODWORTH'S *PSYCHOLOGY:*
THE WORLD'S INTRODUCTORY TEXT

Psychology: A Study of Mental Life first appeared in 1921 and was revised four times (Woodworth, 1921, 1929, 1934, 1940b; Woodworth & Marquis, 1947). Printings of the fifth edition were still in use as late as the 1960s. Records from the publisher indicate that the first three editions sold more than 400,000 copies, an extraordinary number for the 1920s and 1930s (Winston, 1990). E. G. Boring (1950, p. 565) declared that for the first 25 years of its print run, it had no rivals. The book was translated into dozens of languages and was used around the world. *Psychology* served as a model for later introductory texts, particularly in terms of the wide range of topics and openness to a variety of viewpoints. As with the *Dynamics of Behavior*, Woodworth provided an antidote to what he perceived as the narrow vision of Titchener, Watson, and McDougall. Compared to the more Titchenerian texts of the time, Woodworth's emphasized "motor reactions" more than sensations. He included a full chapter on intelligence, including the intercorrelation of different intelligence tests, evidence for a general factor, the role of heredity in intelligence, and the limitations of the tests. Animal research was included in many sections, and two chapters stand out from other texts of the time: "Imagination," with discussion of children, play, empathy, worry, dreams, Freud, creativity, and art; and "Personality," with discussion of temperament, self, and Freud and the unconscious.

In striving for clarity, Woodworth introduced the kind of discussion of *methods* that became common in subsequent decades. As in the *Dynamics of Behavior*, he argued that both "objective observation" and "introspection" are useful approaches, and both could be used in experiments. Woodworth contrasted the "experimental attack" with the "comparative method," in which actions of individuals, classes, or species would be compared for likenesses, differences, norms, and averages. Testing and correlational studies came under this heading, and were said to rank "on a par with a strict experimental method" (p. 15). Woodworth described two other methodological approaches: the genetic method of "tracing the mental development of the individual or race" and the pathological method of tracing the "decay or demoralization of mental life" (pp. 15–16). Thus the physiological experiments he had done with Sherrington, the study of movement, Thorndike's studies of cats in puzzle boxes, the Personal Data Sheet, baby biographies, and psychiatric case histories were all included in the discipline.

But in subsequent editions, Woodworth began to stress experimentation above other methods, and in the third edition of 1934, he introduced a linguistic convention that later became universal in psychology textbooks, and one that is learned by every psychology major: He defined experimentation as the manipulation of an "independent variable" while holding all other factors constant and observing the effect on a "dependent variable." Up until 1934, Woodworth used a broader definition of experiment, which might include tests or comparing children of different ages. But in the 1934 edition, only studies with manipulation of a variable would count as experiments. Woodworth was not the first to use this definition. In his *The Physical Dimensions of Consciousness*, E. G. Boring (1933), defined *experiment* in this way, and Edward Chase Tolman (1932) used the terms *independent variables* and *dependent variables* to provide a framework for inquiry, as did the young B. F. Skinner, at about the same time (Winston, 1988, 1990, 2004). The terms were not invented by psychologists; they had been in use in mathematics for nearly 100 years. They were introduced by John Radford Young in the *The Elements of the Differential Calculus* (1833): "On account of this dependence of the value of the function upon that of the variable the former, that is *y*, is called the *dependent* variable, and the latter, *x*, the *independent* variable" (p. 2). These terms described a purely mathematical relationship, a function of the form $y = f(x)$. Woodworth was well versed in the mathematics of functions, and it is likely that his background as a mathematics teacher made this formulation a clear and comfortable one for him. The use of these terms to define psychology experiments implied something new: The independent variable could be thought of as the "cause" of behavior, and all psychological problems could be formulated in terms of variables. Although psychologists often treated Woodworth's definition of experiment as a kind of universal scientific method, this definition was not typically used by other disciplines (Winston & Blais, 1996).

Woodworth introduced another influential notation in his introductory textbook. Starting in 1929, he described the fundamental model for psychology as S–O–R, stimulus–organism–response, to emphasize the contribution of the organism, especially in terms of motivation and individual differences, and the necessity of considering intervening processes. This simple terminology was Woodworth's way of overcoming the deficiencies of Watsonian S–R behaviorism, and Woodworth later emphasized the continuous, reciprocal interaction between the person and the environment. The S–O–R formulation was taken up by textbook authors (e.g., Munn, 1966) and is still used in contemporary theoretical discussions (e.g., Kwee & Ellis, 1997).

THE "COLUMBIA BIBLE"

The book that most clearly influenced generations of new psychologists was Woodworth's *Experimental Psychology* (1938), also known as the "Columbia Bible" (Winston, 1990). According to Woodworth's personal records, he taught experimental psychology every year from 1905 to 1917, and taught advanced experimental psychology from 1918 to 1920 and from 1928 to 1930. Early on, Woodworth began assembling his notes, summarizing the findings in all fields of experimental research, to create a textbook. By 1912, he began to circulate mimeographed portions of the "bible" to his students. Albert Poffenberger, Woodworth's student, assistant, and successor as chair at Columbia, shared in the effort to create a comprehensive volume, resulting in a 1920 mimeographed edition distributed and treasured by Columbia graduate students. But administrative duties and other pressures prevented Woodworth from fulfilling his 1922 book contract until 1938, when he was nearly 70 years old. As he put it, "the experimental literature was increasing by leaps and bounds, so that while I was making progress, I was falling further behind" (1938, p. iii). So well known and anticipated was Woodworth's effort that when the book finally appeared, it was announced that "the bible is out" (Estes, 1981). The bible was a successor to Ladd and Woodworth (1911), but with physiological psychology and experimental psychology now clearly separated and the philosophical concerns of Ladd (1887) eliminated entirely.

Between 1938 and 1954, nearly 44,000 copies of *Experimental Psychology* were sold in the United States and Canada, according to Woodworth's royalty statements. The revised edition (Woodworth & Schlosberg, 1954) sold more than 23,000 copies between 1954 and 1959, and a revision of the Woodworth and Schlosberg edition by Kling and Riggs (1971) was also widely used. Assuming conservatively that half of the books were reused by other students, nearly 100,000 North American psychology majors and graduate students used Woodworth as their guide for experimental research during the period 1939 to 1959. The book was translated into a number of languages, from Spanish to Slovak. For at least the first decade of its publication, *Experimental Psychology* had no serious competitors. Although the book lacked any overall theoretical framework, it covered a broad range of topics in a way that was eminently useful for researchers (Estes, 1981). The interpretive summaries of the literature showed the careful and balanced analysis of what was understood and what needed further explanation. The book provided a model for the careful weighing of evidence, and confirmed Woodworth's position as the premier generalist of experimental psychology.

In the introduction, Woodworth defined the nature and scope of experimental psychology by drawing a clear distinction between experimental and correlational research in a manner later adopted by most textbook authors.

> To be distinguished from the experimental method, and standing on a par with it in value, rather than above or below, is the comparative and correlational method. It takes its start from individual differences. By use of suitable tests, it measures the individuals in a sample of some population, distributes these measures, and finds their average, scatter, etc. Measuring two or more characteristics of the same individuals it computes the correlation of these characteristics and goes on to factor analysis. This method does not introduce an "experimental factor"; it has no "independent variable" but treats all the measured variables alike. It does not directly study cause and effect. The experimentalist's independent variable is antecedent to his dependent variable; one is cause (or part of the cause) and the other effect. The correlationist studies the interrelation of different effects. (Woodworth, 1938, p. 3)

Mental testing and individual differences were excluded from *Experimental Psychology*. Despite Woodworth's assertion that the two approaches are "on a par in value," only experiments provide the key to cause and effect. Given that Woodworth had emphasized the question of "why" in his dynamic approach, the unstated implication is that laboratory experimentation provides knowledge that simply could not be obtained with other strategies, and yields knowledge of greater scientific value.

The notion that manipulation and control are essential to science was not new, and was a central feature of the philosophical traditions that began with Sir Francis Bacon and continued with Ernst Mach (see Smith, 1992; Winston, 2001). But Woodworth's distinction between experimental and correlational strategies made explicit a difference in the potential for causal knowledge. This view was taken up by subsequent authors of both introductory and experimental textbooks, and Woodworth's position became the common justification for asserting the superiority of experimental over nonexperimental work. The standard phrase learned by all psychology students became, "correlation does not show causation." The question of how nonexperimental sciences, such as astronomy, are able to explain and progress was rarely asked. Such a view also helped psychologists to establish a distinct identity: Sociologists and anthropologists also study human actions, but their studies are uncontrolled, at least in the eyes of psychologists. Asserting the superiority of experimentation also may have helped to justify the choice of laboratory animals as subjects for a widening range of problems, in that animals would permit the degree of manipulation and control necessary for causal inference (Winston, 1990). Woodworth would not have supported this restrictive use of his definition of experiment. Throughout his career, he encouraged and inspired work in almost every area of psychology, with diverse populations and methods. In distinguishing experimentation from correlation, he was striving for clarity, rather than a hierarchy of method. But the unreflective adoption of his distinction may have contributed to the methodological narrowness that developed in social psychology and other areas in the 1950s (see MacMartin & Winston, 2000).

WOODWORTH AS A DISCIPLINE BUILDER AND MENTOR

Woodworth influenced the development of psychology through many administrative positions. Extremely proud to be elected as the 23rd president of the APA in 1914, he used his presidential address to argue for a resolution to the acrimonious debate over "imageless thought" (Woodworth, 1915). Devoted to the organization, he was an important figure in APA affairs and governance for decades. He also worked to increase the recognition of psychology within the broader scientific community through the National Research Council, the research and advisory body of the National Academy of Sciences. While chair of the Division of Anthropology and Psychology of the National Research Council, he helped lay the groundwork for the founding of the Society for Research in Child Development, which became the leading organization for the promotion and dissemination of developmental work. Woodworth's election in 1931 to president of the Social Science Research Council, a prestigious, interdisciplinary group of scholars, showed that he could effectively communicate with sociologists, economists, and political scientists, as well as physiologists. He understood that building a discipline required publication outlets, and in 1906 he created the *Archives of Psychology* especially, but not exclusively, for publishing doctoral dissertations. For doctoral students who were required to publish their dissertations to receive their degree, the *Archives* was often the only means of publication they could afford. He continued to edit and manage the *Archives of Psychology* until 1948, when he turned the *Archives* over to the APA. He served on the editorial board of the *Psychological Bulletin* and other major journals. Woodworth's steady manner and careful treatment of evidence was highly respected, and his advice on what should be published and who should be hired was widely sought.

As Cattell's successor at Columbia, he guided the Psychology Department during its period of greatest prestige, when it produced many future APA presidents and leaders in both basic and applied work. Frederick Thorne, who was both an undergraduate and graduate student at Columbia, credited Woodworth as responsible for recruiting the excellent faculty and coordinating the undergraduate and graduate program staffs. Thorne (1976) referred to the period under Woodworth's stewardship as a "golden age."

Woodworth was considered a great teacher, but not because of his dynamic classroom performance. Gardner Murphy (1963) recalled the experience of being in Woodworth's class in 1919.

> Entering the classroom in an unpressed, baggy old suit, and wearing army shoes, Woodworth would make his way to the blackboard, not quite sure how to begin. He would mumble; then stop dead; fail to find the phrase he wanted; turn and look at the class in a helpless sort of way; go back to the blackboard, and then utter some inimitable word of insight or whimsy, which would go into our notebooks to be remembered in the decades that followed. (p. 132)

While admitting his lackluster style, Woodworth's students found him full of love for his subject, dedicated, accessible, and supportive. According to Seward (1958), when a graduate student presented a seemingly hopeless research plan to the faculty, Woodworth would often manage, "in his quiet, hesitating voice, to pull the whole thing together and save the problem" (p. 11).

Despite the encouraging atmosphere at Columbia in the 1920s and 1930s, the situation was not a golden age for all. Columbia attracted a number of Jewish graduate students. Given the climate of increasing antisemitism after World War I, these students encountered serious barriers to academic jobs. In their letters of recommendation, many faculty in psychology and other disciplines felt an unwritten obligation to tell prospective employers that the applicant was Jewish. For example, Woodworth (1940a) wrote to Gladys Tallman the following.

> Dr. Heinz Ansbacher wishes to offer himself as a candidate for one of your Fellowships. I know him quite well and would recommend him heartily. Among our Jewish graduates he has about the best social background. . . . I have never seen any objectionable traits.

These letters often took the form of, "he is a Jew, but . . . ," followed by a denial that the candidate had the "unpleasant" or "objectionable" traits that Jews were thought by some to share (Winston, 1996, 1998a). Woodworth, E. G. Boring, and the other major figures who wrote such letters knew that raising the issue would mean that the student was unlikely to be hired, and they sometimes discouraged Jewish applicants to graduate school on the grounds that they could not be placed. Woodworth participated in this system of exclusion, even if he did not support it. He held some stereotyped notions about Jews, but was very encouraging to some of his Jewish students, such as Otto Klineberg, who was eventually hired at Columbia, and Ansbacher, who obtained an academic position at the University of Vermont after World War II, when antisemitism in the United States declined. For some students, the situation with regard to bigotry was much worse. Mamie Phipps Clark, the first African American woman to obtain a doctorate in psychology at Columbia, was unable to secure an academic position of any kind, even after her noted work on children's racial identity.

Many of the students whom Woodworth taught or supervised made important contributions. Harold Jones, a leader in child development research at Berkeley, and Gardner Murphy, a major contributor to personality, social psychology, and research on psychic phenomena, are examples of his successful mentoring. Woodworth's student and successor as department chair, Poffenberger, made notable contributions to applied psychology, especially advertising. Klineberg transformed the treatment of race in psychology, helped to create the field of cross-cultural psychology, and helped to found the Society for the Psychological Study of Social Issues. Not all of Woodworth's students made positive contributions: Henry E. Garrett, who was Poffenberger's successor as head of the department, promoted racial segregation and ideas of innate White superiority (see Winston, 1998b). Garrett stands as a reminder that one cannot necessarily give either credit or blame to the supervisor for the subsequent work of the student. But the collection of essays assembled in Woodworth's honor by Seward and Seward (1958) shows the range and extent of his influence, and illustrates how Woodworth's dynamic S–O–R approach provided a general framework of great heuristic value. Woodworth so loved teaching that after he became professor emeritus in 1942, he continued to teach until 3 years before his death at the age of 90.

CONCLUSION

Woodworth was a modest person. When he accepted the American Psychological Foundation Gold Medal in 1956, he did not make a speech summarizing his own accomplishments. Instead, he reflected on his cohort of approximately 30 young psychologists who entered the field around 1900. He described them as the third generation, after the first generation of William James and G. Stanley Hall, and the second generation who headed the laboratories in 1900. He gave a selection of their names and *their* accomplishments, and presented himself as their "visible representative" (Woodworth, 1956). Earlier, when evaluating his career, Woodworth (1930) noted that although he had advised and guided the research of many students, "I have done comparatively little investigation on my own account" (p. 376). He was disappointed that he had not made any specific discoveries for which he would be known. In self-deprecating fashion, he referred to his varied research topics as "this sad array of scattered interests" (p. 372) and wrote that "I rate my achievement very low, believing that I am one of the sort whose name will soon be forgotten" (quoted in Poffenberger, 1962, p. 687).

The honors and awards that Woodworth received show that his colleagues had a much higher opinion of his contributions. Woodworth underestimated the value of his careful summaries of research, analyses of difficult problems, and his synthesis of divergent views. These efforts helped hold together a fractionated discipline. Throughout his career, Woodworth promoted an antidoctrinaire, eclectic empiricism that encouraged and foreshadowed the great diversity of modern psychology. He steadfastly rejected restrictions on the scope of the field.

> My bogey men—the men who most irritated me, and from whose domination I was most anxious to keep free—were those who assumed to prescribe in advance what types of results a psychologist must find and within what limits he must remain. Münsterberg was such a one, with his assertion that a scientific psychology could never envisage real life. Titchener was such a one, in insisting that all the genuine findings of psychology must consist of sensations. Watson was such a one, when he announced that introspection must not be employed, and only motor (and glandular) activities must be discovered. I always rebelled at any such epistemological table of commandments. (Woodworth, 1930, p. 376)

Woodworth's interests, activities, and authority spanned across the discipline to a degree impossible for subsequent generations of psychologists. He was eclectic, but this did not mean he was uncritical. He knew more psychology than his colleagues, and his books show that he was a most admirable generalist. Given the extraordinarily widespread use of his textbooks, Woodworth was *the* leading teacher of psychology in his time, not just to Columbia students but to the world.

REFERENCES

Boring, E. G. (1933). *The physical dimensions of consciousness.* New York: Century.

Boring, E. G. (1950). *A history of experimental psychology* (2nd ed.). New York: Appleton-Century-Crofts.

Crane, A. L. (1923). Race differences in inhibition. *Archives of psychology, 63,* v–vii, 9–84.

Estes, W. K. (1981). The Bible is out. *Contemporary Psychology, 26,* 327–330.

Hollingworth, L. (1914). *Functional periodicity. An experimental study of the mental and motor abilities of women during menstruation.* New York: Teachers College Press.

James, W. (1890). *The principles of psychology* (2 vols.). New York: Holt.

Klein, D. B. (1958). Psychopathology. In G. S. Seward & J. P. Seward (Eds.), *Current psychological issues: Essays in honor of Robert S. Woodworth* (pp. 303–328). New York: Holt.

Kling, J. W., & Riggs, L. A. (1971). *Woodworth & Schlosberg's experimental psychology* (3rd ed.). New York: Holt.

Kwee, M. G. T., & Ellis, A. (1997). Can multimodal and rational emotive behavior therapy be reconciled? *Journal of Rational–Emotive and Cognitive Behavior Therapy, 15,* 95–132.

Ladd, G. T. (1887). *Elements of physiological psychology.* New York: Scribner.

Ladd, G. T., & Woodworth, R. S. (1911). *Elements of physiological psychology.* New York: Scribner.

MacMartin, C., & Winston, A. S. (2000). The rhetoric of experimental social psychology, 1930–1960: From caution to enthusiasm. *Journal of the History of the Behavioral Sciences, 36,* 349–364.

Munn, N. (1966). *Psychology: The fundamentals of human adjustment* (5th ed.). New York: Houghton Mifflin.

Murphy, G. (1963). Robert Sessions Woodworth, 1869–1962. *American Psychologist, 18,* 131–133.

Poffenberger, A. (1962). Robert Sessions Woodworth: 1869–1962. *American Journal of Psychology, 75,* 677–692.

Seward, G. S. (1958). Woodworth, the man: A case history. In G. S. Seward & J. P. Seward (Eds.), *Current psychological issues: Essays in honor of Robert S. Woodworth* (pp. 3–20). New York: Holt.

Seward, G. S., & Seward, J. P. (Eds.). (1958). *Current psychological issues: Essays in honor of Robert S. Woodworth.* New York: Holt.

Shaffer, L. F. (1956). Presentation of the First Gold Medal Award. *American Psychologist, 11,* 587–588.

Smith, L. D. (1992). On prediction and control: B. F. Skinner and the technological idea of science. *American Psychologist, 47,* 216–223.

Sokal, M. M. (1988). James McKeen Cattell and the failure of anthropometric testing, 1890–1901. In L. T. Benjamin, Jr. (Ed.), *A history of psychology: Original sources and contemporary research* (pp. 310–319). New York: McGraw-Hill.

Thorndike, E. L., & Woodworth, R. S. (1901a). The influence of improvement in one mental function upon the efficiency of other functions I. Functions involving attention, observation and discrimination. *Psychological Review, 8,* 247–261.

Thorndike, E. L., & Woodworth, R. S. (1901b). The influence of improvement in one mental function upon the efficiency of other functions, II. The estimation of magnitudes. *Psychological Review, 8,* 384–395.

Thorndike, E. L., & Woodworth, R. S. (1901c). The influence of improvement in one mental function upon the efficiency of other functions. III. Functions involving attention, observation and discrimination. *Psychological Review, 8,* 553–564.

Thorne, F. C. (1976). Reflections on the golden age of Columbia psychology. *Journal of the History of the Behavioral Sciences, 12,* 159–165.

Tolman, E. C. (1932). *Purposive behavior in animals and men.* New York: Appleton Century Crofts.

Winston, A. S. (1988). "Cause" and "experiment" in introductory psychology: An analysis of R. S. Woodworth's textbooks. *Teaching of Psychology, 15,* 79–83.

Winston, A. S. (1990). Robert Sessions Woodworth and the "Columbia Bible": How the psychological experiment was redefined. *American Journal of Psychology, 103,* 391–401.

Winston, A. S. (1996). "As his name indicates": R. S. Woodworth's letters of reference and employment for Jewish psychologists in the 1930s. *Journal of the History of the Behavioral Sciences, 32,* 30–43.

Winston, A. S. (1998a). "The defects of his race . . .": E. G. Boring and antisemitism in American psychology, 1923–1953. *History of Psychology, 1,* 27–51.

Winston, A. S. (1998b). Science in the service of the far right: Henry Garrett, the IAAEE, and the Liberty Lobby. *Journal of Social Issues, 54,* 179–210.

Winston, A. S. (2001). Cause into function: Ernst Mach and the reconstruction of explanation in psychology. In C. D. Green, M. Shore, & T. Teo (Eds.), *The transformation of psychology: Influences of 19th-century philosophy, technology, and natural science* (pp. 107–131). Washington, DC: American Psychological Association.

Winston, A. S. (2004). Controlling the metalanguage: Authority and acquiescence in the history of method. In A. Brock, J. Louw, & W. van Hoorn (Eds.), *Rediscovering the history of psychology: Essays inspired by the work of Kurt Danziger* (pp. 53–74). New York: Kluwer.

Winston, A. S., & Blais, D. J. (1996). What counts as an experiment: A transdisciplinary analysis of textbooks, 1930–1970. *American Journal of Psychology, 109,* 599–616.

Winston, A. S., Butzer, B., & Ferris, M. (2004). Constructing difference: Intelligence, heredity, and race in textbooks, 1930–1970. In A. S. Winston (Ed.), *Defining difference: Race and racism in the history of psychology* (pp. 199–230). Washington, DC: American Psychological Association.

Woodworth, R. S. (1899). The best movement for handwriting. *Science, 10,* 679–680.

Woodworth, R. S. (1903). *Le mouvement.* Paris: Doin.

Woodworth, R. S. (1910). Racial differences in mental traits. *Science, 31,* 171–186.

Woodworth, R. S. (1915). A revision of imageless thought. *Psychological Review, 22,* 1–27.

Woodworth, R. S. (1918). *Dynamic psychology.* New York: Columbia University Press.

Woodworth, R. S. (1921). *Psychology: A science of mental life.* New York: Holt.

Woodworth, R. S. (1929). *Psychology* (2nd ed.). New York: Holt.

Woodworth, R. S. (1930). "Robert S. Woodworth." In C. Murchison (Ed.), *A history of psychology in autobiography* (Vol. 2, pp. 359–380). Worcester, MA: Clark University Press.

Woodworth, R. S. (1934). *Psychology* (3rd ed.). New York: Holt.

Woodworth, R. S. (1938). *Experimental psychology.* New York: Holt.

Woodworth, R. S. (1940a, March 31). Letter to Gladys Tallman. Robert S. Woodworth Papers, Columbia University Archives.

Woodworth, R. S. (1940b). *Psychology* (4th ed.). New York: Holt.

Woodworth, R. S. (1941). *Heredity and environment: A critical survey of recently published material on twins and foster children* (Bulletin 47, Social Science Research Council). New York: Social Science Research Council.

Woodworth, R. S. (1956). Acceptance of the Gold Medal of the American Psychological Foundation. *American Psychologist, 11,* 588–589.

Woodworth, R. S. (1958). *Dynamics of behavior.* New York: Holt.

Woodworth, R. S., & Marquis, D. (1947). *Psychology* (5th ed.). New York: Holt.

Woodworth, R. S., & Schlosberg, H. (1954). *Experimental psychology* (2nd ed.). New York: Holt.

Woodworth, R. S., & Thorndike, E. L. (1901). The influence of improvement in one mental function upon the efficiency of other functions. I. *Psychological Review, 8,* 247–261.

Young, J. R. (1833). *The elements of the differential calculus.* London: John Souter.

Karl M. Dallenbach (Photo courtesy of Rand B. Evans)

Chapter 5

Karl M. Dallenbach:
The Lure of the Empirical

Rand B. Evans

Karl M. Dallenbach (1887–1971) is most easily recognized by present-day students of psychology for his classic experiment with J. G. Jenkins on the effects of sleep versus activity on the retention of learned materials (Jenkins & Dallenbach, 1924). Their finding of interference effects on memory is still discussed in introductory and memory texts even 80 years after it was published. Psychologists of earlier generations knew Dallenbach as the editor of the *American Journal of Psychology*, a position he held from the 1920s through the 1960s. He is also known for some of the scientific instruments he invented or modified that were standard in their day. His name is closely associated with that of Edward Bradford Titchener because he remained as perhaps Titchener's most devoted student (Boring, 1958). For better or worse, that association and the influence of Titchener's personality and ideals cast a long shadow on Dallenbach's life and career, one from which he never totally freed himself.

EARLY LIFE

Dallenbach was a midwesterner, born in Champaign, Illinois, on October 20, 1887 (Boring, 1958; Dallenbach, 1967; Evans, 1972). He was the second son of John and Anna Mittendorf Dallenbach. John Dallenbach was a successful businessman in Champaign. The Dällenbachs, Karl's great-grandparents, had emigrated to the United States from Switzerland in the 1820s and the Mittendorf side of the family from Germany in the 1850s. As a child Dallenbach was serious and perhaps lugubrious—even in his mother's description of him. A certain seriousness of mind and a touch of formality, particularly on first acquaintance, would stay with him throughout his life.

Because his mother wanted a girl and Karl had naturally curly hair, in his early years he was made to wear dresses and wore his curls long. As a consequence, he played only with girls because the boys would have nothing to do with him. Later when he graduated from dresses to knee pants, he still was required to keep his long curls. Now able to play with boys, Dallenbach found that he was at the bottom of the boys' social order because the curls put him at a great disadvantage in roughhousing and competing with the other boys. When, finally, his mother allowed his curls to be cut, his combative personality and physical size and strength allowed him to rise to the top of their social group once the disadvantage of long hair was removed. His natural aggressiveness and determination to win and his general tenacity remained a part of his personality throughout life.

THE UNIVERSITY OF ILLINOIS AND
THE UNIVERSITY OF PITTSBURGH

Dallenbach attended college at the nearby University of Illinois in the pre-law curriculum. Although outstanding in sports in school he was not allowed by his parents to take part in sports in college until he showed he could do the academic work. As a substitute he joined the Adelphi Literary Society. While Dallenbach participated in all the activities of the group, one area in which he did not excel was debate. Dallenbach wrote the following:

> My failure was due chiefly to my inability to shift loyalties. After I had studied a question and had evaluated the arguments pro and con and had come to a conclusion that I thought was right, I could not, with conviction, argue for the other side. (Dallenbach, 1967, p. 72)

Intense loyalty, both to ideas and individuals, would also mark and shape his life and career. His grades were good, and Dallenbach's parents at last allowed him to play sports in which his natural aggressiveness made him a star player in football.

Dallenbach took his first course in psychology hesitantly. He identified psychology with phrenology and pseudoscience and had no interest in such trumpery. It was a fraternity advisor who suggested he take John Wallace Baird's introductory course in psychology. Baird, an excellent lecturer, was a student of Titchener of Cornell, so the psychology Dallenbach learned was based on Titchener's system, the text being Titchener's *An Outline of Psychology* (1899). He found

Baird's course the most interesting he had ever taken. It was, as he said, "science" (Dallenbach, 1967, p. 72).

A year later, after taking other psychology courses, Dallenbach elected to take Baird's course in experimental psychology. Baird used the "Qualitative Students' Manual" of Titchener's *Experimental Psychology* (1902). Dallenbach found the course enjoyable and worked particularly hard on his reports, both typing them and illustrating them with drawings of apparatus, charts, diagrams, and graphs. He did the same in the next semester of experimental psychology. Baird was so impressed by the reports that he had them bound, and they were kept for years at Illinois as models of student lab reports.

In March of Dallenbach's junior year, Titchener gave a series of lectures at the University of Illinois, later published as *Experimental Psychology of the Thought Processes* (Titchener, 1908). Dallenbach attended all the lectures and was enthralled, although he admitted that he did not understand at the time Titchener's arguments against imageless thought. Later, when Titchener saw Dallenbach's laboratory reports, he was sufficiently impressed to suggest that Dallenbach attend Cornell for a doctorate in psychology. Much to Dallenbach's own surprise, he later did just that. Baird made Dallenbach the laboratory assistant in the experimental psychology course even though he was not a psychology major.

Midway through Dallenbach's senior year at Illinois, Baird accepted a call to Clark University as chair of the department of psychology, replacing E. C. Sanford. The second semester of his senior year, Dallenbach was put in charge of the experimental laboratory because Baird's replacement, Arthur Sutherland, was not an experimentalist and did not know how to use the equipment. Dallenbach had enough credits to graduate at the end of the fall term but wanted to retain his eligibility for spring sports and graduate with his class. Because he had completed all the undergraduate requirements for graduation, he entered the graduate school in psychology at the University of Illinois that spring and began a master's thesis under Frederick Kuhlmann. The study would be published later as "The Relation of Memory Error to Time Interval" (Dallenbach, 1913b).

Dallenbach was still torn between a career in psychology and one in law. He saw a notice for a fellowship at the masters program in psychology at the University of Pittsburgh. He decided to let fate take charge. He asked Baird to write a letter of recommendation for him. If he was accepted, he would go to Pitt and psychology. If not, he would go to Harvard for law school. He got the fellowship and so went to Pitt for a master's degree in psychology but he also took courses in the Pitt medical school. There he met and became friends with Karl Lashley. Indeed, Lashley took his first psychology course from Dallenbach at Pitt, a course in experimental psychology. Dallenbach set up the demonstrational laboratory in psychology. Among his other activities was playing on Pitt's undefeated and unscored-on football team of 1910.

Dallenbach had already completed all the master's-level courses at Illinois that were available for him at Pitt, so he gained permission to take courses in the Medical School. His master's thesis work at Pitt was based on the research he had begun with Kuhlmann in his last year at the University of Illinois. Medical school fascinated him and replaced law as a competitor with psychology for his life's work. As he had done with law versus psychology, Dallenbach allowed fate to intervene. He remembered Titchener's interest in him and so applied for only one program in psychology: the Sage Fellowship in Psychology at Cornell. If he received the fellowship he would go to Cornell in psychology. If not, then he would go to medical school.

TO CORNELL

Dallenbach's first meeting with Titchener was his interview for the Sage Fellowship, which was held at Titchener's home in Ithaca, New York. Dallenbach remembered the interview, during which he was asked about his work and activities, as lasting all afternoon. It was in that interview that Dallenbach discovered Titchener's attitude toward applied psychology. After Dallenbach described his master's work, Titchener responded in a disparaging tone with, "Oh, a study in applied psychology." When asked about which theory of vision he believed in, Titchener responded in typical fashion: "Believe? Why, I don't believe in any." What followed was a discourse on theory and its place in science. It was there that Titchener gave Dallenbach one of the pieces of advice that would become a permanent part of his professional life: "Carry your theories lightly" (Dallenbach, 1967; see also Dallenbach, 1953a).

To his surprise, Dallenbach did receive the Sage Fellowship in Psychology, and in the fall of 1911 went to Titchener's Cornell. Titchener ran the doctoral program in psychology like a relatively benign despot. Following the German model, students at Cornell were not required to attend classes, and there were no graduate courses to take except for one seminar in the second term. There was only the dissertation and an oral exam. The student was able to meet with Titchener in his home for discussion of the dissertation topic. Dallenbach remembered it as follows:

> The graduate student was allowed perfect freedom to prepare himself for his final oral examination in any way he wished: by studying in the library, by experimenting in the laboratory, or by attending undergraduate courses of his choice. Many students were unable to survive this degree of freedom; they required the compulsion of a teacher. Those who did survive, who learned to depend on their own initiative, were the productive scholars of the future. (Dallenbach, 1967, p. 81)

In addition to his major, experimental psychology, Dallenbach selected two minors, educational psychology and medicine. Educational psychology was taught in the school of education by Guy M. Whipple. Whipple's *Manual of Mental and Physical Tests* (1910) had just appeared. It was a manual of educational tests and measures that was the equivalent in educational measurement of Titchener's *Experimental Psychology* (1902). From Whipple, Dallenbach gained insights into how psychophysical measurement could be applied in educational tests. Although Titchener had disparaged applied psychology, Dallenbach was curious about it. It is perhaps this connection with Whipple and his later work on psychological testing in the Army that led Dallenbach to define for his own students experimental psychology not as a subject-matter but as a method.

Still thinking of the possibility of medical school, Dallenbach's second minor was in histology and embryology under Benjamin Kingsbury in the Cornell Medical School. It was an unusual selection for a doctoral student of Titchener, but he approved it.

During that year, while taking Madison Bentley's undergraduate course in psychophysics, Dallenbach met Edwin G. Boring. They were the only students in the class and there began an abiding friendship. Dallenbach also gained a lifelong respect for the acerbic but methodologically meticulous Bentley.

Titchener typically selected dissertation topics for his PhD students. Following the German model he had experienced at Leipzig, Titchener rarely did research himself but directed his students in doing studies according to his formulation. The researches were selected by Titchener much like moves in a chess game, intended to support one strategy and then another of Titchener's psychological system against the systems of opposing camps. The topic of attention played an important role in Titchener's systematic strategy in those years. Attention was one of many areas in which Titchener's system differed from that of Wundt. Titchener included attention as a directly observable attribute of sensation: clearness. Wundt brought attention into his system through an elaborate process that made up his doctrine of apprehension. Titchener's *Textbook of Psychology* (1910) had appeared just the year before Dallenbach arrived at Cornell. In that text Titchener carried through his positivistic reformulation of Wundt's attributes by adding space, time, and attention as directly observable states in the description of sensations. Attention appeared as "attributive clearness," the degree to which one aspect of the experiential pattern stands out against the vagueness of other parts. Titchener was still working out the details of differing levels of clearness and so it was natural that Dallenbach was assigned the topic of "The Measurement of Attention" (Dallenbach, 1913a).

Titchener's student, L. R. Geissler, had been given the task of studying this kind of attention with respect to visual sensations. Dallenbach was given the same task but using auditory stimuli and distraction. Dallenbach found, as did Geissler, that it was possible using the introspective method to measure attention in terms of "attributive clearness." Dallenbach would later pursue the study of attention with respect to touch and imagery (Dallenbach, 1916).

Attention would become, for almost 40 years, one of Dallenbach's major interests. He became perhaps the foremost expert on attention as a conscious sensory process. In doing this, Dallenbach was following another of Titchener's admonitions, one that Dallenbach would also impart to his own students: To become well known in a discipline, it is important to be an expert in something. Pick some topic, regardless how small, and study it more thoroughly and know more about it than anyone else (Dallenbach, personal communication to Rand B. Evans, 1966). Dallenbach gave the same admonition to his own students with a modification: It does not take a lot more additional knowledge from the second best to become "the" expert. Just know a little more than anyone else.

STUDY AT BONN

Dallenbach did not accept Titchener's ideas blindly, however. He typically tried to verify the opinions of others by his own experience. Dallenbach had been puzzled by Titchener's criticism of the work of Oswald Külpe's students on imageless thought. When, on traveling to Germany in the summer of 1912, he found he was unable to study with Wundt in Leipzig. He went instead to Bonn to hear Külpe lecture. Dallenbach developed a warm relationship with Külpe and other students who were there at the time. Dallenbach was always proud that he was the only one of the students who had the courage to go to Külpe and ask him for his photograph. Robert S. Woodworth, who was also there hearing Külpe, became like an older brother to him, and the two formed a friendship that lasted the rest of their lives (Dallenbach, 1967, p. 88).

LAUNCHING AN ACADEMIC CAREER

Dallenbach returned to Cornell in the fall of 1912 and completed his dissertation the following spring. His doctoral examination lasted longer than any other in the history of Cornell up to that point, about 6 hours. The reason for this was that, as he explained later, each of the professors tried to outdo all the others in testing him in their fields of study. Now Dallenbach found himself in a position to follow a career in either of two directions: psychology or medicine.

Dallenbach had completed at Cornell his first 2 years of medical school through his minor in medicine. He was inclined to go to medical school and gain an MD degree. It was then that Dallenbach experienced the "Titchenerian imperative." Titchener would have none of it. He had already selected a place for Dallenbach at the University of Oregon and he was not going to have his training go to waste. So Dallenbach went to Eugene.

Dallenbach spent 2 years at Oregon. After he achieved an academic position, he married his college sweetheart, Ethel Douglas. They were both fond of Eugene, recalling that it was a lovely place with a highly social and friendly faculty, with dinner parties in formal dress (Dallenbach, personal communication, 1966). The problem for Dallenbach was that there was no research going on in the department and there was no real support or incentive to do research. He feared that without research he would soon "go to seed" there. It was simply too comfortable. Dallenbach misinterpreted an inquiry from the University of Minnesota as an offer and so resigned his position at Oregon—without a contract in hand. But it was not a true offer, and so Dallenbach again pursued going to medical school. Titchener, on hearing of this, intervened again. This time he contacted G. F. Arps at Ohio State and arranged for a position there for Dallenbach. After a year at Ohio State University, Titchener called Dallenbach back to Cornell for a position in the Department of Psychology. Dallenbach would stay there until 1948, with the exception of involvement in two world wars and a 2-year sabbatical at Columbia.

The first 2 years back at Cornell were filled with research, interrupted only by his volunteering and serving in the Army during World War I. Even with a 2-year break for the war, during the first decade after his degree, he published 28 articles, most of them in the *American Journal of Psychology* (McGrade, 1958).

A LIFE OF RESEARCH

Dallenbach believed fervently in the experimental method. He believed that theory is the summarization of empirical findings and that theory follows and is subservient to observation and method. The experimental method was the center of the psychological enterprise for Dallenbach. He, following Titchener's admonition to carry one's theories lightly, did so far more than did his master. He used the experimental method throughout his career to steer among the various theories, often using the method to design crucial experiments to enlighten theoretical controversy.

Attention

Between 1913 and 1930 Dallenbach published approximately 24 articles, most of them experimental, on the topic of attention. Boring believed Dallenbach could have written the definitive book on the subject (Boring, 1958, p. 25)—as did Dallenbach himself (Dallenbach, personal communication, 1966). It was Dallenbach who finally succeeded in making the distinction stick between attention as a cognitive process and as an attribute of sensory experience (Dallenbach, 1920; Gill & Dallenbach, 1926; Glanville & Dallenbach, 1929). The problem for Dallenbach was that, in following Titchener's lead, he had selected the aspect of attention, that of attention as an attribute of sensory experience, that would not survive in the mainstream of experimental psychology. His steadfast devotion to Titchener and his ideas prevented Dallenbach from pursuing the other tradition of attention, attention as a cognitive process, which would lead to the work of Broadbent and others in what is currently called the psychology of attention. Dallenbach recognized at some point that attention as a sensory process had reached a dead end, and he moved on to other interests.

Psychology of Touch

Another area in which Dallenbach gained expert status was in the study of touch. The dozen or more studies published between 1922 and 1943 were pioneering studies, both methodologically and theoretically important in their day (Boring, 1958, pp. 26–28; McGrade, 1958). He developed methods for mapping the warm and cold spots on the skin (Dallenbach, 1931). He invented the Dallenbach temperature stimulator for producing precisely controlled punctate temperatures on the skin (Dallenbach, 1923). He also developed a "heat" grill, a device made up of two coils of copper tubing run close together, each maintained at constant temperatures by means of a constant flow of warm and cold water. When this grill was pressed against the skin, it produced an experience of "hot," although neither coil was of high temperature (Burnett & Dallenbach, 1927). These instruments were important in Dallenbach's pioneering research on the experience of heat. These instruments and several others became commercially available from the Christian Stoelting Company (Stoelting & Co., 1930, p. 50), and were standard instruments in the field for decades.

Interference in Learning

Another study of major significance was Dallenbach's work on human forgetting. Two competing theories at the time to explain forgetting were the theory of disuse and the theory of interference. Ebbinghaus (1885) had propounded a theory of disuse to explain how we forget; Müller and Pilzecker (1900) had propounded a theory of interference. Dallenbach, with his student John G. Jenkins, undertook their now-classic experiment on the effects of sleep versus activity on retention of learned material (Jenkins & Dallenbach, 1924). It was published in the *American Journal of Psychology* as a "minor study," but was anything but minor. Its finding that activity after learning interfered more with recall of information than did rest was an important empirical confirmation of the interference theory. This research stimulated both experimental and theoretical work by others for decades.

In 1946 Dallenbach would redo the study, this time using cockroaches as his experimental subjects (Minami & Dallenbach, 1946). In part, Dallenbach said, it was to show that he could do an animal experiment if he really wanted to. He devised an ingenious cockroach treadmill in the experiment for the activity condition. The authors also solved a problem that had prevented the use of cockroaches for this purpose, how to get them to sleep. Dallenbach discovered that a roach placed in a snug, confined space effectively switches itself off. A padded match box worked perfectly for this purpose. The results confirmed Jenkins and Dallenbach's earlier study of interference.

Facial Vision

Another example of Dallenbach's use of the experimental method to settle long-standing theoretical questions was his work on "facial vision." This research was performed in the 1940s, during his last decade at Cornell. The question of how blind individuals avoid objects without touching them dates from the time of Diderot (1749). A common belief was that blind individuals localize objects in space by pressure impressions on the face. Even many blind individuals described the experience of localization as a "pressury" experience on the face. William James went so far as to postulate that it was caused by some special pressure sense in the ears, apparently at the tympanic membrane, although not by hearing (James, 1910, II, p. 139). In the 50 years since James's *Principles of Psychology* appeared the question had gone largely unresolved. Dallenbach's stated goal was "to resolve the contradictions between theory and experimental result" (Supa, Cotzin, & Dallenback, 1944, p. 138).

> We hoped, despite–or because of—our theoretical biases, which differed greatly among us, to follow without prejudice the lead of the experimental facts and to determine the necessary and sufficient conditions for the perception of obstacles by the blind. (Supa, Cotzin, & Dallenbach, 1944, p. 138)

Supa, a graduate student at Cornell who had been blind since early childhood, came with the belief in some facial pressure sense as the source of his ability to avoid obstacles. Cotzin, a sighted Cornell graduate student, came naive to the problem and without a predisposition. Dallenbach, because he had worked with a blind student in 1914 in an unpublished experiment, was predisposed to a facial-pressure hypothesis.

In a relentlessly methodical series of articles, Dallenbach and graduate students pinned down just about every conceivable hypothesis about the way in which blind individuals avoid obstacles. The series is a case study in the application of the experimental method to a difficult problem. As a result Dallenbach and his students demonstrated that blind individuals avoid objects by reacting to echoes produced by footsteps or other relatively high-frequency sounds. These studies were fundamental contributions to the experimental and applied literature (Griffin, 1958).

THE *AMERICAN JOURNAL OF PSYCHOLOGY*

Perhaps Dallenbach's most spectacular demonstration of devotion to Titchener and his memory is reflected in Dallenbach's acquisition and stewardship of the *American Journal of Psychology* (Boring, 1958; Dallenbach, 1937; Evans & Cohen, 1987). Dallenbach had returned back to his old position at Cornell after his service in World War I. Because of his expertise in psychological testing both from his work with Whipple and from his work in the Psychological Testing Corps during the war, Dallenbach was offered a position in Chicago to administer personnel tests for a trolley company. Although he was offered twice his Cornell salary, he turned it down to return to Titchener's Cornell and to science (Dallenbach, personal communication, 1966).

Titchener was teaching what was his famous sophomore elementary psychology course in those days, and all the instructors and graduate students typically assembled before his class for a time of discussion. They would form a procession into the classroom, with Titchener mounting the podium in his academic regalia to lecture. They all sat through the lectures and for many years Dallenbach continued to take notes. It was there that they often heard about Titchener's latest thoughts on his systematic psychology. In one of those prelecture discussions the *American Journal of Psychology* came up. It was concluded by the instructors and Titchener alike that G. Stanley Hall was letting the *Journal* "go to Hell." The question was what to do about it. Titchener was one of the cooperating editors of the *Journal* but always harbored the desire to edit it alone. It was Dallenbach who suggested that the journal should be bought from Hall and that Titchener be made sole editor. This was accepted enthusiastically, and Dallenbach was appointed to look into the matter. The idea was for the Cornell faculty to form a cooperative and buy it. To Hall, Dallenbach represented the purchase as from an "unidentified" party. The details of the story have been told elsewhere (Boring, 1958; Dallenbach, 1967; Evans & Cohen, 1987), but suffice it to say that Dallenbach carried out intense negotiations with Hall that led Hall to agree to sell the *American Journal of Psychology*. He required earnest money, however, and therefore Dallenbach put up his own money. Returning to Cornell, he found that no one else had any property to mortgage or any sufficient cash to consummate the purchase. Titchener was unwilling to mortgage his home—and he was the only one of the group with any property at all. Dallenbach, undaunted, went to his father and asked to borrow the sum against his inheritance. His father agreed so that his son would not lose his earnest money. The sum had to be paid back with interest, however; it was no gift. So, with that, Dallenbach delivered to Titchener the *American Journal of Psychology*, which Titchener was to edit as he pleased. Dallenbach became business manager. There was never any written agreement between Titchener and Dallenbach on the *Journal*. Dallenbach was the owner, although he looked on the ownership as a stewardship and had no intention of making a profit from the publication. Titchener was happy with the arrangement for a while but, by 1924, things began going sour. Titchener, perhaps realizing that he was, technically, working for an "underling," proposed that the *American Journal of Psychology* be turned over to a nonprofit organization, perhaps even to Cornell University, once the loan was paid off. Dallenbach responded that he had no desire to sell the *Journal* and certainly could not give it away. After a long interchange and attempts by Dallenbach to mollify Titchener, Titchener resigned as editor.

So Dallenbach found himself not only the owner of the *American Journal of Psychology* but its editor as well. He pulled together a group of psychologists—Boring of Harvard University, Bentley of the University of Illinois, Margaret Washburn of Vassar College, and himself—to carry out the editorial work of the *Journal*. Titchener thought that they would be unable to work together for any length of time. He was wrong, however, and the *Journal* was edited in this manner for several decades.

Titchener was unrelenting in his animosity toward Dallenbach and the *Journal* in the years to follow, a bad situation for a junior faculty member whose academic position was now in jeopardy of being lost. Dallenbach, characteristically, threw himself into his work, managing and coediting the *American Journal of Psychology* as well as carrying out all his normal teaching and research duties. Between 1924 when Titchener resigned his editorship and 1927 when Titchener suddenly died of a cerebral hemorrhage, Dallenbach had published 32 notes and articles.

CORNELL AFTER TITCHENER

After Titchener's death, Dallenbach rationalized Titchener's questionable behavior concerning the *Journal* as being due to the tumor that produced the hemorrhage. That may be partly correct because the tumor was a slow-growing variety. All the old admiration and loyalty returned. Dallenbach always remained faithful to his agreements with Titchener about the *Journal*. He never sold it or gained personal profit from it but, 40 years after Titchener's death, when he felt he could no longer carry on with the editorship, Dallenbach gave the *Journal* to his *alma mater*, the University of Illinois, where it still resides. He also gave with it the total of the *Journal's* bank account plus a gift sufficient to guarantee its survival indefinitely.

The *American Journal of Psychology* was always a competitor with research and teaching for Dallenbach's time and energy. Regardless of who did the reviewing for publication, Dallenbach would check each reference against the publications in his own library. He often expressed astonishment about how careless researchers were in their references. Fully 10 percent of the references he checked, he said, were incorrect (Dallenbach, personal communication, 1966). He also did the annual indexes for decades under his pseudonym, Charles Valley Brook, the literal translation of his German name into English.

He once lamented that the pressures of editing did not allow him to write his book on attention or one on psychophysics. In the 1920s, when J. P. Guilford was a graduate student at Cornell, he took Dallenbach's course on psychophysics and urged Dallenbach to write up the lectures as a textbook on psychophysics. Dallenbach responded that he simply did not have the time and that Guilford should do it himself. Guilford did just that, although expanding it considerably beyond the dimensions of Dallenbach's course, and published it as *Psychometric Methods* (Guilford, 1936, p. xi; also Dallenbach, personal communication, 1966), the standard text in the subject for approximately 30 years.

THE TEXAS YEARS

In 1948 Dallenbach left Cornell for the position of distinguished professor of psychology at the University of Texas in Austin. Cornell had never been the same after Dallenbach returned from his service in World War II. He had made several attempts to move to other universities in the eastern United States after the war. Unknown to Dallenbach, these moves often were thwarted by Boring's negative recommendations. Finally, Dallenbach received and accepted the call to Austin. There he became department chair and designed a new building, some would say in the image of Titchener's laboratory at Cornell (Dallenbach, 1953b). That was certainly an exaggeration, but it must be admitted that there was the flavor of Titchener's Cornell in Mezes Hall. For 10 years, Dallenbach chaired the department, edited the *American Journal of Psychology*, did research with graduate students, and all the while carried a teaching overload so that courses he felt should be taught would be taught.

Dallenbach's reverence for good experimental methodology continued in all these efforts. An example is of his editing of Irvin Rock's article, "The Role of Repetition in Associative Learning" (Rock, 1957). The manuscript had been turned down by other publications before it was sent to the *American Journal of Psychology*. Rock's work on single-trial learning was inventive and sound in Dallenbach's view. That it flew in the face of current theory was less important to Dallenbach than that the methodology was sound and that the generalizations based on the findings were appropriate. Unable to find any fault with his method or generalizations, Dallenbach published Rock's paper, an important contribution to the psychology of learning in its time. There are many other examples of decisions to published material Dallenbach made based strictly on the quality of the methodology.

Even after the normal retirement age, Dallenbach continued teaching under "modified service." This allowed him to work with students and teach, until he finally completely retired at the age of 81. He continued to be productive throughout this period. In his late 70s I collaborated with him in publishing a study of single-trial learning, including a stochastic model for verbal learning (Evans & Dallenbach, 1965).

He was well known in those last years for his undergraduate course in the history of psychology. It was Dallenbach who introduced me to the history of psychology and imprinted on me that same cluster of admonitions that Titchener had imprinted on him, adding a few of his own.

In the spring after his 80th birthday, the Southwestern Psychological Association held a special session in Dallenbach's honor in which past students discussed his influence on them. After a few papers, it became obvious how regularly Dallenbach passed on those attitudes and how well they stuck. The following are paraphrases of some that this author recalls, some clearly derived from Titchener, but others pure Dallenbach:

1. Carry your theories lightly. You may wake up tomorrow and find your most cherished theories have evaporated overnight (Titchener).
2. Be led by the data. Theory is made from data, not the reverse (Dallenbach).
3. Experimental psychology is a method, not a subject matter (Dallenbach).
4. Experimental results are a function of method. The instrument used is part of the method (Titchener).
5. Psychological facts are best understood historically. Unless you can understand how an idea developed you will never understand its implications (Titchener).
6. Be careful in your choice of language when writing. The difference in the right word and almost the right word is the difference between lightning and lightning bug (Dallenbach, crediting Mark Twain, his favorite author).
7. Criticism of another's work can be treacherous. It is always dangerous to call someone's "brain child" an idiot (Dallenbach).
8. Description in psychology should be so precise that, when describing an object, it is possible for someone to reproduce that object without understanding what it is for (Titchener).
9. When you go into a meeting, always have a proposal in hand, preferably in writing. That way you set the agenda for the final result. The discussion will always start with your position (Dallenbach).
10. Become an expert in one or more areas of the field. It does not matter how small that area is. Learn a little more about that area than anyone else. Then the world will come to you (Titchener).

CONCLUSION

Dallenbach may not have exhibited the brilliance of someone like Titchener but he made up for this with solid competence, determination, and hard work. He is the perfect example of a scientific overachiever. He was ethically as solid and straight as anyone could be. If he had faults, they were due to a tendency to tenacity and inertia that sometimes prevented him from seeing all the alternatives at a given choice point. He was unfalteringly loyal and never forgot a favor. The greatest compliment he could give someone was that he or she was consecrated to science. He was at first formal in his demeanor when meeting with people but quickly opened up once he knew someone. He was consistently kind and thoughtful toward his students, inviting his history of psychology and psychophysics classes to his home at the end of each term for a party. He and Mrs. Dallenbach tended to "adopt" his graduate students, treating them much like members of the family.

Dallenbach died on December 23, 1971. He was buried near the University of Illinois campus, at a site within the sound of the Illini bells.[1]

REFERENCES

Boring, E. G. (1958). Karl M. Dallenbach. *American Journal of Psychology*, *71*, 1–49.

Burnett, N. C., & Dallenbach, K. M. (1927). The experience of heat. *American Journal of Psychology*, *38*, 418–431.

Dallenbach, K. M. (1913a).The measurement of attention. *American Journal of Psychology*, *24*, 465–507.

Dallenbach, K. M. (1913b). The relation of memory error to time interval. *Psychological Record*, *20*, 323–337.

Dallenbach, K. M. (1916). The measurement of attention in the field of cutaneous sensation. *American Journal of Psychology*, *27*, 445–460.

Dallenbach, K. M. (1920). Attributive vs. cognitive clearness. *American Journal of Psychology*, *3*, 183–230.

Dallenbach, K. M. (1923). Some new apparatus: II. A thermal stimulator. *American Journal of Psychology*, *34*, 92–94.

Dallenbach, K. M. (1931). A method of marking the skin. *American Journal of Psychology*, *43*, 287.

Dallenbach, K. M. (1937). The *American Journal of Psychology*: 1887–1937. *American Journal of Psychology*, *50*, 489–506.

Dallenbach, K. M. (1953a). The place of theory in science. *Psychological Review*, *60*, 33–39.

Dallenbach, K. M. (1953b). The psychological laboratory of the University of Texas. *American Journal of Psychology*, *66*, 90–104.

Dallenbach, K. M. (1967). Karl M. Dallenbach. In E. G. Boring & G. Lindzey (Eds.), *A history of psychology in autobiography* (Vol. V, pp. 59–93). New York: Appleton-Century-Crofts.

Diderot, D. (1749). *Lettre sur les aveugles* [A letter on the blind]. Paris: Durand.

Ebbinghaus, H. (1885). *Ueber das Gedaechtnis. Untersuchungen zur experimentellen psychologie* [On memory. Investigations on experimental psychology]. Leipzig, Germany: Duncker & Humblot.

Evans, R. B. (1972). Karl M. Dallenbach: 1887–1971. *American Journal of Psychology*, *85*, 463–476.

Evans, R. B., & Cohen, J. B. (1987). The *American Journal of Psychology*: A retrospective. *American Journal of Psychology*, *100*, 321–362.

Evans, R. B., & Dallenbach, K. M. (1965). Single-trial learning: A stochastic model for the recall of individual words. *American Journal of Psychology*, *78*, 545–556.

---

[1] The Illini bells are bells that ring on the University of Illinois campus.

Gill, N. F., & Dallenbach, K. M. (1926). A preliminary study of the range of attention. *American Journal of Psychology*, *37*, 247–256.

Glanville, A. D., & Dallenbach, K. M. (1929). The range of attention. *American Journal of Psychology*, *41*, 432–441.

Griffin, D. R. (1958). *Listening in the dark: The acoustic orientation of bats and men*. New Haven, CT: Yale University Press.

Guilford, J. P. (1936). *Psychometric methods*. New York: McGraw-Hill.

James, W. (1910). *Principles of psychology. Vol. II*. New York: Holt.

Jenkins, J. G., & Dallenbach, K. M. (1924). Obliviscence during sleep and waking. *American Journal of Psychology*, *35*, 605–612.

McGrade, M. (1958). A bibliography of the writings of Karl M. Dallenbach. *American Journal of Psychology*, *71*, 41–49.

Minami, H., & Dallenbach, K. M. (1946). The effect of activity upon learning and retention in the cockroach. *American Journal of Psychology*, *59*, 1–58.

Müller, G. E., & Pilzecker, A. (1900). *Experimentelle Beiträge zur Lehre vom Gedächtnis* [Experimental contributions to the theory of memory]. *Zeitschrift für Psychologie*, *1*.

Rock, I. (1957). The role of repetition in associative learning. *American Journal of Psychology*, *70*, 186–193.

Stoelting, C. H., & Company. (1930). *Apparatus, tests and supplies*. Chicago: Author.

Supa, M., Cotzin, M., & Dallenbach, K. M. (1944). "Facial vision" The perception of obstacles by the blind. *American Journal of Psychology*, *62*, 133–183.

Titchener, E. B. (1899). *An outline of psychology*. New York: Macmillan.

Titchener, E. B. (1902). *Experimental psychology: A manual of laboratory practice, vol. I: Qualitative experiments, part I. Student's manual*. New York: Macmillan.

Titchener, E. B. (1908). *Experimental psychology of the thought processes*. New York: Macmillan.

Titchener, E. B. (1910). *A textbook of psychology*. New York: Macmillan.

Whipple, G. M. (1910). *Manual of mental and physical tests*. Baltimore: Warwick & York.

Frieda Fromm-Reichmann (Photographer unknown)

Chapter 6

Frieda Fromm-Reichmann: Pioneer in the Psychotherapy of Psychosis

Gail A. Hornstein

Frieda Fromm-Reichmann is renowned for doing what Freud and the psychiatric establishment thought impossible: successfully treating the most seriously disturbed mental patients—those diagnosed with schizophrenia and other psychoses—by means of intensive psychotherapy instead of shock treatment, lobotomy, or drugs. Dead since 1957, she is still talked about in hushed tones. Her admirers often make her sound like St. Catherine, able to heal the afflicted with the power of her gaze. Her critics ridicule her devotion to patients long considered beyond reach. Neither group seems willing to let go of Fromm-Reichmann as a symbol of their deepest hopes or fears.

I was 6 years old when Fromm-Reichmann died, so I wasn't fortunate enough to meet her in this life. But I've spent more than a decade reconstructing her background, her personal and intellectual influences, and her way of treating patients, during her early years in Germany and then later in the United States. This task was difficult, because many of the relevant records had been destroyed and more than a dozen people had already tried and failed to write her biography (see Hornstein, 2000, 2001).

Fromm-Reichmann has remained an icon in psychiatry partly because she has seemed so mysterious. For decades, her colleagues and friends have protected her privacy obsessively, as if revealing even the tiniest fact about her life would be tantamount to betraying her. Her enemies have speculated wildly, spinning tales filled with innuendo and lies. For a person who lived practically her whole life in the 20th century, there is a strange absence of the usual sorts of source materials, and a constant, unnerving sense of erasure of most of the details of her life and work.

Fromm-Reichmann's mythic image is also partly the result of her having been reborn, 7 years after her death, as a character in fiction. When Joanne Greenberg, her former patient, published *I Never Promised You a Rose Garden* in 1964, Fromm-Reichmann was transformed into Dr. Fried, the heroic therapist who helped Greenberg recover from schizophrenia (Green, 1964). *Rose Garden* has sold close to six million copies, been translated into a dozen languages, and stayed in print continuously for more than 40 years. Millions of people know Fromm-Reichmann only as the fictional Dr. Fried, and even her friends and colleagues find Greenberg's creation more powerful than their own memories. At this point, she has been Dr. Fried for so long—even to those who knew her best—that her life seems too "invented" to have happened. But actually, she is most inspiring when we get to know her as a real person.

TRAINING AND CORE INFLUENCES

Fromm-Reichmann had an unusual background for a psychoanalyst (especially compared with other prominent women of her generation, such as Karen Horney, Anna Freud, or Melanie Klein), and these early experiences powerfully shaped her way of working with patients. Born Frieda Reichmann on October 23, 1889, in Karlsruhe, a city in southwest Germany near the border with France, she was the eldest of three daughters in a middle-class Orthodox Jewish family. From earliest childhood, she demonstrated an extraordinary sensitivity to nuances of behavior, seeming always to know what was happening in the family without anyone telling her. Clearly the favorite of both her parents, she was raised in an indulgent yet disciplined style that simultaneously endowed her with an unshakable sense of self-confidence and entitlement and a deep devotion to serving others less fortunate.

At the age of 6, Fromm-Reichmann moved with her family to Königsberg, in East Prussia, the farthest point in the sprawling German empire, and she remained there for the next 20 years. A brilliant student from an early age, she was trained privately at home by her mother (because girls were not yet being admitted to the *Gymnasium* in that region), and then entered medical school in 1908, the first year women were admitted to advanced study in Prussian universities. She received her MD in 1913, and soon took up psychiatry when evidence of her unusual ability to relate to severely disturbed patients convinced her she could help them in ways others could not.

One powerful experience took place in her final year of medical school. She had been sitting with the handful of other women students in the back row of a huge amphitheater. (They were not allowed to sit with the men.) A manic–depressive patient was being led down the aisle for that day's demonstration.

(Turn-of-the-century medical instruction featured hapless patients forced to perform their symptoms on demand before hundreds of students.) As the patient passed Fromm-Reichmann's seat, he blurted out excitedly to her, "Bertie, at last I find you again!" Fromm-Reichmann, who described herself as extremely shy and dutiful in every way to her parents and teachers, was as astonished as everyone else by this outburst. Yet without realizing what she was doing, she turned to the patient. A voice she did not recognize as her own, entirely free of shyness, said, "Yes, that's fine. I'm very glad too, but you know now the professor wants to talk to you. I'll come and see you later." Amazed by her own behavior, Fromm-Reichmann stood up at the end of the lecture and declared, "I must go and see that man, I have promised him" (Fromm-Reichmann, 1956, n.p.). She began sitting by the beds of psychotic patients, just listening to them. Sometimes she stayed all night, as they screamed or raved or lay mute and unresponsive to everyone. She became convinced that buried inside the avalanche of illness is a terrified person crying out for help. Her job was to do whatever was necessary to get that person out. She did not think of this as heroic or even particularly worthy of note: A physician's responsibility is to help patients, and she had chosen to do that work.

In 1914, when World War I broke out, Fromm-Reichmann was asked to organize a neurological clinic at the University of Königsberg hospital. An unprecedented number of brain injuries were resulting from the artillery fusillades and shell splinters of industrialized warfare, and physicians were scrambling to cope with casualties totally different from anything for which they had trained. Even though she had just graduated from medical school and knew little about neurology, Fromm-Reichmann quickly became the unofficial director of a 100-bed hospital for brain-injured soldiers (as a woman and observant Jew, she could never have been the formally appointed head of a Prussian military installation). When the fighting ended, she became an assistant physician at her mentor Kurt Goldstein's Frankfurt clinic. By 1920, she had published 20 articles on brain injury (eight coauthored with Goldstein or his colleagues), demonstrating a far greater mastery of neurological issues than most doctors in Europe.

The "irrationality" of brain injury had always baffled physicians. Symptoms could take an extraordinary variety of forms and often failed to correspond to known anatomical pathways. Casualties of war were even more puzzling, because the speed and trajectory of a bullet or a piece of shrapnel are completely unpredictable, creating what appears to be a pattern of symptoms unique to each patient. Wards were a bizarre mix: men compulsively laughing or crying; tilting their arms at odd angles; or walking in jerky, uncoordinated fashion. A patient might be mute and stuporous or delirious and excitable. He might writhe in pain from a place where no wound could be found or be utterly insensitive, smiling when stuck with pins during an examination.

Meticulous studies of thousands of these brain-injured soldiers—who were completely healthy except for their injuries, unlike the typical neurological patient afflicted with stroke or tumor—led Goldstein to reconceive core assumptions of his discipline. He distinguished symptoms caused by the injury from those that express "the struggle of the changed personality to cope with demands it can no longer meet" (Goldstein, 1942, p. 69). Goldstein drew attention to how patients alter their environments to avoid exposing their disabilities. He emphasized the extraordinary creativity of human beings forced to craft new solutions to problems, seeing brain-injured people as particularly inventive.

Most neurologists took just the opposite view, casting their patients as rigid and stereotypical. Goldstein thought this was because they were so distracted by the strangeness of the symptoms that they could not see past them to the person underneath. By focusing on capacities that remained intact even after severe injury, he embraced a flexible biology whose main characteristic was adaptation to change. "He never forgot that he addressed an individual, not a brain," remarked one appreciative student (Riese, 1968, p. 25). It was up to the physician, Goldstein insisted, to figure out what a patient could or could not do, not the patient's job to fit his symptoms to standardized measures. Goldstein maintained that just because a patient's behavior is difficult to understand does not mean he cannot be treated. It is the physician's responsibility to meet the patients where they are and to help them confront the obstacles that now face them. If a patient feels hopeless and despairs of ever getting well, it is up to the doctor to offer a "loan of conviction" that improvement might eventually occur (Dyrud, 1989, p. 486).

Fromm-Reichmann's whole approach to treatment emerged from her research with Goldstein, and it is impossible to understand her later work with psychotic patients without appreciating this fact. Years of daily contact with brain-injured patients accustomed her to so wide a range of symptoms that schizophrenia never seemed especially bizarre to her (as it did to most psychoanalysts, trained solely in work with outpatient neurotics). Goldstein's insistence that there is no such thing as "the" brain-injured patient made Fromm-Reichmann highly sensitive to individual differences, and his ingenuity in using a wide range of techniques to locate strengths in even the most severely impaired person taught her never to regard any one method as sacrosanct. And Goldstein's active, empathic response to patients, based on his nonverbal understanding of their needs, taught Fromm-Reichmann to trust her own instincts as a healer instead of hiding behind the persona of the dispassionate physician. Most important, Goldstein's appreciation of patients' resourcefulness, creativity, and resilience taught her to respect even seriously disturbed people and to think of them essentially as her teachers.

Between 1924 and 1928, Fromm-Reichmann founded and ran a private sanitarium in Heidelberg, Germany (becoming the first woman in the history of psychiatry to create a treatment center). This utopian endeavor was guided by her commitments both to psychoanalysis and to Orthodox Judaism (Scholem, 1980). During this period, she also completed formal training at the Berlin Psychoanalytic Institute, helped to found the Frankfurt Psychoanalytic Institute, and married Erich Fromm (and from then on, she was known as Frieda Fromm-Reichmann).

Of all the creative and visionary figures with whom she was closely associated in these years (Martin Buber, Franz Rosenzweig, Max Horkheimer, Karen Horney), the person who influenced her most powerfully was her friend and colleague Georg Groddeck, who ran a sanitarium in nearby Baden-Baden.

Groddeck's view of the unconscious was both more respectful and more optimistic than Freud's. Instead of conceiving of the unconscious as a dangerous force that needs to be controlled, Groddeck saw it as a constructive ally that could create the conditions for the patient's recovery. His only rule was to use whatever means are necessary—however extreme or unusual—to call forth the person's inherent capacities for healing. Seeing himself as a servant of the It (as he called the unconscious), not as an independent actor with an agenda of his own making, Groddeck wrote in a key clinical paper, "It does not matter to therapy whether the doctor's action is correct or not. All that matters is that the patient should make use of this action in order to get himself well" (Groddeck, 1977, p. 210). Insisting that no patient is ever beyond hope, Groddeck told Freud in a letter, "Failure is due to the doctor. It is not inherent in the illness" (Groddeck, 1977, p. 85).

Fromm-Reichmann never felt comfortable emulating Groddeck's outrageousness or thumbing her nose at the psychoanalytic establishment, as he constantly did (calling himself "the wild analyst," he claimed that psychoanalysis could potentially cure cancer and near-sightedness). But she wholeheartedly embraced his iconoclasm, which, stripped of its excess, closely matched her own attitudes. Groddeck's insistence that every patient is potentially capable of cure fit her own quieter ambition, and his unshakable faith in the healing powers of the organism reinforced much of what she had learned from Goldstein. But more than anything else, Groddeck confirmed Fromm-Reichmann's belief that technique is merely a means to an end. The goal is to help the patient, not to stay loyal to any one method. As one of Groddeck's admirers noted, "The fate of his patients concerned him far more than that of his theories" (Groddeck, 1934, p. 28).

Fromm-Reichmann was absolutely convinced that buried inside even the sickest patients is a natural resiliency that can help them heal. This "tendency toward order," as Goldstein called it, did not need to be expressed in mystical terms; it is the same inherent capacity that knits broken bones together or causes burned skin to peel. Although she never stressed the point as strongly as Groddeck or Jung did, Fromm-Reichmann clearly thought of the therapist primarily as a facilitator of the work. She could not heal a patient on her own, the way a surgeon could; she could only guide the patient toward the inner resources that lessen his or her need to stay ill. Later, in America, Fromm-Reichmann would embrace her colleague Harry Stack Sullivan's image of the therapist as participant–observer because it captured precisely this sense of being necessary but not sufficient. Patients could not recover simply because she willed them to do so; neither could they cure themselves without help from her. Therapist and patient are collaborators, working toward a common goal, and it was her responsibility to accept the patient's guidance and convey her confidence in the ultimate success of their work.

In 1933, shortly after Hitler came to power, Fromm-Reichmann was forced to flee Heidelberg. She and Fromm had separated by then (although they remained close friends and colleagues for the rest of their lives). Warned that she was likely to be arrested by the Nazis—she was a prominent Jewish physician and had been a consultant to a progressive school that had been banned—Fromm-Reichmann escaped secretly to Strasbourg (just over the border into France), pretending to be on a weekend trip. She left behind a 15-room house and all the comforts of 4 decades of life in the middle-class. For 2 years she kept a low profile, living and working at various places in Alsace and Palestine. Then in April 1935, thanks to Fromm's help, she managed to get a visa to come to the United States. A few months after arriving, she went to Chestnut Lodge, a tiny private asylum just outside Washington, DC, as the temporary replacement for a doctor on vacation. Hired initially for only 2 months, she ended up staying for 2 decades and totally transforming the institution.

Her luck in immediately finding a job that precisely fit her talents, combined with her knack for making herself indispensable (as she had done in every place she had ever worked), made Fromm-Reichmann's life in exile quite different from that of other refugees. Unlike fellow Jews who, forbidden to take any money out of Germany, were forced to work as dishwashers or maids, Fromm-Reichmann was able to support herself doing the psychiatric work for which she was trained. And in contrast to other exiled analysts such as Otto Fenichel, who never found positions in America commensurate with what they had previously enjoyed, Fromm-Reichmann thrived professionally in her new post.

Working closely with Dexter Bullard, Chestnut Lodge's director, and Harry Stack Sullivan, who quickly became her close friend and colleague, Fromm-Reichmann spent the rest of her life helping to turn the Lodge into the only mental hospital in the world to specialize in the psychoanalytic treatment of psychosis. Within 4 years of arriving in the United States, she was elected president of the Washington–Baltimore Psychoanalytic Institute, and for more than 20 years was a training analyst and teacher there. In the mid-1940s, with Fromm and three other colleagues, she helped to found the William Alanson White Institute in New York. On April 28, 1957, she died suddenly of a heart attack at her home on the Lodge grounds.

DISTINGUISHING FEATURES OF HER APPROACH

Fromm-Reichmann cannot be said to have developed a theory; rather, she forged a unique viewpoint merging ideas typically seen as unrelated. A follower of no school but a student of many, she drew on an unusually wide range of sources, combining them idiosyncratically, like a sculptor working with found objects or a chef creating bouillabaisse.

Unlike most physicians, Fromm-Reichmann was willing to try anything to help a patient, regardless of whether it was sanctioned by authority, an attitude that did little to endear her to conservative analytic colleagues. She saw one patient at 10:00 p.m. because that was when he was most likely to talk. She took others on walks around hospital grounds, or to symphony concerts, or to country inns for lunch. If a patient was too distraught to leave at the end of an hour, she might simply extend the session until he or she felt calmer. When patients were violent and could not be let off the wards, she went to their rooms or saw them in restraints if necessary. As her former patient Joanne Greenberg later put it, "Frieda would have swung from the chandelier like Tarzan if she thought it would help" (Green, 1967, p. 76). A colleague remarked, *not* admiringly, that Fromm-Reichmann's patients got better because she simply gave them no other choice (Hornstein, 2000).

According to legend, when Fromm-Reichmann marched onto the disturbed ward, the whole floor suddenly calmed. Perhaps this is exaggerated. But the image captures the intensity of her presence, a force field so concentrated it absorbed the available energy in a room. Greenberg likened the scene to "the parting of the Red Sea," with nurses and attendants falling all over themselves, as if Fromm-Reichmann were the queen, arriving at court. With patients, however, such theatrics disappeared. As Greenberg recalled, "As soon as she got down to business, she changed. Almost visibly" (Hornstein, 2000, p. 225). Having spent her whole life defusing tension, Fromm-Reichmann did it automatically, and patients appreciated the habit.

She saw Freud's lack of interest in treating psychotic patients as motivated less by clinical issues than by his fear of losing control. But she never rebutted him directly, as, for example, Horney so often did. Rather, Fromm-Reichmann pointed to historical and cultural changes in the types of patients being treated and the settings in which analysis took place, suggesting, for example, that the sudden forced migration of analysts to America during the Nazi years necessitated changes in technique, changes Freud could never have anticipated. She said that no method as dependent on language and meaning as psychoanalysis is could possibly be transplanted to so different a culture without requiring modification (Fromm-Reichmann, 1939a).

She thought it was irrational to reenact compulsively every detail of Freud's technique, regardless of its sense or appropriateness. For example, within a few years of arriving in the United States, she shifted her chair from behind the couch "to a point level with and some distance away from its foot, where the patient could look at her or away with equal ease," arguing that this facilitates treatment (Cohen, 1982, p. 92). She pointed out matter-of-factly that Freud had positioned himself behind his patients only because he disliked "being stared at for eight hours a day" (Fromm-Reichman, 1950, p. 100). She, in contrast, enjoyed sitting face-to-face, and found eye contact a highly useful source of information. Attacked for this "deviation" by classical colleagues, she retorted that such rules protect analysts more than they help patients. She cautioned students against "lonely, dissatisfied" therapists who unconsciously encourage elaborate transference fantasies as a "substitute with impunity" for inadequacies in their own lives (Fromm-Reichmann, 1950, p. 100).

Her view of the therapeutic relationship was particularly controversial because she insisted that it is *the analyst's* problems, not the patient's, that prevent successful treatment of psychosis. "If the schizophrenic's reactions are more stormy and seemingly unpredictable than those of the neurotic," she wrote in a key clinical paper, "I believe it to be due to the inevitable errors in the analyst's approach to the schizophrenic, of which he himself may be unaware, rather than to the unreliability of the patient's emotional response" (Fromm-Reichmann, 1939b, p. 119). She thought analysts ought to be able to tolerate these outbursts the way they would any transference reaction. Compulsively attempting to interpret a psychotic patient's every utterance, action, and feeling is simply another way to protect the therapist from the anguish of the work. "The psychoanalyst's job," she reminded colleagues, quoting Freud, "is to help the patient, not to demonstrate how clever the doctor is" (Fromm-Reichmann, 1950, p. 19).

Insisting that "the less fear patients sense in the therapist, the less dangerous they are," Fromm-Reichmann urged her colleagues to forge ahead, worry less about technical details, and focus on genuinely accepting the "fellow sufferer" who was appealing for their help (Fromm-Reichmann, 1959, p. 125). Patients could not see themselves as capable of recovery unless their therapists could first conceive of them as capable of being well. The key to success with severely disturbed patients lies less in specific technique than in being less afraid, more willing to experiment. Fromm-Reichmann knew she was often as much in the dark as her mainstream colleagues were; she was just not as frightened by this. As she told students, "I used to have strong feelings about technical details such as seeing patients only in the office, walking around with them, seeing them for non-scheduled interviews. . . . Now I consider [these details] unimportant" (Fromm-Reichmann, 1954, p. 207). What matters is trust. Almost anything a patient might do during a session, short of actual violence, is tolerable so long as it fosters a trusting relationship that could create the conditions for change.

Fromm-Reichmann never assumed that every patient would recover, especially if he or she had been ill for a long time. But she took even subtle signs of improvement seriously, and thought it presumptuous to think that anyone could tell in advance which patient would respond to which treatment. When a violent woman she saw on the disturbed ward snarled, "I could kill you if I wanted to," Fromm-Reichmann quietly answered, "It doesn't seem to me that this would help either of us." The patient sat stunned for several minutes, and then started talking about her problems in a thoughtful way, to the astonishment of ward staff (Fromm-Reichmann, 1959, pp. 147–148).

Therapists could, however, sabotage treatment if their "inner attitude towards psychiatric symptomatology" made them recoil from the very people they were supposed to be helping. Patients who did things like smearing feces, for example, often seemed too repulsive to be considered human. Fromm-Reichmann felt just as disgusted by such acts as her colleagues; the difference was that she regarded this response as indulgent and unprofessional, like a surgeon who would not operate because the wound was fetid or covered with pus. She discovered that by wearing "worn out, long-sleeved washable dresses" with patients who threw food or smeared feces, she was able to focus on their humiliation, rather than on her own feelings (Fromm-Reichmann, 1959, p. 200). This change in attitude often facilitated treatment: Sensing that she understood how vile they felt, patients did not have to make themselves filthy to convey their desperation.

Years of spending time with people in disturbed states proved to Fromm-Reichmann that the "seemingly meaningless and stereotyped actions of schizophrenic patients are meaningful, as are the rest of their communications." Most therapists did not know this because they spent so little time actually on the wards. Psychotic patients unconsciously colluded with this avoidance, "remaining cryptic and ambiguous" to protect themselves from the "danger of being misunderstood" (Fromm-Reichmann, 1942, pp. 130–132). But of course they did not get any better with doctors too impatient or irritated to see through these defenses to the terrified, needy person trapped beneath.

Her colleague at Chestnut Lodge, Robert Cohen (1982, p. 98), contrasted Fromm-Reichmann's style with the classical view of analysis as a process that frees the patient "from his chains by a brilliant, powerful and beneficent figure." Fromm-Reichmann's way of working was precisely the opposite—"sharing the examination of successively deeper layers, with the patient often in the lead." Cohen said treatment with Fromm-Reichmann was like "actively finding one's way through a seemingly trackless wilderness with the help of a resourceful and fearless companion" (p. 98).

This way of working, which Donald Schön has called "reflection-in-action," relies on a tacit knowledge that is "*in* the action" and cannot be articulated fully, as when a baseball player gets "a feel for the ball" or a jazz musician "finds the groove." The key to such "artistry," Schön (1983, p. 50) argued, is an exploratory attitude. Shaping your next action to fit the unique contours of what is happening at that moment keeps your style deeply responsive, never rote or automatic. The problem is that such "intuitive knowing is always richer in information than any description of it," making attempts to distill the principles of the practice or teach them to others only partly successful (Schön, 1983, pp. 54–55). When Fromm-Reichmann urged her patients to "take her along" into their experience, she was simultaneously conveying her humility about the complexities of mental illness, her willingness to let the patient guide the process, and her own unshakable belief in psychotherapy as "a mutual enterprise, if not a mutual adventure" (Fromm-Reichmann, 1950, p. 45).

Fundamental to Fromm-Reichmann's model of therapy with people suffering from psychosis was a deep respect for the patient. She took for granted that even bizarre behavior could potentially be interpreted and that patients' feelings are meaningful. Rose Spiegel, a younger colleague, remembered how Fromm-Reichmann knocked on the door of one patient's room daily "for something like six months without his speaking to her, so that he would get to trust her persistence enough to let her in" (Hornstein, 2000, p. 139). Like Groddeck, she often inherited cases that proved too challenging for others. For example, a patient who showed up for her session with New York analyst Clara Thompson carrying a loaded pistol was immediately referred to Fromm-Reichmann (Silver, 1992).

Ultimately, she thought treatment of psychosis is like physical therapy after stroke—a painstaking exercise in hope. Improvement is unpredictable, and is often followed by relapse or deterioration. Progress, when present, proceeds at an agonizingly slow pace. It is natural for the therapist to have periods of discouragement, even real despair, but she cannot afford to give up, no matter how many setbacks there are. Patients have to have at least one person who can imagine the possibility of their getting well. Fromm-Reichmann thought that the reason most psychiatrists failed at their work was not because their methods were ineffective but because they gave up too soon. Their belief in their own potential to help the patient was so weak that as soon as they encountered a serious setback, they declared the illness "chronic" and abandoned the treatment. Unlike surgeons, who often do their best work when a patient is gravely ill, or oncologists, who pride themselves on creatively adapting their methods to the uniqueness of each case, psychiatrists tend to try one thing, which either works or it does not. But having learned from Goldstein that even people with brain injuries could sometimes respond to treatment, she insisted that psychotic patients should never be considered unreachable.

PERSONAL QUALITIES AND PRIVATE STRUGGLES

The down-to-earth quality of Fromm-Reichmann's style was crucial to its power. Heavy-set and frumpy by American standards, she was often mistaken for the housekeeper; as a result, people who were intimidated by what she said often found her grandmotherly appearance reassuring. Students at her lectures remember the odd juxtaposition of images: Fromm-Reichmann, who at 4'10" sometimes had to stand on a box to be seen over the top of the podium, teaching classes that were "vast, really vast . . . [often filling] huge lecture halls" (Liebenberg, 1989, p. 93). She had the ability to say iconoclastic things in a matter-of-fact style that made them seem obvious and natural, and her fundamental respect for even the most disturbed patients made it hard to dismiss them as untreatable. Perhaps more than any other analyst, Fromm-Reichmann made intensive psychotherapy with schizophrenic patients seem reasonable. As one of her colleagues put it,

"Fromm-Reichmann wasn't a nut. That helped. That helped a hell of a lot" (Hornstein, 2000, p. 285).

Fromm-Reichmann knew how to bring out the best in patients, which meant she saw a side of them that others could not—or would not—even imagine. She thought psychiatrists who drugged their patients or kept them in restraints got what they asked for: people who were violent and out of control. By treating patients with the respect they would have gotten had they not been ill, her belief in their recovery became a realistic hope, not the delusion her critics sometimes made it appear. Of course this attitude brought its own rewards. Seeing psychotic patients as acerbic commentators on hospital culture, or witty, insightful reporters of conflicts among staff made working with them refreshing, even enjoyable, a fact that few other psychiatrists could even fathom.

At times, Fromm-Reichmann used the disarming combination of her short stature and powerful presence to defuse tense situations. Dexter Bullard liked to tell stories like these that follow:

> A patient was bitching, a huge paranoid man, angry with Fromm-Reichmann, angry with the Lodge, asserting he was God and nobody could tell him anything. Fromm-Reichmann, who was all of 4'10", smiled up at him after he stopped roaring and said: "You have my permission to be God."
>
> Another angry man waved his cigar in her face and sneered: "How would you like this, Dr. Fromm-Reichmann?" Fromm-Reichmann reached into a drawer, pulled out a large box of cigars, and said offhandedly: "Just put it in here with the others." (cited in Fort, 1989, p. 249)

Her noncompetitive style of relating to colleagues allowed Fromm-Reichmann to work toward long-term goals she never could have achieved single-handedly. She knew that it was impossible for one person—even someone as indefatigable as she was—to do everything the institution needed. Collaborative relationships were essential if she were to succeed in creating a hospital close to her ideal. In dramatic contrast to someone like Karen Horney, who was always elbowing other people out of her way, or Melanie Klein, who at every possible opportunity asserted the primacy of *her* work and *her* ideas, Fromm-Reichmann pioneered an alternative model of women's leadership. As one of her colleagues put it, Fromm-Reichmann "had a strength of personality which she seemed to assume everyone else possessed, or could possess." She neither "worried about hurting a fellow colleague's feelings, nor was she condescendingly gentle with her patients" (Silver & Freuer, 1989, p. 25).

However, her refusal ever to give in to her own weaknesses and her insistence on maintaining a nonstop work pace—a style she had absorbed from her mother in early childhood and took completely for granted—could sometimes dismay her younger colleagues. Otto Will never forgot the time he was exhausted and disheartened and called Fromm-Reichmann to say he could not come in that day:

In a chilly tone she responded, "You are a doctor. This is your work. You are needed." Ashamed, Will reported for duty and never again tried to shirk his responsibilities (Will, 1989, pp. 133–134).

In praising a biography of Thomas Edison, one reviewer said it "demythologized the man and left the genius bigger than life" (Gates, 1995, p. 64). For Edison, who called genius "1 percent inspiration and 99 percent perspiration," this is fitting praise. It applies equally to Fromm-Reichmann, a woman others called "gifted" but who thought of herself simply as determined and hard working. With Edison, it does not make much difference whether we give the larger role to talent or to struggle; his successes can be measured in material terms. But for someone like Fromm-Reichmann, the question of genius becomes a moral one: If psychiatrists could successfully treat psychotic patients by working harder, maybe we should ask why they could not.

It sounds flattering to call a person "gifted" but it is often a way of discounting what she does. If only "gifted" psychiatrists are successful, then nobody is to blame for the failures of the discipline. By taking responsibility for her failures, Fromm-Reichmann also claimed the right to succeed; when a patient did well, she could attribute his or her improvement to their hard work together, not to some "spontaneous" cure.

This is not to say that talent does not exist. A person with perfect pitch is not someone who just listens exceptionally hard. Natural abilities are clearly evident in fields from mathematics to track, and it is silly to pretend, on grounds of democracy, that they are not. Fromm-Reichmann's intuitive ability was the psychic equivalent of perfect pitch. Reading transcripts of her sessions with schizophrenic patients or listening to tapes of her work, we stand amazed as she asks precisely the right question, or says something exactly on the mark. There is an elegance to her creativity that sets it apart. Yet she herself insisted that any therapist who worked as hard as she did could accomplish as much.

Fromm-Reichmann was no saint. She got exasperated and angry with patients. She made many mistakes. But her boundaries were clear, and she never let people take advantage of her. Every therapist, she warned colleagues, has to come to "an unmasochistic awareness of the limits of his endurance" (Fromm-Reichmann, 1947, p. 345). She did not underestimate the stress and exhaustion of working with psychotic patients. But she refused to blame patients for their symptoms or write them off as unreachable.

"If you want something for my epitaph," Fromm-Reichmann told friends a year before her death, "you could say I wasn't lazy and I had lots of fun, but of another type as compared with many other people. It was a very special type of fun" (Fromm-Reichmann, 1956, n.p.). These are striking statements from a woman hailed by colleagues and students as a clinical genius, whose intuitive gifts seemed unrelated to diligence. Yet Fromm-Reichmann was absolutely convinced, as her close friend and colleague Sullivan always said, that psychotherapy is simply hard work. Her major book, *Principles of Intensive Psychotherapy*, published in 1950 and representing the culmination of her 40 years of clinical experience in Germany and the United States, is a manual on technique devoted to demystifying the notion that therapy requires any kind of special "gift." By insisting that psychotherapy, even with schizophrenic patients, is a learnable skill, Fromm-Reichmann challenged the standard claim that certain kinds of patients are "unanalyzable" and demonstrated that even people given up for lost could fully recover.

Fromm-Reichmann's decision to concentrate on the sickest possible patients— brain-injured soldiers, chronic schizophrenics, manic depressives—made her a target of widespread attack, adding to the weight of her symbolic role. Colleagues who had fled into private practice to treat the "worried well" hated her for making them look timid and ineffectual. Those who argued that only shock treatment or lobotomy is appropriate with psychotic patients found her embrace of psychotherapy infuriating.

But devoting her whole life to such seriously disturbed patients eventually took its toll. In her 60s, Fromm-Reichmann increasingly suffered from the hereditary deafness that had afflicted both her parents, and this painfully isolated her from patients and colleagues. She spent most of her last years struggling to finish a long paper on loneliness and, in hindsight, we can see that she was partly writing about herself. Never satisfied with what she had formulated, this was the only article she wrote that was not submitted for publication. What survives is the draft found in her desk after she died. It stands as a silent rebuke to those who saw her only as the well-defended, self-reliant figure she had always appeared to be.

Loneliness pervaded Fromm-Reichmann's life, but to realize this requires that we refocus our gaze, the way looking at the negative space of a painting turns the light areas dark and the dark ones light. Suddenly we see how cut off she was throughout her life—from her two younger sisters, taught early on to idolize her, from her parents, who poured their own stifled ambitions into the eager mind of their eldest child. By the time she was an adult, Fromm-Reichmann's own needs had been totally subsumed by caring for others. This self-sacrifice had its price. A forceful woman in so many ways, she often seemed paradoxically to unfortify her own mind. Burying her ideas inside the theories of great men, disclaiming even obvious accomplishments, she acted as if independent thought were dangerous and could be allowed into her work only in disguise. Instead of seeing herself as the equal of such colleagues as Groddeck, Sullivan, or Fromm, she hailed their brilliance and saw herself merely as a hard worker (Hornstein, 1994). At the same time, she was also ambitious and competitive and enjoyed running things. By perfecting the art of showing men off to their best advantage while choreographing events from behind the curtain, she managed a compromise so exquisite it surely would have pleased Freud—"retreating into the limelight," thereby managing to satisfy both needs at the same time (Liebenberg, 1989, p. 91).

And no matter what the circumstance—a supervisory session with students, a party, dinner with friends, even her marriage—she remained the analyst, listening attentively to others, her own needs invisible. Having always been the confidante, the older sister, the responsible one, she never really developed the capacity for peer relationships. One of her cousins remembers that even as a child, he was struck by Fromm-Reichmann's presence: "She was the oracle of the family, always in control, always in the limelight. Mutuality is not what I experienced" (Hornstein, 2000, p. 221). From earliest childhood, she had been listening to people's secrets, making sense of the inexplicable. She herself once laughingly said, "I became a psychiatrist when I was three" (Fromm-Reichmann, 1956, n.p.). As an adult, she spent practically every waking hour seeing patients, and many of her closest friends and even her husband had at one time been in treatment with her. No one, in other words, ever saw a Frieda Fromm-Reichmann outside the persona of the dedicated psychoanalyst. As her Chestnut Lodge colleague Margaret Rioch once put it, "You would never say about Frieda that she was not a caring person, but there was a particular quality to it that was totally unequal; Frieda helped you in the way she decided you needed help" (Hornstein, 2000, p. 221).

Being everyone's therapist also had the effect of making her an even more intense figure in their imaginations. Over the years, people have had all kinds of fantasies about Fromm-Reichmann—that she had been involved with a woman, that her life was miserable, that her parents were wealthy, that she killed herself—but none of these claims turn out to have any relation to her actual experience. To a striking extent, she really was the person that she appeared to be: a real-life Dr. Fried.

CONCLUSION

Fromm-Reichmann's commitment to doing absolutely everything she could think of to help emotionally distressed people and her unshakable belief in the underlying humanity of even the most regressed or violent patients may strike us today as idealistic, perhaps even naive. But she herself insisted that these attitudes were not "humanitarian or charitable hypotheses, but scientific convictions," based on decades of careful observation and analysis (Fromm-Reichmann, 1950, pp. xi–xii).

These days, psychiatry and much of clinical psychology are so narrowly conceived, so wedded to biological views of mental illness, that psychotherapy is not even taught as a method of treating psychosis. But Fromm-Reichmann's legacy shows us that no matter what the causes of severe mental illness turn out to be—brain pathology, genetic defects, family conflict, trauma—people suffering from psychosis are in anguish, and treating them as human beings capable of full recovery can help them regain their sense of themselves.

The lives of psychoanalysts have become a source of fascination in a culture where therapists have replaced priests, and stripping away the layers of silence in which they have shrouded themselves seems tantalizing. But Fromm-Reichmann is not like other psychoanalysts, especially the women. She wrote about schizophrenia, not femininity or children. She lived on the grounds of mental institutions, not in elegant apartments, and she devoted herself to patients who smeared feces or muttered incoherently or tried to attack her. Her formative intellectual experiences took place on a ward for brain-injured soldiers, not in Freud's living room. She acted as if men and children were distractions, with no real place in a life like hers, dedicated to serious work. She was an Orthodox Jew at a time of assimilation. In a field famous for "excommunicating heretics" and given to interminable "civil wars," she took pains never to disparage even her sharpest critics. And she had no interest in the theoretical disputes that obsessed most of her psychoanalytic colleagues; curing patients was her consuming goal.

So here we have the life of a woman who denied that she had accomplished much, who most people think is a fictional character, whose intellectual legacy is ambiguous, and whose work stands in contradiction to everything contemporary psychiatry believes in. Yet the ideal that guided her life and work remains intensely powerful even in our jaded lives: To redeem one person is to redeem the world.

REFERENCES

Cohen, R. A. (1982). Notes on the life and work of Frieda Fromm-Reichmann. *Psychiatry, 45*, 90–98.

Dyrud, J. E. (1989). The early Frieda, and traces of her in her later writings. In A.-L. S. Silver (Ed.), *Psychoanalysis and psychosis* (pp. 483–493). Madison, CT: International Universities Press.

Fort, J. P. (1989). Present-day treatment of schizophrenia. In A.-L. S. Silver (Ed.), *Psychoanalysis and psychosis* (pp. 249–270). Madison, CT: International Universities Press.

Fromm-Reichmann, F. (1939a). Notes on some cultural differences between the attitudes of American and European psychoanalytic patients and physicians. Unpublished lecture, Chestnut Lodge Archive, Rockville, MD.

Fromm-Reichmann, F. (1939b). Transference problems in schizophrenics. *Psychoanalytic Quarterly, 8*, 117–128.

Fromm-Reichmann, F. (1942). A preliminary note on the emotional significance of stereotypes in schizophrenics. *Bulletin of the Forest Sanitarium, 1*, 129–132.

Fromm-Reichmann, F. (1947). Problems of therapeutic management in a psychoanalytical hospital. *Psychoanalytic Quarterly, 16*, 325–356.

Fromm-Reichmann, F. (1950). *Principles of intensive psychotherapy.* Chicago: University of Chicago Press.

Fromm-Reichmann, F. (1954). Psychotherapy of schizophrenia. *American Journal of Psychiatry, 3*, 194–209.

Fromm-Reichmann, F. (1956). Unpublished transcript of autobiographical interview, recorded in Palo Alto, CA. Chestnut Lodge Archive, Rockville, MD.

Fromm-Reichmann, F. (1959). *Psychoanalysis and psychotherapy: Selected papers of Frieda Fromm-Reichmann* (D. M. Bullard, Ed.). Chicago: University of Chicago Press.

Gates, D. (1995, March 20). Wizard of Menlo Park. *Newsweek*, p. 64.

Goldstein, K. (1942). *Aftereffects of brain injuries in war: Their evaluation and treatment.* New York: Grune & Stratton.

Green, H. (1964). *I never promised you a rose garden.* New York: New American Library.

Green, H. (1967). In praise of my doctor—Frieda Fromm-Reichmann. *Contemporary Psychoanalysis, 4,* 73–77.

Groddeck, G. (1934). *The world of man.* London: C. W. Daniel.

Groddeck, G. (1977). *The meaning of illness: Selected psychoanalytical writings.* New York: International Universities Press.

Hornstein, G. A. (1994). The ethics of ambiguity: Feminists writing women's lives. In C. E. Franz & A. J. Stewart (Eds.), *Women creating lives: Identities, resilience, and resistance* (pp. 51–68). Boulder, CO: Westview Press.

Hornstein, G. A. (2000). *To redeem one person is to redeem the world: The life of Frieda Fromm-Reichmann.* New York: Free Press.

Hornstein, G. A. (2001, February 9). Frieda Fromm-Reichmann and the accidental biographer. *Chronicle Review*, pp. B7–B9.

Liebenberg, B. (1989). Fromm-Reichmann at the Washington School of Psychiatry. In A.-L. S. Silver (Ed), *Psychoanalysis and psychosis* (pp. 91–94). Madison, CT: International Universities Press.

Riese, W. (1968). Kurt Goldstein—The man and his work. In M. L. Simmel (Ed.), *The reach of mind: Essays in memory of Kurt Goldstein* (pp. 17–29). New York: Springer.

Scholem, G. (1980). How I came to the Kabbalah. *Commentary, 69,* 42.

Schön, D. A. (1983). *The reflective practitioner: How professionals think in action.* New York: Basic Books.

Silver, A.-L. S. (1992, November 17). *Frieda Fromm-Reichmann: Her life before coming to the Lodge.* Paper presented at the meeting of the Historical Committee of the Washington Psychoanalytic Institute.

Silver, A-L. S., & Freuer, P. C. (1989). Fromm-Reichmann's contributions at staff conferences. In A.-L. S. Silver (Ed.), *Psychoanalysis and psychosis* (pp. 23–45). Madison, CT: International Universities Press.

Will, O. A., Jr. (1989). In memory of Frieda. In A.-L. S. Silver (Ed.), *Psychoanalysis and psychosis* (pp. 131–144). Madison, CT: International Universities Press.

Marion Almira Bills (Photo courtesy of Bentley Historical Library,
University of Michigan)

Chapter 7

Marion Almira Bills: Industrial Psychology Pioneer Bridging Science and Practice

Laura L. Koppes and Adrienne M. Bauer

A theme of bridging the work of scientists and practitioners pervaded Marion A. Bills's entire career. She advocated that a scientific approach would improve each person's work, and believed in the application of psychological research to solve business and industry problems. Whenever possible, Bills promoted the expertise of psychologists and discussed their contributions to organizations. She worked full-time in industry, wrote publications read by executives, and published extensively in scientific journals on psychological research in applied settings. Bills successfully linked science and practice by studying real business problems using empirical research methods, then applying the research results to address the problem in the organization. She was one of few psychologists who worked for the first not-for-profit cooperative venture between industry and a university, and she also had a career of applying psychology in a private organization. Her long-term research on selection of clerical and sales personnel for the life insurance industry is considered one of the first congenial collaborations between business individuals and psychologists (Ferguson, 1952), and was considered at the forefront of selection research during the time period. She also studied uncharted territory, including job permanency and compensation. This chapter includes a brief biographical background with a more in-depth review of her contributions to demonstrate her pioneering role in building a bridge between science and practice and to the early development of an applied psychology, industrial psychology (now known as industrial–organizational psychology).

CONTEXT OF HER WORK

Historical accounts of early industrial psychology generally describe male psychologists as the primary contributors to the discipline (e.g., Baritz, 1960; Hilgard, 1987; Katzell & Austin, 1992; Landy, 1993); however, recent research reveals that women psychologists were also pioneers of applying psychological science to the workplace (e.g., Koppes, 1997; Vinchur & Koppes, 2006). Scarborough and Furumoto (1987), for example, noted that women made up the majority of psychologists moving into applied work at the beginning of the 20th century.

Why did women psychologists work in applied settings? One possible explanation is the doctrine of separate spheres (Furumoto, 1992; Russo & Denmark, 1987; Scarborough & Furumoto, 1987) that existed at the turn of the century. This doctrine refers to the distinction between "women's work" and "men's work," with women's work being within the home and men's work being outside the home. As a consequence, the formal and institutional challenges faced by women when pursuing an academic career in psychology were substantial during this period. Male psychologists prevailed in universities, and female psychologists worked in employment settings that reflected societal stereotypes of the women's sphere (Russo & Denmark, 1987).

O'Connell and Russo (1988) noted that, despite the doctrine of separate spheres, the early 20th century was positive and productive for female professionals, partly as a result of the women's suffrage movement at the turn of the century. During this time, a particular need surfaced for female psychologists' involvement in work outside the home. Russo (1988) stated, "The goal of melding science and motherhood in the service of child welfare provided a rationale for women's higher education and legitimized women's participation in the world of work" (p. 10).

Furthermore, at the beginning of the 20th century, other changes in American society and in psychological thought (from structuralism to functionalism) contributed to the creation of the new science, applied psychology (Katzell & Austin, 1992; Napoli, 1981). Opportunities in alternative settings became available because experts with scientific credentials were sought to address individual and social problems, and a few university psychologists were proactive in being involved with society. For example, with the growth of industrialization, organizations expanded in size and complexity, and the need for qualified employees surfaced; as a consequence, a demand for skills available from applied psychologists increased (Napoli, 1981). The burgeoning of capitalism and an emphasis on efficiency warranted assistance from applied psychologists to select hardworking and committed employees (Katzell & Austin, 1992).

Pulled by the demands and expectations of industry and by an ever-changing society and economy (e.g., Baritz, 1960), psychologists firmly established the economic objectives of industrial psychology, and in many cases naively adopted capitalist objectives (Koppes & Pickren, 2006). As early as 1913, Hugo Münsterberg stated, "Our aim is to sketch the outlines of a new psychology which is to intermediate between the modern laboratory psychology and the problems of economics: the psychological experiment is systematically placed at the service of commerce and industry" (p. 3). Several early industrial psychologists professed that psychology could improve business and that the results of industrial psychology would benefit workers as well as employees (Münsterberg, 1913). Bills was one of these experts who pioneered the application of psychological theory and science to solve business problems.

BIOGRAPHY

Bills was born in Allegan, Michigan, on July 5, 1889. Her mother was Martha Rood, and she married Marion's father Walter H. Bills. Marion Bills earned a bachelor's degree in 1908 from the University of Michigan. In 1911, she then enrolled in the experimental psychology doctoral program at Bryn Mawr College, where she completed her PhD in 1917. While attending Bryn Mawr, Bills studied with Clarence E. Ferree, a student of E. B. Titchener and a widely published expert on visual perception (Austin & Waung, 1994). Ferree and his wife, Gertrude Rand, are noted for their research in visual processes in industrial and applied settings (Zusne, 1975). Bryn Mawr's faculty was largely made up of women, and in addition to Rand, Kate Gordon, an associate professor in the Education Department from 1912 to 1916, likely served as a role model for Bills (Austin & Waung, 1994).

Bills's dissertation, titled "The Lag of Visual Sensation in Its Relation to Wave Lengths and Intensity of Light," was published as an American Psychological Association (APA) monograph (Bills, 1920). After completing her doctorate, Bills held a series of academic appointments. She was a professor at Miami University (Oxford, Ohio; 1917–1918), and an associate professor of psychology at the University of Kansas (1918–1919).

Following these academic positions, Bills began a long and productive career in applied settings, where she used psychological research methods and theory to study business issues. One early not-for-profit program to promote applied psychology was the Division of Applied Psychology at Carnegie Institute of Technology (CIT; now Carnegie–Mellon University), which was established in 1915 with Walter Van Dyke Bingham as the director (Hilgard, 1987). This cooperative venture between industry and a university was important for facilitating the development of an early industrial psychology and for preparing psychologists, particularly women, for industry (Hilgard, 1987). Its initial purpose was to train applied psychologists, but eventually the division evolved into helping businesses and government agencies. Bingham hired Bills as a research assistant for the Bureau of Personnel Research, a component of the Division of Applied Psychology. The Bureau was then directed by C. S. Yoakum (and formerly called the Bureau of Salesmanship Research when headed by W. D. Scott). Later, from 1919 to 1923, Bills became an associate director of the Bureau and consulted businesses on selection, training, and supervision.

Between 1922 and 1925, the Bureau of Personnel Research became the Life Insurance Sales Research Bureau (LISRB), which is currently known as the Life Insurance Marketing and Research Association (LIMRA). From 1923 to 1925, Bills was a consultant in office management and then continued to work for LISRB after it relocated to Hartford, Connecticut. In this context she consulted with several companies on personnel issues.

In 1926, Bills agreed to join Aetna Life Insurance Company as an assistant secretary with the condition that she be made a voting officer (Patricia Cain Smith, personal communication, June 14, 1996). She also served as a consultant to top management at Aetna (Austin & Waung, 1994). After a long and successful 30-year career at the Aetna Life Insurance Company (with retirement in 1955), Bills was diagnosed with Parkinson's disease and then passed away in 1970 in Hartford. She never married (Patricia Cain Smith, personal communication, June 14, 1996).

APPLICATIONS OF PSYCHOLOGICAL RESEARCH AND THEORY

As stated in the introduction to this chapter, Bills bridged science and practice by working full-time in industry, writing for executive publications, and publishing in research journals. Topics of her practice and research included job analysis, selection, job permanency, compensation, measurement of office work, and fair personnel policies. She wrote regularly for the *American Management Association Office Executive Series, American Management Association Office Management Series, American Management Association Marketing Series,* and *Life Office Management Association* (e.g., Bills, 1926, 1927a, 1928a, 1928b, 1929, 1941b). In addition, she published empirical research in periodicals such as *Journal of Applied Psychology, Journal of Personnel Research* (later *Personnel Journal*), *Personnel, Psychological Bulletin,* and *Journal of Consulting Psychology* (e.g., Bills, 1925, 1927a, 1927c, 1933, 1938a, 1938b, 1941a, 1944, 1953; Bills & Davidson, 1938; Bills & Taylor, 1953; Bills & Ward, 1936; Pond & Bills, 1933); and she contributed chapters to the *Annals of the American Academy of Political and Social Science* (Yoakum & Bills, 1923), the *Handbook of Applied Psychology* (Bills, 1950), and *Applications of Psychology: Essays to Honor W.V. Bingham* (Bills, 1952). Her writings consistently exhibited a practical perspective or orientation. Her research samples were typically large, the measures were of top quality for the time period, the analyses were suitable, and her discussions were thoughtful and reasoned (Austin & Waung, 1994).

In several articles, Bills highlighted the ways that psychologists use psychological research and principles in organizations. In her presidential address, as the seventh president of the Division of Industrial and Business Psychology, Bills stressed the contributions of psychologists, stating, "We have a mighty heritage of at least seventy-five years of psychological research back of us to which is constantly being added new and valuable data and ideas" (Bills, 1953, p. 144). She discussed how research revealed that the selection interview was an ineffective selection tool but could be improved, that tests can be helpful, and particular approaches to scoring an application blank form would indicate success or failures. The next section provides examples of studies in which Bills used scientific research methods and theory to examine business problems while employed at the Bureau of Personnel Research of CIT and later the Aetna Life Insurance Company.

BUREAU OF PERSONNEL RESEARCH, DIVISION OF APPLIED PSYCHOLOGY, CARNEGIE INSTITUTE OF TECHNOLOGY

Bills conducted several studies on selection, which was a topic frequently studied during the early years of industrial psychology. According to Vinchur (2006),

> Central to the development of early industrial psychology, employee selection has been a core activity in the field of industrial–organizational psychology for close to 100 years. What the early industrial psychologists brought to selection was a particular approach, relying on the scientific methodology of the new experimental psychology and grounded in the measurement of individual differences, of empirically verifying the efficacy of their efforts.

While working for the Bureau of Personnel Research, Bills and her colleagues devised a multiple-component selection system for sales personnel that included a personal history blank form (biodata), a standard interview, a reference form, and a mental alertness test. Bills conducted two frequently cited studies on the selection of comptometer operators and stenographers (1921a, 1921b; note that a comptometer was a calculating machine). The purpose of the 1921a article was twofold: First, Bills was interested in determining whether tests could be used to select applicants for technical school courses in stenography and comptometer operation, and second, whether successful comptometer and stenographic operators could be selected from this group of applicants. Bills stated, "the first purpose demanded that failures be eliminated and the second that sure successes be selected" (1921a, p. 275). Participants were 139 technical night school students of various ages. Teachers from the technical school and employees of a manufacturing firm served as judges. The judges used multiple predictors (general intelligence test, aptitude test, and the will–temperament test) to determine participants' quality of work and evaluate whether the student was suited for one of the lines of work. Failures and successes in the different courses were the criteria. For example, a student was considered to fail if the teacher did not recommend that the student continue the coursework or take an advanced course. A successful student was evaluated as being able to continue the work. Bills stated that both purposes were achieved, such that the tests became part of the entrance requirements for students at the technical school and were used as guidelines by the hiring officials of the manufacturing firm. Bills concluded that failures can be better eliminated and successes can be better selected from a battery of tests rather than from a single examination. She also determined that successful stenographers can be selected with this approach. This study is particularly important because Bills researched multiple predictors for selection purposes and examined the use of critical scores for examining the validity of tests in selection, unusual practices in industry at that time.

In addition to selection research, Bills conducted research studies on what she labeled "permanency" (now known as retention or turnover; e.g., Bills, 1923b, 1925). Job permanency (retention) was a novel idea in the 1920s, and continues to be a research topic in the field of industrial–organizational psychology today (e.g., Boath & Smith, 2004). The focus of this research was on determining factors that predicted length of service in a job. Who stayed in a certain position and who left? What factors were used in advance (selection) to avoid problems in the future (poor performance, turnover)? Bills assessed several factors when studying permanency, including mental alertness, social status, age at employment, gender, and achievement orientation. For instance, in her 1923 article, "Relation of Mental Alertness Test Score to Positions and Permanency in Company," Bills examined the mental alertness scores of 133 clerical employees (1923b). She proposed that natural selection would take place in relation to job permanency. Bills's use of the phrase *natural selection* reflects the prevalent thought of the time—specifically, Charles Darwin's theory of evolution by natural selection. Bills hypothesized that individuals with low mental alertness would not be able to handle difficult clerical positions and would therefore leave; similarly, individuals with a high mental alertness score would be dissatisfied with low-difficulty clerical positions and would leave. She predicted that after 2½ years on the job, those with high mental alertness would be in high-difficulty jobs and those with low mental alertness would be in low-difficulty jobs. Bills discussed how this information could be used by the company in selecting clerical staff.

Bills studied classification methods with regard to compensation, in addition to the selection and job permanency research. In a 1923 article, "A Method for Classifying the Jobs and Rating the Efficiency of Clerical Workers," Bills discussed the methodology she used as an external consultant for a large company (1923a). She was asked by the client to classify 300 clerical jobs and to establish equitable employee salaries based on this information. In developing job classifications and this employee-efficiency rating scheme, Bills emphasized the importance of following key principles; these principles were based on research regarding successful development of rating scales, which continue to be followed today. She noted that ratings must have three qualities.

First, it must be a rating on the qualities vital to the efficiency of a clerk. Second, it must be the opinion of more than one judge on the efficiency of the clerk. Third, it must provide, as far as possible, for the elimination of individual tendencies of the raters to over or underrate. (Bills, 1923a, p. 385)

Furthermore, Bills (1923a) recognized the importance of basing classifications on job analyses rather than on personal opinions about the job.

The classification model proposed by Bills included variables ranging from supervisory responsibilities, decision making, and manual dexterity to knowledge of a large number of rules and regulations. Bills then conducted internal and external salary reviews to set the salary limits for each clerical pay grade. In addition, she developed a graphic rating scale with differentially weighted items to measure employee efficiency. Efficiency was defined by eight qualities: appearance, ability to learn, accuracy, dependability, speed, cooperativeness, constructive thinking, and ability to direct the work of others. Based on the managers' ratings of employee efficiency, salaries were adjusted. In this example, Bills developed a standardized process for rating employee performance and a process for determining classification and compensation of the company's entire clerical force.

The three areas of primary research (selection, job permanency, and compensation) conducted at the Bureau of Personnel Research are good examples of applying psychological methods, theory, and principles in organizational settings. Bills conducted similar research throughout her career with the Aetna Life Insurance Company.

AETNA LIFE INSURANCE COMPANY

Throughout her career at Aetna, Bills's job title of assistant secretary did not accurately reflect her contributions. Crissey wrote,

At Aetna, the impact of your work, as well as your personal charm and understanding counseling, has been tremendous. It should be a source of deep job satisfaction to see the job classification method for clerical jobs still in successful use, not only at Aetna but in other insurance companies as well. Likewise, your clerical wage incentive system is also unique. Your studies in selection for clerical jobs and insurance salesmen, as well as other research, have been frequently quoted. (1957, n.p.)

Bills continued to do research on selection predictors in the context of the Aetna Life Insurance Company. For example, in a 1941 study, scores on four types of tests were examined, including the Strong's *Vocational Interest Blank*, the *Bernreuter Personality Inventory*, a personal history blank, and a mental alertness test (cited in Bills, 1941a). Scores were compared to criteria, which were managers' ratings of productivity as either *outstanding, probably successful,* or *probably failure.* The participants were 700 students (100% men) enrolled in the casualty insurance school at Aetna. The Strong's *Vocational Interest Blank* and the personal history blank were found as the most useful predictors. Based on the analyses conducted for this research, Bills concluded that the utility of a predictor will vary depending on the variable of interest. For instance, education level was a stronger predictor for individuals falling in the age range of 24 years or younger. In addition, many items on Strong's *Vocational Interest Blank* were better predictors for those more than 30 years of age than for younger groups. It was a typical approach then to examine demographic variables such as marital status, age, and family size. For example, Bills noted,

> For those under 25, too few were married or had dependents to make a scoring possible, but those over 30, a married man with one or two dependents was more apt to succeed than a single person with no dependents and much more apt to succeed than the person who had been divorced or separated, regardless of the number of dependents. (1941a, p. 8)

Study of the correlations between selection predictors and performance criteria continues to be important today, although it should be acknowledged that demographic variables are usually excluded from selection decisions given the legal ramifications in the current work environment.

While working for Aetna, Bills further examined the concept of job permanency (e.g., 1927b, 1927c, 1928a). In a 1927 study, Bills examined the relationship between age and permanency of service, with particular attention to gender differences (1927c). Using age at employment for 420 women and 196 men employed at Aetna Life Insurance Company, Bills observed a difference between men and women with regard to staying with the company. She then offered several explanations. In doing so, she was ahead of her time in recognizing another variable, job satisfaction, which later industrial psychologists studied in subsequent years.

As with her research in selection, Bills incorporated the results of her job-permanency studies in the practices of the company with which she was employed; for instance, she used mental alertness scores and job difficulty level in the selection process of clerical employees because she found these variables to be related to permanency on the job. In fact, Austin and Waung (1994) noted that the extent of Bills's influence at Aetna was enhanced because of her persistence in using empirical data for understanding tenure and retention, especially with regard to gender differences.

Other important contributions by Bills at Aetna included the development of a unique wage incentive system for clerical positions, creation of a job classification method, and the implementation of a job evaluation program (Austin & Waung, 1994). She continued to advocate for psychologists in industry. In a 1944 article, "Psychology Applied to Problems of Office Personnel," Bills defined three types of psychological services that are typically rendered by organizations: consultant, psychologist hired for a particular job, and staff psychologist. Bills also discussed the range of contributions provided by the psychologists within the spectrum of office personnel, such as a classification or job evaluation scale for clerical work, selection tests such as mental alertness and work samples, and recommendations for the effects of noise on work efficiency. In a 1953 article, Bills provided explanations for how psychologists became involved with management programs. She noted that management turned to psychologists for problems because psychology was a new and vague science and field that seemed to hold promise. In turn, Bills observed that psychologists willingly responded to management's requests because psychologists viewed their involvement as a compliment. She stated,

> I believe the most important is that as we go into managerial work we carry with us many fundamental psychological principles, and so influence management in the way that as psychologists we feel they should be influenced and our influence is greater because we do not wear a tag which says "psychologists." What are these principles that we carry over? I believe one of the most important is the principle of "Stop, look and listen" that as scientists has been ground into us in all of our training. (Bills, 1953, p. 143)

Bills (1953) determined that the primary role of psychologists in industry is to serve as liaisons between scientists and management. In this role, psychologists would inform both sides to establish and maintain connections between science and practice.

INVOLVEMENT IN PROFESSIONAL ASSOCIATIONS

Bills played a critical role in bringing together individuals who were applying psychology in industry during those early years. She was an active participant in the committee that formed the original APA Division 14 (see Benjamin, 1997, for a history of Division 14, now known as the Society for Industrial and Organizational Psychology). Before this division was established, Bills served on the newly formed Board of Governors of the American Association of Applied Psychology (AAAP) during 1939, on the conference program committees, and as the recording secretary of the Industrial and Business Section.

Bills was the founder of an informal group called Psychologists Employed Full-Time in Industry, which met at APA meetings. Several working groups evolved from this first group (e.g., the Dearborn and Mayflower Groups; Meyer, 2006).

Orlo Crissey provided an informal history of this group in a letter to Bills. This letter was about an event to recognize Bills for being the catalyst in forming the group; the recognition occurred at the group's annual meeting. Crissey (1957) wrote,

> As I remember it, the first meeting I attended was in 1947, and some 8 or 10 people gathered in your hotel suite. It was a nice chance for persons devoting full-time to psychological work in business or industry to get to know each other and to talk informally about what they were doing. From small beginnings the group has grown until today some 200 names are on the mailing list. (n.p.)

In a response to Crissey, Bills revealed her modesty. She stated,

> I think it is always a privilege to be in on the ground floor of any adventure. When practically nothing has been done previously it is very easy to accomplish something, because anything that one does is better than the nothing which has been done before. The greatest credit should go to those who improve and carry through an undertaking. That involves harder work and more critical thought and ingenuity. Therefore I should like to hand back to all of the industrial psychologists signing the letter my knowledge and realization that they have done much more than I ever did. (Bills, 1957)

In addition to industrial psychology, Bills was involved with other professional psychological organizations on a national level. She was a charter trustee for the American Board of Examiners in Professional Psychology (ABEPP). She served on the APA Council of Representatives (1945), and was a member of the Policy and Planning Board of the APA (1945–1947), the Committee on Academic Freedom and Conditions of Employment (1952), and the Conference of State Psychological Associations.

At the state level, Bills was a founder of the Connecticut Valley Association of Psychologists and its successor, the Connecticut State Psychological Society. She helped create the Connecticut Certified Psychologists Act, and facilitated the development of the Connecticut Board for Certification of Psychologists, serving as a charter member of the board and as its secretary in 1945 to 1950. She served as the second president of the Connecticut State Psychological Society from 1945 to 1946.

CONCLUSION

Bills's efforts to bridge science and practice are clearly reflected in her work. Her research studies were directed at the relevant issues of the time and addressed problems of the company for which she was employed. Her ability to integrate

science and practice is especially noteworthy given the male-dominated environment in which she was employed and the issues women in the workforce faced
during the 1920s. Not only did she succeed in a male-dominated hierarchical
organization, but she faced organizational constraints, such as time pressures,
project deadlines, budgetary limits, and supervisor demands. Despite these obstacles, Bills was able to identify organizational needs, conduct empirical research
on employees, recommend specific changes to improve organizational processes,
and implement changes for improvement within the organization.

In addition to advocating for the application of psychological research in
industry throughout her lifetime, Bills also recognized the challenges of doing so.
Bills (1953) observed a disconnect between psychologists working in university
settings and those working in private industry. (Indeed, a disconnect between
scientists and practitioners continues to characterize the field of industrial–
organizational psychology today [Zickar & Gibby, 2006].) One explanation for
this disconnect was the lack of recognition of applied contributions because of
the paucity of publications and reports produced by psychologists in industry.
"Many valuable data are being lost because of the lack of the urge to publicize
on the part of the staff psychologist" (Bills, 1944, p. 162). Bills acknowledged
the importance of publishing research results, but indicated, "Perhaps since we
do not need to publish to advance in our work, and since we are fairly busy, we
get a little lazy and do not take the time and energy to clarify our thinking and
put it down on paper for others to read and maybe profit by. But the fact remains—
we do not publish" (Bills, 1953, p. 145).

Bills highlighted possible explanations for why psychologists in industry were
not reporting results of their research. Because most of their research was conducted in organizations, compared to a controlled experiment in a laboratory,
there was hesitance to publish research with such potential confounds. What
was noteworthy according to industry standards may not have been statistically
significant. Bills (1953) recalled that statisticians could have shot holes in her
statistical analyses; however, such skeptics would miss the real point of her
studies—the use of quasi-experimental data for solving business problems. This
concept of being valuable regardless of its statistical significance is referred
to today as being *practically meaningful* (Rosenthal & Rosnow, 1991). In an
organizational setting, psychologists are often faced with providing a workable
solution (a solution that is "good enough") to meet company deadlines, so they
sacrifice publishing their results. Bills recognized that reaching workable solutions
in a timely fashion is more valuable than publishing (Bills, 1953). As a trained
scientist, however, Bills pondered her contributions to a scientific discipline. She
questioned, "Would our publications in this less rigid field (management) add
anything to the fundamental knowledge of psychology?" (Bills, 1953, p. 145).
After further exploring this explanation and other responsibilities, Bills (1953)
concluded,

psychologists in private industry are only about 100 strong and we need the advice of our consulting friends and especially of our academic ones to help us to see clearly where our greatest contribution to a young but fast growing science lies. (p. 145)

Bills's use of scientific research methods and psychological principles and theory to examine typical as well as novel concepts within work settings, her prominent role in the Division of Applied Psychology at Carnegie Institute of Psychology, her influential impact at Aetna Life Insurance, and her substantive involvement with professional organizations distinguish her as a pioneer of psychology. She was included in Cattell's *American Men of Science*, and in 1940, she received the Leffingwell Medal from the National Office Management Association for her work with personnel management.

REFERENCES

Austin, J. T., & Waung, M. P. (1994, April). Dr. Marion A. Bills: Allegan to Aetna. In L. Koppes (Chair), *The founding mothers: Female I/O psychologists in the early years*. Symposium conducted at the Ninth Annual Conference of the Society for Industrial and Organizational Psychology, Inc., Nashville, TN.

Baritz, L. (1960). *The servants of power*. New York: Wiley.

Benjamin, L. T., Jr. (1997). A history of Division 14 (The Society for Industrial and Organizational Psychology). In D. A. Dewsbury (Ed.), *Unification through division: Histories of the divisions of the American Psychological Association* (Vol. 2, pp. 101–126). Washington, DC: American Psychological Association.

Bills, M. A. (1920). The lag of visual sensation in its relation to wave lengths and intensity of light. *Psychological Monographs, 28*, 101.

Bills, M. A. (1921a). Methods for the selection of comptometer operators and stenographers. *Journal of Applied Psychology, 5*, 275–283.

Bills, M. A. (1921b). A test for use in the selection of stenographers. *Journal of Applied Psychology, 5*, 373–377.

Bills, M. A. (1923a). A method for classifying the jobs and rating the efficiency of clerical workers. *Journal of Personnel Research, 1*, 384–393.

Bills, M. A. (1923b). Relation of mental alertness test score to positions and permanency in company. *Journal of Applied Psychology, 7*, 154–156.

Bills, M. A. (1925). Social status of the clerical worker and his permanence on the job. *Journal of Applied Psychology, 9*, 424–427.

Bills, M. A. (1926). The status of measuring office work. *American Management Association, Office Executive Series, 16*, 3–12.

Bills, M. A. (1927a). An application of principles of the individual bonus plan to home office clerical work. *Life Office Management Association, 192*, 153–159.

Bills, M. A. (1927b). Permanence of men and women office workers. *Journal of Personnel Research, 5*, 402–404.

Bills, M. A. (1927c). Stability of office workers and age at employment. *Journal of Personnel Research, 5*, 475–477.

Bills, M. A. (1928a). Relative permanency of men and women office workers. *American Management Association, 5,* 207–208.

Bills, M. A. (1928b). Time study as a basis of measuring office output. *American Management Association (Office Management Series,* No. 32), 3–22.

Bills, M. A. (1929). Measuring, standardizing and compensating for office operations. *American Management Association (Office Management Series,* No. 44). 3–22.

Bills, M. A. (1933). Rate of promotion of clerical forces. *Psychological Bulletin, 30,* 731–732.

Bills, M. A. (1938a). Present trends in selection for employment. *Personnel, 15,* 184–193.

Bills, M. A. (1938b). Relation of scores in Strong's Interest Analysis Blank to success in selling casualty insurance. *Journal of Applied Psychology, 22,* 97–104.

Bills, M. A. (1941a). Selection of casualty and life insurance agents. *Journal of Applied Psychology, 25,* 6–10.

Bills, M. A. (1941b). Tests that have failed—and why. *American Management Association (Marketing Series,* No. 45), 32–35.

Bills, M. A. (1944). Psychology applied to problems of office personnel. *Journal of Consulting Psychology, 8,* 160–164.

Bills, M. A. (1950). Field salesmen. In D. H. Fryer & E. Henry (Eds.), *Handbook of applied psychology* (Vol. 1, pp. 212–215). New York: Rinehart.

Bills, M. A. (1952). A tool for selection that has stood the test of time. In L. L. Thurstone (Ed.), *Applications of psychology: Essays to honor Walter V. Bingham* (pp. 131–138). New York: Harper.

Bills, M. A. (1953). Our expanding responsibilities. *Journal of Applied Psychology, 37,* 142–145.

Bills, M. A. (1957, October 23). Letter to O. L. Crissey. Marie Crissey Collection, Box M2054, Folder 4, Archives of the History of American Psychology, University of Akron, Akron, OH.

Bills, M. A., & Davidson, C. M. (1938). Study of interrelation of items on Bernreuter Personality Inventory and Strong's Interest Analysis Test, part VIII, and their relation to success and failure in selling casualty insurance. *Psychological Bulletin, 35,* 677.

Bills, M. A., & Taylor, J. (1953). Over and under achievement in a sales school in relation to future production. *Journal of Applied Psychology, 37,* 21–23.

Bills, M. A., & Ward, L. W. (1936). Testing salesmen of casualty insurance. *Personnel Psychology, 15,* 55–58.

Boath, D., & Smith, D. Y. (2004). When your best people leave, will their knowledge leave too? *Harvard Management Update, 9,* 6–8.

Crissey, O. L. (1957, October 19). Letter to M. A. Bills. Marie Crissey Collection, Box M2054, Folder 4, Archives of the History of American Psychology, University of Akron, Akron, OH.

Ferguson, L. W. (1952). A look across the years 1920 to 1950. In L. L. Thurstone (Ed.), *Applications of psychology: Essays to honor Walter V. Bingham* (pp. 1–17). New York: Harper.

Furumoto, L. (1992). Joining separate spheres—Christine Ladd-Franklin, woman-scientist (1847–1930). *American Psychologist, 47,* 175–182.

Hilgard, E. R. (1987). *Psychology in America: A historical survey.* San Diego, CA: Harcourt Brace Jovanovich.

Katzell, R. A., & Austin, J. T. (1992). From then to now: The development of industrial–organizational psychology in the United States. *Journal of Applied Psychology, 77,* 803–835.

Koppes, L. L. (1997). American female pioneers of industrial and organizational psychology during the early years. *Journal of Applied Psychology, 82,* 500–515.

Koppes, L. L., & Pickren, W. (2006). Industrial and organizational psychology: An evolving science and practice. In L. L. Koppes (Ed.), *Historical perspectives in industrial and organizational psychology.* Mahwah, NJ: Erlbaum.

Landy, F. J. (1993). Early influences on the development of industrial/organizational psychology. In T. K. Fagan & G. R. VandenBos (Eds.), *Exploring applied psychology: Origins and critical analyses* (pp. 83–118). Washington, DC: American Psychological Association.

Meyer, H. H. (2006). The influence of formal and informal organizations on the development of I–O psychology. In L. L. Koppes (Ed.), *Historical perspectives in industrial and organizational psychology*. Mahwah, NJ: Erlbaum.

Münsterberg, H. (1913). *Psychology and industrial efficiency*. Boston: Houghton Mifflin.

Napoli, D. S. (1981). *Architects of adjustment: The history of the psychological profession in the United States*. Port Washington, NY: Kennikat Press.

O'Connell, A. N., & Russo, N. F. (Eds.). (1988). *Models of achievement: Reflections of eminent women in psychology* (Vol. 2). Hillsdale, NJ: Erlbaum.

Pond, M. A., & Bills, M. A. (1933). Intelligence and clerical jobs: Two studies of relation of test score to job held. *Personnel Journal, 12*, 41–56.

Rosenthal, R., & Rosnow, R. L. (1991). *Essentials of behavioral research: Methods and data analysis* (2nd ed.). Boston: McGraw-Hill.

Russo, N. F. (1988). Women's participation in psychology: Reflecting and shaping the social context. In A. N. O'Connell & N. F. Russo (Eds.), *Models of achievement: Reflections of eminent women in psychology* (Vol. 2, pp. 9–27). Hillsdale, NJ: Erlbaum.

Russo, N. F., & Denmark, F. L. (1987). Contributions of women to psychology. *Annual Review of Psychology, 38*, 279–298.

Scarborough, E., & Furumoto, L. (1987). *Untold lives: The first generation of American women psychologists*. New York: Columbia University Press.

Vinchur, A. (2006). A history of psychology applied to employee selection. In L. L. Koppes (Ed.), *Historical perspectives in industrial and organizational psychology*. Mahwah, NJ: Erlbaum.

Vinchur, A., & Koppes, L. L. (2006). Early contributors to the science and practice of industrial psychology. In L. L. Koppes (Ed.), *Historical perspectives in industrial and organizational psychology*. Mahwah, NJ: Erlbaum.

Yoakum, C. S., & Bills, M. A. (1923). Tests for office occupations. *Annals of the American Academy of Political and Social Science, 110*, 1–14.

Zickar, M. J., & Gibby, R. E. (2006). Four persistent themes throughout the history of I–O psychology in the U.S. In L. L. Koppes (Ed.), *Historical perspectives in industrial and organizational psychology*. Mahwah, NJ: Erlbaum.

Zusne, L. (1975). *Names in the history of psychology: A biographical sourcebook*. New York: Halstead.

Calvin Perry Stone (Photo courtesy of the APA Archives)

Chapter 8

Calvin Perry Stone:
Solid Citizen and Scientist

Wade E. Pickren

Imagine being 5 years old. Your father has died and your mother and seven siblings are at the funeral and for some unknown reason have left you at home alone. While they are away, you smell smoke, see flames, and before you can get anyone's attention, the house has burned down. This is what happened to Calvin Perry Stone on a bitterly cold winter day near Portland, Indiana, a small town near the border with Ohio. The resilience and persistence demonstrated by Stone and his family in rebuilding their home and remaking their lives after that dark day were hallmarks of Stone throughout his life.

Stone was born on February 28, 1892, near Portland, Indiana, and died of a heart attack on December 28, 1954, half a continent away in Palo Alto, California. From humble origins, he became a college professor, member of the National Academy of Sciences, and president of the American Psychological Association (APA). His was not a glamorous life marked by sudden ascendancy or startling accomplishment. Rather, his story illustrates what determination and persistence can accomplish when joined with intelligence, open-mindedness, useful personal connections, and a solid institutional base.

A DETERMINATION TO SUCCEED:
EDUCATION AND HARD WORK

Stone was the seventh of eight children born to his parents, Ezekial and Emily (Brinkerhoff) Stone. According to an autobiographical sketch Stone prepared in

119

the 1940s, his paternal lineage was English and his maternal lineage was Dutch. His recent heritage was entirely agrarian, as he put it, and his parents and grandparents were "educated only in rural schools, of moderate circumstances, never well-to-do" (Stone, c. 1940s, p. 1). He recalled that none of his uncles or aunts became professionals. However, that changed in Stone's generation, as many of his cousins and four of his siblings became schoolteachers. At one point in the early 20th century, there were 15 of Stone's relatives teaching in the Jay County, Indiana, schools. Stone believed that education was the key to improving one's possibilities in life, and he and his family worked hard to obtain an education.

After the fire burned down the family home, relatives urged Stone's mother to move the family. She, however, was determined that adversity was not going to best her or rob her children of life's opportunities. With the help of family and neighbors, his mother rebuilt the family home. The three older children were unable to continue their education beyond grammar school, but their hard work and sacrifice made it possible for the five youngest children to go beyond the education locally available and earn college and postbaccalaureate degrees. All had to work at something, however, to earn enough money to get through school. In Stone's case, at age 10 he began hiring himself out to neighboring farmers during the summer. At age 11, he went to live with another family, the Griles, during the school year to earn enough money helping around their house to buy his clothes and pay his school costs. He remained with the Griles for 3 school years, working for extra wages in the fields during summers, and graduated from 8th grade in May 1905 at age 13.

Two years later, Stone became the principal farmer of his family's land, even renting additional land from a neighbor, and that fall borrowed money to enter Valparaiso University, a Lutheran teacher training college. While there, he completed high school and earned approximately 3 years of university credit. Once Stone completed high school, he was qualified to be a high school teacher. At age 18, in 1910 Stone became the principal at Deer Creek High School. He continued to attend Valparaiso University in the summer and earned the AB in classics in 1913. That year he was class poet. He then enrolled at Indiana University to work on his master's degree, but was also superintendent of Stillwell High School. The summer of 1914 was spent selling home medical books in Iowa and Stone found, much to his surprise, that he was good at sales. In the fall of 1914, Stone enrolled at Indiana University with primary interests in medicine and the social sciences. Although he never lost interest in medicine and related sciences, study with philosopher Ernest H. Lindley and psychologist Melvin Haggerty directed Stone's interest increasingly toward psychology. He earned a second AB in 1915, and under Haggerty's direction, Stone completed work in 1916 for a master's degree with a thesis titled, "Notes on Light Discrimination in Dogs."

Haggerty had been a graduate student at Harvard with the comparative psychologist Robert M. Yerkes, and initially pursued comparative work when he came to Indiana University. However, Haggerty, along with his mentor and many other comparative psychologists of his generation (e.g., John B. Watson), felt enormous pressure to do research that had practical, useful applications (Dewsbury, 1992). This pressure eventuated in Haggerty's move into educational psychology. Haggerty left Indiana in 1915 to become a professor of educational psychology at the University of Minnesota and persuaded Stone to come with him to Minnesota to complete his doctoral degree (Hearst & Capshew, 1988). Although Stone spent a semester as a teaching fellow at Minnesota in 1916, he deferred his doctoral work there to serve a year as a director of research at a penal institution and 2 years as a psychological examiner in the U.S. military during World War I. Both positions provided experiences that were crucial in sparking his lifelong interest in psychopathology.

INSIDE INSTITUTIONS: REFORMATORY AND MILITARY, 1916 TO 1919

Perhaps it was a desire to remain closer to his sweetheart, Minnie Ruth Kemper, whom he had met at Valparaiso University in 1913, but Stone was not ready to depart Indiana. In September 1916, with marriage on his mind, he sought to improve his finances by accepting a position as psychological research director with the Indiana State Reformatory in Jeffersonville, just across the Ohio River from Louisville. He and Ruth were married on June 30, 1917, and eventually had two sons and a daughter.

The Reformatory was for young men, ages 16 to 32, and Stone found the work fascinating because it exposed him to individuals with varying degrees of mental disorder for the first time in his life. The entry of the United States into World War I led him to resign his position in August 1917 and to enter the U.S. military in September of that year.

Stone wrote an account of his experiences in the military for his young son in 1919. According to the account, he entered the Army after much debate and conflicting advice from his superiors at the Reformatory. On August 27, 1917, Stone said goodbye to his new bride and, in the company of his former college roommate, entered the Officer Training School at Fort Benjamin Harrison, Indiana. On October 11, 1917, Yerkes received a telegram from Lt. Marion Trabue, head of the psychological examiners unit at Camp Taylor, requesting that Yerkes have Stone commissioned as an officer at once. Trabue wrote Yerkes that "preliminary work here has shown that Calvin P. Stone has extraordinary ability in psychological examining. Work will be seriously hindered unless he remains" (Trabue, 1917). Still, the commission as first lieutenant did not come through until February 1918, when Stone was transferred to Camp Greenleaf, Georgia.

In January 1918, Stone and Lt. Heber Cummings did what they called a "Barnum and Bailey tour." They traveled from Kentucky to military camps in Michigan, Illinois, Iowa, and Kansas to examine officer candidates. More than 2,000 men were examined, tests were scored, and reports were made in 2 weeks. Calvin indicated that what he found most remarkable was the variance in temperature among the sites: In Illinois, the temperature was 22 degrees below zero, whereas in Kansas it was in the 70s and some farmers were already plowing. Striking about Stone's account of this program is the haste with which everything was done.

Once Stone transferred to Camp Greenleaf in Georgia, he was commissioned as a first lieutenant and eventually promoted to captain. While there, he completed his officer training and served as the adjutant to the camp commander. In April 1918, he was assigned to Camp Pike, Arkansas. There, Stone became primarily responsible for psychological assessment of those suspected of having mental disorders. Curious today is the fact that conscientious objectors were first on the list of those suspected of psychopathology. Stone's staff in Arkansas was quite large, and included three officers, several noncommissioned officers, and between 12 to 30 individuals who were responsible for scoring the tests. From June through September 1918, Stone's group screened 75,000 men for psychopathology and eliminated 2,500 as unfit to serve. For Stone, this experience served to bolster his interest in the field of abnormal psychology.

In August 1919, Stone was sent to Walter Reed Hospital to work in the rehabilitation of soldiers. In September he was discharged from the military and resumed his doctoral work at the University of Minnesota.

ANIMALS, SEX, AND MEDICINE: 1919 TO 1921

When Stone returned to graduate school at Minnesota, he was much more experienced in the ways of the world than the young farm boy he had been in 1916. He had traveled across much of the United States, served with distinction in the military where he developed a keen eye for the absurdities and pomposities of those in authority, and struggled with married life and the responsibilities of parenthood. The psychology department at Minnesota had changed as well. Karl S. Lashley returned as a faculty member in 1920, and it was Lashley who became Stone's mentor, instead of Melvin Haggerty.

Lashley, a native of West Virginia, had obtained his doctoral degree in genetics with H. S. Jennings at Johns Hopkins University in 1914. Before and after his degree he worked closely with John B. Watson. Lashley and Watson collaborated on a project to evaluate the effects of venereal-disease films on soldiers for the U.S. Interdepartmental Social Hygiene Board (Lashley & Watson, 1920). In

1920, they published the results of a lengthy questionnaire on physicians' views on sex and sex education, which revealed a startling paucity of sex knowledge among physicians (Watson & Lashley, 1920). Their research provided a critical impetus for the initiation of the scientific sex research community in America; as a result, Stone became an important member of the sex-research community.

Lashley first taught at the University of Minnesota in 1917, but left for war-related work. He finally returned to Minnesota in 1920 and stayed until 1926. During these years he served as a consultant in the development of a national interdisciplinary approach to sex research funded by the Rockefeller Foundation. Although sex research was not a major research interest for Lashley, he was highly interested in the scientific study of sex. His article titled, "Physiological Analysis of the Libido" was a powerful statement of the need to tie theorizing about sexual behavior and interests to demonstrable physiological functions (Lashley, 1924). In the article he frequently cited Stone's work.

When Stone resumed his graduate work, he almost chose medicine as his field rather than psychology. His graduate transcript shows a number of courses in neurology, histology, anatomy, and other medical subjects. But the enormous preparation necessary for a medical degree apparently discouraged him, because he already had a family, with another child on the way. Lashley may also have influenced him to remain in psychology. Under Lashley's tutelage, Stone completed his dissertation on the topic, "An Experimental Analysis of the Congenital Sexual Behavior of the Male Albino Rat" (see Stone, 1922). He was awarded the doctoral degree in 1921, and remained at Minnesota for the next academic year.

Lewis M. Terman, chair of the psychology department, recruited Stone to Stanford University in 1922. Lashley strongly recommended Stone, remarking in a letter to Terman that "we have all been very favorably impressed with his work here . . . in research he has shown a good bit of originality, and very great perseverance" (Lashley, 1922, cited in Hilgard, 1994, p. 403). Lashley also described Stone's personality in his recommendation letter. Stone, Lashley wrote, "is rather quiet and unassuming, slow in speech, and outwardly unemotional" (Lashley, 1922, cited in Hilgard, 1994, p. 403). After Terman met Stone in April 1922, he described him as "solid and substantial" and possessed of a pleasant personality (Terman, cited in Minton, 1988, p. 134). Stone was described as balanced, of sound judgment, sympathetic and helpful to his students, and with other phrases that depict a steady, stable person.

Stone was a faculty member at Stanford for his entire academic career. His primary work was as a comparative psychologist, and he was the first American psychologist to develop a sex-research program (Pickren, 1997).

Stone initiated a program of research that crossed disciplinary boundaries and exemplified the cooperative ethos of research that was favored by the newly influential philanthropic foundations. Stone's work will be better understood with a little background on the emergence of the emphasis on cooperative research and the role that philanthropies played in encouraging it.

SEX RESEARCH AND COOPERATIVE SCIENCE
BETWEEN THE WORLD WARS

Cooperation in science in the post–World War I era was stimulated by scientists' involvement in the war effort and by new sources of support from philanthropies, such as the Rockefeller Foundation. The Rockefeller Foundation was a joint project by prominent scientists and philanthropic foundation officers to minimize the importance of disciplinary boundaries to maximize the application of science to issues of human importance. The National Research Council (NRC) had been organized in 1916 to provide scientific assistance to the government as the nation prepared to mobilize for war. The cooperation among scientists during the war was of immediate value to the war effort. What perhaps was of more lasting value were the lessons learned about the power of organization of scientific research. The hope of such cooperative science, at least in the medical, biological, and social sciences, has been characterized as social control, social engineering, and human engineering (e.g., Haraway, 1989, chap. 4).

James Rowland Angell, psychologist and then chair of the NRC, sought to discount the fears of central control over research ideas while promoting the value of cooperative research as a method of increasing productivity and efficiency of scientific work. "Organization is the clue," Angell wrote, to ensuring that full use is made of the "intellectual capital" of the nation's scientists (Angell, 1920, p. 252). Similar articles appeared in a variety of journals and magazines that reached audiences in industry, science, and the public. This was a concerted effort on the part of NRC officials to sell their agenda for cooperation in scientific research. Concomitant with the push for cooperation was the encouragement of interdisciplinary research, for scientists from disparate but related fields to collaborate in the investigation of scientific issues that concerned them both. What is taken for granted by many scientists today—the need for interdisciplinary research—was a novel and stimulating idea to many scientists in the 1920s and 1930s.

The research agenda of the NRC was linked to the efforts of philanthropists to build a scientific community for the advancement of knowledge and the amelioration of social problems. This new cooperation followed a period of suspicion between the managers of the new national philanthropies and the scientists. Scientists were accustomed to few funds for their research and were also accustomed to obtaining any available funds on an individual basis. With the advent of large-scale philanthropy, there arose a new system of patronage with a concomitant rise in a new system of professional managers of the funds. In the decade following the war, these managers and their clients in science worked out a new relationship, with the primary goal being the general advancement of knowledge (Geiger, 1986).

Research fellowships and cooperative research projects were two of the methods that were used to facilitate the mutual goals of the scientists and the foundation managers. Although the advancement of knowledge was the overarching goal, both scientists and managers believed that scientific knowledge was the key to the amelioration of pressing social problems. One such set of problems concerned sex; initially the concerns were eugenic—that sexual mores were changing amid the influx of immigrants from eastern and southern Europe and the migration of African Americans to the northern United States. The old northern European and Anglo Saxon elites worried that the "great White race" would be overwhelmed (Grant, 1916). By the 1920s, these elites in industry, academia, and philanthropies turned to science for answers to this perceived problem. The NRC established the Committee for Research in Problems of Sex (CRPS) in 1921 to encourage and coordinate research and to distribute funds for support of sex research (Aberle & Corner, 1953). The Rockefeller Foundation's Bureau of Social Hygiene provided the money. The development of a community of interest in sex problems illustrates the desire of foundation managers and scientists to bring to bear the promise of cooperative science on social problems.

The committee was chaired by Yerkes and supported sex research of scientists from different fields, including physicians, physiologists, embryologists, anatomists, zoologists, psychologists, and anthropologists. Research by comparative psychologists, such as Stone, was well funded in the committee's first decade. In fact, Stone was funded by the committee almost continuously from 1922 until 1940, receiving a total of $18,650 in those years.[1] The funding he received from the committee was critical for the sustenance of his program, and his work extended the scientific understanding of sex, while it also served to support the agenda of social control pursued by scientific and cultural elites.

STONE'S COMPARATIVE APPROACH TO SEX RESEARCH

Stone's graduate mentor, Lashley, proved to be an important connection both to sex research and to support from the CRPS. On the former, Lashley wrote Stone in early 1920 suggesting that one way to do research on topics relevant both to medicine and psychology was to study the emerging field of hormonal effects on behavior. He suggested that Stone study "the effects of internal secretions [hormones] upon specific reactions—for example, attempts to induce maternal behavior in virgin females [rats] by injection or implantation of a pregnant uterus . . . positive results would be pretty sure to make a man in psychology" (cited in Beach, 1981, p. 355). Stone followed up Lashley's suggestion by studying the effects of testicular hormones (Stone, 1923a). In the fall of 1922, Lashley asked the CRPS for permission to divert a portion of his $3,500 grant to Stone. Although the committee declined to divert any of Lashley's funds, it did make

---

[1]$18,650 in 1940 is roughly equivalent to $244,297 in 2003.

a special appropriation of $250 to Stone. It could be argued from this that Stone's sex research was funded from the beginning by the CRPS.

Stone turned the money to good use; he was a diligent researcher who produced a steady stream of research publications. Although the dollar amounts of his grants seem small when compared to post–World War II research support, the funds were critical to Stone's ability to do quality work. Stone also used committee funds to support the work of his graduate students. Stone and his students published their work in psychological and physiological journals, thus illustrating the plan of the CRPS to foster interdisciplinary research.

Stone's publication, "The Congenital Sexual Behavior of the Young Male Albino Rat," is considered a classic of comparative research (see Dewsbury, 1984). Stone's article was part of the lively debate about instincts then occurring in the social and behavioral sciences (e.g., Kuo, 1921). Kuo sparked the debate by arguing that environmental factors are the critical determinants of human development and behavior, rendering the concept of instincts unnecessary in psychology. Stone's paper was part of the early response to Kuo's more extreme position (Dewsbury, 1984). Stone concluded that the copulatory act in young male rats does not depend on previous learning or environmental experience. Stone's article also reflected his interest in development; he noted that sexual behavior is not initiated until the young rat is physiologically mature. That is, the presence of a female rat in heat does not elicit premature, undeveloped attempts at copulation by young rats. From these observations Stone directed a criticism against Freudian ideas of infantile sexuality, noting that his (Stone's) research did not support the Freudian view. But Stone did have an eye toward human applications in his article. He compared his findings to the work of Havelock Ellis on the role of external stimulation in sexual arousal. This first publication by Stone demonstrated his experimental rigor and careful analysis of findings. It is also an adumbration of some of the themes he would develop over the next 20 years and illustrates the close connection between comparative research and human application that was so desired by the CRPS.

Stone offered a comprehensive review of extant literature on the role of neural and hormonal factors in male sexual behavior (1923a). Physiologists, anatomists, and nascent endocrinologists were just beginning to develop this as a research area (see Clarke, 1991). Stone argued that neural and hormonal control of sexual behavior is a fit subject for experimental psychology, and most of his publications over the next 20 years were in this research area.

In the 1920s, Stone employed both ablation and castration techniques to determine neural and hormonal control of sexual behavior (Stone, 1923b, 1926, 1927). From the ablation research, it seemed that sexual behavior was due to subcortical brain regions rather than cortical areas, at least in the species he worked with. Stone used castration to assay potential hormonal influences on sexual behavior in the rat. Stone argued that his work had importance in the light of claims of physical and sexual rejuvenation of human males when injected with testicular substances, claims that had been made as early as the mid-19th century and continued well into the 20th century (see Beach, 1981; Wyndham, 2003). Although Stone's work can be considered basic research, it is clear that it was valuable for understanding human sexual behavior, as was much of the work sponsored by the CRPS. During this decade, Stone also investigated the effects of diet on copulatory ability and on female reproductive behavior, and with his graduate student, Mary Sturman-Hulbe, investigated the maternal behavior of rats (Sturman-Hulbe & Stone, 1929).

As noted earlier, Stone was generous in using external funding to support the research of his graduate students. By all accounts, he was also considerate and helpful to his students (Hilgard, 1994; Rosvold, 1955). His student George T. Avery investigated copulation in both male and female guinea pigs; Avery was the first to use guinea pigs in sex-behavior research (e.g., Avery, 1925). William Dollard Commins's research studied the effects of castration at various ages (e.g., Commins, 1932). With Stone as her coauthor, Lois Doe-Kuhlmann investigated premature pubertal development in boys and girls (Doe-Kuhlman & Stone, 1927). With Roger Barker, who later came to prominence, Stone investigated the effects of menarche on intellectual and personality development (Stone & Barker, 1937). Harry Harlow conducted his dissertation work on eating behavior in rats, and later cited Stone as his research mentor (Sidowski & Lindsley, 1989).

Clarence Ray Carpenter became one of the most visible of Stone's graduate students at Stanford. Under Stone and using Stone's CRPS funds, Carpenter researched the effect of castration on pigeons (e.g., Carpenter, 1933). Stone, who by this time was well connected in the psychological establishment, helped Carpenter make connections with funding sources and other important psychologists. On completing his dissertation, Carpenter won a National Research Fellowship to work with Yerkes at the Yale Laboratories of Comparative Psychobiology. This was critical during the Great Depression, because jobs were few and research support was increasingly scarce. Under Yerkes's tutelage, Carpenter began field research with primates. His work, like that of his mentor Stone, was noted for its thoroughness and detail and became "the major driving force behind primate field biology" (Dewsbury, 1984, p. 103). Like Stone, Yerkes, and other scientific sex researchers, Carpenter's work was part of the effort to extend scientific control to all of life, with sex and mind providing keys to that control (Haraway, 1989).

Sex research was a new area of investigation that was open to any qualified investigator, regardless of disciplinary affiliation. Stone fit well within this nontraditional community of interest (Long, 1987). Within this community, he demonstrated how experimental psychology could provide key insights into a topic that had important social implications. In doing so, he helped enlarge the scope of psychological science.

STONE'S INTEREST IN ABNORMAL BEHAVIOR AND FREUD

Stone's experience with individuals with psychological disorders began early in his career, at the state reformatory and in some of his military work, as mentioned earlier. It may well have been in these same settings that he first became acquainted with the work of Sigmund Freud (Hale, 1995; Shakow & Rapaport, 1964). It was during World War II that the theories and treatment developed by Freud began to gain adherents in the wider medical and psychological communities (Shephard, 2000). Both interests remained with Stone throughout his career.

In Stone's second academic year at Stanford, he offered what is often identified as being the first course on Freudian psychology in the regular curriculum of an American university (Street, 1994). In an early publication (Stone, 1922), Stone criticized Freud's view on infantile sexuality, asserting that his research results did not support it. The lecture notes from his course on Freudian psychology have survived and offer an interesting insight into his approach. He developed charts indicating the concurrent events in other fields of science and medicine along with events in Freud's development of his work. In this way it was possible to see the relationship between Freud and other scientists. Stone's actual lecture notes indicate how careful and precise he sought to be in his statements, a characteristic remarked on by those who knew him well (Hilgard, 1994; Rosvold, 1955).

Like other psychologists of the time (e.g., Woodworth, 1917), Stone found much to be critical of in Freud's writings: Freud overgeneralized, emphasized sexual factors too much, changed his theories to suit his findings, and so forth. Still, Stone, like many of his contemporaries, found Freud impossible to ignore (Hornstein, 1992). Stone also spent a morning in intense conversation with Freud's British disciple, Ernest Jones, during his long visit to Europe in the spring of 1932. Stone's notes from the meeting show that he was deeply impressed by Jones and by Freud's concepts, although he expressed reservations about the mixture of theory and therapy in analytical writings. In the last few weeks of his life Stone was thoroughly engrossed in a recent edition of Freud's letters that had recently been published. In a letter to E. G. Boring, in which he commented on the letters, Stone included both negative and positive comments about Freud and his work. He faulted Freud for "being greedy for immortality" and suspected that Freud was a "very neurotic man." He wrote that Freud "has always been a vigorous hater." On the other hand, he praised Freud for being a fine linguist and translator, as well as being "a very studious library man" (Stone, 1954).

Stone's interest and work in abnormal psychology paralleled his interest in Freud's work. As stated, he had his first experiences with individuals suffering from mental disorders when he worked in the reformatory and while serving in World War I. Stone offered a course in abnormal psychology in his first year as a professor at Stanford (1922–1923). This was at a time when psychologists were just beginning to incorporate coursework on abnormal psychology into the undergraduate curriculum and when the first textbooks on abnormal psychology written by psychologists were beginning to appear (e.g., Bridges, 1921; Conklin, 1927; McDougall, 1926).

Stone spent the academic year of 1928 to 1929 on sabbatical at the Institute of Juvenile Research in Chicago, where his old mentor, Lashley, held a position. The Institute was begun in 1909 as a service of the Cook County Juvenile Court and was taken over by the state of Illinois in 1917. It was one of the first places dedicated both to service and research in problems of child and adolescent development and was a progenitor of both clinical and forensic psychology (Perce, 1954). Stone had the opportunity in this year to interact with others who were working on issues related to the social problem of juvenile delinquency. His seminal chapter on wildness and savageness in rats came out of this year, suggesting that he considered his topic relevant to the problem of delinquency (Stone, Darrow, Landis, & Heath, 1932). Although Stone did not publish much over the next decade related to psychopathology, it was clear that he was still invested in the topic. In 1943, he extracted from multiple sources 86 case histories of individuals with mental disorders that was meant to serve as an aid to students (Stone, 1943a).

In 1945, Stone spent a 6-month sabbatical at the New York State Psychiatric Institute, where Carney Landis was the principal research psychologist. Landis and a talented group of psychologists had an outstanding record of psychopathology research (Zubin & Zubin, 1977). While there Stone assisted David Wechsler in the development of an improved version of the Wechsler Memory Scale. Stone focused primarily on the effects of electroconvulsive shock therapy (ECT) on cognitive abilities in both humans and rats in the 6 months he spent at the psychiatric institute (Stone, 1947, 1948). In general, he found that scores, whether on a memory test or general intelligence test or a parallel test with rats, declined during the therapy, then improved afterward.

PROFESSIONAL SERVICE CONTRIBUTIONS

Stone had the honor of being elected president of the APA from 1941 to 1942. However, wartime exigencies forced the cancellation of the national convention, and he was unable to deliver his presidential address, although he did publish it (Stone, 1943b). In this article, he reminded psychologists of the importance of evolutionary theory to their work, and used the term *behavioral ecology* perhaps for the first time (Dewsbury, personal communication, October 2004). As a wartime president of the APA, he worked on involving psychologists in the war effort. This included establishing the Office of Psychological Personnel (OPP) in Washington, DC. The OPP was responsible for keeping a census of all American psychologists and their areas of expertise. The census helped the federal government locate and contact psychologists for assistance on war-related work. Stone also initiated a committee to plan for the rehabilitation of soldiers during and after the war.

Of greatest long-term consequence was Stone's involvement in the long-range planning group organized by Yerkes in 1942 under the auspices of the Emergency Committee in Psychology. Members of the group, in addition to Stone and Yerkes, were Carl Rogers, Boring, Richard Elliott, Edgar Doll, Alice Bryan, and Ernest R. Hilgard. Based on the recommendations of this group, all the psychological organizations were called together to plan for the future of psychology. It was this larger meeting that led to the reorganization of the APA. The newly reorganized APA expanded its mission beyond the promotion of psychology as a science to include the promotion of psychology as a profession and as a means of promoting human welfare (Capshew & Hilgard, 1992). The reorganization strengthened organized American psychology but also held within itself the seeds of discontent and conflict that extended into the 21st century.

At the end of World War II, Stone was approached by psychologist Walter Bingham on behalf of the U.S. surgeon general about becoming the head of the U.S. Army's new program in clinical psychology. The position's responsibilities included developing and coordinating both service and research. Stone decided to decline the offer. He was reluctant to leave Stanford and his friends and family there.

CONCLUSION

In December 1948, Stone suffered a major heart attack. He was able to recover well enough to resume research and teaching. He continued his work on ECT; edited a new edition of his book, *Comparative Psychology* (1951); and became the first editor of a new series, *Annual Review in Psychology*. In the early 1950s, he began a new program of research on the pituitary gland and its relationship to sexual behavior. He remarked to friends how exciting it was to have a new lease on research life. This work filled the remainder of his research career. In the last week of his life, he was busy reading a new edition of Freud's letters and engaging in correspondence with friends about their contents. On December 28, 1954, Stone suffered a second heart attack, this one fatal.

The life and career of Stone were marked by stability, steadfastness, and solid intellectual judgment. He was an excellent scientist, although perhaps not of the first-rank when compared with other members of the National Academy of Sciences. He was, by all accounts, a good mentor to his students, loved by his children, and a good companion to his wife. It is individuals such as Stone who, in the end, are the core of any scientific discipline. American psychological science was better for his presence.

REFERENCES

Aberle, S. D., & Corner, G. W. (1953). *Twenty-five years of sex research: History of the National Research Council Committee for Research in Problems of Sex, 1922–1947*. Philadelphia: W.B. Saunders.

Angell, J. R. (1920). Organization in scientific research. *Review, 2*, 251–254.

Avery, G. T. (1925). Notes on reproduction in guinea pigs. *Journal of Comparative Psychology, 5*, 373–396.

Beach, F. A. (1981). Historical origins of modern research on hormones and behavior. *Hormones and Behavior, 15*, 325–376.

Bridges, J. W. (1921). *Outline of abnormal psychology*. Columbus, OH: R. G. Adams.

Capshew, J. H., & Hilgard, E. R. (1992). The power of service: World War II and professional reform in the American Psychological Association. In R. B. Evans, V. S. Sexton, & T. C. Cadwallader (Eds.), *100 years, The American Psychological Association, A historical perspective* (pp. 149–175). Washington, DC: American Psychological Association.

Carpenter, C. R. (1933). Psychobiological studies of social behavior in Aves. I. The effect of complete and incomplete gonadectomy on the primary sexual activity of the male pigeon. *Journal of Comparative Psychology, 16*, 25–57.

Clarke, A. (1991). Embryology and the rise of American reproductive sciences, circa 1910–1940. In K. R. Benson, J. Maienschein, & R. Rainger (Eds.), *The expansion of American biology* (pp. 107–132). New Brunswick, NJ: Rutgers University Press.

Commins, W. D. (1932). The effect of castration at various ages upon the learning ability of male albino rats. *Journal of Comparative Psychology, 14*, 29–53.

Conklin, E. S. (1927). *Principles of abnormal psychology*. New York: Henry Holt.

Dewsbury, D. A. (1984). *Comparative psychology in the twentieth century*. Stroudsburg, PA: Hutchinson Ross.

Dewsbury, D. A. (1992). Triumph and tribulation in the history of American comparative psychology. *Journal of Comparative Psychology, 106*, 1–19.

Doe-Kuhlman, L., & Stone, C. P. (1927). Notes on the mental development of children exhibiting signs of puberty praecox. *Journal of Abnormal and Social Psychology, 22*, 291–324.

Geiger, R. L. (1986). *To advance knowledge: The growth of American research universities, 1900–1940*. New York: Oxford University Press.

Grant, M. (1916). *The passing of the great race—Or the racial basis of European history*. New York: Charles Scribner's.

Hale, N. G., Jr. (1995). *The rise and crisis of psychoanalysis in the United States*. New York: Oxford University Press.

Haraway, D. (1989). *Primate visions*. New York: Routledge.

Hearst, E., & Capshew, J. H. (1988). *Psychology at Indiana University: A centennial review and compendium*. Bloomington: Indiana University Department of Psychology.

Hilgard, E. R. (1994). Calvin Perry Stone. February 28, 1892–December 28, 1954. In *Biographical memoirs: National Academy of Sciences for the United States of America* (Vol. 64, pp. 397–419). Washington, DC: National Academy Press.

Hornstein, G. (1992). Return of the repressed: Psychology's problematic relations with psychoanalysis, 1909–1960. *American Psychologist, 47*, 254–263.

Kuo, Z. Y. (1921). Giving up instincts in psychology. *Journal of Philosophy, Psychology and Scientific Method, 18,* 645–664.

Lashley, K. S. (1924). Physiological analysis of the libido. *Psychological Review, 31,* 192–202.

Lashley, K. S., & Watson, J. B. (1920). A psychological study of motion pictures in relation to venereal disease campaigns. *Journal of Social Hygiene 7,* 181–219.

Long, D. E. (1987). Physiological identity of American sex researchers between the two World Wars. In G. L. Geison (Ed.), *Physiology in the American context, 1850–1940* (pp. 263–278). Bethesda, MD: American Physiological Society.

McDougall, W. (1926). *Outline of abnormal psychology.* New York: Charles Scribners.

Minton, H. L. (1988). *Lewis M. Terman: Pioneer in psychological testing.* New York: New York University Press.

Perce, F. C. (1954). Institute for Juvenile Research, State of Illinois. In E. A. Rubinstein & M. Lorr (Eds.), *A survey of clinical practice in psychology* (pp. 19–31). New York: International Universities Press.

Pickren, W. E. (1997). Robert Yerkes, Calvin Stone, and the beginning of programmatic sex research by psychologists, 1921–1930. *American Journal of Psychology, 110,* 603–619.

Rosvold, H. E. (1955). Calvin Perry Stone: 1892–1954. *American Journal of Psychology, 68,* 326–329.

Shakow, D., & Rapaport, D. (1964). *The influence of Freud on American psychology.* New York: International Universities Press.

Shephard, B. (2000). *A war of nerves: Soldiers and psychiatrists in the twentieth century.* Cambridge, MA: Harvard University Press.

Sidowski, J. B., & Lindsley, D. B. (1989). Harry Frederick Harlow. In *Biographical memoirs: National Academy of Sciences of the United States of America* (Vol. 58, pp. 218–257). Washington, DC: National Academy Press.

Stone, C. P. (1922). The congenital sexual behavior of the young male albino rat. *Journal of Comparative Psychology, 2,* 95–153.

Stone, C. P. (1923a). Experimental studies of two important factors underlying masculine sexual behavior: The nervous system and the internal secretion of the testis. *Journal of Experimental Psychology, 6,* 84–106.

Stone, C. P. (1923b). Further study of sensory functions in the activation of sexual behavior in the young male albino rat. *Journal of Comparative Psychology, 3,* 469–473.

Stone, C. P. (1926). The effects of cerebral destruction on the sexual behavior of male rabbits. III. The frontal, parietal, and occipital regions. *Journal of Comparative Psychology, 6,* 435–448.

Stone, C. P. (1927). The retention of copulatory ability in male rats following castration. *Journal of Comparative Psychology, 7,* 369–387.

Stone, C. P. (c. 1940s). Transcript of autobiographical statement. Calvin P. Stone Papers, Stanford University Archives.

Stone, C. P. (1943a). *Case histories in abnormal psychology.* Palo Alto, CA: Stanford University Press.

Stone, C. P. (1943b). Multiply, vary, let the strongest live and the weakest die—Charles Darwin. *Psychological Bulletin, 40,* 1–24.

Stone, C. P. (1947). Losses and gains in cognitive functions as related to electro–convulsive shocks. *Journal of Abnormal and Social Psychology, 42,* 206–214.

Stone, C. P. (1948). Deficits in maze learning by rats tested from two and one-half to three months after a course of electro–convulsive shocks. *American Psychologist, 3,* 237.

Stone, C. P. (Ed.). (1951). *Comparative psychology* (3rd ed.). Oxford, England: Prentice-Hall.

Stone, C. P. (1954, December 21). Letter to E. G. Boring. Calvin P. Stone Papers, Stanford University Archives, Stanford, CA.

Stone, C. P., & Barker, R. S. (1937). Aspects of personality and intelligence in postmenarcheal and premenarcheal girls of the same chronological age. *Journal of Comparative Psychology, 23,* 439–445.

Stone, C. P., Darrow, C. W., Landis, C., & Heath, L. L. (1932). *Studies in the dynamics of behavior*. Chicago: University of Chicago Press.

Street, W. R. (1994). *Chronology of noteworthy events in American psychology*. Washington, DC: American Psychological Association.

Sturman-Hulbe, M., & Stone, C. P. (1929). Maternal behavior in the albino rat. *Journal of Comparative Psychology, 9*, 203–237.

Trabue, M. (1917, October). Letter to Robert M. Yerkes. Calvin P. Stone Papers, Stanford University Archives.

Watson, J. B., & Lashley, K. S. (1920). A consensus of medical opinion upon questions relating to sex education and venereal disease campaigns. *Mental Hygiene, 4*, 769–847.

Woodworth, R. S. (1917). Some criticisms of the Freudian psychology. *Journal of Abnormal Psychology, 12*, 174–194.

Wyndham, D. (2003). Versemaking and lovemaking—W. B. Yeats's "Strange second puberty": Norman Haire and the Steinach rejuvenation program. *Journal of the History of the Behavioral Sciences, 39*, 25–50.

Zubin, D., & Zubin, J. (1977). From speculation to empiricism in the study of mental disorder: Research at the New York State Psychiatric Institute in the first half of the twentieth century. *Annals of the New York Academy of Sciences, 291*, 104–135.

Donald G. Paterson (Photo courtesy of the Archives of the History of
American Psychology, University of Akron)

Chapter 9

An Individual Difference:
The Career of Donald G. Paterson

David B. Baker

Donald Paterson was said to be fond of the proverb, "A difference, to be a difference, has to make a difference." The proverb is telling. Paterson was a psychologist whose life and career were about differences. In a career that mirrored much of the rise of applied psychology in America, Paterson made original and lasting contributions to the study of individual differences. Intelligence, interests, abilities, and aptitudes were all areas of individual differences that Paterson explored with scientific rigor. He applied his findings to real-life situations in higher education, industry, and government. His legacy is evident in student personnel work, vocational psychology, counseling psychology, industrial–organizational psychology, and human engineering, yet it is a legacy that is largely unknown.

BACKGROUND

Donald Gildersleeve Paterson was born in Columbus, Ohio, on January 18, 1892. He was one of five children born to Robert Gildersleeve Paterson and Rosaltha Olds Paterson. Both parents were deaf. His father, who lost his hearing at the age of 12, attended Gallaudet University and went on to become the principal of the Ohio School for the Deaf, where he developed the school's first formal curriculum (Gordon, 2000; Osier & Bahnemann, 2003).

Education was an important part of the Paterson household. Young Donald attended a large public high school in Cincinnati, Ohio, where he discovered an interest in law and the courts. His interest was keen enough that as a high school student he often attended civil trials (Paterson, 1958/1976). When it came time to attend college, Paterson selected Olivet College in Olivet, Michigan. It was an interesting choice. The orientation at Olivet was decidedly progressive. It made no distinctions based on gender, ethnicity, or ability to pay, and it sought to provide students with the "means of intellectual, moral, and spiritual improvement, and to teach them the Divine art and science of doing good to others" (Olivet College, 2004, n.p.). At Olivet, Paterson became acquainted with the work of the progressive social reformer Frank Parsons. Known as the founder of the vocational guidance movement, Parsons believed that knowledge of oneself when mated with knowledge of occupations would produce a satisfying career choice. A Boston attorney, Parsons believed that a thorough individual assessment should include the best measurement that science had to offer. In the early 20th century such measures were few and the prospect of designing such an efficient system of occupational guidance led to skepticism in the young Paterson.

> My information told me Parsons was engaged in an impossible task and his efforts would prove to be futile. This stuck in my mind as a real challenge because it seemed to me that it is the business of science—social science as well as natural science—to do the impossible. I still believe this to be a fundamental assumption inherent in all scientific endeavors. (Paterson, 1958/1976, p. 381)

It was an issue to which Paterson would devote considerable time and attention throughout his career.

AN INTRODUCTION TO PSYCHOLOGY

Paterson stayed at Olivet College from 1910 to 1912, and then transferred to the Ohio State University, where he completed his undergraduate degree in 1914. He stayed at Ohio State as a graduate assistant to A. P. Weiss in the Department of Psychology. Weiss, a recently minted PhD from the University of Missouri, brought a rugged behaviorism to Ohio State. In Weiss, Paterson found an answer to his questions about the objective examination of students.

> I didn't know how this could be accomplished until I became an assistant to Dr. A. P. Weiss. He was a disciple of Max Meyer's "pipeline of behaviorism." Meyer believed not only in getting rid of introspection in psychology but also in getting rid of subjective examinations by means of short-answer and completion-type examinations. I became enthusiastic about this technique. (Paterson, 1958/1976, p. 381)

Although Paterson acknowledged the influence of Weiss, his most productive relationship was with Rudolf Pintner, a Leipzig PhD who came to the United States in 1912. Arriving in New York City, Pintner befriended such notables as Harry Hollingworth and Edward. L. Thorndike. A faculty appointment at the University of Toledo brought Pintner to Ohio, and he soon transferred to the psychology department of Ohio State, where he met graduate student Paterson. Pintner's interest in performance-based measures of intelligence, along with Paterson's knowledge of sign language and deaf culture, produced an extensive body of research on testing children with special needs. Most notably Pintner and Paterson developed the Scale of Performance Tests (Pintner & Paterson, 1917), a performance-based measure of intelligence for the assessment of hearing-impaired children. It was work that would earn Pintner an honorary degree from the alma mater of Paterson's father, Gallaudet University, in 1931 (Boake, 2002; Pintner & Paterson, 1917).

A basic conclusion of Pintner and Paterson was that hearing-impaired children are intellectually deficient.[1]

> Although the reasons for the mental retardation of the deaf are unknown, the fact that they are, as a group, mentally backward is quite evident. This has been the outstanding result of all the mental tests. The deaf child is, on average, two to three years retarded in mental development as contrasted with the hearing child. (Pintner & Paterson, 1918, p. 11)

By 1919, 15 articles and a book later, the collaboration between Paterson and Pintner was over. Having earned his MA in 1916, Paterson left Ohio State for a position as an instructor in the psychology department at the University of Kansas. At Kansas he met Margaret Young, who later became his wife and the mother of their two children.

Walter Hunter was a sizeable presence in the psychology department at Kansas, and Paterson was soon under his influence. In Hunter, Paterson found a psychology more consistent with that of Weiss, a science of behavior that stressed rigorous observation and verification. Shadowing Hunter's interest in animal learning, Paterson produced his first solo publication, a critique of circular maze studies that appeared in the *Psychological Bulletin* (Paterson, 1917). Surprisingly, Hunter was unable to answer some of Paterson's questions about the reliabilities of mazes, and it was agreed that Paterson would conduct a study on the topic as a doctoral dissertation under the supervision of Harvey Carr and James Rowland Angell at the University of Chicago. He was to have done the work at Kansas but receive his PhD from Chicago (Hunter, 1952). But it never happened.

---

[1]The conclusion reached by Pintner and Paterson is now refuted. See Williams and Finnegan (2003).

EXAMINING A NATION

Like many young psychologists of the day, Paterson enlisted in the army to serve in World War I. Paterson's background in psychology, especially his work with Pintner on intelligence testing, helped to earn him the rank of captain and an assignment to the U.S. Army Committee on the Psychological Examining of Recruits under the direction of Robert M. Yerkes. For 2½ years he served as a psychological examiner with a group that included Lewis Terman, Edwin G. Boring, Walter Dill Scott, and Richard M. Elliott (Yerkes, 1930). The intelligence testing program that Yerkes assembled was a massive effort, testing approximately 1.7 million recruits. Its leaders made bold statements about doubts concerning the intellectual ability of young Americans and a need for educational reforms while at the same time reinforcing stereotypes of racial and ethnic inferiority (Guthrie, 1998; Sokal, 1987).

In addition to the mass intellectual testing of recruits, there was a considerable program of personnel assessment under the direction of Scott, a Leipzig-trained psychologist who was no stranger to the classification business. Before the war, he had worked on the psychology of advertising and was a member of a pioneering group of applied psychologists at the Carnegie Institute of Technology in Pittsburgh, Pennsylvania. The first applied psychology program in America, the group was active in the development of tests of selection and classification for use in business. During the war, Scott's unit assessed abilities, aptitudes, and interests and combined them with academic, social, and employment histories to find the right soldier for the right job. By most standards, the testing programs were a tremendous success and served to create an industry and culture of testing in America that has continued unabated (Benjamin & Baker, 2004).

Paterson was a beneficiary of being in the right place at the right time. By the age of 27 he knew many of the major players in American psychology, especially in the new and growing field of applied psychology. After the war, in 1919, he joined Scott's firm in Philadelphia (the Scott Company) and continued to apply scientific methods to problems of personnel selection. It was then that Paterson had an insight that would foretell much of his future in psychology:

> An appalling amount of occupational maladjustment and ineffective management existed in business and industry. This was revealed by excessive labor turnover, absenteeism, grievances, and strikes. This crystallized in me the conviction that colleges and universities could do much more to develop and train professional personnel workers sorely needed as staff men in building genuine personnel programs in business and industry. This also developed in me a conviction that our educational system needed to do a far better job of preparing pupils at all educational levels for entry into the labor market. (Paterson, 1958/1976, p. 382)

With this mindset, Paterson accepted a position as an associate professor in the psychology department at the University of Minnesota.

THE MINNESOTA POINT OF VIEW

The University of Minnesota was carved out of the ideals of the Land Grant College Act of 1862, which also created the University of Wisconsin, the University of Missouri, Iowa State, Kansas State, and Michigan State, among many others. Engineered to serve pragmatic and egalitarian principles, these universities were envisioned as being of the people and for the people. They were created with the promise of bringing a better life to all through education. Propelled by a progressive ideology that sought to couple the advance of science with the need for promoting human welfare, land grant universities such as Minnesota embraced the new science of psychology. The result was "dustbowl empiricism," a point of view that held that the subject matter and principles of psychology should be determined through empirical means. Theory was sidelined while observation, quantification, measurement, and testing took center field.

Some of the biggest names in experimental and applied psychology populated departments of psychology and education in the Midwest. Not only did they influence psychology at the local level, they influenced the field as a whole. The fusion of this pragmatic psychology with a humanistic vision of higher education was fertile ground for developing and expanding an applied psychology based on individual differences. At the University of Minnesota, science and practice mingled to address problems of unemployment, personality and vocational assessment, rehabilitation, student personnel work, and personal counseling (Baker, 2002).

Paterson's appointment to the Minnesota faculty came amid much activity among a group of psychologists well known to Paterson. The psychology department at Minnesota was established in 1919, an act of secession from the department of philosophy. Such splits were becoming commonplace as the new science of psychology gained a foothold in colleges and universities across the United States. The dean of the College of Science, Literature and the Arts at the time, John Black Johnston, was a supporter of, and a believer in, the ability of the new psychology to help students find an appropriate place in the academic world and, by extension, the world of work. A neurologist by training, Johnston thought he had secured Yerkes as head of the newly formed department of psychology. When it was clear that Yerkes's postwar duties would keep him in Washington as head of the new National Research Council (NRC), Yerkes suggested colleague Richard Elliott instead (Keyes, 2004).

Like Paterson, Elliott was a psychological examiner during World War I. In fact, Elliott's first assignment was under the supervision of Paterson at Camp Wadsworth. Elliott, a Harvard PhD, had been a student of Hugo Münsterberg's and an assistant to Yerkes. Both had a major influence on Elliott. From Münsterberg, Elliott inherited a true believer's faith in applied psychology; from Yerkes, Elliott adopted behavioral psychology as well as a direct line to federal funds. At the University of Minnesota, Elliott was pleased to be able to bring Paterson on board.

I had served as a psychological examiner under "Pat" in the army, had followed in a general way his work in personnel psychology from the Scott Company and, when Dr. Mabel Fernald resigned the position in individual differences in 1921, knew at once whom we wanted if we could get him. (Elliott, 1952, p. 91)

Paterson got to work quickly. The environment was a receptive one. The postwar years brought a steady stream of enrollments, which meant entering students needed to be assessed and properly placed in the curriculum. Department chair Elliott retained a strong interest in applied psychology and testing, and Dean Johnston had a progressive spirit that sought to apply science to the prediction of student success. There was abundant support for, and interest in, the development of student services. The University of Minnesota soon became a national leader in the newly emerging student personnel movement. Before Paterson's arrival, Johnston had been conducting research on the relationship between high school performance and college performance. He developed a system for converting high school grades into ranks that could be combined with college ability tests to predict student success. The data that he generated led to a host of programs designed to support both low- and high-ability students. It also contributed to statewide testing and guidance programs in secondary schools. The emphasis on testing and placement became incorporated into what was known as the "Minnesota Point of View."

> Together Donald Paterson and Dean Johnston helped orient the University experience to the needs of individual students. The result of their efforts was the creation of the Minnesota Point of View. The Minnesota Point of View adopted three guiding principles: First, it promoted a concern for the individual student as a unique combination of abilities and interests. Second, it advocated respect for objective data and the methods of data collection. And lastly the Minnesota Point of View advocated that data and test results could produce a sound basis for action. (Osier & Bahnemann, 2003, pp. 2–3)

Paterson stayed busy with student personnel work at the University of Minnesota for a decade. His work earned the respect of his colleagues, and in 1923 he was promoted to full professor. He was known to be an engaging and popular teacher. His course, "Individual Differences," was legendary. It enrolled many students who would go on to make their mark on American psychology, including William Estes, Howard Hunt, Marvin Dunnette, John Holland, Leona Tyler, Harrison Gough, James Jenkins, Paul Meehl, Jane Loevinger, and Starke Hathaway.

In the decade of the 1920s Paterson and his colleagues at the university conceived a program of student personnel work that was comprehensive, inclusive, and above all else geared toward the individual student. The concept of individual differences at Minnesota meant that students received individual attention and assessment, and this concept was supported in finding the best fit between students' aptitude, interests, and abilities and the available curriculum. Every member of the faculty, administration, and staff played a role in student services. Vocational and personal guidance, financial aid, student health, curriculum planning, grading, recreation, and housing were all included under the umbrella of student personnel services. The plans developed and implemented by the Minnesota group in the 1930s served as a model for providing student personnel services in universities across the United States (Beck, 1982; Williamson, 1947).

In 1923, the University Testing Bureau was established and was headed by one of Paterson's graduate students, E. G. Williamson. At mid-century, Williamson would emerge as one of the key figures in establishing counseling psychology as a domain of professional psychology.

The emphasis on testing and assessment was fundamental to the Minnesota Point of View and to Paterson's insistence on empirical evidence. For better or worse, testing became synonymous with the Minnesota approach to student personnel work, especially in vocational guidance and counseling. To some, the Minnesota Point of View was no more than a "test them and tell them" program of vocational guidance. Indeed, testing of abilities, aptitudes, and interests was commonplace at Minnesota, but it was not all that was done (Williamson, 1947).

Like many in the progressive movement, Paterson saw the need to improve human efficiency through the humane application of science and technology. The great mass of factories and workers that quickly populated large urban centers during the industrial revolution created a demand for a system of classification of school-aged children that would ensure every student the fullest measure of the ideals of democratic life. Speaking before the Minnesota Education Association in 1922, Paterson pointed out the following.

> It must be recognized clearly that vocational success depends on a variety of independent factors. If success depended strictly upon one's vocational capacity, intelligence, and other tested abilities, then tests and measurements would be all-important in vocational training and guidance. Success is not conditioned in so simple a way. It is dependent upon one's health and physical fitness, upon financial ability to get proper training, upon the help one's family and friends can give, upon the demand for one's product, etc. Vocational advice must take all of these factors into account fully and adequately. For these reasons, it is obvious that tests are not all-important but are important only insofar as they supplement and make more accurate the judgments that are made in advising a pupil to enter a training course or take a job in industry. (Paterson, 1923, p. 296)

Typical of Paterson's early efforts at the University of Minnesota was the Committee of Faculty Counselors. Under Paterson's direction this committee selected faculty members who were trained as student counselors and charged with assisting students presenting a variety of concerns. True to his empirical base, Paterson fastidiously collected and reported data on the program. The data provided an interesting snapshot of student counseling in 1929. Not unlike today, referral questions often involved vocational choice, course selection, and emotional problems (Paterson, Schneidler, & Williamson, 1935).

UNEMPLOYMENT TESTING

Testing of abilities, aptitudes, and interests continued unabated at the University of Minnesota, and soon Paterson's ideas and influence extended to a much larger national stage. Concerned with issues of mass migration after World War I, the NRC appointed a committee to study problems of human migration and the measurement of human traits and abilities. It was hoped that the findings would help delineate a sound immigration policy. One line of work concerned the measurement of mechanical ability. Yerkes, the NRC director, knew just whom to tap for the assignment: Elliott and Paterson.

With NRC funding, the Minnesota Mechanical Ability Investigation began a 4-year examination of the characteristics of mechanical ability and its measurement. Beyond establishing the existence of mechanical ability and effective means for its measurement, the program did not answer many of the questions that the NRC had originally asked, such as the existence and inheritance of racial and national differences in mechanical ability. Nonetheless, Yerkes maintained a strong enthusiasm for the undertaking, "It is difficult for me to write calmly and objectively of this report, so stirred am I by its contributions of fact, method, and insight, and its promise of developments which should significantly improve educational, vocational, and industrial procedures" (Yerkes, 1930, p. iii).

Paterson and colleagues at Minnesota were showing the world what they had known for a long time: Individual differences in abilities and aptitudes could be reliably measured and used in the efficient classification of workers. For them the timing was good; for the nation it was not. The stock market crash of 1929 ushered in the Great Depression of the 1930s. The size and magnitude of the Depression is hard to comprehend. Roughly 25% of the population was out of work, industry stood idle, and a severe drought ruined agriculture production in the Midwest. However, the Depression that brought so much hardship to so many provided ample opportunities for measurement and classification work.

When he was elected president in 1932, Franklin D. Roosevelt instituted a series of reforms aimed at rejuvenating the economy. Many of Roosevelt's initiatives involved work programs and resulted in establishing agencies such as the U.S. Employment Service, the Occupational Information and Guidance Service, and the Occupational Outlook Service, as well as in publishing the *Dictionary of Occupational Titles* (Johnson & Johnson, 1958). It also brought Paterson into national prominence as he earned appointments to the U.S. Department of Labor, the Veterans Administration, and the NRC.

At the local level, federal initiatives aimed at reducing unemployment led to establishing the Minnesota Employment Stabilization Research Institute. The goal of the institute was the scientific study of occupations and employment and the procurement of jobs for the area's unemployed individuals. Paterson was named chair of the institute's Committee on Individual Diagnosis and Training. His efforts continued to be successful, and the program clearly demonstrated the efficacy of occupational guidance and employment selection techniques. During the period 1931 to 1945, the Minnesota Employment Stabilization Program produced a significant number of publications dealing with issues related to employment. The program strongly advocated for centralized public employment services and the continued development of occupational assessment. The term *occupational ability pattern* entered the lexicon as a result of the Minnesota Employment Stabilization Program. This term represented an ideal for Paterson: the use of empirical data derived from tests of individual differences to match individuals to the demands of the world of work. A 1933 publication of the Employment Stabilization Research Institute defined occupational ability patterns as follows:

> the numerical, objective descriptions of a given type of work in terms of measurable human abilities necessary for success in that work. They are derived from test data on representative workers of known occupational success in the job under analysis. After the test results have been related to satisfactory measures of job ability, it is possible to translate the test scores into graphic form on a percentile chart. This graph, or "profile," then represents the range and patterns of ability necessary for success in the occupation thus studied. (Darley, Paterson, & Peterson, 1933, p. 37)

The work of Paterson's team on individual diagnosis and training helped to establish a set of principles for personnel selection and vocational guidance that became the norm in industry and education, which culminated in his book, *Men, Women, and Jobs: A Study in Human Engineering* (Paterson & Darley, 1936). It also served to strengthen his conviction about the scientific measurement of human traits and abilities.

REAL SCIENCE

The pseudosciences of physiognomy, phrenology, and related practices that had characterized much of 19th-century vocational guidance and counseling were anathema to Paterson, who saw in these practices a threat to the rigorous scientific traditions he espoused. One example was the character analysis system of physician Katherine Blackford, the author of many popular books on character analysis. Blackford's method of personnel selection was based on an analysis of physical features such as face shape and hair color. For example, she claimed that people with convex faces are typically keen, alert, quick, aggressive and impatient, whereas people with concave faces are more likely to be careful, reasoning, deliberate, and persistent (Blackford & Newcomb, 1914). Blondes and brunettes were also said to possess certain personality traits that Blackford considered to be enduring. She used adjectives such as *dynamic, driving, aggressive, domineering, impatient, active, quick, hopeful, speculative, changeable,* and *variety-loving* to describe blondes and *negative, static, conservative, imitative, submissive, cautious, painstaking, patient, plodding, slow, deliberate, serious,* and *thoughtful* to describe brunettes (Blackford & Newcomb, 1916). Although this all sounds silly now, Blackford's system of personnel selection found its way into such corporate offices as Westinghouse (Farr, 1997).

Paterson devoted considerable energy to debunking pseudosciences that claimed to measure human traits and abilities. In 1922, he published a study that clearly showed no differences between blondes and brunettes on many of the traits that Blackford so firmly declared are different in the two groups (Paterson & Ludgate, 1922). Paterson was not ready to let the issue go. In 1930, in *Physique and Intellect,* Paterson showed that claims of a relationship between physical traits and intellectual ability were unfounded (Paterson, 1930).

ADVANCING APPLIED PSYCHOLOGY

Paterson's influence was growing steadily. Through a combination of intelligence, hard work, good timing, and important connections he was on the leading edge of the applied psychology movement in America. His contributions to personnel work were recognized in industry, education, and government. His work informed social policy and affected the lives of millions. Clearly he was shaping and defining applied psychology, and he soon took on administrative and service roles that complemented his record of research.

The election of Walter Hunter to the presidency of the American Psychological Association (APA) in 1931 brought Paterson into the organization as secretary. In the position until 1937, Paterson served alongside APA presidents Walter Miles, L. L. Thurstone, John Peterson, A. T. Poffenberger, Clark L. Hull, and E. C. Tolman.

As secretary, Paterson was responsible for many of the details associated with the annual meeting of the APA. It was a position not without its frustrations, because many of the meeting details such as room assignments, program printing, and selecting session chairs fell to the secretary. In an era devoid of electronic communication, arrangements had to be painstakingly worked out, often over multiple correspondences. For example, for a session on learning at the 1932 convention at Cornell Paterson had hoped to secure E. G. Boring for the spot. However, Boring refused, citing his poor health, the health problems of his son, and noting, "I am not sure that I shall ever come to a September A.P.A. meeting now that it has turned out that they must happen before the 15th. This is just my hay-fever time, and the one period in the year when I have no interest in anything" (Boring, 1932, n.p.). But headaches of schedules aside, Paterson's work as secretary brought him into contact with an ever widening circle of American psychologists.

Leaving APA service in 1937, Paterson was quickly caught up in the formal organization of the rapidly expanding applied psychology movement. The growth and political power of applied psychology had been rising for years. Attempts to organize psychologists with applied interests both inside and outside the APA had met with mixed success but, by 1937, the organizations that did exist agreed to merge into one national association, the American Association for Applied Psychology (AAAP). The AAAP comprised four sections: business and industrial, clinical, consulting, and educational psychology. Considering Paterson's contributions to each section it was not surprising that he was elected president of the AAAP in 1938 (Benjamin & Baker, 2004).

Within a few years, the AAAP was the largest organization of psychologists outside of the APA. However, America's entry into World War II brought with it an overwhelming need for the expertise of psychologists both in applied areas and in basic research. The result was the reorganization of the APA in 1945. Joining together with the AAAP, a new APA emerged, one that included a divisional structure whereby the diverse interests of all the membership could be represented (Benjamin & Baker, 2004).

The reorganization of the APA in 1945 was accomplished in part by having psychologists identify the areas that best represented their interests and work. The result was the differentiation of psychology with the APA into the divisional structure we know today. In the process, psychologists had to select a primary affiliation. For Paterson that affiliation would be with Division 17, The Division of Personnel and Guidance Psychologists (now known as the Society for Counseling Psychology). The division came into existence in large part because of the long history of leadership of the University of Minnesota in student personnel work and the efforts of Minnesota faculty members such as E. G. Williamson and John Darley, who had studied and worked with Paterson at the University of Minnesota for many years. For Paterson the counseling psychologist embodied all that he had tried to achieve in applied psychology.

> The counseling psychologist is held accountable for knowledge and competence in personnel psychology, vocational and occupational psychology, occupational counseling, industrial and human engineering psychology, tests and measurements of special value in education and vocational counseling, plus suitable practicum training. (Paterson, 1958/1976, p. 384)

After World War II, Paterson had plenty to keep him busy. From 1943 to 1954 he served as the editor of the *Journal of Applied Psychology*. At the University of Minnesota he served as a charter member of the newly formed Industrial Research Center. The center, still in operation, was created in 1945 to bridge the gap between management and labor through leadership training and research.

Paterson devoted significant energies to the University of Minnesota psychology department. During his tenure he supervised approximately 300 master's-level and 88 doctoral students. His list of publications numbered more than 300, and many included students and colleagues as coauthors. In 1952, 35 years after he left his dissertation research behind at the University of Kansas, he was awarded an honorary LLD degree from Ohio State (Osier & Bahneman, 2003).

The same progressive spirit that brought a young Paterson to Olivet College in 1910 was evident in his civic activities as an older adult. Paterson was an active member in the Citizens League and the American Civil Liberties Union. A local activist, he rallied his neighbors to fight the encroachment of a freeway into their Minneapolis neighborhood (Devonis, 2001).

Paterson retired from the University of Minnesota in 1960. He continued working, consulting with various organizations and agencies including his father's alma mater, Gallaudet University. After participating in the 14th International Congress of Applied Psychology in Copenhagen in 1961, he was diagnosed with cancer. He died a short time later on October 4, 1961.

CONCLUSION

Paterson made enviable use of the time he had in life. He was brought along on a current of change in American psychology, and he adapted to it. Predisposed to a progressive world view, he found a home in the emerging applied psychology movement of the early 20th century and grew to make an important mark on it. Throughout the cataclysmic changes wrought by World War I, the Great Depression, and Word War II, Paterson was there as a participant–observer who helped craft a science of applied psychology that had myriad applications to assessing a wide range of human differences. He had open access to much that was new and that mattered. His contributions to the study of individual differences, especially as it applied to the world of work, contributed to many lasting concepts and practices in personnel work. A Festschrift in his honor, published on his retirement in 1960, described Paterson's work this way.

> Throughout all of his research and teaching have been two principal skeins, the theme of individual differences and the theme of occupational adjustment. People are born different and they remain different. These differences are influenced, and often expanded, by the experiences of the person, and these differences have great relevance for the life of the person, particularly for his occupational life. These differences are measurable, they are predictable, and they themselves have predictive usefulness. Differences in ability, interests, and values transcend differences in race, sex, and physique, but frequently they are influenced by these latter differences

and research, not dogma, must reveal the nature and extent of these influences. (Department of Psychology, 1960, p. ii)

After Paterson retired he wrote to his close colleagues to thank them for their well wishes and bid them farewell. In the closing paragraph of that letter he wrote, "Keep up the good work. Saw wood. And, above all, continue Anton Carlson's dictum *'Was ist die evidence?'"* (Paterson, 1960). In summing up the life of Paterson it is fair to say that the evidence shows he made a difference.

REFERENCES

Baker, D. B. (2002). Child saving and the emergence of vocational counseling. *Journal of Vocational Behavior, 60,* 374–381.

Beck, R. H. (1982). *Beyond pedagogy: A history of the University of Minnesota College of Education.* St. Paul, MN: North Central.

Benjamin, L. T., & Baker, D. B. (2004). *From séance to science: A history of the profession of psychology in America.* Belmont, CA: Wadsworth.

Blackford, K. M. H., & Newcomb, A. (1914). *The job, the man, the boss.* New York: Doubleday & Page.

Blackford, K. M. H., & Newcomb, A. (1916). *Analyzing character: The new science of judging men, misfits in business, the home, and social life* (2nd ed.). New York: Review of Reviews.

Boake, C. (2002). From the Binet–Simon to the Wechsler–Bellevue: Tracing the history of intelligence testing. *Journal of Clinical and Experimental Neuropsychology, 24,* 383–405.

Boring, E. G. (1932, June 21). Letter to Donald G. Paterson. Olson Papers, M146, Archives of the History of American Psychology, The University of Akron, Akron, OH.

Darley, J. G., Paterson, D. G., & Peterson, I. E. (1933). Occupational testing and the Public Employment Service. *Bulletin of the Employment Stabilization Research Institute, 2,* 35–54.

Department of Psychology, University of Minnesota. (1960). *In honor of Donald G. Paterson.* Mimeographed Program. Tyler Papers, Tyler Depot Box, Archives of the History of American Psychology, The University of Akron, Akron, OH.

Devonis, D. C. (2001, June 21–24). *Donald G. Paterson vs. I-94: A psychologist in the path of progress.* Paper presented at Cheiron (International Society for the History of the Behavioral and Social Sciences), Bloomington, IN.

Elliott, R. M. (1952). Richard M. Elliott. In E. G. Boring, H. S. Langfeld, H. Werner, & R. M. Yerkes (Eds.), *A history of psychology in autobiography* (Vol. 4, pp. 75–95). Worcester, MA: Clark University Press.

Farr, J. L. (1997). *Organized I/O psychology: Past, present, and future.* Retrieved August 29, 2004, from http://siop.org/tip/backissues/tipjul97/Farr.html

Gordon, J. (2000). *History of OSD.* Retrieved July 12, 2004, from http://www.ohioschoolforthe deaf.org/history/

Guthrie, R. V. (1998). *Even the rat was white: A historical view of psychology* (2nd ed.). Boston: Allyn & Bacon.

Hunter, W. S. (1952). Walter S. Hunter. In E. G. Boring, H. S. Langfeld, H. Werner, & R. M. Yerkes (Eds.), *A history of psychology in autobiography* (Vol. 4, pp. 163–187). Worcester, MA: Clark University Press.

Johnson, R. G., & Johnson, W. F. (1958). The vocational guidance movement. *National Business Education Quarterly, 12,* 13–21.

Keyes, M. (2004). *A synopsis of our history.* Retrieved August 21, 2004, from http://www.psych. umn.edu/courses/about/index.htm

Olivet College. (2004). *About Olivet: Olivet history.* Retrieved June 19, 2004, from http://www. olivetcollege.edu

Osier, D., & Bahnemann, G. (2003). *Inventory of the Donald G. Paterson Papers.* Retrieved May, 21, 2004, from http://special.lib.umn.edu/findaid/xml/uarc00762.xml

Paterson, D. G. (1917). The Johns Hopkins circular maze studies. *Psychological Bulletin, 14,* 294–297.

Paterson, D. G. (1923). The vocational testing movement. *Journal of Personnel Research, 2,* 295–305.

Paterson, D. G. (1930). *Physique and intellect.* New York: Century.

Paterson, D. G. (1960). Letter to colleagues. Tyler Papers, Tyler Depot Box, Archives of the History of American Psychology, The University of Akron, Akron, OH.

Paterson, D. G. (1976). Reminiscences concerning the development of student personnel work at the University of Minnesota. *Journal of College Student Personnel, 17,* 380–385. (Posthumous publication of a 1958 speech)

Paterson, D. G., & Darley, J. G. (1936). *Men, women, and jobs: A study in human engineering: A review of the studies of the Committee on Individual Diagnosis and Training.* Minneapolis: University of Minnesota Press.

Paterson, D. G., & Ludgate, K. (1922). Blonde and brunette traits: A quantitative study. *Journal of Personnel Research, 1,* 122–127.

Paterson, D. G., Schneidler, G., & Williamson, E. G. (1935). *Student personnel procedures and techniques used by faculty counselors at the University of Minnesota.* Minneapolis: University of Minnesota Mimeograph Department.

Pintner, R., & Paterson, D. G. (1917). *A scale of performance tests.* New York: Appleton.

Pintner, R., & Paterson, D. G. (1918). Some conclusions from psychological tests of the deaf. *Volta Review, 20,* 10–14.

Sokal, M. M. (1987). James McKeen Cattell and mental anthropometry: Nineteenth-century science and reform and the origins of psychological testing. In M. Sokal (Ed.), *Psychological testing and American society, 1890–1930* (pp. 21–45). New Brunswick, NJ: Rutgers University Press.

Williams, C., & Finnegan, M. (2003). From myth to reality: Sound information for teachers about students who are deaf. *Teaching Exceptional Children, 35,* 40–45.

Williamson, E. G. (1947). Counseling and the Minnesota point of view. *Educational and Psychological Measurement, 7,* 141–155.

Yerkes, R. M. (1930). Foreword. In D. G. Paterson, R. M. Elliott, L. D. Anderson, H. A. Toops, & E. Heidbreder (Eds.), *Minnesota Mechanical Ability Tests: The report of a research investigation subsidized by the Committee on Human Migrations of the National Research Council and conducted in the Department of Psychology at the University of Minnesota* (p. iii). Minneapolis: University of Minnesota Press.

Coleman Roberts Griffith (Photo courtesy of the University of Illinois at Urbana–Champaign Archives)

Chapter 10

Coleman Roberts Griffith: "Adopted" Father of Sport Psychology

Christopher D. Green

Coleman Roberts Griffith is often called the "father" of American sport psychology. A quick search of the World Wide Web will confirm that Griffith and his work are the starting points for numerous college courses on the topic. The Association for the Advancement of Applied Sport Psychology has named their most prestigious invited lecture in honor of Griffith's memory. Indeed, Griffith has a strong prima facie claim to the title of "father" of the discipline: He opened the first American laboratory dedicated specifically to investigating psychological aspects of sport, and he wrote the first American textbooks on the topic. Like many things historical, however, matters are more complicated than they might appear at first glance. Unlike other disciplinary fathers such as Wilhelm Wundt, Griffith's laboratory was in operation for less than a decade, and he produced no doctoral students in sport psychology who (like, for instance, Wundt's students) would go on to found their own laboratories, publish their own textbooks, create a community of scholars, and ultimately found a discipline. No journals dedicated to sport psychology would appear until the decade after Griffith's death (*International Journal of Sport Psychology,* founded in 1970), and no American journal would debut until 1973 (*Psychology of Motor Behavior and Sport*). In fact, it was the generation of American sport psychologists that coalesced after Griffith's

Thanks to the personnel at the University of Illinois Archives, where the papers of Coleman R. Griffith are housed. They were most helpful, and frequently went beyond the call of duty. Thanks are also due my graduate student Cathy Faye, who assisted me with this research, and to Coleman Griffith's son and granddaughter, Wayland Griffith and Susan Griffith, who both kindly wrote me helpful and informative letters.

death in the last third of the 20th century, looking for historical precedents to their own research, that "rediscovered" Griffith's work of nearly a half century earlier, "adopted" him as the father of sport psychology, and bestowed on him a prominence that he had not attained during his own lifetime (see, e.g., Benjamin & Baker, 2004, pp. 205–207; Gould & Pick, 1995; Kroll & Lewis, 1970/1978; LeUnes, 2000; see also chap. 12, this volume; and see Singer, 1989, and Swoap, 1999, for brief historical overviews).[1]

GRIFFITH'S EARLY LIFE AND CAREER

Griffith was born on May 22, 1893, in Guthrie Center, Iowa, about 50 miles from Des Moines. His father was a Methodist minister. His family moved widely during his childhood. Although details are scarce, Griffith described his early education as having been "in the public and private schools of California, South Dakota, and Illinois" (Griffith, ca. 1945). In 1911, he entered Greenville College in Illinois, a school affiliated with the Free Methodist Church, earning an AB degree (cum laude) in 1915. As an undergraduate, he was devoted to athletics and outdoor activities, an interest that continued throughout his life.[2] After teaching at Greenville for 1 year, he began graduate school at the University of Illinois under the supervision of Madison Bentley.

Bentley had studied under two of Wilhelm Wundt's American students—first H. K. Wolfe at Nebraska and later E. B. Titchener at Cornell—receiving his doctorate in 1899. Bentley taught at Cornell for more than a decade before being called to head the psychology department at Illinois in 1912.[3] At the outbreak of World War I, only a year after Griffith's arrival at Illinois, Bentley volunteered for the Air Corps, conducting research on the vestibular organs of the ear. This was the environment in which Griffith conducted his own graduate research. Bentley, who had been a cooperating editor of the *American Journal of Psychology* since 1903, the editor of the *Psychological Index* since 1916, and who would soon become editor of the *Journal of Comparative Psychology* (in 1921) and of the *Journal of Experimental Psychology* (in 1926), proved to be an invaluable contact for Griffith as well.

---

[1] It is interesting to note, as a measure of the recency of the growth of Griffith's prominence, that his name does not appear in Zusne's *Biographical Dictionary of Psychology* (1984).

[2] Gould and Pick (1995) published photographs of Griffith in his baseball uniform and in his hiking gear. The Griffith papers contain many letters about his fishing trips and vacations to wilderness areas. He also mentions having purchased a shotgun, although it is unclear whether he became a regular sport hunter.

[3] The psychological laboratory at Illinois was founded in 1892 by William O. Krohn, only the 17th in North America, according to Garvey (1929).

Griffith's (1919) first publication was in *Science,* an article in which he took up the possibility that rats' fear of cats is instinctive. The year 1920 saw Griffith emerge as a significant scholar in his own right: In January he was elected a member of the American Association for the Advancement of Science. In May he defended his dissertation and, over the course of the year, produced six journal articles based on his doctoral research on the impact on rats' sense of balance of raising them entirely on a rotating platform. He also published a seventh article that year, again on the instinctiveness of rats' fear of cats. Bentley appointed Griffith assistant editor of the *Psychological Index,* and he was promoted from an "assistant" to an "instructor" in the psychology department (see Griffith, ca. 1931a). Griffith's star was on the rise. The University of Minnesota attempted to hire him away from Illinois, but to no avail. In 1921, he published two more articles, including a call for a history specifically of experimental psychology (Griffith, 1921), some 8 years before E. G. Boring's (1929), Gardner Murphy's (1929), and Walter Pillsbury's (1929) celebrated textbooks on the topic.

Surviving letters from Griffith to his students show him to have been a man with a wry sense of humor, always prodding them to do better. To one he wrote, "Someone is always taking the joy out of life. Your Mathematics 4 seems to be the offender this time. ... Suppose you try an extra fifteen minutes a day" (Griffith, 1922g). To another, "I see by your report for the first six weeks that you have been applying the principles of economics to the time you spend studying Economics 8. I wonder if you couldn't spend a little more time on Economics and remove the only bad mark against you" (Griffith, 1922f).

The year 1922 was a turning point in Griffith's career. In addition to two more journal articles, including a second one on the history of psychology (Griffith, 1922b), it saw the publication of Griffith's first book, *An Historical Survey of Vestibular Equilibration* (Griffith, 1922c). Griffith also demonstrated his penchant for technological innovation by employing, in his study of disequilibrated rats, "ultra-rapid moving pictures," a technique he would later bring to the field of sport. His reputation was growing, and Griffith was courted by a variety of Midwestern universities during the course of 1922. University of Chicago, Ohio State, and Minnesota (again) made him offers. He even taught at Chicago for part of the summer of 1922. To keep him, Illinois promoted Griffith to assistant professor of psychology, appointed him to the graduate faculty, and made him the acting head of the department during Bentley's sabbatical of 1922 to 1923. In addition, Bentley appointed him acting editor of the *Psychological Index* during Bentley's absence. Furthermore, Griffith had written a textbook on psychology that had sold more than 1,000 copies in privately mimeographed form over the previous few years (Griffith, 1922i). By December of 1922 he found a publisher, and the book appeared the following year under the title, *General Introduction to Psychology* (Griffith, 1923a). According to Griffith, it was immediately adopted by 125 colleges and universities. He would produce a revised edition just 5 years later (Griffith, 1928a).[4]

Perhaps the most interesting aspect of Griffith's activities in 1922 was his handling of a serendipitous finding with his disequilibrated rats that seemed to run contrary to received scientific opinion. Griffith found that a certain proportion of the offspring of rats that had been raised in his rotating cages appeared to be born with equilibrium problems of their own. In short, it seemed that they had inherited characteristics that had been acquired during the lifetimes of their parents, contrary to the dictates of Darwinian evolutionary theory. Griffith, clearly concerned for his reputation, was reluctant to publish results "so at variance with common biological belief" (Griffith, 1922d). He arranged for a distant colleague— J. A. Detlefsen of the Wistar Institute for Anatomy and Biology in Philadelphia— to begin a replication of his research, sending Detlefsen not only his equipment and films but also samples of rats he had raised in his rotating cage.[5] Detlefsen seems to have presented the preliminary results of Griffith's work in a talk at the meeting of the American Society of Naturalists late in 1921. Immediately Griffith began receiving requests for details, including one from the newly formed Science Service in Washington, DC. When Griffith delayed, the Science Service asked to reprint a report of his results that appeared in an early 1922 issue of the *Eugenical News,* a bulletin published by the Eugenical Research Association and other groups.[6] Griffith, apparently previously unaware of this published report, immediately wrote the editor of *Eugenical News,* protesting what he called its "unauthorized and incorrect" account of the phenomenon (Griffith, 1922e). Throughout the summer he agonized about whether to publish the controversial finding. Finally, in October, he asked Detlefsen to read over a short piece he

---

[4]His publisher, Macmillan, demanded that he omit his chapter on the history of psychology, complaining that it was too long. Two chapters on the history of psychology appeared in the second edition, however (Griffith, 1928a). It is not clear to what degree these were restorations from the original manuscript and to what degree they were new material written, perhaps as a result of the research conducted during his Guggenheim fellowship of 1926 to 1927. Thanks to David Winter of the University of Michigan for his assistance on this point.

[5]See Griffith (1923c). He also seems to have arranged for replications by Irving Hardesty of the Tulane College of Medicine (see Griffith, 1923b). Detlefsen (1923) published a partial replication in which he found some similarities between the rats' symptoms and those of simple "mastoid" cases. The hypothesis that such infections were passed from rotated parents to nonrotated offspring, however, could not account for Griffith's finding that the *lateralization* (left–right) of vestibular dysfunction seemed to be passed from parent to offspring as well. In this publication, Detlefsen said that he had not yet bred his rotated rats to see if Griffith's "Lamarckian" finding would be confirmed. Detlefsen (1925) published a long article on acquired characteristics in which he mentioned Griffith's work once more along with his infection hypothesis, which he again admitted could not wholly account for the data. I have not found a published report of Detlefsen's attempt to breed rotated rats. Thanks to Roger Thomas of the University of Georgia for helping me locate the Detlefsen (1923, 1925) reports.

[6]I have been unable to locate a copy of this issue of the *Eugenical News.* I thank Andrew S. Winston of the University of Guelph for providing me with information about its background.

had prepared for *Science* (Griffith, 1922h). With Detlefsen's support, he submitted it to James McKeen Cattell (Cattell, 1922), then *Science*'s owner and editor, who in turn ran it in the December issue (Griffith, 1922a). The tone of the article is quite tentative, and it is not clear exactly what effect, if any, the report had on the scientific community. In any case, its publication would essentially mark the end of his work on vestibular equilibrium.[7]

THE PSYCHOLOGY OF SPORT

Griffith was already developing a new research program that would occupy the next decade of his life. Since 1918, he had been conducting psychological research, still unpublished, on athletes. The exact nature of these studies is not clear, but Griffith would later write that he began with "problems of vision and shifting attention," and "passing notice . . . of those shifting moods and attitudes which go so far toward keeping men on a winning streak or beguiling them into an unexpected defeat" (Griffith, 1930, p. 35). By 1920, he was lugging a "Sanborn reaction time outfit" to the football field to test players' quickness. He found, perhaps not surprisingly, that when practice squads were organized around the results of these tests, the squads with lower reaction times were more successful on the field. Naturally, this caught the attention of the Illinois football coach Robert Zuppke and the director of athletics George Huff. A special section of Griffith's introductory psychology course was soon organized exclusively for athletes. In late 1921, Griffith gave what appears to have been his first public talk on psychology and athletics at a meeting of a local honorary psychology fraternity called Psi Xi (Wright, 1921; see Brown, 1923, p. 677, for basic information about Psi Xi). By early 1922, his work on athletics had already begun to attract national attention, meriting a short piece in the *New York Times*. In 1923 he offered, for the first time, a course called "Psychology and Athletics" (Griffith, 1930). The material for this course soon became the basis of Griffith's third book, *Psychology of Coaching* (Griffith, 1926).

Late in 1924, he began what is now a well-known correspondence with Notre Dame's legendary football coach Knute Rockne about the psychological side of coaching: Do you "key up" players before games, or just select those who "play the game joyously for its own sake"? (Griffith, 1924a; see also Benjamin, 1993, pp. 149–150, for published excerpts of this communication). What is less well-known is that this exchange seems to have prompted Griffith to write to college

---

[7]Two years later (Griffith, 1924), there was an article on the topic published in the *Journal of Comparative Psychology*, then edited by Bentley. There were also two review articles in the *Psychological Bulletin* (Griffith, 1929, 1932).

football coaches throughout the Midwest and Northeast,[8] asking them roughly the same questions.

In 1925, Griffith's first published article on the topic of sport appeared, titled "Psychology and Its Relation to Athletic Competition" (Griffith, 1925) that had been read by Zuppke at the previous year's meeting of the Society of Physical Education. Although the text of this work contains some lay descriptions of basic psychomotor factors that had been at the core of Griffith's research to this point, it is interesting to note that the basis of his appeal to coaches—in this instance and throughout his career—was essentially moral in character. Griffith's fundamental proposition was that

> the more mind is made use of in athletic competition, the greater will be the skill of our athletes, the finer will be the contest, the higher will be the ideals of sportsmanship displayed, the longer will our games persist in our national life, and the more truly will they lead to those rich personal and social products which we ought to expect of them. (Griffith, 1925, p. 193)

The question of the "justification" of athletics, especially in the college context, was frequently at the center of his message: "Competition does justify itself because the football field is the place where morale, spirit, courage, honor, sportsmanship, fair play, team work, and the like, are directly taught. We do not learn these things in our courses in mathematics, English, or history" (Griffith, 1925, p. 198).

This apparently all sat quite well with the university director of athletics, George Huff, who proposed the founding of an athletic research laboratory, with Griffith as the director. The plan was approved by the university Board of Trustees in September 1925, and Griffith's celebrated laboratory became a reality. What has not been reported as often is that in this same year the university constructed an enormous new athletic complex (White, 1926) of which Griffith's facilities seem to have been but a relatively small part.

Although Griffith's lab was the first in North America, it was not the first in the world. About 1 year earlier, Robert Werner Schulte founded a laboratory in Berlin for the "psycho-technical study of gymnastics, games, and sports" (Schulte, 1925, cited in Bäumler, 1997, p. 488). Even in the United States, there had been investigations into psychological aspects of sport before Griffith's, including Griffith's. There was the famous "social facilitation" study of bicyclists by Indiana psychologist Norman Triplett (1898). In Griffith's home state of Iowa, G. T. W. Patrick (1903) conducted research on psychological aspects of the football crowd.

---

[8] See, for example, Griffith (1924b). There are identical letters from the same date (just 6 days after Rockne had written his first reply to Griffith) to the coaches of Harvard, Dartmouth, Pennsylvania, Yale, Cornell, Minnesota, Princeton, Michigan, Indiana, Chicago, Iowa, Ohio State, Northwestern, Purdue, and Wisconsin.

At Johns Hopkins, Karl Lashley (1915) studied the effect of practice on archery (cited in Bäumler, 1997). Outside of the United States, especially in Italy and France, there were studies of the psychology of sport dating back to the mid-1890s. Founder of the modern Olympics Pierre de Coubertin had even used the French equivalent of the phrase "sport psychology" in the title of one of his works (1913). Nevertheless, despite the fact that it did not last for long, Griffith's setup seems to have been more elaborate and longer lasting than those of any of his predecessors.

Along with the directorship of the new laboratory, Griffith was promoted to associate professor and his appointment assigned to the College of Education, rather than to the Department of Psychology. Lists of many possible research programs for the laboratory were rapidly drawn up. They were to involve everything from studies of general health, conditioning, and sleep to habit-learning, the effects of drugs and emotional stress on athletic performance, as well as sex differences. The sports to be studied ranged across basketball, soccer, gymnastics, baseball, football, track, golf, swimming, and diving. Before the lab had published any research results, however, Griffith won a prestigious Guggenheim Fellowship to study in Germany for a year. Although he initially won the award in 1925 (Moe, 1925), he appears to have delayed taking it up for a year to get the new laboratory up and running.[9]

Griffith proposed a three-part project for his Guggenheim fellowship: (a) to study the history of German psychology, spending up to 2 weeks each at the universities of Leipzig, Bonn, Heidelberg, Munich, Berlin, and Giessen, among others; (b) to study the work of Preyer, Stern, Bühler, and Koffka on the "genetic" and "evolutionary principles" underlying animal and child psychology; and (c) to study the phenomenon of "sudden learning" in children using the methods Thorndike and Köhler had developed for animals (Griffith, ca. 1924). It is not clear how much of this proposal he completed. Thereafter he always referred to having gone to Berlin for his fellowship, not to the other cities named. Although the history of psychology had long been an interest of his, Griffith would not later publish anything substantial on the topic (apart from chapters in his textbooks). The influence of Gestalt psychology and of Lewin's field theory can be seen in some of his later work in educational psychology, but I know of no direct evidence that he met with the Gestaltists while in Berlin, nor that he published research on Köhler's "insight" with children.[10] Perhaps most interesting of all,

---

[9] Griffith was first granted a leave by the University Board of Trustees on July 28, 1925, and then again on May 15, 1926 (University of Illinois Board of Trustees, 1924–1926). Another factor in the delay may have been that his only child, Wayland Griffith, was born on June 26, 1925.

[10] It is interesting to note that Griffith (ca. 1931a) lists an article titled, "An Empirical Study of Insight" as being "in press" in the *American Journal of Psychology*. No such article appeared in that publication, nor have I found it published elsewhere.

there is no indication that he met Schulte or visited his sport laboratory while in Berlin.

Griffith returned to Illinois in 1927, but it was not until the following year that publications began to come from Griffith's typewriter (excluding Griffith, 1927). The most important of these publications was his fourth book, *Psychology and Athletics* (Griffith, 1928b), but it was not based on work in his laboratory. He had written it before the opening of the laboratory and it had been circulating in mimeographed form since about 1924. Both Macmillan, the publisher of his general textbook, and Knopf had refused to publish it, expressing doubt that there was sufficient market for such a book (Latham, 1924; Thomas, 1925). It was ultimately published by Scribner's, who had brought out Griffith's book on coaching 2 years before. The expanded revision of his general textbook appeared in 1928 as well (Griffith, 1928a), along with a minor piece on high school sports "pep" sessions (Griffith, 1928c).

The year 1928 also saw the first of eight articles Griffith would publish over the next 4 years in the *Athletic Journal.* The history of the *Athletic Journal* is worthy of some note. It was founded by a midwesterner named John L. Griffith (no apparent relation to Coleman Griffith). John Griffith was born in Illinois in 1880 and educated at Beloit College in Wisconsin, graduating in 1902. In 1908, he became a history teacher, athletic director, and football and track coach at Drake University in Des Moines, Iowa, where he earned a reputation as a promoter of intercollegiate sports. After serving in World War I, he became athletic director at the University of Illinois, Champaign, where, in 1920, he founded the *Athletic Journal,* which described itself as a "national" magazine for coaches. It was filled mainly with news of college athletic programs around the country, articles by coaches about new types of plays and strategies in a variety of sports, and John Griffith's own editorials. In June of 1922, John Griffith was appointed head of the Big Ten intercollegiate athletic conference,[11] a position he would hold until his death in 1944. He left Champaign to take up his new duties in Chicago, taking the journal with him. Although the editorship of the *Athletic Journal* seems to have fallen to a committee after 1922, John Griffith remained a prominent member of its editorial group and a regular contributor to its pages.

The two Griffiths almost certainly knew each other well, and the younger Griffith appears to have been welcomed to contribute regularly to the older Griffith's journal as the "scientist" in the midst of the coaches. None of Coleman Griffith's many contributions to the *Athletic Journal* were technical in nature. They seem, rather, to have been attempts to bring the conclusions of his research and his psychological insights into the purview of coaches, rather than reporting

---

[11] In 1922, the members of the Big Ten were Chicago, Illinois, Indiana, Iowa State, Michigan, Minnesota, Northwestern, Ohio State, Purdue, and Wisconsin. Chicago dropped out in 1946; Michigan State joined in 1949 (see http://bigten.collegesports.com/trads/big10-trads.html).

the details of the research itself. Although this is perhaps to be expected, given the journal's character, it appears that full "scientific" reports on Griffith's laboratory research were not published anywhere.

Although Griffith's total publication output in these years was prodigious, the character of his publications showed a marked change from earlier in his career. Compared with the early 1920s, Griffith's appearance in scientific journals shows a sharp decline in the late 1920s and early 1930s in favor of less academic vehicles. Even when he did publish in traditional scholarly journals, his contributions were usually literature reviews (Griffith, 1929, 1932), book reviews (e.g., Griffith, 1931c), or short technical pieces (Griffith, 1931b, 1931c; Griffith & Eddy, 1931), rather than reports of original research. It is not clear whether this change was the result of the scientific journals of the day being unwilling to publish his work on the psychology of sport or whether it reflected a conscious effort on Griffith's part to bring the results of his athletics research first to the attention of coaches, rather than to psychologists. For instance, in 1930, five two-page reports that seem to describe research conducted in the Athletics Research Laboratory appeared in the Proceedings of the IXth International Congress of Psychology (ICP),[12] but none seem to have ultimately been developed into a journal article. One short piece on athletics appeared that same year in the first volume of *Journal of Health and Physical Education.* In 1931, he made four contributions to the *American Journal of Psychology*—one a book review and the other three short notes on improvements to well-known experimental apparatuses. Apart from those already mentioned, Griffith's publication vehicles during the period 1929 through 1931 included *Proceedings of the Illinois Academy of Sciences, Biological Abstracts, Greenville College Quarterly, Phi Delta Kappan, Chicago Schools Journal,* and *Optometry Weekly.*

One of the more striking aspects of the curriculum vitae contained in Griffith's (ca. 1931a) papers is that six articles—at least three of them sport-related—are described as being "in press" in the *American Journal of Psychology,* the *Journal of Applied Psychology,*[13] the *Journal of Genetic Psychology,* and the *Journal of Experimental Psychology* but never ultimately appeared in those publications. In addition, in the same document seven books were characterized by Griffith as "contracted for and undergoing final editing for the press," whereas another six were said to be "contracted for and in active preparation." As best as I can determine, of these 13 books, no more than three—textbooks on applied psychology and educational psychology and his major work on "systematic" psychology—ever made it to publication. Four of the books listed were to have

---

[12] Held in early September 1929 at Yale University, the first ICP to be held in the United States.
[13] This article ultimately appeared in the first volume of the physical education journal entitled *Research Quarterly* (Griffith, 1930).

been on topics related to sport, including a book on football coauthored by Illinois football coach Robert Zuppke.[14] None of these ever appeared in print, however.

Although Griffith and his students seem to have been quite active—six master's theses had been completed by about 1931 and three more were in progress at this time (Griffith, ca. 1931b)—there appears to have been some serious snag along the path to founding the new subdiscipline of sport psychology. Although Griffith published two books on the topic (1926, 1928b), few of his articles appeared in traditional academic journals, and there were no new doctorates[15] to set up their own laboratories elsewhere, generate their own research, and graduate their own students. Thus, the critical mass necessary for the founding of a journal dedicated to the psychology of sport, often the sign that a subdiscipline has "arrived," did not occur until decades later and under the leadership of other individuals.

TEXTBOOK WRITER AND ADMINISTRATOR

In 1932, Griffith's athletic research laboratory was closed by the University of Illinois. There have been two explanations: One is that, with the onset of the Depression, shrinking revenues forced the university to cut back, and Griffith's laboratory was simply one of the victims (Seidler, 1948, cited in Kroll & Lewis, 1970/1978). The other story is that his research program had lost the confidence of Coach Zuppke (Kroll, 1971, cited in Gould & Pick, 1995). Whatever the reason, essentially in exchange for his laboratory, Griffith was given an administrative post as the director of the Bureau of Institutional Research at the university, a body that collected and analyzed statistics on things such as teacher–student ratios and teaching load, and then reported to the university president. Although he seems to have taken to his new duties zealously, he continued to find the time to publish four more books over a 9-year period: *An Introduction to Applied Psychology* (1934), *An Introduction to Educational Psychology* (1935), *Psychology Applied to Teaching and Learning* (1939), and *Principles of Systematic Psychology* (1943). Over the course of these four books—nearly 2,700 published pages—one can see Griffith's interest in the details of sport psychology waning and his interest growing, first, in general educational psychology and, finally, in broad theoretical questions about the foundations of psychology as a science. Although he was always careful to accept the behaviorist methodological impera-

---

[14] Fragments of many of these works, some several hundred pages of typescript in length, are contained in Coleman Roberts Griffith Papers at the University of Illinois Archives, Boxes 13 to 17 and 19.

[15] At least one of Griffith's students completed a doctorate: Stephen Maxwell Corey had a successful academic career, but he specialized in educational psychology rather than in the psychology of sport.

tives of his era, he was wary of "radical" behaviorists (by which term he meant primarily Watson and his followers; this was largely prior to the emergence of Skinner as a major force in the field), and he appreciated the contributions of Woodworth's "dynamic" psychology, what he called the "configurational" psychologies (Gestalt, Lewin's "field theory"), and especially the "genetic" approach to psychology (i.e., developmental). His magnum opus, *Principles of Systematic Psychology,* constituted an attempt to synthesize what Griffith termed "patterns and points of reference" among seven different schools of psychology into a common system that would be agreeable to everyone.

> With respect to a wide range of data, postulates, and conclusions, an orderly pattern of basic points of reference can and must be found which will adequately define the domain of psychological science, identify its indigenous types of data, lay bare the express or implied assumptions about the domain, designate the methods to be used, and illuminate the various ways in which resulting facts and generalizations are dynamically related to one another in their role as parts of an organic unity. (Griffith, 1943, p. 9)

The book was an enormous undertaking. E. G. Boring, to whom Griffith sent a copy, showed it to some colleagues who declared it to be "Psychology's largest book" (Boring, 1943).

One last opportunity to return to applied sports psychology appeared when Philip K. Wrigley, owner of the Chicago Cubs baseball club, contacted Griffith about working with the Cubs through the 1938 season. Griffith did so, hiring an assistant and setting up a laboratory at Wrigley's expense, traveling to their spring training camp on Santa Catalina Island, California, to test and train players, and then returning to Illinois for the regular season, where he continued to monitor their progress from Urbana–Champaign via his assistant. The team did well in 1938, making it to the World Series. He continued on with the Cubs in a somewhat reduced capacity in 1939 and 1940. There was, however, a great deal of resistance from the team's managers to cooperate with Griffith or to implement his recommendations. The project—probably the first in which a professional psychologist worked with a professional sports team for an extended period of time—ended in frustration (see Green, 2003).

In 1944, Griffith accepted the office of provost (the chief academic officer) for the University of Illinois. With that, administrative duties came to consume his entire professional existence. To his former mentor, Bentley, he wrote, "I mourn the complete cessation of psychological studies. . . . Scarcely have I read a thing since last fall when the provosting began" (Griffith, 1945a). Of his research on sport, he soon wrote of himself only that "for a short period he [Griffith] carried on special studies in the psychology of athletics" (Griffith, ca. 1945). Griffith also soon became frustrated with the conservative university administration of which he had become a senior member (Griffith, 1945b), which seemed opposed to any modernizing of the school's curriculum or methods.

Matters changed dramatically, however, the day in 1946 that George D. Stoddard (1897–1981) was appointed president of the university. Stoddard was a liberal-minded educator of high reputation who had served for many years as director of the Iowa Child Welfare Research Station. Griffith must have seen Stoddard as a kindred spirit. In 1949, he wrote to a friend that "the more I hear Stoddard, read his letters and take note of his speeches, the more I am convinced that, in educational and social philosophy, we are dealing with a great man" (Griffith, 1949). Griffith became Stoddard's right-hand man, frequently being asked to reply to general inquiries addressed to the president and occasionally making appearances or giving speeches in Stoddard's stead.

Although exciting, the Stoddard era at Illinois was not a harmonious one. There were major controversies over new appointments in the School of Music and in the College of Commerce (see Solberg & Tomlinson, 1997). Stoddard's educational innovations often did not sit well with the old faculty members, and he often was not inclined to accommodate those who did not fit well into his new order. Stoddard frequently feuded with Chicago Republicans who did not approve of his ideas or his methods. Finally there was a public flap over research being conducted on a putative cancer treatment, krebiozen, which turned out to be quackery. The promoter of the substance was a university vice president who was supported by the Board of Trustees. Stoddard, frustrated with the Board's apparent blindness to the effect the controversy was having on the school's reputation, simply eliminated the man's administrative position. In response, some members of the Board called a snap meeting in July 1953 and approved motions of nonconfidence in both Stoddard and Griffith. Both men immediately resigned. It is often said that the krebiozen affair was the "cause" of Stoddard's and Griffith's downfall, but newspaper articles of the time suggest that Stoddard's days had been numbered from the moment that Republicans had taken control of the Board of Trustees nearly 3 years earlier (see Cleveland, 1950). What is surprising is not that Stoddard was forced to resign but that he hung on for as long as he did. Griffith had, by then, become so closely identified with the Stoddard regime that he was bound to be targeted as well.

After his resignation as provost, Griffith returned to the College of Education at the University of Illinois, continuing to serve as a regular professor until his retirement in 1961. Griffith continued to work after his retirement from Illinois, taking on a position in the Oregon State System of Higher Education the following year. He passed away in 1966, just 4 years before Kroll and Lewis (1970/1978) declared him to be the "father" of the "new" field of sport psychology.

CONCLUSION

Griffith's life teaches us some things about the nature of history in general. Had it not been for the rise of sport psychology in the 1970s, Griffith would not now be considered a significant "pioneer" of psychology, even though his career would have unfolded in exactly the same way. Only later events, over which he had no control, made him and his work on sport historically salient. Consider, for instance, that his research on the vestibular system does not appear to qualify him for historical standing even though it is the topic on which he published most of his academic papers and in which he established his scientific reputation. Looking at the matter from the other chronological end, so to speak, as new disciplines emerge, their founders often look for past "precedents"—even ones that are historically unconnected to their own work but for a similarity of topic— to build a case for the new discipline's importance on a kind of historical legitimacy. Kroll and Lewis (1978) and the other modern sport psychologists did not cite Griffith's work simply as a matter of courtesy to an earlier researcher in the same area. The references to Griffith were intended to establish the credibility of sport psychology by demonstrating that the topic, despite seeming new (and, thus, possibly ephemeral), was in fact part of a venerable tradition with which one must come to terms. One sees this sort of "boundary work"—delimiting the edges of a discipline's intellectual "property"—in many fields. Only rarely can it be seen as it happens.

REFERENCES

Bäumler, G. (1997). Sports psychology. In W. G. Bringmann, H. E. Lück, R. Miller, & C. E. Early (Eds.), *A pictorial history of psychology* (pp. 485–489). Carol Stream, IL: Quintessence.

Benjamin, L. T. (1993). *A history of psychology in letters.* Boston: McGraw-Hill.

Benjamin, L. T., & Baker, D. B. (2004). *From séance to science: A history of the profession of psychology in America.* Belmont, CA: Thompson-Wadsworth.

Boring, E. G. (1929). *A history of experimental psychology.* New York: Appleton-Century.

Boring, E. G. (1943, August 10). Letter to C. R. Griffith. Coleman R. Griffith Papers, Box 1, Griffith, C. R. (Personal) 1942–1947, University of Illinois Archives, Urbana.

Brown, J. T. (1923). *Baird's manual of American college fraternities.* New York: James T. Brown.

Cattell, J. M. (1922, October 30). Letter to C. R. Griffith. Coleman R. Griffith Papers, Box 1, General Correspondence, 1922–1924, C–F, University of Illinois Archives, Urbana.

Cleveland, C. B. (1950, November 29). Next few months to decide Stoddard's future at U. of I. *Chicago Daily News.*

de Coubertin, P. (1913). *Essais de psychologie sportive* [Essays on sport psychology]. Paris: Payot.

Detlefsen, J. A. (1923). Are the effects of long-continued rotation in rats inherited? *Proceedings of the American Philosophical Society, 62,* 292–300.

Detlefsen, J. A. (1925). The inheritance of acquired characters. *Physiological Reviews, 5,* 224–278.

Garvey, C. R. (1929). List of American psychology laboratories. *Psychological Bulletin, 26,* 652–660.

Gould, D., & Pick, S. (1995). Sport psychology: The Griffith era, 1920–1940. *Sport Psychologist, 9,* 391–405.

Green, C. D. (2003). Psychology strikes out: Coleman Griffith and the Chicago Cubs. *History of Psychology, 6,* 267–283

Griffith, C. R. (1919). A possible case of instinctive behavior in the white rat. *Science, 50,* 166–167.

Griffith, C. R. (1921). Some neglected aspects of a history of psychology. *Psychological Monographs, 30*, 17–29.

Griffith, C. R. (1922a). Are disturbances of equilibration inherited? *Science, 56*, 676–678.

Griffith, C. R. (1922b). Contributions to the history of psychology, 1916–1921. *Psychological Bulletin, 19*, 411–428.

Griffith, C. R. (1922c). *An historical survey of vestibular equilibration*. Urbana: University of Illinois Press.

Griffith, C. R. (1922d, February 14). Letter to Science Service. Coleman R. Griffith Papers, Box 1, General Correspondence, 1921–1922, L–Z, University of Illinois Archives, Urbana.

Griffith, C. R. (1922e, March 1). Letter to Watson Davis. Coleman R. Griffith Papers, Box 1, General Correspondence, 1921–1922, A–K, University of Illinois Archives, Urbana.

Griffith, C. R. (1922f, March 29). Letter to H. E. Beane. Coleman R. Griffith Papers, Box 1, General Correspondence 1921–1922, A–K, University of Illinois Archives, Urbana.

Griffith, C. R. (1922g, March 30). Letter to A. H. Alisky. Coleman R. Griffith Papers, Box 1, General Correspondence 1921–1922, A–K, University of Illinois Archives, Urbana.

Griffith, C. R. (1922h, October 16). Letter to J. A. Detlefsen. Coleman R. Griffith Papers, Box 1, General Correspondence, 1922–1924, C–F, University of Illinois Archives, Urbana, IL.

Griffith, C. R. (1922i, December 22). Letter to Edwards Brothers. Coleman R. Griffith Papers, Box 1, General Correspondence, 1922–1924, C–F, University of Illinois Archives, Urbana.

Griffith, C. R. (1923a). *General introduction to psychology*. New York: Macmillan.

Griffith, C. R. (1923b, January 2). Letter to Irving Hardesty. Coleman R. Griffith Papers, Box 1, General Correspondence, 1922–1924, G–J, University of Illinois Archives, Urbana.

Griffith, C. R. (1923c, April 4). Letter to G. F. Paul. Coleman R. Griffith Papers, Box 1, General Correspondence, 1922–1924, N–R, University of Illinois Archives, Urbana.

Griffith, C. R. (1924a, December 9). Letter to K. Rockne. Coleman R. Griffith Papers, Box 1, General Correspondence, 1924–1925, J–Z, University of Illinois Archives, Urbana.

Griffith, C. R. (1924b, December 19). Letter to J. Hawley. Coleman Roberts Griffith Papers, Box 1, General Correspondence, 1924–1925, A–I, University of Illinois Archives, Urbana.

Griffith, C. R. (1924c). A note on the persistence of the practice-effect in rotation experiments. *Journal of Comparative Psychology, 4*, 137–150.

Griffith, C. R. (ca. 1924). "I hereby make the following proposals. . . ." Coleman Roberts Griffith Papers, Box 1, General Correspondence, 1924–1925, A–I, University of Illinois Archives, Urbana.

Griffith, C. R. (1925). Psychology and its relation to athletic competition. *American Physical Education Review, 30*, 193–199.

Griffith, C. R. (1926). *Psychology of coaching: A study of coaching methods from the point of view of psychology*. New York: Scribner's.

Griffith, C. R. (1927). Mental hygiene in everyday life. *Electric Journal, 24*, 100–107.

Griffith, C. R. (1928a). *General introduction to psychology* (Rev. ed.). New York: Macmillan.

Griffith, C. R. (1928b). *Psychology and athletics: A general survey for athletes and coaches*. New York: Scribner's.

Griffith, C. R. (1928c). The psychology of "pep" sessions. *High School Teacher, 4*, 366–367.

Griffith, C. R. (1929). Vestibular sensations and the mechanisms of balance. *Psychological Bulletin, 26*, 549–565.

Griffith, C. R. (1930). A laboratory for research in athletics. *Research Quarterly, 1*, 34–40.

Griffith, C. R. (1931a). A flexible form of the Carr slot maze. *American Journal of Psychology, 43*, 283–285.

Griffith, C. R. (1931b). A new method for administering shock in animal experimentation. *American Journal of Psychology, 43*, 286–287.

Griffith, C. R. (1931c). Review of Bretagnier, L. *L'activité psychique chez les animaux: Instinct et intelligence* [Psychological activity in animals: Instinct and intelligence]. *American Journal of Psychology, 43*, 422–424.

Griffith, C. R. (ca. 1931a). Curriculum vitae. Coleman R. Griffith Papers, Box 3, Experimental Charts, etc. 1931–1933, University of Illinois Archives, Urbana.

Griffith, C. R. (ca. 1931b). The Laboratories for Research in Athletics. Coleman R. Griffith Papers, Box 3, Experimental Charts, etc., 1931–1933, University of Illinois Archives, Urbana.

Griffith, C. R. (1932). The perceptions and mechanisms of vestibular equilibration. *Psychological Bulletin, 29,* 279–303.

Griffith, C. R. (1934). *An introduction to applied psychology.* New York: Macmillan.

Griffith, C. R. (1935). *An introduction to educational psychology.* New York: Farrar & Reinhart.

Griffith, C. R. (1939). *Psychology applied to teaching and learning: A first book in the field of educational psychology.* New York: Farrar & Rinehart.

Griffith, C. R. (1943). *Principles of systematic psychology.* Champaign: University of Illinois Press.

Griffith, C. R. (1945a, March 21). Letter to M. Bentley. Coleman R. Griffith Papers, Box 1, Griffith, C. R. (Personal) 1942–1947, University of Illinois Archives, Urbana.

Griffith, C. R. (1945b, July 5). Letter to Kenneth Williamson. Coleman R. Griffith Papers, Box 1, Griffith, C. R. (Personal) 1942–1947, University of Illinois Archives, Urbana.

Griffith, C. R. (ca. 1945). A biographical blurb for a book entitled: Coleman R. Griffith. Coleman R. Griffith Papers, Box 1 (CRG Personal), 1945–1950. University of Illinois Archives, Urbana.

Griffith, C. R. (1949, October 12). Letter to Tony (no further name given). Coleman R. Griffith Papers, Box 1 (CRG Personal), 1945–1950. University of Illinois Archives, Urbana, IL.

Griffith, C. R., & Eddy, J. R. D. (1931). An improvement in the Seashore serial discriminator. *American Journal of Psychology, 43,* 435–437.

Kroll, W. (1971). *Perspectives in physical education.* New York: Academic Press.

Kroll, W., & Lewis, G. (1978). America's first sport psychologist. In W. F. Straub (Ed.), *Sport psychology: An analysis of athlete behavior* (pp. 16–19). Ithaca, NY: Mouvement. (Original work published 1970)

Lashley, K. S. (1915). The acquisition of skill in archery. *Papers from the Department of Marine Biology of the Carnegie Institution of Washington, 7,* 105–128.

Latham, H. S. (1924, September 2). Letter to C. R. Griffith. Coleman Roberts Griffith Papers, Box 1, General Correspondence, 1924–1925, J–Z, University of Illinois Archives, Urbana.

LeUnes, A. (2000). Griffith, Coleman Roberts. In A. E. Kazdin (Ed.), *Encyclopedia of psychology* (Vol. 4, pp. 14–15). Washington, DC: American Psychological Association.

Moe, H. A. (1925, June 4). Letter to C. R. Griffith. Coleman R. Griffith Papers, Box 1, General Correspondence, 1924–1925, A–I, University of Illinois Archives, Urbana.

Murphy, G. (1929). *Historical introduction to modern psychology.* New York: Harcourt, Brace.

Patrick, G. T. W. (1903). The psychology of football. *American Journal of Psychology, 14,* 368–381.

Pillsbury, W. B. (1929). *The history of psychology.* New York: Norton.

Schulte, R. W. (1925). *Eignungs- und Leistungssteigerung im Sport* [Enhancement of ability and achievement in sport]. Berlin, Germany: Hackebeil.

Seidler, A. H. (1948). *A history of the professional training in physical education for men at the University of Illinois.* Unpublished master's thesis, University of Illinois, Urbana-Champaign.

Singer, R. N. (1989). Applied sport psychology in the United States. *Journal of Applied Sport Psychology, 1,* 61–80.

Solberg, W. U., & Tomlinson, R. W. (1997). Academic McCarthyism and Keynesian economics: The Bowen controversy at the University of Illinois. *History of Political Economy, 29,* 55–81.

Swoap, R. A. (1999). A history of Division 47: Exercise and sport psychology. In D. A. Dewsbury (Ed.), *Unification through division: Histories of the divisions of the American Psychological Association* (Vol. 4, pp. 151–173). Washington, DC: American Psychological Association.

Thomas, P. B. (1925, January 31). Letter to C. R. Griffith. Coleman Roberts Griffith Papers, Box 1, General Correspondence, 1924–1925, J–Z, University of Illinois Archives, Urbana.

Triplett, N. (1898). The dynamogenic factors in pacemaking and competition. *American Journal of Psychology, 9,* 507–533.

University of Illinois Board of Trustees. (1924–1926). *Twenty-third report.* Urbana, IL: Author.

White, J. M. (1926). The new gymnasium at Illinois. *Athletic Journal, 6*(9), 11–13.

Wright, J. F. (1921, December 12). Letter to C. R. Griffith. Coleman Roberts Griffith Papers, Box 1, General Correspondence, 1921–1922, L–Z, University of Illinois Archives, Urbana.

Zusne, L. (1984). *Biographical dictionary of psychology.* Westport, CT: Greenwood.

Henry A. Murray (Photos courtesy of the
Harvard University Archives)

Chapter 11

Henry A. Murray: Personology as Biography, Science, and Art

Nicole B. Barenbaum

In the fall of 1926, Henry A. Murray began work as assistant to the director of the Harvard Psychological Clinic, a newly founded branch of the Department of Philosophy and Psychology at Harvard University dedicated to the study of abnormal and dynamic psychology. Although not an unusual subfield of academic psychology today, abnormal psychology at that time was still considered a medical specialty. Indeed, according to prominent Boston psychopathologist Morton Prince, the first director of the Clinic, Harvard was "the pioneer American University to introduce this field of research and instruction into its curriculum" (Editorial, 1926, p. 3). Prince had arranged an endowment to establish a chair of abnormal and dynamic psychology and a small clinic as "a part of the general psychological department" (p. 1). President A. Lawrence Lowell of Harvard had appointed Prince to the new chair and established the Clinic without consulting the department faculty, who viewed the enterprise with some skepticism (Triplet, 1983).

The mission of the Clinic was threefold: (a) to offer instruction in psychopathology, (b) to conduct scientific research, and (c) to investigate and treat selected cases of psychopathology (Murray, 1929). For Murray, who succeeded Prince as director in 1928, these aims were part of a larger purpose—"to achieve a deeper insight into human nature" (1935/1957, p. 16). This purpose, in Murray's view, was central to psychology, which he had originally identified with the "depth psychology" (1940, p. 153) of Sigmund Freud, Carl Jung, and other specialists in psychopathology. But as I shall explain, Murray's encounter with academic psychology constituted a rude awakening.

Trained in medicine and in biochemistry, Murray had only a brief acquaintance with academic psychology before 1926. As an undergraduate at Harvard between 1911 and 1915, he attended two introductory lectures by Hugo Münsterberg, an experience he later recalled as having nipped in the bud his interest in psychology and sent him "looking for the nearest exit" (1940, p. 152). But in the early 1920s, Murray began to explore the ideas of Freud and Jung and became fascinated with the unconscious. After meeting Jung in Zurich in 1925, he embarked on a career as a depth psychologist without fully realizing the gulf that separated psychoanalysis from academic psychology. To his dismay, he discovered not only that academic psychologists were more preoccupied with questions of perception, consciousness, and animal behavior than with unconscious motives but also that most of them took a dim view of psychodynamic approaches.

Murray's criticisms of academic psychology, soon to become more explicit, were foreshadowed in an article he wrote for the Harvard newspaper the *Crimson* in 1929. Noting that the Clinic had been "sloughed out of Emerson Hall and quartered upon the most remote plot of land owned by the University," he described the new quarters at 19 Beaver Street as "a livable house with no mammoth marble columns to remind us of the Roman Parthenon or the First National Bank, and no reinforced concrete to establish in our minds conceptual images of ourselves as factory workers" (p. 4). Murray's disparaging description of academic buildings—perhaps a veiled reference to the brick columns and the style of Emerson Hall, home of academic psychology at Harvard—suggested his distaste for approaches he considered outdated and mechanistic and his preference for psychoanalytic approaches based on "close contact with reality" (p. 4).

Defining psychology as "the science which describes people and explains why they perceive, feel, think, and act as they do," Murray complained that "no science of the kind exists" (1935/1981, p. 338). He poked fun at the proliferation of work in academic psychology on such problems as "the bodily turn of the white rat in a straight alley" and "the theory of happiness as bright pressure in the epigastrium," concluding, "From all this web of activity, consideration of man as a human being has somehow escaped" (p. 339). In the following much-quoted passage, he wrote,

> The truth which the informed are hesitant to reveal and the uninformed are amazed to discover is that academic psychology has contributed practically nothing to the knowledge of human nature. It has not only failed to bring light to the great, hauntingly recurrent problems, but it has no intention, one is shocked to realize, of attempting to investigate them. Indeed—and this is the cream of a wry jest— an unconcerned detachment from the natural history of ordinary mortals has become a source of pride to many psychologists. (p. 339)

Even psychologists who were interested in personality had missed their mark, Murray suggested. "Armed with questionnaires, rating scales, pop-guns, mazes, peg-boards and numberless other mechanical contraptions, the testers have borne down on their subjects—so heavily, in fact, that the souls of their subjects have been forced to shelter" (p. 341).

In Murray's view, medical psychologists and psychoanalysts had achieved a greater understanding of human nature and of "the lives of individual persons ... chiefly because they have been patient enough to listen every day over periods of months or of years to persons talking about themselves" (1935/1981, pp. 341–342). But he thought these practitioners, untrained in "the fundamental sciences," held biased theories that resembled "myths or metaphysical doctrines rather than authentic scientific formulations" (p. 343). What was needed, Murray argued, was an approach that combined the scientific methods of academic psychology with a focus on the important problems of medical psychology. By the early 1930s, he had begun to implement such an approach, collaborating with an interdisciplinary team of researchers on a project that would culminate in the pioneering volume *Explorations in Personality* (Murray, 1938a). Murray adopted the term "personology," coined by Jan Christiaan Smuts (1926, p. 262; see Rosenzweig, 1985) to refer to the study of personality, for "the branch of psychology which principally concerns itself with the study of human lives and the factors that influence their course, [and] which investigates individual differences and types of personality" (Murray, 1938a, p. 4).

With the Clinic researchers, Murray strove to administer a standard set of procedures and to develop a comprehensive system of theoretical concepts, analogous to the classification schemes of chemistry or anatomy, for the description and interpretation of personalities. Thus his approach was self-consciously scientific. However, he drew inspiration from concepts in psychoanalysis and psychopathology, focusing on "the search for covert springs of fantasy and action" (1938a, p. xii). Unlike mainstream academic psychologists who conducted group studies using psychometric tests, he proposed that in personology "the objects of study are individual organisms, not aggregates of organisms" (p. 38). He insisted, "The life cycle of a single individual should be taken as a unit, the *long unit* for psychology. . . . The history of the organism *is* the organism. This proposition calls for biographical studies" (p. 39; emphasis in original).

As these remarks suggest, Murray's theory and his methods of investigating personality reflected the influence of several fields of study, beginning with history and biography, his "earliest avenue of approach to psychology" (1967b, p. 287). "My principal interests centre around psychology, biological and medical science and literature," he noted in 1925 (quoted in Robinson, 1992, p. 89). This unusual combination of interests persisted throughout his career. Beginning with a brief biographical sketch, this chapter examines Murray's major psychological contributions, with particular attention to interdisciplinary influences on his work. I conclude with examples of Murray's case studies and biographical works that illustrate his interdisciplinary approach to the study of individual lives. The final case study, Murray's (1967b) autobiographical "Case of

Murr," exhibits his recognition that scientific theories reflect the personalities of their creators.

BIOGRAPHY

Murray was born in New York City on May 13, 1893. The second child and firstborn son of wealthy parents, Murray later described his childhood as that of "an average, privileged American boy" (1967b, p. 298). He enjoyed outdoor activities and adventure stories and traveled to Europe with his family; his heroes were primarily explorers and pioneers. Murray explained these interests in part as efforts to counteract a "marrow of misery and melancholy" (p. 300) stemming from his painful relationship with his mother. Believing that she favored his older sister and his younger brother, he cultivated a sense of "emotional self-sufficiency" and "venturesome autonomy" (p. 299). Murray also struggled to overcome a stutter and had poor hand–eye coordination resulting from a visual defect. To these early experiences he attributed his "affinity for the darker, blinder strata of feeling" (p. 300) and his sympathy with the sufferings of others, sources of his interests in medicine and in psychology. Murray's privileged background contributed to his unusual career trajectory. He attended exclusive private grammar and high schools, and in 1911 entered Harvard College, where, according to his own report, he was a mediocre student who "majored in the three Rs— Rum, Rowing, and Romanticism" (Robinson, 1992, p. 27). He had rooms in "the most desirable of the 'Gold Coast' dormitories" (p. 29) and served in his senior year as captain of the Harvard crew team. He concentrated in history, graduating in 1915 to pursue a medical degree at the Columbia College of Physicians and Surgeons. In 1916, Murray married Josephine Rantoul, the daughter of a prominent Boston family; the marriage lasted until her death in 1962. The Murrays' daughter Josephine was born in 1921.

Experiencing an intellectual awakening during medical school, Murray supplemented a rigorous schedule of study with hours of reading and discussion of literature, philosophy, and politics (Robinson, 1992). He graduated at the top of his class in 1919, earned a master's degree in biology at Columbia University in 1920, and spent a semester at Harvard working with the eminent biochemist and physiologist Lawrence J. Henderson, whose research examined the interrelations of the components of blood (see Henderson, 1928). In 1922, Murray completed a surgical internship at Presbyterian Hospital in New York and accepted a fellowship at the Rockefeller Institute for Medical Research, where he studied biochemical and metabolic changes in chicken embryos.

Murray described a "profound affectional upheaval," beginning in 1923, that "swept [him] into the unruly domain of psychology" (1967b, p. 290). Abandoning the conservative religious and political values he had absorbed as a child, he began to explore the world of the emotions and the unconscious through art, literature, and the psychodynamic theories of Freud and Jung. Among the colleagues and friends with whom he shared these discoveries, a primary figure was Christiana Morgan, who first sparked his interest in Jung in 1923. Murray was drawn to Morgan, who shared his passionate interests in Romantic literature and in exploring the unconscious, but he also had a strong attachment to his wife Jo, with whom he shared an affectionate marriage and a comfortable family life. In 1924, while sailing to Europe to pursue a doctorate in biochemistry at Cambridge University, Murray read *Moby-Dick*. He became fascinated with Herman Melville, in whose works he saw precursors of psychoanalytic insights and expressions of personal and romantic conflicts very similar to his own; he soon began work on a biographical study of Melville (Douglas, 1993; Robinson, 1992).

In the spring of 1925, Murray spent 3 weeks in Zurich with Jung (Robinson, 1992). To his "astonishment," he "*experienced* the unconscious," and he found solutions to "a score of bi-horned problems" (Murray, 1940, p. 153; emphasis in original), not the least of which was the conflict between his marriage and his growing love for Morgan. Murray learned that Jung had resolved a similar dilemma; with his wife's consent, he maintained a relationship with another woman, Toni Wolff, whom he saw as his guide to the unconscious. Although Jung warned that it would be difficult, Murray adopted Jung's solution. With Jo's reluctant consent, he and Morgan soon became partners in a turbulent personal and professional relationship that lasted until Morgan's death in 1967 (Robinson, 1992). Having "emerged a reborn man" (1967b, p. 287) from his encounter with Jung, Murray decided to become a depth psychologist. In 1926, he completed the work for his doctorate in biochemistry at the Rockefeller Institute and accepted the position of research fellow at the Harvard Psychological Clinic. Morgan subsequently joined the Clinic staff as a volunteer (Robinson, 1992).

After replacing Prince as director in 1928, Murray shifted the primary emphasis of teaching and research at the Clinic from medical psychopathology to psychoanalysis (Triplet, 1983). He sought psychoanalytic training and became a founding member of the Boston Psychoanalytic Society (Robinson, 1992). In the early 1930s, he assembled an interdisciplinary group of researchers who became collaborators in an intensive study of 51 young men (see the discussion of the *Explorations* project later in the chapter), combining techniques developed by psychoanalysts and by academic psychologists.

We might say that our work is the natural child of the deep, significant, metaphorical, provocative and questionable speculations of psycho-analysis and the precise, systematic, statistical, trivial and artificial methods of academic personology. Our hope is that we have inherited more of the virtues than the vices of our parents. (Murray, 1938a, pp. 33–34)

A charismatic leader, Murray established a stimulating atmosphere at the Clinic. He furnished the new quarters, a two-story house at 64 Plympton Street, with antiques and artwork and supplied two Clinic libraries with works of psychology, fiction, and biography (Robinson, 1992; Sanford, 1980). He invited public figures, writers, and scholars from many disciplines, many of whom were his friends, to frequent luncheons at the Clinic, which became occasions for lively intellectual exchange.

Like his research, Murray's teaching emphasized insights from depth psychology and focused on the whole person. Soon after he replaced Prince, his course in abnormal psychology became one of the most popular psychology courses offered by the Department of Philosophy and Psychology (Triplet, 1983). Murray's attempt to persuade his colleagues to expand the focus of the introductory psychology course was not so successful. Despite his suggestion that an elementary course presenting "a dynamic concept" of "the mind as a whole" should precede "the special psychologies of sensation, perception, affection, conation, cognition, etc." (Murray, 1930), the course remained unchanged for several years. Apparently, undergraduate students agreed with Murray. Especially critical of the introductory course, they considered psychology "over-technical and quite beyond the attainments of most beginners" (Students lecture teachers, 1936). The 1936 *Crimson Confidential Guide to Freshman Courses and Fields of Concentration* praised Murray's courses and those of his fellow personality psychologist Gordon Allport but characterized other department members as "narrowly specialized psycho-physicists 'still following the subject-matter of the 19th century'" (Robinson, 1992, p. 173).

The popularity of Murray's courses raised suspicions among members of the Harvard administration, who equated popularity with lack of rigor (Triplet, 1983). Moreover, Murray's psychoanalytic orientation, his lack of training in academic psychology, and his upper-class lifestyle and disregard of official procedures created controversy, and his caustic remarks regarding their field (e.g., Murray, 1935/1981) offended mainstream academic psychologists. E. G. Boring, chair of the Department of Psychology, who favored a rigorously scientific approach, opposed Murray's bid for tenure in 1936 (Robinson, 1992). During the protracted deliberations over his case, Murray's colleagues took opposite sides, with neuropsychologist Karl Lashley threatening to resign if tenure was granted and personality psychologist Allport supporting Murray.[1] Eventually Murray was

---

[1] Although some sources state that Allport threatened to resign if Murray's tenure was not approved (e.g., Robinson, 1992), Allport's correspondence with E. G. Boring does not support such a claim. Concerned that a negative decision might suggest that his own work was no longer welcome at Harvard, Allport did consider a job offer from Clark University at the time of the deliberations over Murray's tenure case. However, after learning that the value of his own work was not in question, Allport rejected the offer from Clark before the deliberations concluded (Allport, 1937).

promoted without tenure, his continuing appointment supported by grants from
the Rockefeller Foundation (Triplet, 1983). Murray was finally granted tenure
in 1948.

From 1937 until his retirement from Harvard, Murray continued to occupy
a somewhat marginal position in relation to the Department of Psychology
(Robinson, 1992). He took frequent leaves of absence, including several years
during World War II. From 1943 to 1948 he directed an assessment service for
the U.S. Office of Strategic Services (OSS), forerunner of the Central Intelligence
Agency (CIA). Murray was one of several faculty members involved in the
creation of the Harvard Department of Social Relations. Consisting of faculty
drawn from the Departments of Anthropology, Sociology, and Psychology, this
interdisciplinary unit remained active from 1946 to 1972. Murray (1941–1965)
conducted several studies modeled on the *Explorations* project, but these involved
fewer research participants and did not result in major published works.

Murray continued to revise and expand his theoretical system throughout his
career (e.g., 1959, 1968). After World War II, he turned toward such broad
cultural issues as religious values and mythology (e.g., 1960). Murray also became
known for his research on Melville. Although he did not complete the biography
that occupied him for many years, he published several psychobiographical
interpretations and helped to revive interest in Melville's writings (Murray, 1949,
1951, 1966, 1967a; see Robinson, 1992). Murray retired from Harvard in 1962.
He married psychologist Caroline Chandler Fish in 1969. He suffered a number
of strokes and other health problems during his later years, but remained creative
and intellectually engaged. He died in Cambridge, Massachusetts, on June 23,
1988 (Robinson, 1992).

Murray's colleagues and friends characterized him as charismatic, charming,
and witty, and as a Renaissance man whose many fields of interest informed his
imaginative and creative constructions of human personality (Robinson, 1992).
His mischievous sense of humor was evident not only in his outspoken attacks
on mainstream academic psychology (e.g., 1935/1981) but also in his autobiographical accounts (1940, 1959, 1967b). His complex view of personality reflected
clearly his own multiple lives.

> A personality is a full Congress of orators and pressure-groups, of children, dema-
> gogues, communists, isolationists, war-mongers, mugwumps, grafters, log-rollers,
> lobbyists, Caesars and Christs, Machiavels and Judases, Tories and Promethean
> revolutionists. And a psychologist who does not know this in himself, whose mind
> is locked against the flux of images and feelings, should be encouraged to make
> friends . . . with the various members of his household. (1940, pp. 160–161)

For biographical works on Murray, see Anderson (1990), Elms (1987), and
Robinson (1992).

MURRAY'S MAJOR PSYCHOLOGICAL CONTRIBUTIONS

Murray is best known for his contributions to the landmark *Explorations in Personality* (1938a) and the Thematic Apperception Test, for the catalog of variables and the "multiform method" of assessment that emerged from the *Explorations* project, and for promoting intensive studies of individual lives. Each of these contributions reflected his interests in literature and biography and his interdisciplinary training in history, medicine, biochemistry, and psychology.

The *Explorations* Project

At the Harvard Psychological Clinic, Murray assembled an interdisciplinary group of more than two dozen researchers; among these were Erik Homburger (later known as Erik Erikson), Donald MacKinnon, Saul Rosenzweig, Nevitt Sanford, and Robert White, all of whom went on to pursue distinguished careers as personality psychologists. Although they shared an interest in unconscious or covert psychological processes, the researchers initially worked separately, with each investigator focusing on a different aspect of personality. Their studies were generally designed "to compare the responses of a group of subjects in two contrasting situations" (Murray, 1938a, p. viii). However, Murray and his colleagues soon found the results of these studies unsatisfactory. Group averages left unexplained not only "minority" (uncommon) responses, but also participants' individual reasons for giving the "majority" response; thus they failed "to reveal the complex interaction of forces which determines each concrete event" (p. viii). Drawing on his training in medicine, Murray suggested that the researchers study the same group of "subjects" using multiple methods. The participants were 51 men of college age; 12 were unemployed and 39 were Harvard students who had applied for work at the Employment Office (p. xi). Each man was interviewed and tested over a period of several weeks in multiple sessions conducted by different researchers. "The purpose of the entire procedure," Murray explained, "was to place at the disposal of each experimenter a wealth of information about his subjects and thus to assist him in interpreting his results and arriving at generally valid psychological laws" (p. ix). Like medical specialists conferring on a case (Murray, 1959; see also Triplet, 1983), the researchers held a meeting on each participant to share the results of their specific procedures, compare tentative personality diagnoses, and hear a "biographer" present a "portrait" based on the case material (Murray, 1938a, p. 604). After a general discussion, a five-member Diagnostic Council of experienced investigators voted on final ratings for the individual on all personality variables.

"Variables of Personality"

One influential outcome of the *Explorations* project was Murray's catalog of "variables of personality" (the title of chap. 3 of *Explorations in Personality*), presented in an effort to create a common conceptual scheme for personologists. According to historian Kurt Danziger (1997), the number of references in the psychological literature to "variables of personality" increased greatly following the publication of *Explorations in Personality* (Murray, 1938a). Murray's list of psychological "needs" (including the need for achievement and the need for affiliation) forms the basis of several widely used personality questionnaires (Barenbaum & Winter, 2003).

Murray's efforts to define a comprehensive system of variables reflected a recognition, grounded in his training in medicine and in biochemistry and influenced by Henderson's organismic approach, that like physical bodies and blood, personality is composed of multiple interacting elements (Triplet, 1983). Anticipating contemporary biopsychosocial and systems approaches (Zucker, 1990), Murray insisted, "The organism and its milieu must be considered together" (1938a, p. 40). His model included environmental tendencies, or press—both actual conditions (alpha press) and the individual's perceptions of the environment (beta press). His later work also emphasized aspects of culture and society (e.g., Kluckhohn & Murray, 1948). Murray expanded and revised his personological system throughout his career (e.g., 1959, 1968).

The "Multiform Method"

Another important contribution from the *Explorations* project is Murray's "multiform method" of assessment (1959, p. 11), the measurement of numerous aspects of each personality by a team of investigators who use multiple methods. As noted, the Diagnostic Council drew on these assessments to reach a consensus in rating the personality on a large number of variables. During World War II, Murray adapted the multiform method in his work for the OSS, developing a program to select intelligence personnel for secret missions. The method has also been influential in such settings as the Institute of Personality Assessment and Research (IPAR) at the University of California, Berkeley, and in centers designed to assess managerial talent among business personnel (Barenbaum & Winter, 2003).

The Thematic Apperception Test

Drawing on psychodynamic theories, Murray and his coworkers investigated fantasies—especially in the form of literary creations—to reveal unconscious aspects of personality (Murray, 1938a, 1943b). The Thematic Apperception Test (TAT), Murray's best-known measure, was one of several methods designed to elicit fantasies. Developed in collaboration with Christiana Morgan (Morgan & Murray, 1935/1981), the TAT is a series of ambiguous picture cues presented to research participants or patients, who tell or write a creative story based on each picture. Participants project their own "circumstances, experiences or preoccupations" into the cues (p. 392); thus, TAT stories may reveal "the deeper layers of a personality" (p. 408). Psychologists have developed many ways to interpret and score TAT stories (see Gieser & Stein, 1999), ranging from global clinical interpretations to empirically derived measures of motives. The TAT continues to be used widely in clinical and in research settings.

Murray suggested that the immediate source of inspiration for the TAT was the account of a student, Cecilia Roberts, whose son had invented creative stories based on pictures from a book or a magazine (Anderson, 1999; Douglas, 1993). However, the TAT may also have literary sources in works by two of Murray's favorite authors. According to Murray's former student Sanford (1980), one possible source was Thomas Wolfe's (1929) novel *Look Homeward, Angel,* which Murray was reading in 1930 around the time that he developed an early version of the TAT (see also Gieser & Morgan, 1999). In one scene in the novel, Eugene Gant, the protagonist, enters a contest in which participants write their interpretations of a picture, *The Song of the Lark.* Like the instructions in Wolfe's contest, the original instructions for the TAT asked participants "to interpret the action in each picture"; Morgan and Murray modified the instructions after realizing that "more of the personality is revealed if the S [i.e., subject] is asked to create a dramatic fiction rather than to guess the probable facts" (1938, p. 531; see Gieser & Morgan, 1999).

Michael Vannoy Adams (1998) has suggested another possible literary source of inspiration for the TAT—a chapter from Melville's *Moby-Dick.* In the chapter titled "The Doubloon," Captain Ahab and several of his crew members in turn examine a gold doubloon, each offering his own interpretation of the images stamped on the coin. As Adams noted, the scene portrays, "in effect, a projective test"; indeed, one sailor comments, "There's another rendering now; but still one text" (Melville, 1851/1952, p. 434; as quoted in Adams, 1998, p. 6). Perhaps even more striking is Ahab's remark,

> The firm tower, that is Ahab; the volcano, that is Ahab; the courageous, the undaunted, and victorious fowl, that too, is Ahab; all are Ahab; and this round gold is but the image of the rounder globe, which, like a magician's glass, to each and every man in turn but mirrors back his own mysterious self. (Melville, 1851/1952, p. 428)

In a film on Melville's life and work (Squier & Thomas, 1985), Murray himself commented that in the chapter Melville "has each of his personages on the ship go up to the doubloon and look into it and, as it were, describe the doubloon, and they describe themselves, and each one sees something that's like what's in his own mind." Not coincidentally, Murray discussed Melville and Wolfe in his paper, "Personality and Creative Imagination," where he noted that he had designed the TAT as a method of "deducing the personality of an author from his writings" (1943b, p. 143) to support his interpretations of the "autobiographical"

(p. 150) novels of Wolfe and, ultimately, of Melville, whose works and character Murray described as "my first and last problem" (p. 143).

Expansion of Disciplinary Boundaries

Perhaps most influential among Murray's larger contributions is one that is difficult to recognize today—his role in expanding the disciplinary boundaries of academic psychology (Triplet, 1983). Today, courses in abnormal and clinical psychology and references to psychoanalytic concepts appear so routinely in academic departments of psychology that it is difficult to imagine that these topics have not always been considered part of the discipline. As noted, however, Murray pioneered efforts to integrate concepts from psychoanalysis and other depth approaches with methods from academic psychology. His aim in doing so was to promote the intensive study of the whole person, an approach he described as biographical.

MURRAY'S BIOGRAPHICAL STUDIES

Murray's biographical approach to personality, inspired in part by his efforts to write a biography of Melville, reflected the influence of his training in history, in medicine, and in psychopathology. Although mainstream psychologists generally dismissed case studies as unscientific (Barenbaum & Winter, 2003), Murray adopted from medicine a view of the "ultimate scientific value of . . . case histories" (1959, p. 11), and he promoted biographical studies throughout his career. The following examples of case studies illustrate the evolution of Murray's multidisciplinary approach to the study of individual lives and the central role of case studies in the development and testing of his personological system.

A Medical Case Study: Alice Henry

Murray's medical training at the Columbia College of Physicians and Surgeons included visits to different hospitals, where he practiced his diagnostic skills with patients from many walks of life. On rounds at the City Hospital on Blackwell's Island in 1918, he met Alice Henry, a patient his professor declared a hopeless case of syphilis. Although Murray agreed with the diagnosis, he was dismayed by the callous attitude of his professor and his fellow medical students. He questioned Alice and returned the next day to hear her life story. An Irish immigrant, Alice had become embroiled in the New York crime scene. Forced to work in a house of prostitution, she had been arrested more than once and subjected to physical abuse; her medical history included treatment not only for complications of syphilis but also for injuries, drug abuse, and a suicide attempt (Murray, 1918; Robinson, 1992).

Murray wrote two versions of Alice's case. A thorough medical history, complete with diagrams, lists of symptoms, and diagnoses, began with Alice's life story and cited correspondence, interviews, and other documents Murray had gathered from members of her family and from medical and legal personnel. In a second, incomplete account, apparently intended as a short story, Murray revealed his strong empathy toward Alice and his critical view not only of the criminals who had abused her but also of his medical professor and of Alice's former employer, privileged people who had treated her without respect or care. Murray's budding interest in psychology was evident in this version of the case. He wrote,

> Of the sincerity and honesty of my patient I was quite convinced—a student of medicine must also necessarily be a student of psychology and physiognomy. After obtaining any history about a patient the doctor should always make a note as to the reliability of the information obtained. After Alice Henry's story I wrote "[She] is apparently sincere honest [sic] and in normal mind and there is no reason to doubt the accuracy of her story." (Murray, 1918, n.p.)

Murray's early medical case anticipates several features of his personological studies, including his effort to integrate views of several experts—an early version of the "multiform method"—and his attention to the life history and to subjective reports. Later, Murray (e.g., 1959) frequently criticized psychologists, particularly behaviorists, for refusing to consider the subjective reports of research "subjects"; he pointed out that physicians, far from relying solely on overt physical signs, often made accurate diagnoses based on patients' reports of covert symptoms.

A Psychological Biography: Herman Melville

As mentioned earlier, Murray saw Melville as a great explorer of the unconscious, and he "zestfully embarked on a biography of that alienated genius" (1967b, p. 287), beginning in 1925 (Robinson, 1992). After completing *Explorations in Personality* (Murray, 1938a), he produced a draft of the biography, some three volumes in manuscript. In the preface, Murray (1938b) attributed to *Moby-Dick* his decision to become a psychologist, explaining his desire to understand Melville's personality and to examine the relationship between the author's life and his writings. Murray (1943b) later noted that his questions regarding Melville lay behind his research on the expression of personality in fantasy using such methods as the TAT. In the unpublished biography, Murray (1938b) adopted two different methods of interpretation: (a) an empathic or intuitive approach based on his extensive knowledge of Melville's life and on his identification with the author and (b) an analysis using psychoanalytic concepts and personality variables from *Explorations in Personality* to construct an abstract portrait of Melville. Presented in a separate chapter, the portrait reveals not only the close relationship between Murray's theory and his biographical work on Melville but also the parallels he perceived between Melville's life and his own. For example, he suggested that Melville's strong need for autonomy and his fascination with his own inner world were in part reactions to feeling rejected by his mother. Although Murray's identification with Melville, whose life ended in tragedy, prevented him from completing the biography (Robinson, 1992), he published several well-known interpretations of psychological themes in Melville's works. He argued that *Moby-Dick* symbolized "an insurgent Id in mortal conflict with an oppressive cultural Superego" (Murray, 1951, p. 446) and that Melville's *Pierre* was "his spiritual autobiography in the form of a novel" (Murray, 1852/ 1949, p. xxiv; see also 1966, 1967a).

Explorations in Personality: Introduction to the Case of Earnst

The case of Earnst is the only full case history published in *Explorations in Personality* (Murray, 1938a). The case material included reports of 22 sets of tests, interviews, and experimental procedures as well as a biography prepared by former student White. Murray's principal contribution to the case was an introduction describing the construction of biographies and presenting a rationale for case studies. Explaining that the biographer's function was to construct a "convincing portrait" from the case material, he remarked, "A 'portrait' meant a 'biography,' since the notion was accepted generally that the history of a personality *is* the personality" (1938a, p. 604; emphasis in original). An important focus of many biographies, he noted, was the *"unity-thema,"* a pattern of needs and press, established in early childhood, that provides "the key to [the individual's] unique nature" and "repeats itself in many forms in later life" (pp. 604–605; emphasis in original). Murray noted that unlike other psychologists who defined "psychograph" as a profile of trait scores, he used the term to refer to the "abstract biography" (pp. 605–606). His definition apparently derived from the work of popular biographer Gamaliel Bradford, who referred to his own portraits as psychographs (Johnston, 1927; Murray [1935/1957], quoted from Bradford's Foreword to Johnston's 1927 book).

Murray regretted that only one case history could be included in the volume. "Case histories are the proof of the pudding," he wrote. "That is to say, a personological theory can be tested best by utilizing it in the writing of biographies" (1938a, p. 606). He expressed a hope that psychologists of the future would develop a system of technical notation that could be used to represent the important episodes of a person's life, just as a musical score represents a piece of music. "Nowadays," he argued, "the psychologist is forced to employ non-technical language and consequently the writing of case histories (which should provide the factual substance for a true science of psychology) must lie somewhere on the continuum between biology (science) and literature (art)" (p. 607). A complete scheme of theoretical constructs was a first step toward a system of notation, but "when it came to the test of writing biographies," the researchers had compromised between rigidly applying their theory, thus "squeez[ing] the life out of our subjects," and "using what literary ability we possessed to catch some of the conceptually unmanageable life" (p. 608). "A psychologist who believes that he can tell the truth without being 'literary,'" Murray remarked, "has only to try writing a case history or biography, and then compare what he has done to a character sketch by any novelist of the first order" (pp. 608–609). The introduction to the case of Earnst highlighted not only Murray's attention to literature but also the centrality of biographical studies to his creation and revision of theory.

Psychological Warfare: The Case of Adolf Hitler

Before joining the OSS assessment team, Murray prepared, in response to a request from Walter Langer at the OSS, a detailed case study of Adolf Hitler based on biographical information and on interpretations of the imagery in Hitler's writings (Robinson, 1992). Drawing on his personological concepts, Murray (1943a) suggested that Hitler had developed strong needs for dominance, superiority, aggression, and revenge to counteract feelings of inferiority and humiliation. The report concluded with predictions of Hitler's behavior, including a possible suicide, and suggestions for handling him after Germany surrendered. Murray expected the OSS staff to combine his own report and others in a final analysis of Hitler, but copies of his study were destroyed, and he did not see the final report. Years later, Langer (1972) published a "secret wartime report" of Hitler's personality that duplicated, without acknowledgment, many of Murray's insights and predictions (Robinson, 1992). Still, Murray's case of Hitler suggested the practical utility of personological case studies, soon to be tested in the OSS assessment program.

Elaborating a Complex: American Icarus

"American Icarus" is the case study of "Grope," one of a group of Harvard students assessed with the multiform method in the 1950s. Generally recognized as Murray's first published account of the Icarus complex, a "unity thema" (1955/1981, p. 536) named after the mythological figure who fell after flying too near the sun, the case actually elaborates a complex identified earlier. In the last chapter of *Explorations in Personality,* Murray described two "cases" suffering from

> traumas and fears involving physical Insupport, followed by counteractive attempts to conquer gravity, to move far and high in space. This combination may be termed an *Icarus* complex. As an example of its sublimation we may cite Nietzsche who with such passion, especially in *Zarathustra,* eulogized seamen, voyagers, mountain climbers, dancers, tight-rope walkers and eagles. (1938a, p. 731; emphasis in original)

Murray (1955/1981) described a more extensive complex, determined in part by early frustration of oral and affectional needs—a compound of "the wish to overcome gravity" (also expressed in "passionate enthusiasm"), concerns with falling, "cynosural narcism" ("a craving for unsolicited attention and admiration"), and a love of fire (pp. 548–549). Grope's case also revealed "an abundance of water imagery," "a craving for immortality," and "a conception of women as objects to be utilized for narcistic gains" (pp. 554–555). "American Icarus" exemplifies Murray's use of case studies to develop, expand, and revise his personological concepts. Continuing the Murray tradition, Ogilvie (2004) recently presented an interpretation of "Icarian" flying fantasies.

Murray's work on the Icarus complex also reflected the personal side of the psychological phenomena he chose to study. He considered himself an embodiment of the complex (Robinson, 1992), and in an autobiographical essay originally titled "Narcism Re-Exhibited" (p. 384), he described his own early deprivation of oral and affectional needs and his "counteracting disposition of sanguine and expansive buoyancy" (Murray, 1967b, p. 300).

The Case of Murr

Perhaps his most interesting case study, Murray's (1967b) autobiography presents "The Case of Murr," a fanciful third-person account in the style of a research case. The essay depicts Murray's multiple selves and illustrates his belief that "the history of a personality *is* the personality" (1938a, p. 604, emphasis in original), examining multiple determinants of his own personality and of his theoretical and methodological preferences in psychology. Appearing in the narrative as both researcher and subject, Murray introduces "The Case of Murr" by describing the conflicting plans of his "expansive, omnivorous, sanguine disposition," an aspect of "the larger Self" that leads him "to start by envisaging every new, appealing undertaking in the most voluminous dimensions," and the governor of his "conscious ego system (the little self)" (1967b, p. 285), who advocates a more limited agenda. Heeding the "little self," he resolves to avoid discussing both his new theoretical concepts and his childhood and to limit his focus to four topics: Murr's career choice, his view of his role in psychology, his achievements, and his evaluation of his contributions. Murray examines multiple determinants of his vocational choice and his role as an "eccentric" who rebelled against prevailing views in academic psychology (p. 291); he describes his successive lives as college athlete, physician, and biochemist and the "profound affectional upheaval" (p. 290) that led to his fascination with the unconscious.

Reflecting his historical view of personality, Murray as narrator traces the consequences of various early experiences in his later life and work, shifting time perspectives frequently so that the past appears to live on in the present. As if to parallel the affectional upheaval in his life, he interrupts his autobiography with a "flash-back" that he attributes to "the caucus of friends who frequent my boardinghouse" (p. 295). The number of selves multiplies as Murray quotes Murr, who occasionally refers to himself in the third person as he discusses his parents and his childhood memories, providing his "free associations" (p. 299) and psychodynamic interpretations of his personality. Murr examines several consequences of the "marrow of misery and melancholy" that resulted from his troubled relationship with his mother: his career choice; his attraction to "tragic themes in literature" (p. 300) and to "the darker, blinder recesses of the psyche" (p. 293); his counteracting "sanguine and expansive" disposition (p. 300), pride, "emotional self-sufficiency," and "venturesome autonomy" (p. 299); and such theoretical concepts as nurturance (p. 300).

Murray's (1967b) attention to early determinants of his interest in depth psychology contrasts sharply with his brief mention of Morgan, whom he identifies explicitly only as one of several "kindred spirits" (p. 291) and as a collaborator at the Harvard Psychological Clinic. According to his own biographer, Forrest Robinson, Murray's vital but difficult relationship with Morgan was at the center of much of his psychological work and his work on Melville, but his ambivalence regarding Morgan and his family produced "competing compulsions to reveal and to conceal" (1992, p. 311) the relationship and the worldview it inspired. Robinson suggested that Murray's autobiography grapples obliquely with his "failures in love" (p. 384), which Murray as narrator attributes to the early loss of his mother's affection. However, the autobiography, like Melville's novel *Pierre,* also includes a number of intentional clues to "the hushed story of his life" (Murray, 1852/1949, p. xxiii), beginning in the prologue, where Murray assumes "the task of steering a fitting course for Murr between the Scylla of concealment and mendacity and the Charybdis of the 'meanest mortal's scorn'" (1967b, p. 286). The uncited quote from Melville's remark in *Pierre*—"He who shall be wholly honest . . . shall stand in danger of the meanest mortal's scorn" (1852/1949, p. 127)—concludes a passage that reveals Pierre's erotic attraction to the dark and mysterious Isabel. Murray and Morgan saw themselves in these characters (Robinson, 1992), and Murray argued that Melville, championing heart over head, intended *Pierre* as "the legend of his heart, the biography of Eros" (1949, p. xxiii). Thus, from the beginning of his autobiography, Murray (1967b) hints at the importance of his relationship with Morgan. Echoing his interpretation of *Pierre*, Murray emphasizes repeatedly his own experience of a separation or a conflict between head and heart, variously represented as "conscious ego" and "sanguine surplus"—his hearty "disposition" (p. 285)—or as separate "mental and emotional metamorphoses" (p. 290). He, too, champions heart over head; his affectional upheaval changes the course of his life and propels him toward psychological approaches that examine "feelings" rather than "the full light of consciousness" (p. 293). In the end, the "sanguine surplus" prevails; the flashback occupies a third of "The Case of Murr," and although Murray returns to the conscious agenda of "the little self" to describe his achievements, he claims to have reached the page limit with no room for the final evaluative section, "the forehead and crown of the portrait" (p. 308).

CONCLUSION

In this chapter I have examined Murray's major psychological contributions, with particular attention to his biographical studies and to personal and interdisciplinary influences on his work. Trained in history, medicine, and biochemistry and drawn to psychology through his interests in his own emotional life, in Melville, and in psychoanalysis, Murray explicitly combined aspects of science and art in his personological theory and research. His emphasis on the study of the whole person and his complex model of personality as a system of multiple interacting variables have had an enduring influence on the field of personality psychology. Murray's legacy ranges from specific concepts and methods to general goals for the study of personality and to the integration of psychodynamic concepts in academic psychology. As noted earlier, Murray's concepts of motives, including the needs for affiliation and for achievement, have inspired a continuing tradition of research. The TAT and other projective methods are still widely used in clinical practice and in research, and the multiform method of assessment continues to inform work in research settings and in centers for the assessment of business personnel. Through his own work and that of his many students, including MacKinnon, Rosenzweig, Sanford, and White, Murray played a central role in expanding the disciplinary boundaries of psychology to include abnormal psychology and studies of psychodynamic concepts (Triplet, 1983) and of the creative process (Zucker, 1990). Finally, as suggested by the focus on Murray's case studies in this chapter, a resurgence of interest in studies of individual lives and in narrative and interpretive methods in contemporary personality psychology (Barenbaum & Winter, 2003) reflects the legacy of Murray's personology.

REFERENCES

Adams, M. V. (1998). For love of the imagination. In J. Reppen (Ed.), *Why I became a psychotherapist* (pp. 1–14). Northvale, NJ: Jason Aronson.
Allport, G. W. (1937, January 12–13, 21, 28). Letters to E. G. Boring. Edwin G. Boring Papers, Harvard University Archives, Cambridge, MA.
Anderson, J. W. (1990). The life of Henry A. Murray: 1893–1988. In A. I. Rabin, R. A. Zucker, R. A. Emmons, & S. Frank (Eds.), *Studying persons and lives* (pp. 304–334). New York: Springer.
Anderson, J. W. (1999). Henry A. Murray and the creation of the Thematic Apperception Test. In L. Gieser & M. I. Stein (Eds.), *Evocative images: The Thematic Apperception Test and the art of projection* (pp. 23–38). Washington, DC: American Psychological Association.
Barenbaum, N. B., & Winter, D. G. (2003). Personality. In I. B. Weiner (Series Ed.) & D. K. Freedheim (Vol. Ed.), *Handbook of psychology: Vol. 1. History of psychology* (pp. 177–203). New York: Wiley.

186   NICOLE B. BARENBAUM

Danziger, K. (1997). *Naming the mind: How psychology found its language.* Thousand Oaks, CA: Sage.

Douglas, C. (1993). *Translate this darkness: The life of Christiana Morgan.* New York: Simon & Schuster.

Editorial: Research and instruction in abnormal psychology at Harvard. (1926). *Journal of Abnormal and Social Psychology, 21,* 1–3.

Elms, A. C. (1987). The personalities of Henry A. Murray. In R. Hogan & W. H. Jones (Eds.), *Perspectives in personality* (Vol. 2, pp. 1–14). Greenwich, CT: JAI Press.

Gieser, L., & Morgan, W. G. (1999). Look homeward, Harry: Literary influence on the development of the Thematic Apperception Test. In L. Gieser & M. I. Stein (Eds.), *Evocative images: The Thematic Apperception Test and the art of projection* (pp. 53–64). Washington, DC: American Psychological Association.

Gieser, L., & Stein, M. I. (1999). *Evocative images: The Thematic Apperception Test and the art of projection.* Washington, DC: American Psychological Association.

Henderson, L. J. (1928). *Blood: A study in general physiology.* New Haven, CT: Yale University Press.

Johnston, J. C. (1927). *Biography: The literature of personality.* New York: Century.

Kluckhohn, C., & Murray, H. A. (1948). *Personality in nature, society, and culture.* New York: A. A. Knopf.

Langer, W. C. (1972). *The mind of Adolf Hitler: The secret wartime report.* New York: Basic Books.

Melville, H. (1949). *Pierre, or the ambiguities* (H. A. Murray, Ed.). New York: Hendricks House. (Original work published 1852)

Melville, H. (1952). *Moby-Dick; or, the whale.* New York: Hendricks House. (Original work published 1851)

Morgan, C. D., & Murray, H. A. (1938). Thematic Apperception Test. In H. A. Murray (Ed.), *Explorations in personality: A clinical and experimental study of fifty men of college age* (pp. 530–545). New York: Oxford University Press.

Morgan, C. D., & Murray, H. A. (1981). A method for investigating fantasies: The Thematic Apperception Test. In E. S. Shneidman (Ed.), *Endeavors in psychology* (pp. 390–408). New York: Harper & Row. (Original work published 1935)

Murray, H. A. (1918). Alice Henry. Murray/Robinson Papers, Accession 13406, Box 3, Folder A.16, Harvard University Archives, Cambridge, MA.

Murray, H. A. (1929, January 12). Professor Murray describes Department of Abnormal Psychology. *Harvard Crimson,* p. 4.

Murray, H. A. (1930, December 2). Letter to E. G. Boring. Edwin G. Boring Papers, Harvard University Archives, Cambridge, MA.

Murray, H. A. (Ed.). (1938a). *Explorations in personality: A clinical and experimental study of fifty men of college age.* New York: Oxford University Press.

Murray, H. A. (1938b). Manuscript biography of Herman Melville. Henry A. Murray Papers, Harvard University Archives, Cambridge, MA.

Murray, H. A. (1940). What should psychologists do about psychoanalysis? *Journal of Abnormal and Social Psychology, 35,* 150–175.

Murray, H. A. (1941–1965). Multiform assessments of personality development among gifted college men. Unpublished raw data, Henry A. Murray Research Center, Radcliffe Institute for Advanced Study, Harvard University, Cambridge, MA

Murray, H. A. (1943a). *Analysis of the personality of Adolph Hitler.* Unpublished report, Franklin D. Roosevelt Library, Hyde Park, NY.

Murray, H. A. (1943b). Personality and creative imagination. In R. Kirk (Ed.), *English Institute essays 1942* (pp. 139–162). New York: Columbia University Press.

Murray, H. A. (1949). Introduction. In H. Melville, *Pierre, or the ambiguities* (H. A. Murray, Ed.; pp. xiii–ciii). New York: Hendricks House.

Murray, H. A. (1951). In nomine Diaboli. *New England Quarterly, 24,* 435–452.

Murray, H. A. (1957). The Harvard Psychological Clinic. In A. Wessman (Ed.), *Harvard Psychological Clinic, 1927–1957: Its founder, aims, methods, members, graduates and contributions to knowledge* (pp. 11–22). Cambridge, MA: Privately published. (Original work published 1935)

Murray, H. A. (1959). Preparations for the scaffold of a comprehensive system. In S. Koch (Ed.), *Psychology: A study of a science* (Vol. 3, pp. 7–54). New York: McGraw-Hill.

Murray, H. A. (1960). The possible nature of a "mythology" to come. In H. A. Murray (Ed.), *Myth and mythmaking* (pp. 300–353). New York: George Braziller.

Murray, H. A. (1966). Bartleby and I. In H. P. Vincent (Ed.), *A symposium: Bartleby the scrivener* (pp. 3–24). Kent, OH: Kent State University Press.

Murray, H. A. (1967a). Dead to the world: The passions of Herman Melville. In E. S. Shneidman (Ed.), *Essays in self-destruction* (pp. 7–29). New York: Science House.

Murray, H. A. (1967b). Henry A. Murray. In E. G. Boring & G. Lindzey (Eds.), *A history of psychology in autobiography* (Vol. 5, pp. 283–310). New York: Appleton-Century-Crofts.

Murray, H. A. (1968). Components of an evolving personological system. In D. L. Sills (Ed.), *International Encyclopedia of the Social Sciences* (Vol. 12, pp. 5–13). New York: Macmillan-Free Press.

Murray, H. A. (1981a). American Icarus. In E. S. Shneidman (Ed.), *Endeavors in psychology* (pp. 535–556). New York: Harper & Row. (Original work published 1955)

Murray, H. A. (1981b). Psychology and the university. In E. S. Shneidman (Ed.), *Endeavors in psychology* (pp. 337–351). New York: Harper & Row. (Original work published 1935)

Ogilvie, D. M. (2004). *Fantasies of flight.* New York: Oxford University Press.

Robinson, F. G. (1992). *Love's story told: A life of Henry A. Murray.* Cambridge, MA: Harvard University Press.

Rosenzweig, S. (1985). Freud and experimental psychology: The emergence of idiodynamics. In S. Koch & D. E. Leary (Eds.), *A century of psychology as science* (pp. 135–207). New York: McGraw-Hill.

Sanford, R. N. (1980). Murray's clinic as a place to learn. In C. Comstock (Ed.), *Learning after college* (pp. 104–114). Orinda, CA: Montaigne.

Smuts, J. C. (1926). *Holism and evolution.* New York: Macmillan.

Squier, R. D. (Producer/Director), & Thomas, K. (Producer). (1985). *Herman Melville, damned in paradise* [Videotape]. Santa Monica, CA: Pyramid Film & Video.

Students lecture teachers. (1936, May 1). *Harvard Crimson.* Retrieved July 21, 2004, from http://www.thecrimson.com/article.aspx?ref=182143

Triplet, R. G. (1983). *Henry A. Murray and the Harvard Psychological Clinic, 1926–1938: A struggle to expand the disciplinary boundaries of academic psychology.* Unpublished doctoral dissertation, University of New Hampshire, Durham.

Wolfe, T. (1929). *Look homeward, angel.* New York: Modern Library.

Zucker, R. A. (1990). Henry Murray's legacy: An epilogue. In A. I. Rabin, R. A. Zucker, R. A. Emmons, & S. Frank (Eds.), *Studying persons and lives* (pp. 335–340). New York: Springer.

Mary Cover Jones (Photo courtesy of the Archives of the History of American Psychology, University of Akron)

Chapter 12

Mother of Behavior Therapy and Beyond: Mary Cover Jones and the Study of the "Whole Child"

Alexandra Rutherford

Mary Cover Jones (1896–1987) was christened the "mother of behavior therapy" in the early 1970s by her colleague and friend Joseph Wolpe,[1] and has been portrayed throughout the psychological literature as a pioneer in this field because of her seminal work on the unconditioning of the fear reaction in infants (see M. C. Jones, 1924a, 1924b). Jones's well-known study of the 3-year-old named Peter (completed under the supervision of behaviorist John B. Watson while she was a graduate student at Columbia University) was selected by the behavior therapists of the 1970s as signifying the birth, or origin, of their field. As a result, the "Little Peter study" has probably been cited more extensively than any other aspect of her work, leading most introductory psychology students to assume that this was her major professional accomplishment. A closer examination of her research, however, reveals a rich and eclectic approach to the study of development across the lifespan, in which she consistently emphasized the importance of individual differences in understanding growth and development. These

---

[1] Sources are mixed regarding exactly when Wolpe bestowed this title on Jones. Reiss (1990, p. 358) and Krasner (1988, p. 102) report that Wolpe first used this title in reference to Jones at the First Temple University Conference in Behavior Therapy and Behavior Modification held in Philadelphia, November 14 to 17, 1974. Wolpe was a faculty member at Temple at the time, and Jones was invited to give the conference's keynote address, in which she reflected on her experiences with Watson and the Peter study. This address was later published in the *Journal of Behavior Therapy and Experimental Psychiatry* as "A 1924 pioneer looks at behavior therapy" (Jones, 1975). Gieser (1993), however, dates the appellation earlier, to Wolpe's 1969 remarks at the First Annual Southern California Conference on Behavior Modification at Los Angeles.

aspects of her work have been overshadowed by the mythic status of the Peter study and her association with Watson in the early years of her career.

In this chapter, I describe and analyze the personal and professional contributions of Jones to provide a more comprehensive account of her place in psychology. This examination of her life and work is intended both to help redress the narrow scope of her representations in introductory texts and to contextualize her work within the broader themes and currents that characterized the child development movement in North America during the middle of the 20th century.

EARLY LIFE, FAMILY, AND EDUCATION

Jones was born in Johnstown, Pennsylvania, on September 1, 1897, the middle child of Carrie Louise (Higson) Cover and Charles Blair Cover. Her parents, although not themselves educated beyond high school, placed a high value on education and regularly took the family to the Chautauqua Summer Institutes held on the shores of Lake Erie. There, young Jones was a member of the girls' club, swam at the lake, and completed nature studies. She also recalled seeing Theodore Roosevelt and hearing a number of other interesting speakers. In reminiscing about her summers at Chautauqua she recalled the following "scandalous" incident that revealed the social mores of the time.

> I remember one afternoon when the girls' club was going swimming. I went in my bathing suit, which was a big dress with a skirt. And I didn't have any stockings on. I was twelve years old. They wouldn't let me be on the beach without stockings. I had to go back and get stockings . . . so we were very proper at that place. (M. C. Jones, 1983, p. 9)

In addition to the stimulating summers at Chautauqua, Jones recalled a supportive and nurturant upbringing. Her mother was a devoted homemaker and amateur singer. Her father was a businessman who was insistent that all of his children should have every educational opportunity. With the encouragement of their parents and their own love of learning, all of the Cover children completed both undergraduate and graduate studies. Jones's older brother John, who was a positive influence on her throughout her life, became a professor of economics. Her younger sister, Anna Louise, became a naturalist and writer. For Jones, psychology became her lifelong passion.

JONES AND WATSON: BEHAVIORIST BEGINNINGS

In 1915, after graduating from Johnstown High School, Jones began her career in psychology as an undergraduate at Vassar College, where she took "every psychology course offered"—except one (Reiss, 1990, p. 205). She had completed an introductory laboratory course in her sophomore year with professor Margaret Floy Washburn, who was the first woman to receive her PhD in psychology. Because of Jones's own and her lab partner's indifference to the subject matter, they both finished with only a C in the course. This grade proved influential in keeping her out of Washburn's senior seminar in psychology. When pressed, Washburn declared to Jones, "You wouldn't enjoy the Senior Seminar, it's just like that Sophomore lab course that you didn't like!" (as reported in Reiss, 1990, p. 206). As a result, Jones was unable to enroll in the class. Despite this, she later remarked that Washburn was an excellent teacher who inspired her interest in psychology.

Given the eventual focus of Jones's career in child development, it was perhaps propitious that her association with Washburn was curtailed. Washburn was a committed experimentalist who, as head of the Psychology Department, vehemently opposed the proposal that Vassar open a nursery school to contribute to studies in child psychology. As a result of her opposition, the Child Study Department was set up as a separate department at Vassar in 1927 (Senn, 1975), and was eventually funded by the Josiah Macy Jr. Foundation (Frank, 1962). Joseph Stone, one of the developmental psychologists associated with the Vassar project, suggested that a possible reason for Washburn's position on the nursery school issue was that "she was one of the ardent feminists at Vassar and this [the nursery school] was a backdoor to *Küche, Kirche,* and *Kinder*" (i.e., the kitchen, the church, and children; Stone, as cited in Senn, 1975, p. 21).

Despite Washburn's rebuff, Jones graduated from Vassar in the spring of 1919, and at least one of her Vassar connections became beneficial when she later pursued graduate studies at Columbia University. While at Vassar, she met fellow student Rosalie Rayner in a developmental psychology class. It was not until after the class had ended, however, that a friendship developed between the classmates. Jones ran into a distraught Rayner immediately after a disciplinary hearing in which Rayner had been punished (although not expelled) for smoking cigarettes in her room. Rayner would soon interview for a graduate assistantship at The Johns Hopkins University, and would start working there with Watson while Jones completed her studies at Vassar.

Meanwhile, a second auspicious event occurred for Jones. In 1919, while on a weekend trip to New York City, she was directed by a friend to a lecture given by Watson. She reported the following:

> I was first introduced to John B. Watson at a lecture, which included motion pictures, in New York City in 1919. I had gone from Vassar College to New York for a weekend and was steered, more or less accidentally, by a friend to this lecture, rather than to the usual Friday night theatre. (M. C. Jones, 1974, p. 581)

In this lecture, Watson presented some of his research on the conditioning of fear in infants undertaken with Jones's Vassar classmate Rayner—the now classic

"Little Albert" study (Watson & Rayner, 1920). The year 1919, however, was Watson's last at Johns Hopkins, as news of his affair with Rayner came to light. Nevertheless, as a result of this lecture, Jones became intrigued by the possibility that a fear, once conditioned, could be removed with procedures similar to those Watson had described. Jones also reported that Watson's lecture was influential in cementing her desire to pursue psychology instead of pediatrics (Reiss, 1990, p. 204).

With her interest in psychology firmly established, Jones began graduate work at Columbia University in the fall of 1919 after interviewing with R. S. Woodworth, whose eclecticism and open-mindedness toward psychological theory appealed to her immensely. Within the year, she met Harold Jones, a fellow graduate student at Columbia, who became both her husband and collaborator. They both completed their master's degrees by the spring of 1920, and were married that summer.

In 1922, Jones received an offer from Helen Thompson Woolley at the Merrill-Palmer Institute in Detroit to take a position as research fellow in their newly established nursery school. Jones's name had been forwarded to Woolley by Watson, who then wrote to Jones noting, "I told her that I knew of no one better fitted to go on with that work than you, and that I would do everything in my power to get you to take the job. . . . " (Watson to Jones, July 5, 1922, as reproduced in Reiss, 1990, n.p.).

Despite Watson's encouragement, Jones declined the offer. It had come at a rather untimely juncture: She was just about to give birth to her first daughter, Barbara. As Watson acknowledged in a subsequent letter, "I do not wonder that under the circumstances you do not care to undertake a winter's work away from your husband. I wish you all the joys of the new duties that are coming to you, and none of the sorrows" (Watson to Jones, July 7, 1922, as reproduced in Reiss, 1990, n.p.).

Other opportunities were quickly forthcoming, however, and in 1923 Jones began an appointment as associate in psychological research at the Institute of Educational Research of Columbia University Teachers College. To facilitate this work, Jones and her new family took up residence in Hecksher House, a facility supported by the Hecksher Foundation, which housed children who had been abandoned by or temporarily separated from their parents. At this point, a number of events converged to determine Jones's further association with Watson and her work with 3-year-old Peter.

In 1924, Lawrence K. Frank approached the dean of Teachers College, James E. Russell, and proposed forming a child study institute with a trial grant from the recently established Laura Spelman Rockefeller Memorial. With the support of Woodworth and E. L. Thorndike, the grant was accepted, and Watson, who had turned to a career in advertising, was recruited to oversee the research. In this consultative capacity, which represented a partial return to academia for Watson, he became Jones's supervisor in her work with Peter, a young resident of Hecksher House, whom she later dubbed "Albert grown a bit older" (M. C. Jones, 1924b, p. 309).

Unlike Albert, Watson and Raynor's experimental subject Peter would have his fear unconditioned rather than conditioned. Jones selected Peter as a candidate for her study because of his extant (and presumably conditioned) fear of a rabbit. For several days, Peter was exposed to the rabbit in the presence of other children who had been carefully selected because of their "entirely fearless attitude toward the rabbit and because of their satisfactory dispositions in general" (M. C. Jones, 1924b, p. 310). Over the course of his exposure in the presence of these fearless models, Peter's initial fear of the rabbit changed into a "tranquil indifference" (p. 312), and lessened to the degree that he would touch the rabbit voluntarily. At this point, Peter came down with scarlet fever and was removed to the hospital for 2 months.

On his return, Peter's fear of the rabbit had regained its original strength, and another procedure, that of "direct conditioning," was tried. This time, the rabbit was presented to Peter at the same time as a pleasant stimulus (food) was also presented. Care was taken to ensure that at each stage fear of the rabbit did not interfere with Peter's eating. Other children who were not afraid of the rabbit were also brought in as positive role models throughout the unconditioning process. Peter was eventually able to tolerate the rabbit in his lap and would play with it for several minutes at a time.

In a subsequent publication (M. C. Jones, 1924a), Jones outlined seven different fear-removal procedures tested on a sample of children (of whom Peter was one) whose fears had been identified (the children selected were variously afraid of rabbits, rats, or frogs). The methods she tested were elimination through disuse, verbal appeal, negative adaptation, repression, distraction, direct conditioning, and social imitation. Jones concluded that only the last two, direct conditioning and social imitation, provided "unqualified success" (p. 390) in the removal of the infants' fear responses.

After she published the case of Peter (1924b), Jones completed her dissertation with the support of Watson. It appeared in *Pedagogical Seminary* in 1926 as "The Development of Early Behavior Patterns in Young Children" (M. C. Jones, 1926). Ironically, her study of children's fears, including the Little Peter study, had not been deemed suitable as a dissertation project because of the small sample size. Jones reported that the work with Peter received little attention when first published: "I still have yellowed stacks of reprints. No one was interested in them at the time" (M. C. Jones, as cited in Logan, 1980, p. 106).

Jones certainly overcame the sample-size problem in her dissertation research, in which she examined 365 infants in three baby welfare stations (centers providing medical examinations and treatment to at-risk infants) in New York City, "with the purpose of determining age norms, and the period of development, for a group of early behavior patterns" (M. C. Jones, 1926, p. 539). Her research was supported by a fellowship in child development from the Laura Spelman

Rockefeller Memorial. Between 1923 and 1930, Laura Spelman Rockefeller funds were instrumental in supporting many of the research programs that would come to define the emerging child development movement (see Lomax, 1977). Jones noted that this was a positive period in her career, and that the fellowship complemented the inner sense of reward she was gaining from her work (Reiss, 1990, p. 254). But Jones had not abandoned the topic of infant emotional reactions, despite the behavioral emphasis of her dissertation research.

THE EMOTIONAL DEVELOPMENT OF INFANTS: BEYOND BEHAVIORISM

Although history and clinical psychology texts have identified Jones as a pioneer of behavior therapy, it is important to examine the extent to which Jones's work and her personal theoretical orientation exemplified a truly behaviorist viewpoint. Although she acknowledged Watson's considerable contributions to psychology and was appreciative of his professional support and encouragement, Jones did remark on his theory in the following way:

> Had Watson stayed in the psychological laboratory, I am sure that his theoretical position would have become more dynamic, more mellow. He would have modified an oversimplification of his concept of native disposition in view of more complex aspects of human development and functioning that were coming to his attention in our studies. (M. C. Jones, 1974, p. 582)

The studies to which Jones was referring were published between 1928 and 1933, authored sometimes by Jones alone and sometimes jointly with her husband Harold Jones (H. E. Jones & M. C. Jones, 1928, 1930; M. C. Jones, 1930, 1933). An examination of these articles reveals that Jones seriously questioned both Watson's view that the infant is born with only three basic emotions (fear, rage, and love) and his view that all other emotional reactions are built up through conditioning. Second, in these articles, Jones refuted Watson's conviction that all innate fear reactions in infants are caused by either a sudden loss of support or loud noises, and supplanted this theory with an alternative explanation that she and Harold Jones developed from their observational and experimental work. In their formulation, fear reactions are caused, more broadly, by the demand for adjustment to novelty or discomfort. Third, she did not subscribe to a strictly behavioristic viewpoint on the origin and treatment of fear in individual cases, emphasizing as well etiological explanations of a psychodynamic nature and a wide range of treatment options, including the promotion of self-confidence and the removal of secondary gain associated with fear expression (M. C. Jones, 1930).

It is clear from a closer examination of Jones's contributions to the literature on the emotional development of infants, and the nature and treatment of fear, that she did not espouse a purely Watsonian viewpoint. At times she clearly opposed aspects of Watson's theorizing. She adhered to more nativistic developmental explanations, and advocated many fear-reducing treatments in addition to unconditioning. When it came to raising her own children, she noted, "I never wanted to follow Watson's advice to parents . . . when it came to his advice to parents, we weren't with him" (M. C. Jones, as cited in Reiss, 1990, p. 290). In reflecting on his relationship and conversations with Jones, a colleague noted, "Although Wolpe had proclaimed Mary 'the Mother of Behavior Therapy' and her scientific methods had helped to establish behavior therapy as a field resting on empirically based interventions, let history note that she never identified herself as a 'behaviorist'" (Gieser, 1993, p. 322).

A NOTE ON HISTORIOGRAPHY

With Jones's early contributions to the field in mind, several questions remain. Why has the case of Peter achieved almost mythic status in psychology? Why was Jones's subsequent work on emotional development overshadowed by the Peter study? Why has unconditioning been touted as Jones's primary contribution to the field, to the exclusion of the other methods of fear reduction that she amply discussed? The answers to these questions may reside in what some historians have referred to as a "myth-making" process in psychology (Baumgardner, 1977; Samelson, 1974). To build a sense of identity and continuity for a new field, researchers often choose classic studies as "origin myths," and unconsciously distort or misrepresent the findings to provide an oversimplified or glorified account of the "birth" of their discipline and its subsequent development (see Kornfeld, 1989, for an extended discussion of this process in the case of Peter; and Harris, 1979, for an analysis of the "Little Albert" study). Although the Peter study was only the starting point marking a series of articles expressing a much more theoretically and clinically eclectic view of the development and treatment of fear, with Wolpe's pronouncement Jones became the unsuspecting mother of behavior therapy, and the case of Peter became one of the seminal studies in the field. As a result, Jones's theoretical divergences from Watson and her expanded account of the nature, development, and treatment of children's fears have remained relatively obscured.

A CAREER IN DEVELOPMENTAL PSYCHOLOGY:
THE LIVES AND TIMES OF THE OAKLAND GROWTH STUDY

As noted earlier, in 1923, while still at Columbia, Jones and her husband met Frank who, with funds from the Laura Spelman Rockefeller Memorial, was putting together a plan to establish an institute in child development on the west coast. Several years later, with the plans in place, Frank approached Harold Jones to take on the role of director of research at the Institute of Child Welfare in Berkeley, California. And so it was that in the summer of 1927, the Jones family, which now included a second daughter, Lesley, packed their bags and headed west.

When the family arrived in California, Mary Jones took a position as research associate in the new institute. She was, however, unable to procure an appointment in the Psychology Department at the University of California in Berkeley because of her husband's position there. At the time, many universities had strict antinepotism rules that precluded spousal appointments. Despite this, Jones lectured frequently in the Psychology Department. It was not until 1952, at the age of 56, that she was eventually made assistant professor in the Department of Education. In this same year, she and her husband Harold produced the first educational television course in child psychology on the west coast, featuring Mary Jones as the host and instructor.

In the meantime, Jones was making important contributions to research in child development. One of her first tasks at the institute was to help set up and run programs in parent education at the new nursery school that would be associated with the institute (the nursery school would eventually be named the "Harold E. Jones Child Study Center"). At around the same time that Jones was involved in this project, two of the three longitudinal studies that would come to be associated with the institute were initiated. The first, the Berkeley Guidance Study, was directed by Jean MacFarlane, a clinical psychologist with a background in developmental psychology who was on the faculty of the University of California Medical School in San Francisco. Nancy Bayley, a psychologist from the University of Wyoming, was recruited to be the research associate for the second study, the Berkeley Growth Study. Finally, the Oakland Growth Study (OGS), with which Jones became most closely affiliated, began in 1932. It was designed to follow a group of approximately 200 fifth- and sixth-grade students from puberty through adolescence (M. C. Jones, 1967). In fact, several follow-up studies were undertaken as members of this group moved well into middle and older adulthood. By the end of her career, Jones had published more than 100 research articles using data from the OGS.

THE EFFECTS OF EARLY AND LATE MATURING: A PROGRAM OF RESEARCH

Starting in 1950, with an article published in collaboration with Bayley, Jones began an investigation of the effects of early and late maturing on the lives of the participants in the OGS. This investigation resulted in several articles. A closer look at a number of these studies uncovers the concern for the individual and the individual's development over time that imbued Jones's work.

In their study of the relationship between rates of physical maturation and social behavior, M. C. Jones and Bayley (1950) chose two groups of boys who fell at the extreme ends of their sample on skeletal age, an index of developmental maturity. Two groups of 16 boys each were selected and followed over a 4½ year period. Jones and Bayley collected behavioral observations in two settings: same-sex free-play situations and mixed-group situations. This second set of observations was collected as the boys socialized in a clubhouse for longitudinal study members maintained by and located near the institute, providing a real-life social setting in which to conduct observational research. The researchers made their interpretive approach clear from the outset of the 1950 article. In noting the importance of investigating the effects of maturation on psychological development during adolescence, they wrote the following:

> Although the psychological accompaniments of these differences in maturing can be examined in terms of mass statistics, this approach to the problem is often disappointing because of its tendency to obscure the intricacies of the growth pattern. . . . Case reports of individual children have been somewhat more successful in their attempts to disclose the processes involved in the attainment of maturity. . . . (M. C. Jones & Bayley, 1950, p. 129)

Although noting the importance of idiographic analysis in understanding the intricacies of the growth process, Jones and Bayley also acknowledged the useful-ness of group differences and attempted to strike a balance between these two levels by including statistical comparisons between the two groups as well as illustrative case material. They concluded from their study that boys who matured early (in terms of skeletal age) were more likely to be accepted and treated by adults and their peers as more emotionally mature and had less need to strive for status. Early maturers were more likely to become student leaders in senior high school. In contrast, late physical maturers were more likely to demonstrate emotionally immature behavior (perhaps arising out of a tendency for adults to treat them more like children because of their physical appearance) and often seemed to compensate for their physical immaturity with greater activity and attention-getting behaviors. To support these conclusions, they presented several case descriptions of late maturers. For example, observations of Tom, "a chubby small boy, very rosy of cheek, sparkling-eyed, laughing and dimpled," were reported over the course of his junior and senior high school years. In describing Tom at 13 years, one observer noted the following:

> Tom Saylor chattered to Jim Cohn about his new job with as much enthusiasm as if he had found a gold mine. He is paid fifty cents a week to pass out handbills for a grocery store; this involves getting up at 5:30 every Friday morning. He was enthusiastic in urging Jim to "get in on it." The latter's indifference seemed to him like mild insanity. (M. C. Jones & Bayley, 1950, p. 141)

In striking contrast to Tom, but in the same late-maturing group, were brothers Glenn and Charles. Instead of conforming to the more active and expressive pattern of behavior characteristic of several late maturers, Jones and Bayley noted that Glenn and Charles were extremely self-contained, quiet, and unsocial. They wrote the following:

> When most youngsters were seeking social satisfactions outside the family, Glenn and Charles were still enjoying fairly congenial recreational interests with their parents. . . . Glenn's response to the question, "Does your mother go camping with you?" was, "Yes, she likes to get away from people, too." (p. 142)

The lives of Tom, Glenn, Charles, and other early and late maturers whose adolescent antics were reported in the 1950 article were followed by Jones through early adulthood. In a 1957 article, she reported on the later careers and adjustments of 20 of the original sample of 32 members described in the 1950 article with Bayley.

In this follow-up, Jones included more case histories, revealing her commitment to the understanding of individual personality development and her idiographic approach. In the concluding section of the article, she made this orientation explicit once again by stating, "The foregoing presentation of data and the case summaries remind us again of the conclusions to the original study which stressed individual differences within each group, resulting from the complex interplay of factors" (M. C. Jones, 1957, p. 127).

In another 1957 article, written with colleague Paul Mussen, Jones explored the self-conceptions, motivations, and interpersonal attitudes of this same sample of early- and late-maturers using Thematic Apperception Test (TAT) data that had been collected when most of the boys were 17 (Mussen & M. C. Jones, 1957). Again, although focusing on general themes that differentiated the two groups, Mussen and Jones noted, "In summary, in understanding any individual case, generalizations based on the data of the present study must be particularized in the light of the individual's past history and present circumstances" (pp. 254–255).

Jones and Mussen also examined the TAT stories of a group of thirty-four 17-year-old girls, 16 of whom had been identified as early maturers and 18 of whom were late maturers. Again, although presenting general trends distinguishing the two groups, including a tendency for late-maturing girls to have higher scores on negative characteristics and need for recognition and achievement than their early-maturing counterparts, the researchers repeatedly stressed the need to pay attention to the unique personality structures of individual members, writing, "In conclusion, it is evident that each individual's unique personality structure is determined by a complex of interacting variables, including rate of maturation" (M. C. Jones & Mussen, 1958, p. 498), and later, "It is obvious that the findings

for this specific group of girls need to be particularized for each individual"
(p. 499).

The frequency, consistency, and forcefulness with which these statements
appeared throughout Jones's published work, in addition to her frequent inclusion
of detailed case material and focus on the complexity of the individual personality,
all attest to the idiographic orientation that she brought to her research. These
same qualities appeared in a later series of articles on the personality correlates
of problem drinking.

DRINKING PATTERNS: EVIDENCE ACROSS THE LIFESPAN

It was not until 1959, only 1 year before her official retirement, that Jones was
granted full professorship in the Department of Education. This allowed her to
hold professor emeritus status after her retirement, and she remained active in
the department for another 20 years. During the early 1960s, after the untimely
death of her husband, Jones was invited to join the research staff at the Institute
for the Study of Human Problems being set up by Nevitt Sanford at Stanford
University. Here she used longitudinal data from the OGS to conduct an investigation of the personality correlates and antecedents of problem drinking (see M. C.
Jones, 1968, 1971, 1981). These articles are noteworthy because of the richness
and depth of the data collected on individual members, as well as the length of
time over which data were available.

In her 1968 article on the personalities of adult male drinkers, Jones presented
results from California Q-sort ratings[2] made of OGS members over three periods:
junior high, senior high, and adulthood. The ratings were made on the basis of
detailed case material drawn from a number of sources.

> In the school years, periodic measurements of interests, attitudes, and physical
> and mental abilities were obtained in the classroom or at the Institute of Human
> Development. . . . Parents contributed family background and home-life informa-
> tion, teachers reported classroom interactions, classmates rated impressions of each
> other. Study members revealed themselves in compositions and interviews, on
> projective measures, and on self-report personality inventories. (M. C. Jones, 1968,
> p. 3)

In addition to these sources of data, at the adult follow-up intensive one-on-one
interviews averaging 12 hours in length were used to make Q-sort classifications.
Clearly, the emphasis of the OGS project, and Jones's involvement in it, was

---

[2]The California Q-sort method was developed by psychologist Jack Block. It is a widely used
personality assessment tool in which cards featuring descriptive personality statements are arranged
by observers according to how well they describe a person.

to collect, organize, and analyze data from the point of view of deeply and comprehensively understanding the individual, in addition to uncovering general developmental patterns and regularities.

In her 1971 article on the relationship between personality variables and drinking patterns in women, Jones again expressed her desire to balance the two levels of analysis, but also belied her preference for an idiographic approach. "Perhaps *more convincing than ratings* are descriptive comments and clinical appraisals of individuals who, in meeting the changing demands of adolescence, reveal tendencies which will later influence drinking habits" (M. C. Jones, 1971, p. 67; emphasis added). Jones then provided case summaries of three women to illustrate the personality configuration of a problem drinker, a heavy drinker, and a light drinker.

Finally, in a 1981 book chapter summarizing the findings from these two studies, Jones once again indulged her preference for individual case analysis. Excerpts from the stories of Ned, Jed, Rob, Sadie, and Naomi added some "'real life' flavor to the statistical analyses" (M. C. Jones, 1981, p. 239). In describing Ned, a problem drinker, she wrote,

> Ned presents a mixed picture—sense of humor, liking people, and yet an undercurrent of anxiety and depression. He seems pretty realistic in talking about his life experiences and yet there is a rigidity, a confusion, and disrupted thought processes that alcohol probably does not help. . . . [He] recounts his drinking adventures with boyish pride. "I can put 'em all down at a party." (pp. 226–227)

Jones reported that Ned had first arrived at the Institute of Human Development as a 10-year-old child. Introductory descriptions from this period, combined with Ned's reflections on them, gave some clues about later aspects of Ned's development.

"Ned is a small, energetic youngster. With these new companions he is completely unafraid, interested, and energetic." When Ned was asked at 38, "What were you like as a child?" he unhesitatingly answered, "Call me active. I didn't pass up many dares" (p. 239).

Clearly, Jones was not only a committed researcher but had a deep and sincere interest in the study of participants as human beings. She, in turn, became an important part of their lives.

THE PROFESSIONAL AND THE PERSONAL

Throughout her work, Jones emphasized the primacy of the individual, and the complexity, depth, and developing nature of personality across the lifespan. This professional orientation extended to her personal life. She served as one of the major sources of continuity on the OGS, keeping in touch on a one-to-one basis with many of the study's members via personal notes and telephone calls until just before her death (Reiss, 1990, p. 274). Logan (1980) noted, "The special relationships she worked to develop between the research staff and the study participants is surely one of the primary reasons for the lack of major attrition, a problem of great magnitude in longitudinal studies" (pp. 112–113).

The intimacy that Jones established with individual OGS members was evident in excerpts from notes she received on the occasion of her 90th birthday, when many members of the study were then in their 60s and Jones had known them for more than 50 years. One member wrote, "The world's a nice place for me because you're in it." Another wrote, "You made a significant contribution to my life. I love you for it" (as reported in Reiss, 1990, Appendix 148). Perhaps the nature of her relationships with the OGS members can best be captured by the inscription on the plaque presented to Jones at the OGS reunion of 1985 (as reported in Reiss, 1990, Appendix 64).

> Our heartfelt appreciation of the combination of professionalism and distinctive personal empathy, for the sincere help and advice from young teens to mature life. This eclipsing over 53 years of service and still ongoing, to a lady who gave of herself to help any and all of the Study Group.

THE STUDY OF THE "WHOLE CHILD": JONES AND THE CHILD DEVELOPMENT MOVEMENT

In 1943, the Society for Research in Child Development, a multidisciplinary association founded in 1934 to promote meetings and publications on child research, published a monograph written by the staff of the Psychological Clinic at Harvard University titled, "Physique, Personality and Scholarship: A Cooperative Study of School Children." Primary among the researchers was Nevitt Sanford, who had worked with Henry Murray on a clinical and experimental study of college-aged men (Murray, 1938). In the introduction to this monograph, Sanford characterized the research as "a clinical and exploratory study of the growth of the 'whole child'" (Sanford, 1943, p. 1). Clearly influenced by the personology of Murray and following closely in his theoretical and methodological footsteps, Sanford wrote,

> Our procedure has been to take the segments of the life cycle that were available for intensive study . . . to formulate the "total picture" as it was during a certain period. . . . Then the question was, how did this "total picture" come to exist and what was it becoming? . . . [W]e resolved to take into account as many factors as possible. . . . Our main concern was to study each of these variables in relation to the others. . . . This is the "whole child" that we have studied. (Sanford, 1943, pp. 2–3)

Sanford, although also an important collegial influence, was a close personal friend of Jones's for more than half of her life. He was instrumental in supporting her postretirement research on the personality correlates of problem drinking.

The eclecticism characteristic of child development research of this era was bolstered by the fact that the movement was, from its inception, intended to be as interdisciplinary as possible. In reflecting on the collegial environment at Berkeley during this era, Jones noted,

> Our objective was to contribute to an understanding of the "whole" individual, a biological organism in a cultural setting: first the infant, then the child, then the adolescent, now the adult. This required an interdisciplinary staff with different theoretical orientations, different techniques for collecting and processing data, for reporting and evaluating findings. (quoted in Reiss, 1990, p. 314)

These different theoretical orientations were supplied, among others, by Erik Erikson (who came to Berkeley in 1939 and had an office next door to Jones) and Egon and Else Frenkel-Brunswik, who became close personal friends and next-door neighbors of the Jones family. Jack Block, the developer of the California Q-sort (1961) and the author of *Lives Through Time* (1971) was another close friend and colleague of Jones's whose orientation was clearly idiographic.

CONCLUSION

In conclusion, despite Jones's intense involvement with the OGS, which resulted in dozens of published research articles, her behaviorist beginnings and her work with Little Peter have continued to garner more attention than her developmental work. In 1974, she was invited to give the keynote address at the first Temple University Conference in Behavior Therapy and Behavior Modification. In reflecting on the question of whether, if she were to begin her career over again with her present background of experience, she would have repeated her 1924 research, she remarked,

> [M]y last 45 years have been spent in longitudinal research in which I have watched the psychobiological development of our study members as they grew from children to adults now in their fifties. . . . My association with this study has broadened and deepened my conception of the human experience. Now I would be less satisfied to treat the fears of a 3-year-old, or of anyone else, without a later follow-up and in isolation from an appreciation of him as a tantalizingly complex person with unique potentials for stability and change. (M. C. Jones, 1975, p. 186)

Jones died in Santa Barbara, California, on July 22, 1987, after a brief illness. Almost 91 years old, she was still actively involved in her work. In addition to her status as the mother of behavior therapy, Jones should also be remembered for her rich, significant, and pioneering contributions to the understanding of development across the lifespan.

REFERENCES

Baumgardner, S. R. (1977). Critical studies in the history of social psychology. *Personality and Social Psychology Bulletin, 3,* 681–687.

Block, J. (1961). *The Q-sort method in personality assessment and psychiatric research.* Springfield, IL: Charles C. Thomas.

Block, J. (1971). *Lives through time.* Berkeley, CA: Bancroft Books.

Frank, L. K. (1962). The beginnings of child development and family life education in the twentieth century. *Merrill-Palmer Quarterly, 8,* 207–227.

Gieser, M. T. (1993). The first behavior therapist as I knew her. *Journal of Behavior Therapy and Experimental Psychiatry, 24,* 321–324.

Harris, B. (1979). Whatever happened to Little Albert? *American Psychologist, 34,* 151–160.

Jones, H. E., & Jones, M. C. (1928). Fear. *Childhood Education, 5,* 136–143.

Jones, H. E., & Jones, M. C. (1930). Genetic studies of emotions. *Psychological Bulletin, 27,* 40–64.

Jones, M. C. (1924a). The elimination of children's fears. *Journal of Experimental Psychology, 7,* 383–390.

Jones, M. C. (1924b). A laboratory study of fear: The case of Peter. *Pedagogical Seminary, 31,* 308–315.

Jones, M. C. (1926). The development of early behavior patterns in young children. *Pedagogical Seminary, 33,* 537–585.

Jones, M. C. (1930). The prevention and treatment of children's fears. In V. F. Calverton & D. Schmalhausen (Eds.), *The new generation* (pp. 445–464). New York: Macauley.

Jones, M. C. (1933). Emotional development. In C. Murchison (Ed.), *A handbook of child psychology* (2nd ed.). New York: Russell & Russell.

Jones, M. C. (1957). The later careers of boys who were early- or late- maturing. *Child Development, 28,* 113–128.

Jones, M. C. (1967). A report on the three growth studies at the University of California. *Gerontologist, 7,* 49–54.

Jones, M. C. (1968). Personality correlates and antecedents of drinking patterns in adult males. *Journal of Consulting and Clinical Psychology, 31,* 2–12.

Jones, M. C. (1971). Personality antecedents and correlates of drinking patterns in women. *Journal of Consulting and Clinical Psychology, 36,* 61–69.

Jones, M. C. (1974). Albert, Peter, and John B. Watson. *American Psychologist, 29,* 581–583.

Jones, M. C. (1975). A 1924 pioneer looks at behavior therapy. *Journal of Behavior Therapy and Experimental Psychiatry, 6,* 181–187.

Jones, M. C. (1981). Midlife drinking patterns: Correlates and antecedents. In D. H. Eichorn, N. Haan, J. A. Clausen, M. P. Honzik, & P. H. Mussen (Eds.), *Present and past in middle life* (pp. 223–242). New York: Academic Press.

Jones, M. C. (1983). Regional Oral History Office, The Bancroft Library, University of California, Berkeley.

Jones, M. C., & Bayley, N. (1950). Physical maturing among boys as related to behavior. *Journal of Educational Psychology, 41,* 129–148.

Jones, M. C., & Mussen, P. H. (1958). Self-conceptions, motivations, and interpersonal attitudes of early- and late- maturing girls. *Child Development, 29,* 491–501.

Kornfeld, A. D. (1989). Mary Cover Jones and the Peter case: Social learning versus conditioning. *Journal of Anxiety Disorders, 3,* 187–195.

Krasner, L. (1988). Mary Cover Jones: A legend in her own time. *Behavior Therapist, 11,* 101–102.

Logan, D. D. (1980). Mary Cover Jones: Feminine as asset. *Psychology of Women Quarterly, 5,* 103–115.

Lomax, E. (1977). The Laura Spelman Rockefeller Memorial: Some of its contributions to early research in child development. *Journal of the History of the Behavioral Sciences, 13,* 283–293.

Murray, H. A. (1938). *Explorations in personality.* New York: Oxford University Press.

Mussen, P. H., & Jones, M. C. (1957). Self-conceptions, motivations, and interpersonal attitudes of late- and early- maturing boys. *Child Development, 28,* 243–256.

Reiss, B. K. (1990). *A biography of Mary Cover Jones.* Unpublished doctoral dissertation, the Wright Institute, Los Angeles.

Samelson, F. (1974). History, origin myth and ideology: "Discovery" of social psychology. *Journal for the Theory of Social Behavior, 4,* 217–231.

Sanford, R. N. (1943). Physique, personality and scholarship: A cooperative study of school children. *Monographs of the Society for Research in Child Development, 8* (1, Serial No. 34).

Senn, M. J. E. (1975). Insights on the child development movement in the United States. *Monographs of the Society for Research in Child Development, 40* (3–4, Serial No. 161).

Watson, J. B., & Rayner, R. (1920). Conditioned emotional reactions. *Journal of Experimental Psychology, 3,* 1–14.

David Shakow (Photo courtesy of the Archives of the History of
American Psychology, University of Akron)

Chapter 13

David Shakow: Architect of Modern Clinical Psychology

Robin L. Cautin

In 1976, David Shakow (1901–1981) became one of only two people ever to win both the American Psychological Association's (APA) Distinguished Scientific Contribution Award (1975) and its Distinguished Professional Contribution Award (1976). With two of its most prestigious awards, the APA affirmed the breadth of the contribution that Shakow himself would try to describe in his unfinished autobiography. Tentatively titled, "Pilgrimages Toward an Experimental–Clinical Psychology—An Autobiography" (Shakow, n.d.), Shakow's sketchy outlines and scribbled notes reflect the nature of his myriad scientific and professional contributions.

The character and status of clinical psychology had changed dramatically in the years following World War II. The nature of this change was owed both to increased demand for psychological services and to the efforts of particular individuals devoted to the professionalization of the field. Probably no one figure deserves more recognition in this regard than does Shakow.

BIOGRAPHICAL OVERVIEW

Early Life

The first child of Russian Jewish immigrants, Shakow was born on January 2, 1901, on New York City's Lower East Side. He was raised in a strictly orthodox household, but as a teenager rejected the formal practice of Orthodox Judaism

(Krawiec, 1976). Anticipating that he would follow in his father's and grand-father's footsteps in a commercial career, Shakow attended the High School of Commerce. After graduation, he worked a year for his uncle, a businessman, while in the evening taking business courses at New York University. But a career in business was not to be. His other early experiences would resonate far more deeply with his nature and have greater impact on his development.

Shakow would come to regard the Lower East Side, with its diversity and fervor, as a propitious environment in which to have developed. From ages 13 to 21, Shakow volunteered at Madison House, a settlement for new immigrants on the Lower East Side. He considered this experience one of the most formative of his early days. There he interacted with an eclectic group of individuals, representing a broad range of interests and backgrounds. Through his associations at Madison House he encountered the ideas of Freud and Jung, ideas that would stimulate Shakow's lifelong interest in psychology. A few years later, Shakow, curious about socialism and the labor movement, was deeply affected by his reading of Cornelia Stratton Parker's *American Idyll* (1919), an account of the author's life with her husband, Carlton Parker. Carlton Parker was an economist interested in applying psychological methods to labor problems. In his works, Parker mentioned John Dewey and William James, whose ideas captured Shakow's interest and devotion. But it was James whom Shakow would come to regard as his "long life hero" (Krawiec, 1976, p. 4).

Education and Early Career

Late in 1920, Shakow, determined to study where his hero had taught, wrote and submitted an essay on James as part of his application to Harvard University. In 1921 he entered Harvard, where he was taught by significant figures such as Floyd Allport, William McDougall, E. G. Boring, Helge Lundholm, Frederick Wells, and Anton Boisen. It was to "the Jamesian influence that had permeated me" that Shakow attributed his enduring interest in psychopathology (Krawiec, 1976, p. 6). He developed this interest throughout his undergraduate career, owing both to the field experience he was able to obtain and to the significant mentors who would train him. The ensuing several years would be a time in which Shakow would come into contact with many of the institutions central to American clinical psychology. During Shakow's freshman year, Lundholm invited him to McLean Hospital to be a psychological assistant; Shakow enthusiastically accepted. In his third year, Shakow accepted Lundholm's invitation to take his place as the psychologist at McLean Hospital while Lundholm took a year-long sabbatical. In his senior year, Shakow was a psychological intern at Boston Psychopathic Institute, where Frederick Wells had a great influence on him.

After earning his undergraduate degree from Harvard in 1924, Shakow worked with Grace Helen Kent at Worcester State Hospital (WSH) in Massachusetts for 15 months. The impact of his experiences under her supervision would be profound.

Shakow began his graduate work in psychology at Harvard in 1925. It was also in that year that he met his future wife, Sophie Harap, whom he married in June 1926 (Shakow, 1974). Shakow earned his master's degree in 1927. But, in 1928, with a young family to support and preliminary dissertation research yielding equivocal results, Shakow left Harvard to take a position as chief psychologist and director of psychological research at WSH. Shakow later spoke gratefully about his early training experiences, but he noted that his training "program," as all others at the time, was of a "do-it-yourself character" (Shakow, 1976, p. 15). He would later reflect on these experiences as he developed a formalized training program for clinical psychologists.

Worcester Years

Shakow's 18-year tenure at WSH proved remarkably productive. As Kent's successor as head of the hospital's Psychology Department, Shakow served as both clinician to the hospital and as the research psychologist to a newly founded interdisciplinary research program dedicated to understanding the nature of schizophrenia. He also initiated and developed a clinical internship-training program that would serve as a model for other institutions. In 1942, 14 years after assuming his position at WSH, Shakow returned to Harvard to earn his doctoral degree with his dissertation, *The Nature of Deterioration in Schizophrenic Conditions* (1946). This work emphasized the importance of attention and mental set in the psychological understanding of schizophrenia. It also represented a pioneering effort in its application of experimental methods to the scientific study of psychopathology.

Chicago Years

Ready for a change, Shakow in 1946 became professor of psychiatry at the University of Illinois Medical School. Two years later, he assumed an additional professorial appointment at the University of Chicago in the Department of Psychology. During his 8 years in Chicago, he suspended his research work in favor of teaching, training, and educational policy and curricular development. In addition to these responsibilities, Shakow participated in multiple professional activities. Involved with several committees and boards of the APA, he would have a profound impact on the problems of education in clinical psychology at both the doctoral and postdoctoral levels. He served as a consultant for various branches of the federal government, including the Public Health Service, the Veterans Administration, and the U.S. Army. Shakow cherished these opportunities to contribute to the development of national policies and make recommendations for specific grants and programs.

NATIONAL INSTITUTE OF MENTAL HEALTH

Ready to immerse himself once more in clinical research and laboratory work, Shakow became the first chief of the Laboratory of Psychology in the Intramural Research Program of the National Institute of Mental Health (NIMH) in 1954. There he collaborated with an interdisciplinary group of scientists, including Robert Cohen, Seymour Kety, and John Eberhart. Their work covered a broad range of topics within psychology, such as neuropathology, perception, psychopathology, social psychology, and creativity. When Shakow retired as laboratory chief in 1966, he was presented with a set of 12 bound volumes that contained the reprints of almost 500 articles, the output of his research team during his stay as chief (Shakow, 1971). Although Shakow retired in 1966, he continued to work at NIMH as a senior research psychologist. He spent a considerable amount of this time writing up results of empirical studies conducted earlier in his career.

Throughout his professional life, Shakow made continual contributions to the study of psychoanalysis, and he facilitated the empirical investigation of its process. He wrote many articles and participated in numerous symposia, discussing theoretical and methodological challenges inherent in psychotherapy research (e.g., Shakow, 1948b, 1960). Perhaps his most ambitious project was his psychoanalytic film study in which he attempted to film an entire course of psychoanalysis in order to examine its process scientifically (Rosner, 2005). For his contributions to the objective evaluation of psychotherapy, Shakow was the recipient of the Helen Sargent Memorial Award of the Menninger Foundation (1965). One of his most influential works on psychoanalysis, a collaborative effort with David Rapaport, was the monograph *The Influence of Freud on American Psychology* (Shakow & Rapaport, 1964).

SHAKOW'S ROLE IN DEFINING THE FIELD OF CLINICAL PSYCHOLOGY

In the early 20th century, applied psychologists held differing conceptions of clinical psychology. Although all existing psychological clinics dealt with practical problems, the nature of these problems varied considerably, as did the activities of clinical psychologists and the settings within which they performed. The formal founding of clinical psychology is usually credited to Lightner Witmer (chap. 5, Portraits II), who in 1896 at the University of Pennsylvania opened the first psychological clinic. Witmer emphasized the treatment of cognitive–intellectual difficulties to the exclusion of affective–personality pathologies. Whereas Witmer's clinic focused on educational problems that were often physical in nature, primarily within the school setting, other noteworthy clinics, such as those of William Healy and Carl Seashore, emphasized psychological and dynamic personality pathologies that brought them into contact with institutions outside the school environment (Shakow, 1948a; Watson, 1977).

For approximately 50 years following its inception, clinical psychology was a field ambiguously defined. Although the practice of psychology had always existed, at the beginning of the 20th century the formalization of its profession had yet to occur. A bona fide profession must include standards of behavior and "the capacity to control the competency of its own members" (Watson, 1977, p. 209); rigorous and specialized training, usually taking several years, and continuing education to ensure that individuals are familiar with the newest theories, methods, and techniques; and the provision of services to the public (Benjamin & Baker, 2004). Thus, according to such criteria, clinical psychology during its first 50 years did not qualify as a profession. Even though self-nominated clinical psychologists provided services to a receptive public, standards guiding training and accreditation did not exist, nor were there means by which to enforce such standards (Shakow, 1976).

To formalize clinical psychology would be no easy assignment; tensions both internal and external to the field of psychology rendered the task most challenging. The APA, originally dedicated to the advancement of laboratory research, generally opposed including the application of psychology as part of its mission. Larger and larger numbers of psychologists would feel their interests underrepresented as they began to devote their efforts to individuals' practical problems. Their discontent provided impetus for the establishment of professional organizations such as the American Association for Applied Psychology (AAAP), founded in 1937, as well as for the founding of professional journals, such as the *Journal of Consulting Psychology*. Thus, within the field, tensions grew as a seemingly divided psychology began to emerge. And although the tensions between science and practice remain palpable today, the field's infancy in the first half of the 20th century rendered such tensions a particularly difficult obstacle.

In addition to tensions within psychology itself, external pressures, largely dealing with the medical specialty of psychiatry, posed challenges to the professionalization of psychology. The medical community became increasingly uncomfortable with what it perceived as an encroachment on its professional domain (Benjamin & Baker, 2004); some contended that clinical psychologists should not practice psychotherapy outside the medical setting (e.g., Menninger, 1950). Thus it was in this cauldron that Shakow would define clinical psychology, specifying its goals and functions, training, and relations with allied professions.

GOALS AND FUNCTIONS OF THE CLINICAL PSYCHOLOGIST

Most early definitions of clinical psychology were broadly conceived as dealing with the practical problems of individuals in a variety of settings, including schools, hospitals, courts, businesses, and private practice. In contrast, other definitions severely restricted the role of the clinical psychologist to psychological testing or to the study of the abnormal. Both kinds of definitions were inadequate, the former being too broad and the latter too narrow (Louttit, 1939). Although acknowledging that a precise and unambiguous definition of clinical psychology was impossible, Shakow discouraged exceedingly narrow conceptions of the clinical psychologist, stating, "'Otis specialists' or even 'Rorschach specialists' are not clinical psychologists" (Shakow, 1948a, p. 246). He argued that narrow definitions neglect certain areas and activities associated with clinical psychology and suppress the field's natural growth. At the same time, exceedingly broad definitions run the risk of intruding on the boundaries of associated disciplines (Shakow, 1952).

It is important to note that Shakow worked primarily in medical–psychiatric settings and worked closely with medical professionals. Thus, his writings on the goals and functions of the clinical psychologist were largely inspired by his experiences in such settings. In environments such as the psychiatric clinic, where the main professionals' jobs tended to overlap in scope, Shakow was able to carve out a unique role for the clinical psychologist. He consistently identified the clinical psychologist with the following three functions: (a) diagnosis; (b) research; and (c) therapy (e.g., Shakow, 1942, 1948a, 1952, 1969a, 1969b).

DIAGNOSIS

According to Shakow, *diagnosis* refers to the determination of the nature and origins—particularly underlying dynamics—of conditions, including hypotheses regarding outcome and disposition. Always emphasizing the substantive as opposed to the superficial and the dynamic as opposed to the structural, Shakow insisted that diagnosis is not simply a matter of labeling a patient. He stressed, moreover, the role of psychological (personality) factors not simply in psychiatric conditions but in more strictly medical illnesses as well (Shakow, 1969b). Thus, he argued that the role of the clinical psychologist and of psychodiagnostics should be recognized in a broad range of contexts.

The predominant diagnostic method used by the clinical psychologist was psychological testing, or psychodiagnostics. Shakow emphasized its scientific aspects, presumably in an effort to distinguish it from the more subjective, qualitative diagnostic methods practiced by the psychiatrist. In so doing, Shakow identified three kinds of controls with respect to psychological testing: (a) pre-examination controls, which refer to the development of valid testing materials and standardized instructions for administering the tests; (b) examination controls, which involve determining the extent to which the patient's present potential and fundamental capacity are actually represented in the patient's test performance; and (c) postexamination controls, which refer to the use of empirically derived norms by which a patient's performance may be compared with that of a particular reference group. By virtue of these controls, Shakow explained, psychodiagnosis reflects a midpoint between the subjectivity of naturalistic observation and the objectivity of the strictly experimental situation (Shakow, 1952).

Although Shakow emphasized the relatively objective components of psychodiagnosis, in no way did he mean to objectify the patient.

> Psychological examining is not a matter of machine-tending; it is a complex human relationship calling for all the skills and sensitivities demanded by any situation requiring the establishment and maintenance of rapport. . . . It is necessary that [the examiner] have a "therapeutic attitude" in . . . testing, that is, one which avoids probing and the carrying-out of misplaced therapy. In keeping with good testing procedure and without violating any controls, [the examiner] must leave the patient better rather than worse for the test experience. (Shakow, 1952, p. 463)

The psychologist's focus thus should always be the patient as opposed to the problem or technique (Shakow, 1969b). In addition, Shakow insisted that one remain cautious about interpreting testing results. He stated that "it would be rather presumptuous to report any findings without some hesitation and reservation, [for] even the most complete verbal report of events cannot adequately convey the whole body of data available to the examiner" (p. 63). Shakow appreciated not only the complexities of the psychodiagnostic process but the complexity of the human being as well.

RESEARCH

Shakow's deep appreciation of the intricacies of the diagnostic process extended into the domain of research. He was well aware of the challenges—technical and attitudinal—involved in conducting research. Of the researcher, Shakow wrote,

> As well as having a sense of personal responsibility about his findings, an appreciation of the fact that his findings make a real difference to a particular individual and his immediate family, the psychologist should recognize that he also carries a broader social and scientific responsibility. He must be aware of the inadequacy of the methods, the data, and the theory in the field. He should, therefore, be constantly sensitive to the research implications of his findings and his techniques, and be on the lookout for significant problems and investigative methods, attacking these problems in order to be able to integrate his data with the fundamental body of psychological knowledge. (1969b, p. 68)

Shakow considered research the primary function of the clinical psychologist; this proceeded from the psychologist's rigorous training in scientific methodology, including the use of statistics (Shakow, 1953). Especially within an interdisciplinary setting, research was the domain of which psychologists could and should

assume leadership. The dearth of fundamental knowledge in the fields of personality and mental health, moreover, rendered this function imperative.

Shakow identified three major areas of research: (a) patient-oriented applied,
(b) administrative applied, and (c) basic (Shakow, 1969b). The first domain of research, patient-oriented applied, involves examining the psychometric properties
of personality measures, conducting follow-ups of cases that do not support
predictions, and investigating all facets of the therapeutic process. He warned
that the repertoire of "therapeutic devices" is far from reliable.

> While both the objective and projective devices we use appear to have logical
> rationales—sampling of behavior under controlled and standardized conditions
> based on norms, on the one hand, and the projective hypothesis added to these, on
> the other—we are far from having established their dependability. (1969b, p. 69)

And he made explicit the various problems inherent in any systematic study
of psychotherapy:

> There are problems of the different varieties of therapy and their appropriate use,
> problems of assessment of change, of controls, of defining the significant variables,
> of analyzing the therapeutic relationship, problems of methods of expression and
> communication, and the problem of the learning processes involved in the therapy
> situation. (1969b, p. 69)

The second area of research, administrative applied, referred to hospital administration, an area conspicuously neglected by industrial psychologists, Shakow
observed (1969a). The psychologist is particularly well equipped to deal with
problems of personnel selection and, in the hospital setting, certain aspects of
residency training. With regard to the latter, psychologists are competent to study
the conditions conducive to learning. Shakow's view was that such problems
should be studied experimentally, so as to control systematically for different
types of causal factors.

The third area, basic research, encompassed a diversity of topics ranging
from learning and memory to social behavior. Although psychology's interest
in research had well been established as a function of its academic heritage, its
focus, Shakow noted, had not been on motivation and the functional aspects
of personality. Shakow considered this gap problematic and encouraged the
development of a comprehensive theory of personality, ideally one based on the
integration of experimental and clinical experience. In particular, he encouraged
that Freudian theory, which was based on clinical experience and theoretical
speculation, be subjected to the rigors of experimental study in order to expand
the field's fundamental knowledge base (Shakow, 1952).

Quality research, Shakow insisted, is inextricably linked to experimental training and clinical experience. Clinical work confers on the psychologist an apprecia-

tion of the complexity and subtleties inherent in human behavior and experience. Without clinical training informing the formulation of research questions and the interpretation of data, research runs the risk of being rendered meaningless, devoid of significance and external validity (Shakow, 1949). Thus, the most important function of clinical psychologists is research, "and it is for this reason primarily that they are interested in therapy" (1949, pp. 392–393).

THERAPY

Shakow wrote relatively little about the therapeutic function of the clinical psychologist independent of the research role. By no means, though, did Shakow oppose an expanding role for psychologists in psychotherapy, and indeed he acknowledged that increasing numbers of clinical psychologists were becoming interested in conducting psychotherapy (Shakow, 1965). In his writings, however, he emphasized the psychotherapeutic function less than psychologists' other two roles in diagnosis and research.

Shakow strongly favored a group approach to treatment. Whereas he understood the allure of private practice—autonomy, profitability, and security—he warned against its dangers and limitations (Shakow, 1965). A group approach better facilitates interdisciplinary communication, increases accountability, and provides more opportunity to contribute to psychology's scientific literature and to society at large. Shakow's view on this issue was not an unpopular one. For many leaders within the mental health field, in fact, the issue of private practice for clinical psychologists raised serious questions about the evaluation of competence and the great need in community agencies for psychological services (Raimy, 1950).

Accordingly, in a retrospective report on his 1947 recommendations for training for clinical psychologists, Shakow stated, "private practice is of minor importance. It should be restricted. It should be limited in every way possible to persons with considerable experience" (Shakow, 1965, p. 354).

Shakow's identification during his time at WSH of diagnosis, research, and therapy as the primary functions of the clinical psychologist explicitly informed the training programs that he developed throughout his career.

TRAINING

Shakow acknowledged that he had begun his clinical training just prior to the transitional period that would accompany clinical psychology's rise to professional status. He mused that perhaps this timing conferred on him a unique and helpful perspective as the burgeoning field of clinical psychology was on the verge of professionalization (Shakow, 1976). Indeed, the 1940s were a time ripe for change. Several interrelated factors converged to create immediate intense concern for the problems of mental health and of training for clinical psychologists. The war produced an unprecedented increase in the need for mental health professionals. This acute demand quickly brought into focus the problem of training. As increasing numbers of clinical psychologists were trained and employed, the responsibility to ensure their competence became compelling. Moreover, Shakow wrote, "The need for applied psychological work is great and unless psychology can provide adequately trained personnel, other disciplines, which recognize both the need and responsibilities, will take over the functions which are more properly the province of the psychologist" (Shakow, 1942, pp. 277–278). To be sure, training for clinical psychologists was available before World War II; however, it was piecemeal and unsystematic. The time for formalized training principles and programs had arrived.

The training of clinical psychologists thus became an immediate priority— and not just within the field of psychology. Governmental agencies such as the U.S. Public Health Service (USPHS) and the Veterans Administration also recognized this imperative; the former was primarily interested in developing a national mental health policy, and the latter in meeting the clinical needs of its clients.

The 1949 Boulder Conference on Graduate Education in Clinical Psychology, subsidized by the USPHS and organized by the APA, represented a milestone in the history of clinical psychology (Raimy, 1950). Seventy-one participants, including Shakow, convened at the University of Colorado to review critically the issue of training and to plan for its future; by all accounts it was an overwhelming success. It is clear that the major resolutions that resulted from the Boulder conference may largely be credited to Shakow; his ideas provided the framework within which training problems were discussed.

It is important to note that the Boulder conference was not the first organized meeting devoted to the training of clinical psychologists; in fact, throughout the 1940s, several committees had been formed, and conferences had been convened, to address the issue (Baker & Benjamin, 2000). Shakow himself had actually begun developing training programs in clinical psychology during his tenure at WSH. In 1941, as a member of the Committee on the Training of Clinical Psychologists convened by the AAAP, Shakow drafted a 4-year training program that integrated academic and clinical work (Shakow, 1942). He wanted to ensure that aspiring clinical psychologists were trained in scientific methodology as well as in psychotherapeutic diagnosis and intervention. Shakow's proposal suggested that the first year of graduate study provide a "systematic foundation of knowledge of psychology and achieve the degree of acquaintance with the medical sciences needed for clinical work" (p. 280). The second year was to be "mainly directed at providing the student with the necessary background in the experimental, psychometric, and therapeutic approaches to the problems of clinical psychology" (p. 281). The third year was to be devoted to the clinical internship, an essential component of training that served the following purposes:

> to give the student *facility in the use of already acquired techniques*. . .[;] to *saturate the student with experience* in the practical aspects of psychopathology. . .[;] to retain and develop that characteristic in which the psychologist by his training is different from the psychiatrist and social worker, namely, in the more *experimental–objective attitude* which he takes. [And] to get the student *acquainted with the types of thinking and the attitudes of his colleagues in other disciplines*. (Shakow, 1938, pp. 74–75; emphasis in original)

The fourth year was to be devoted to completing the dissertation. The committee endorsed Shakow's proposal, which influenced subsequent committee discussions of the same topic—for example, the Committee on Training in Clinical (Applied) Psychology (Baker & Benjamin, 2000).

Following the integration of the AAAP and the APA, the Subcommittee on Graduate Internship Training was formed (Wolfe, 1946). Shakow chaired this committee, which met at the Vineland Training School (located in Vineland, New Jersey) in October 1944 (Baker & Benjamin, 2000). The report that resulted from that meeting—*Graduate Internship Training in Psychology* (Shakow et al., 1945)—reflected Shakow's emphasis on the primary functions of the clinical psychologist: diagnosis, research, and therapy. In March 1947, the APA Board of Directors formed the Committee on Training in Clinical Psychology. Carl R. Rogers, then president of the APA, appointed Shakow to chair the committee. After soliciting feedback from all committee members on the 1945 report, the "Shakow Report," as it became known, was officially endorsed by the APA (APA, 1947; Baker & Benjamin, 2000). Its fundamental principle, combined scientific and professional training, was affirmed at the Boulder conference (Raimy, 1950), the Miami conference (Roe, Gustad, Moore, Ross, & Skodak, 1959), and at several minor subsequent meetings, ensuring the report's profound and lasting impact on the development and professionalization of clinical psychology.

Shakow's vision for training was not without its critics, however. In the years following the Boulder conference, growing dissatisfaction with the model's implementation inspired discussions of an alternative training model. Although Shakow envisioned a 50–50 division between science and practice, critics noted that graduates of extant training programs were not adequately prepared for careers as practitioners. George Albee (1971), an ardent opponent of the Boulder model, further asserted that there exists an inherent incompatibility between the science of psychology and its profession in terms of their epistemologies, goals, and methods. And Albee (1992) continued to take issue with the field's acceptance of the medical model of mental illness, arguing that clinical psychology should instead embrace a social learning model. Other critics argued that the academic departments, where clinical psychology training programs are housed, tended to be disparaging of clinical practice and thereby conferred a disadvantage to clinical psychology students (Peterson, 1976; Stricker, 1975). Detractors thus maintained that adequate and comprehensive clinical training would best be achieved in a professional school setting (e.g., Stricker, 1975). Some argued for a new degree, the doctor of psychology (PsyD), to certify competence in practice (e.g., Peterson, 1976). Although the Boulder model still remains the predominant training model within clinical psychology, the professional school movement, inspired by the critics of Boulder, continues to exert significant influence (Stricker & Cummings, 1992).

RELATIONS WITH ALLIED FIELDS

In delineating the goals, functions, and training requirements of clinical psychologists, Shakow was simultaneously indicating how clinical psychology overlaps, as well as differs from, related fields, specifically psychiatry and social work. In so doing, he addressed palpable tensions that exist among the disciplines. Psychiatrists felt intruded on as psychologists assumed more responsibility for the treatment of patients. Although Shakow deemphasized the psychotherapeutic function of the psychologist, he took umbrage at the suggestion that only psychiatrists are entitled to assume therapeutic responsibilities. He insisted that one's competence, not one's title or professional identification, should determine whether one conducts psychotherapy (Shakow, 1949). Moreover, Shakow went so far as to state that medical training might impede one's effectiveness as a psychotherapist. He wrote,

> In relation to medicine as professional background for psychotherapeutic training, I have often wondered whether conventional medical training does not sometimes serve as a hindrance rather than as an aid to optimal preparation for psychotherapy. . . . [T]here is some danger that acting as a healer of physical ailments may serve to desensitize the student to the subtleties of psychological and social factors. (Shakow, 1969a, p. 64)

One should not conclude, however, that Shakow lacked respect for psychiatry or that he was unwilling to collaborate with psychiatrists. In fact, he considered the team approach superior to any other. The team approach benefits from the various skills and backgrounds of its members. And while it becomes unavoidable in the clinical setting that responsibilities among the various disciplines would overlap, the training of the social worker, psychologist, and psychiatrist, respectively, should dictate the sphere of activity within which leadership should be assumed. For the social worker, it is community relations; for the psychiatrist, it is therapy; and for the psychologist, it is research (Shakow, 1952). And given Shakow's view that clinical experience renders research more meaningful,

Shakow urged the allied professions to "contribute some of their time to the training of the psychologist, in order to give him as full-bodied a background for research as is possible" (Shakow, 1949, p. 394). It is in this multifaceted approach that the very heart of the scientist–practitioner model can be found.

CONCLUSION

Shakow's work and dedication to the professionalization of clinical psychology left an indelible mark on the development and character of the field. In delineating clinical psychology's goals, training, and relations with other professions, Shakow's contributions transformed an ambiguously defined field into a bona fide profession. Working largely in medical–psychiatric settings, Shakow formalized a vision of clinical psychology that reflected his close ties with the medical discipline of psychiatry. The Boulder model of training for the clinical psychologist, most notably, illustrates this alliance. Critics notwithstanding, the Boulder model has served as a reference for all later discussions concerning training in clinical psychology. Moreover, it continues to provide a framework for the majority of training programs in the field (Belar & Perry, 1992).

Throughout his career, Shakow maintained that research should be the primary responsibility of the clinical psychologist, and he emphasized the importance of scientific rigor and experimental analysis. These views speak directly to the ongoing contemporary debate with respect to the nature and future of clinical psychology. In a milieu that includes both psychiatrists and a growing number of master's-level practitioners, Shakow's vision continues to articulate the unique set of skills and abilities that should distinguish the clinical psychologist.

REFERENCES

Albee, G. (1971). The uncertain future of clinical psychology. *American Psychologist, 26*, 1071–1080.

Albee, G. (1992). About Dr. Shakow, the March of Dimes, the triumph of truth, and angel food. *Clinical Psychologist, 29*(1), 9–10.

American Psychological Association, Committee on Training of Clinical Psychologists. (1947). Recommended graduate training program in clinical psychology. *American Psychologist, 2*, 539–558.

Baker, D. B., & Benjamin, L. T., Jr. (2000). Professional psychology at 50: A look back at Boulder. *American Psychologist, 55*, 241–247.

Belar, C. D., & Perry, N. W. (1992). National conference on scientific–practitioner education and training for the professional practice of psychology. *American Psychologist, 47*, 71–75.

Benjamin, L. T., Jr., & Baker, D. B. (2004). *From séance to science: A history of the profession of psychology in America.* Belmont, CA: Wadsworth.

Krawiec, T. S. (1976, September 7). Transcript of taped interview with T. S. Krawiec. Shakow Papers, M1300, Archives of the History of American Psychology, University of Akron, Akron, OH.

Louttit, C. M. (1939). The nature of clinical psychology. *Psychological Bulletin, 36*, 361–389.

Menninger, W. C. (1950). The relationship of clinical psychology and psychiatry. *American Psychologist*, *5*, 3–15.

Parker, C. S. (1919). *American idyll*. Boston: Atlantic Monthly Press.

Peterson, D. R. (1976). Need for the doctor of psychology degree in professional psychology. *American Psychologist*, *31*, 792–798.

Raimy, V. C. (1950). *Training in clinical psychology*. New York: Prentice-Hall.

Roe, A., Gustad, J. W., Moore, B. V., Ross, S., & Skodak, M. (Eds.). (1959). *Graduate education in psychology: Report of the Conference on Graduate Education in Psychology*. Washington, DC: American Psychological Association.

Rosner, R. (2005). Psychotherapy research and the National Institute of Mental Health, 1948–1980. In W. E. Pickren & S. F. Schneider (Eds.), *Psychology and the National Institute of Mental Health: A historical analysis of science, practice, and policy* (pp. 113–150). Washington, DC: American Psychological Association.

Shakow, D. (n.d.). Autobiographical materials. Shakow Papers, M1300, Archives of the History of American Psychology, University of Akron, Akron, OH.

Shakow, D. (1938). An internship year for psychologists. *Journal of Consulting Psychology*, *2*, 73–76.

Shakow, D. (1942). The training of the clinical psychologist. *Journal of Consulting Psychology*, *6*, 277–288.

Shakow, D. (1946). The nature of deterioration in schizophrenic conditions. *Nervous and Mental Disease Monographs*, *70*.

Shakow, D. (1948a). Clinical psychology: An evaluation. In L. G. Lowrey & V. Sloane (Eds.), *Orthopsychiatry, 1923–1948: Retrospect and prospect* (pp. 231–247). New York: American Orthopsychiatric Association.

Shakow, D. (1948b). *The objective evaluation of psychotherapy III: Procedure*. Shakow Papers, M1507. Archives of the History of American Psychology, University of Akron, Akron, OH.

Shakow, D. (1949). Psychology and psychiatry: A dialogue (Parts I and II). *American Journal of Orthopsychiatry*, *19*, 191–258, 381–396.

Shakow, D. (1952). Clinical psychology. In F. Alexander & H. Ross (Eds.), *Dynamic psychiatry* (pp. 449–482). Chicago: University of Chicago Press.

Shakow, D. (1953). Some aspects of mid-century psychiatry: Experimental psychology. In R. R. Grinker (Ed.), *Mid-century psychiatry* (pp. 76–103). Springfield, IL: Charles C. Thomas.

Shakow, D. (1960). The recorded psychoanalytic interview as an objective approach to research in psychoanalysis. *Psychoanalytic Quarterly*, *29*, 82–97.

Shakow, D. (1965). Seventeen years later: Clinical psychology in the light of the 1947 committee on training in clinical psychology report. *American Psychologist*, *20*, 353–362.

Shakow, D. (1969a). Clinical psychology. In D. Shakow, *Clinical psychology as science and profession: A forty-year odyssey* (pp. 38–43). Chicago: Aldine.

Shakow, D. (1969b). The role of the psychologist. In D. Shakow, *Clinical psychology as science and profession: A forty-year odyssey* (pp. 58–70). Chicago: Aldine.

Shakow, D. (1971). *Closing remarks*. Shakow Papers, M1539, Archives of the History of American Psychology, University of Akron, Akron, OH.

Shakow, D. (1974). *Harvard class of 1924: Fiftieth anniversary report*. Shakow Papers, M1300, Archives of the History of American Psychology, University of Akron, Akron, OH.

Shakow, D. (1976). Reflections on a do-it-yourself program in clinical psychology. *Journal of the History of the Behavioral Sciences*, *12*, 14–30.

Shakow, D., Brotemarkle, R. A., Doll, E. A., Kinder, E. F., Moore, B. V., & Smith, S. (1945). Graduate internship training in psychology: Report by the Subcommittee on Graduate Internship Training to the Committees on Graduate and Professional Training of the American Psychological Association and the American Association for Applied Psychology. *Journal of Consulting Psychology*, *9*, 243–266.

Shakow, D., & Rapaport, D. (1964). The influence of Freud on American psychology. *Psychological Issues, 4* (Monograph No. 13).

Stricker, G. (1975). On professional schools and professional degrees. *American Psychologist, 30,* 1062–1066.

Stricker, G., & Cummings, N. A. (1992). The professional school movement. In D. K. Freedheim (Ed.), *History of psychotherapy: A century of change* (pp. 801–828). Washington, DC: American Psychological Association.

Watson, R. I. (1977). A brief history of clinical psychology. In J. Brozek & R. B. Evans (Eds.), *Watson: R. I. Watson's selected papers on the history of psychology* (pp. 195–229). Hanover: University of New Hampshire.

Wolfle, D. (1946). The reorganized American Psychological Association. *American Psychologist, 1,* 3–6.

Magda B. Arnold (Photo courtesy of Stephanie A. Shields)

Chapter 14

Magda B. Arnold:
Pioneer in Research on Emotion

Stephanie A. Shields

I met Magda Arnold (1903–2002) only once, when she was 95 years old. It came about because of a professional meeting that I planned to attend in Tucson. It was my first trip to Tucson, and because I had an address for Dr. Arnold from 10 years earlier when I edited the newsletter for the then new International Society for Research on Emotions, I wrote to her out of the blue, not knowing whether the address was current or even if she was still living. It seemed worth some effort because Arnold is one of the great names in 20th-century emotions research. She is credited with reviving the cognitive approach to emotion, which for years had been eclipsed by behaviorist accounts of emotion (Cornelius, 1996; Lyons, 1980; Roseman & Smith, 2001). Arnold aimed not simply to bring emotion back to psychology, but to develop a theory that would integrate the psychological, neurological, and physiological aspects of affective phenomena to explain the place of emotion in personality organization.

I must admit that I was surprised when I soon received a letter from her, neatly typed, inviting me to contact her when I was in the area. So on a sunny Sunday morning I picked her up at her home—where she was still living on her own—and we drove to a small restaurant for a late breakfast. I had no idea what to expect before meeting Arnold. I was familiar with her work because of my own research on emotions. And I had long felt that she had not gotten credit for initiating the cognitive revolution in emotions research. In addition, I admired her aim to build a theory of emotion that incorporated an understanding of emotion as a dimension of the person as a whole. But what would she be *like*?

I should not have wondered. She was open as she talked about her own life and experiences and enthusiastic about discussing all aspects of emotions research. Since then, as I have been able to learn more about her life and her work, my admiration has grown. Her life and her work tell a story of a person deeply committed to research, whose steadfast belief in herself and the worth of her project enabled her to meet the many challenges of the times and her own circumstances (Shields, 1999a).

Arnold was drawn to study emotion in the early 1940s because of her interest in personality psychology, and by the 1960s she had become a leader in emotions research in the United States. She worked from a distinctly disadvantaged position. She began her studies of emotion when behaviorism was the reigning paradigm, and emotion was definitely out of fashion, more likely to be viewed as a disruptive extreme on an arousal curve (the hypothetical inverted U-shaped curve that describes the relation between level of physical–mental activation and performance–behavioral organization) than as a constructive or positive force in behavior. She was a woman in a field almost completely dominated by men. She was a devout Roman Catholic at a time when the impartiality and quality of science by Catholic scholars was suspect. She was an immigrant to Canada and, later, to the United States, whose early life provided her with no advantages and little opportunity. Finally, she wrote or edited six books and many research papers in English—her third language.

In this overview of Arnold's work, I provide a sense of the scope and complexity of Arnold's thinking and her contributions to research on human emotion, as well as a sense of her life. In this chapter, I aim to situate her life and work in the context of the scientific psychology of the 1950s and 1960s. I am helped in telling Arnold's story by her unpublished autobiography, which she wanted to share with me when we met in Tucson.

BECOMING A PSYCHOLOGIST

In her autobiography, Arnold begins her life story by telling about when her interest in psychology began. "From the time I first read Freud's *Psychopathology of Everyday Life*, at the age of sixteen, I wanted to be a psychologist. There was not the faintest chance, I knew that."[1] Arnold was not a likely candidate for a career in psychology. She was born December 22, 1903, and raised in Mährisch Trübau, a German-speaking rural community in Austria later annexed to Czechoslovakia. Her parents were traveling theater people, and she was raised by two

---

[1] Quotes of Magda Arnold are taken from her unpublished and undated autobiography unless otherwise noted. According to her family and students, the autobiography was initially written in 1987 and edited periodically thereafter. There is no definitive date for the final version, but it is likely to be about 1996. See also Shields and Fields (2003).

women who were admirers of her mother. She grew up with limited means, and that curtailed her opportunities for schooling. Nevertheless, she was an eager student and insatiable reader. Much later, by the time that she had obtained her bachelor's degree in 1939, she was confident that she had read all the important books in psychology. A commercial course taken at a convent school when she was young enabled her to gain a reading knowledge of English and training for clerical work. At the time she read *Psychopathology of Everyday Life,* she was working as a bank clerk.

She later became engaged to Robert Arnold, a university student in Slavic languages, and they married when he received his PhD. From 1925 to 1927 they lived in Prague, where she worked as a secretary and sat in on lectures in psychology at Charles University. Her husband, believing war was imminent and wanting no part of it, immigrated to Canada, and she joined him in Toronto in 1928. In 1935, when she began the study of psychology at the University of Toronto, she was also caring for their three young daughters, one still an infant. She completed her honors bachelor's degree with a Gold Medal (Wright, 1992) in 1939, and then began work on her master's the following autumn. Graduate work came at great cost—Robert, motivated by self-interest, often acted in an erratic and demanding manner. Just as Magda was to begin graduate school, he left her and took their three daughters to live outside of Toronto and limited her visits to them. Legally she had little recourse, and she lived with the pain of separation from her daughters for a decade.

Arnold's scholarly interests and personal principles, on some significant occasions, led her to choose a path that created personal difficulty or put her in opposition to those with greater power. Her master's thesis is one telling example of her willingness to do things the hard way when she believed it was the right thing to do. Arnold wanted to study the psychological effects of muscular tension. For her thesis she proposed to study how muscle tension affects performance. She devised an experiment in which she would compare muscle tension in the working and the nonworking hands of stenographers as the dictating speed increased. The department head, a student of Titchener, had other ideas. He essentially ordered her to work with a single subject rather than data from a group, which would not allow her to answer the central question about individual differences. She opted to do the study as she had planned it and ran her experiment during the Christmas holidays when the labs were empty. The data came out well. But that alone did not assuage the department head's ire, and it was only because she and her advisor argued that her thesis could be published (Arnold, 1944) that the department chair was persuaded to accept the thesis and award the degree.

As Arnold continued her doctoral studies at the University of Toronto, an internship at the Psychiatric Hospital in Hamilton, Ontario, in 1940 gave her the opportunity to do mental testing with psychiatric patients. At that time in Canada psychiatrists alone practiced psychotherapy and performed much of the work and research we associate today with clinical psychology. Psychologists, as the director of internships at Toronto sternly reminded her, were not to mix their task of intelligence testing with activities that should be left to physicians. For the time being she heeded the warning.

Her doctoral dissertation, an investigation of the effects of adrenaline injections on sound-produced seizures in mice, drew on her internship experiences, the results of her master's thesis, and her growing interest in emotion. The project yielded results contrary to what would be predicted by Walter Cannon's (1927) fight-or-flight dictum. Most important, the publications that ensued (Arnold, 1944, 1945) set Arnold on the track to develop what she aimed to be a comprehensive theory of emotion. The key element in her theory was her idea of "appraisal." Most simply stated, emotion is "a felt tendency [action tendency] toward anything appraised as good and away from anything appraised as bad" (personal communication, March 21, 1999). Her insight seems obvious today, and maybe even simple, but it was quite bold for the time because it integrated cognitive processes into an explanation of emotion. Her idea of appraisal, described more fully below, was the basis for a complex and rich theory.

World War II was underway, and men on the faculty were either away in the military or engaged in the war effort at home. The shortage created an opportunity for Arnold, just as it did for many other women in the United States and Canada who entered jobs and professional positions that had been difficult or impossible for women to enter before the war. Opportunities were especially good for Canadian women psychologists (de la Cour, 1987). Arnold was invited to join the faculty as a nontenured lecturer as soon as she received her PhD in 1942. Postwar events later afforded Arnold an opportunity to advance her clinical research. In 1946, when male faculty members had returned to the psychology department, she was no longer needed as a full-time lecturer. She knew that as an immigrant and as a woman, particularly one separated from her husband, there was next to no possibility of a permanent faculty appointment.

That year Arnold was invited to be director of research and training in the newly established Psychological Services of the Canadian Veterans Affairs Department. This work led her to develop a new method for scoring the Thematic Apperception Test (TAT; Arnold, 1962). Her work in Veterans Affairs revealed to her the importance of professional contacts; one result was her involvement in organizing the Ontario Psychological Association. It also revealed that psychologists would need new skills to deal with the needs of war veterans. At that time, Canadian psychologists were trained only in intelligence testing and not in personality testing, so Arnold and her supervisor William Line, who was her mentor at Toronto, planned a workshop and invited psychologists from across Canada. Line was an important figure in the development of community psychology in Canada, and he wanted psychology to contribute to improving the quality of life for military personnel (Babarik, 1979).

Line and Arnold decided that psychologists needed skills in administering and scoring at least one personality test, and so chose the then widely used TAT. In the course of setting up the training workshop, she found that the method of scoring originally developed by Henry Murray was not useful in working with war veterans, the main people she was working to help. She undertook the task of devising a new method of scoring the TAT based on an assessment of the individual's goal-setting.

Over the years Arnold further developed and refined this method (Arnold, 1949, 1962), which she named *story sequence analysis.* In sequence analysis the narrative produced for the TAT picture is described in terms of what the story teller is saying about his or her life situation, then coded in terms of whether the moral of the story (which she termed its *import*) is constructive (i.e., the result of effort, initiative, virtue, or the outcome of a plan that adapts to the circumstances) or destructive. Emotions that occur in the story are interpreted as an indication of the storyteller's motivational patterns. The self-ideal in action is reflected in constructive themes that involve conquering negative emotions (e.g., resentment, disappointment) and fostering positive emotions (e.g., love, cheerfulness). Arnold's story sequence analysis reflects her views on motivation as essentially concerned with growth and the fulfillment of a higher purpose. Her approach was noteworthy for its emphasis on the active engagement of the individual and the central place of values in structuring motivation (Gasper & Bramesfeld, in press).

AN INTELLECTUAL AND PERSONAL TURNING POINT

After having investigated Cannon's ideas about adrenalin and preparation for action in her dissertation, Arnold became interested in Cannon's idea that emotion results when cortical inhibition of emotion is interrupted (Cannon, 1927). It seemed to her that emotion results from activation instead. Her solution, at that time, was to propose that different emotions involve excitation of different brain areas (Arnold, 1950). This first idea, though, did not satisfy her because she believed that she needed evidence to demonstrate the connection between cortical areas and the autonomic nervous system responses and some way to relate how psychological evaluation could mediate bodily arousal. Arnold described her dilemma as follows,

> I had often been thinking about Descartes' notion that emotion is an "affliction" of the soul, and his division of the world into "res cogitans" and "res extensa." To me, the "individual" is just that, *indivisible.* And emotion is not something that happens to us[,] but something we do: we evaluate something as dangerous, and feel fear; as annoying, and feel anger. Although unintended and often unwanted,

emotion is still something we have initiated. Hence we are active in emotion, not passive. We are the actor, the agent; there must be a center of activity within us. Is that perhaps what is meant by "soul," I wondered. (Arnold, n.d., p. 7)

A major change in her theorizing, one that was to inform her work for the rest of her career, occurred when she left behind the questions of physiological reactions and turned to a different way of construing emotion's function. Instead of continuing to grapple with the fight–flight view espoused by Cannon and others, she began to think in terms of the features that distinguish the gradations between human and nonhuman capacities and, thereby, the emotions of humans and other animals.

This shift in thinking was possible through both hard intellectual work and a deeply felt spiritual transformation. Arnold experienced a significant spiritual transformation in 1948 while attending the meeting of the Eastern Psychological Association for the first time. Professional meetings are not usually associated with spiritual transformation, but there was something about the combination of the intellectual liveliness of the meetings, the diversity of people and topics, and her own interest in the nature of consciousness that awakened in her a long-dormant faith. By her account, she had been raised as a not particularly religious Roman Catholic. Moreover, the intolerance she saw in some priests and nuns while she was growing up in Austria repelled her. As an adult she had not given religion much thought. Yet somehow at this moment in the spring of 1948, the significance of Catholic beliefs seemed clear to her and became central to her sense of who she was, offering her a sense of calm purpose. In her autobiography she recalled, "I knew that this experience was bound to change my life. Now I had a firm basis, a firm belief" (n.d., p. 10). For the rest of her life, this uncompromising scientist maintained her deeply felt spiritual values. More than once, these values led her to make choices that would complicate her life and make her commitment to scientific study and writing more difficult to accomplish. (See also Shields, in press.)

EMOTION AND APPRAISAL

The academic year of 1947 to 1948 began an extraordinarily important period of professional opportunity in Arnold's life. She was offered a visiting appointment at Wellesley College, taught a summer course at Harvard University, and was then appointed to an associate professorship of psychology at Bryn Mawr College. During this period she undertook what was the first full formulation of her theory of emotion. A central construct of her theory was appraisal.

Arnold proposed that emotions are generated through a series of steps. First, the emotion object or situation is perceived, a process that she viewed as immediate and automatic. This direct, immediate, and intuitive process does not initially require that we recognize the object, whether the "object" is the self, another individual, or something else in the external or internal environment. This direct process of perception is based on phylogenetically ancient subcortical brain structures. For emotion to be evoked, that object must be appraised by the individual as good or bad for him or her at that moment. A subsequent nondeliberative (i.e., immediate and nonintellectual) appraisal process is initiated almost immediately, and as the self-aware part of emotion, it is the link between emotion and actions, plans, and values. The roots of Arnold's theory can be traced back to phenomenological psychology of the previous century (Reisenzein, in press) in viewing emotions as having objects—that is, as being *about* something and, thus, intentional at some level. Her theory also was grounded in the medieval philosophy of Thomas Aquinas (Cornelius, in press) in emphasizing emotion as an expression of values and the self as an active agent.

This is how the theory works out in everyday life: An object, let us say in this case a cute puppy, can entice a person to approach or retreat. Whether the person is drawn to approach or to move away depends on the meaning of the object for the person in that context—a meaning that is not simply equivalent to liking or disliking but related to one's current motivational state. I may love puppies, but I already have a puppy, I'm very hungry and on my way to dinner, and the puppy in question is covered in some sort of ugly, gooey, smelly substance in which he has rolled. Under other circumstances I would be motivated to cuddle the puppy, but in this one I am motivated to retreat. The direct and immediate evaluative process that occurs for me is, Arnold (1960) would say, automatic.

> The appraisal that arouses an emotion is not abstract; it is not the result of reflection. It is immediate and indeliberate. If we see somebody stab at our eye with his finger, we avoid the threat instantly, even though we may know that he does not intend to hurt, or even to touch us. Before we can make such an instant response, we must have estimated somehow that the stabbing finger could hurt. Since the movement is immediate, unwitting, or even contrary to our better knowledge, this appraisal of possible harm must be similarly immediate. (p. 172)

The immediate appraisals at the sight of the puppy (or the stabbing finger) elicit action tendencies to move away—or more accurately, "diswant" the object (Reisenzein, in press). Emotion is the felt tendency to want or diswant the object. What makes emotion special is that the appraisal of the object is specific with respect to its relationship to *me*. Reflective appraisals immediately follow those that are "direct, immediate, and intuitive" (Arnold, 1960, Vol. 1, p. 172) and can modify them. So, as I think about this puppy, remember a dog I used to have, and remember the waiting appointment, the emotion evoked by initial appraisals can intensify, or attenuate, or even change.[2] Action tendencies also evoke physiological responses, including emotional expression, and perception of those responses as they occur can generate secondary appraisals of bodily responses. Thus, secondary appraisal processes can intensify or even change the original emotion.

Arnold's theory handles the complicated nature of experienced emotion particularly well. Initial appraisals can occur with respect to different aspects of the emotion object, so that the adorable puppiness of the puppy draws me, but the stinky goo that covers the puppy repels me. Arnold's idea about "mixed" emotion was that it reflects the fact that sense judgments (the intuitive appraisals) can be about more than one aspect of a thing or person.

Arnold viewed motivation as the link between the wanting/diswanting-evoked action tendency (that is, emotion) and the actual action. Arnold did not consider emotion a modular system—that is, a system separate and separable from other cognitive and sensory processes. She stressed the interconnections between emotion-relevant structures and processes and the neuropsychology of other capacities, especially perception, memory, and motor activity.

Emotions are important in personality integration because emotional responses are guided by one's higher ideals. Arnold viewed reflective appraisals as ones that help us harness and understand emotion and use it constructively as a motivating force in personality. Personality integration, according to Arnold, is the process by which a person's emotional responses are guided by his or her ideals to achieve harmony between emotional reactions and intellectual understanding (Cornelius, in press). So, for Arnold, emotion was firmly based in our evolutionary history and thus similar to the emotions experienced by other animals. At the same time, however, human emotion is unique given the capacity of humans to think, and plan, and most important, to have a sense of their most enduring and central values.

THE MOOSEHEART AND LOYOLA SYMPOSIA

One of the noteworthy events in Arnold's early professional life was her participation in the first major international conference on emotions research since 1927, one that was intended to bring together significant people from every area of psychology to talk about emotion. The Mooseheart Symposium on Feelings and Emotions in 1948 was a watershed of mid-century emotion research. It was named "Mooseheart" because it was funded by The Loyal Order of Moose and held at Mooseheart, the national orphanage of the Moose fraternal organization. Mooseheart was a self-contained village that included a laboratory for the study

---

[2] Kappas (in press) pointed out that recent disputes among emotions researchers as to whether "appraisal" necessarily involves conscious experience of evaluation would not have occurred had Arnold's insights about the multilevel nature of appraisal been included in the discussion.

of child development. The symposium was organized by the head of the laboratory for child research, developmental psychologist Martin Reymert (Beito, 2000).

Reymert had previously organized the Wittenberg Symposium on Feelings and Emotions in 1927, held at Wittenberg College in Ohio. This had been the first time that scientists studying emotion came together to talk about that field of study (Reymert, 1928). At the time of the 1927 meeting, Reymert had the ambitious goal of bringing together emotions researchers every 10 years. The Great Depression in the United States and World War II intervened, so it was not until the late 1940s that Reymert was able "to call together again the leading scientists in the various disciplines in order to note the progress made within the field of feelings and emotions and to stake out new avenues of approach for future research" (Reymert, 1950, p. ix).

The participants at the Mooseheart Symposium were a who's who of social and behavioral scientists of the day. The names of many participants are familiar from the history of psychology in North America: Dorwin Cartwright, Arnold Gesell, Harold Jones, Donald Lindsley, Robert Malmo, and Gardner Murphy, to name just a few. The demographics of the conference were typical of the time, however. Only three of the 47 papers presented were by women (Margaret Mead, Anne Roe, and Magda Arnold). Arnold's paper, "An Excitatory Theory of Emotion," was based on the examination and critique of Cannon's "thalamic" theory of emotion that she had tested in her doctoral dissertation.

After Mooseheart, Reymert ambitiously aimed for an international conference on emotions every 5 years. Once again, his grand dream was derailed. After Mooseheart emotions research was neglected as scientific psychology came to be thoroughly dominated by a behaviorist paradigm that defined thought, mind, and experience as unobservable and, therefore, outside the boundaries of scientific study. When behaviorists considered emotion at all, they ignored the key role that the individual's perception and evaluation of situations plays in determining when and which emotion occurs. Emotion was thought of as a problematic byproduct of evolution, elicited by learned associations with evoking situations. Emotions research in the United States that was not entirely driven by behaviorism could be found, but few theorists (most notably Arnold and Robert Leeper) ventured into new territory. Theories of emotion in the United States characterized emotion as a manifestation of arousal (e.g., Duffy, 1941) and largely a disorganizing or disruptive process (e.g., Young, 1943, 1961). As Elizabeth Duffy (1941, p. 283) is famously—and often—quoted, "'emotion,' as a scientific concept is worse than useless," by which she meant that a science of behavior could not use constructs that are defined primarily by their experiential properties. From her perspective, feelings or anything else that are essentially subjective, even if they are a part of real, everyday life, cannot be measured directly and so are outside the realm of scientific study.

Arnold described the "Dark Ages" of emotions research that followed Mooseheart in the following way.

A wall of silence began to close off emotion from the general theoretical and experimental endeavor of psychologists, particularly in this country. Behavior theory, as it now began to be called, had finally succeed in banishing all thought of what might be going on in the "black box" by convincing psychologists that any concern with "mentalistic" events was thoroughly unscientific. (Arnold, 1970, p. viii)

Arnold herself organized the next conference in 1968 at Loyola University in Chicago. She modeled it on Reymert's 1948 symposium. The time was ripe for another symposium because "the black box would have to be opened sometime, somehow if the science of psychology was not to become strangled in formalisms" (Arnold, 1970, p. viii). By the time that Arnold planned the symposium, significant articles and books on emotion that opened up that black box had begun to appear (e.g., Candland, 1962; Plutchik, 1962; Schachter & Singer, 1962; Tomkins, 1962). These set the stage for revitalization of emotions research, which has grown consistently and considerably since then.

Arnold kept the Third International Symposium small and largely within psychology to promote discussion, but in the process, she lost the interdisciplinarity of the two previous conferences. She did keep the symposium's international flavor, however, even bringing Pavel Simonov from the Soviet Union, quite a feat in those Cold-War days when there was little scientific communication between Western nations and Communist-dominated Eastern Europe. The late 1960s were also a period that saw widespread protests and demonstrations for social change. Even Arnold's small symposium was affected. In France in May 1968 there were massive university student protests calling for university reorganization. Several French psychologists could not come to Chicago for the conference because of the university reorganization process that had then begun in response to the protests.

Ironically, Arnold was the only woman among the authors of the 20 papers that appeared in the published proceedings. The absence of women may, in part, reflect the general scarcity of women psychologists, given the sharp dip in the proportion of women admitted to graduate training immediately after World War II (Solomon, 1985). After all, until passage of the U.S. Civil Rights Act of 1964 it was perfectly legal for graduate programs to limit the number of women admitted (which they did) and for employers to say "we don't hire women," to pay women less when they were hired, and to promote women more slowly.[3]

---

[3] In 1970, fewer than 15% of tenure-line positions in U.S. higher education were filled by women, with a much lower proportion at research universities and elite colleges (Sexton, 1976). Even though the proportion of women undergraduates and graduate students has increased substantially since then—in the case of psychology quite dramatically—the proportion of tenured women faculty in research universities has scarcely registered this change (Valian, 1998). Women have been earning a higher proportion of PhDs in psychology than men since 1986, yet only one third of the tenure-line faculty in PhD-granting psychology departments is female (American Psychological Association, 2003). Moreover, increasing the proportion of women in the field by itself does not reduce the barriers to women nor rectify the effects of past inequities (Shields, 1999b; Stewart & Shields, 2001). Psychology has not escaped the incursion of sexism and bias in its scientific practice, either (Sherif, 1979).

MEMORY AND THE BRAIN

Arnold continued her quest to explain psychological processes in terms of brain circuits, and wanted to explore the connection of affective memory to memory in general. Work on *Emotion and Personality* (1960) had shown Arnold that tracing the brain pathways involved in emotion processes needed to be considered in relation to pathways mediating other psychological activities. She identified memory, an area in which there was a substantial and growing psychological research literature, as the topic of her next major book, *Memory and the Brain* (1984).

Arnold's laboratory was engaged in the kind of animal experimentation that was typical of physiological psychology at that time, but the development of her theory required a far greater range of information than her own lab was able to produce. Her books relied heavily on critical evaluation and integration of other published work. In those pre-Internet days, Arnold's exploration of others' research relevant to her project meant a lot of time in the library searching through books and journals. She also traveled to gather information. To extend the range of material on which she drew, she wished to learn about recent findings of Russian physiological psychologists. At that time, there was no free movement of scholarship or science between the United States and Soviet countries, so Arnold hoped that a research year in Germany might help her get better access to Russian neuroscience. She applied for, and was awarded, a Fulbright Fellowship to the Max Planck Institute in Munich for the 1962 to 1963 academic year. She was disappointed to find that West German psychology was no help at all and that the Russian work was no more available in West Germany than in the United States.

On one of her annual spring vacation visits to Mobile, Alabama, Arnold had decided that she would settle in the area after retiring from Loyola in 1972. She took part of a sabbatical year at Spring Hill College in Mobile, where her long-time collaborator Arnold Gasson (e.g., Arnold & Gasson, 1954) was a member of the faculty. The following semester she moved to a permanent position at Spring Hill College as head of the Social Sciences Division. Talks with the administrators at Spring Hill had inspired her to apply for a National Science Foundation grant to upgrade the Social Sciences Division of the college. To everyone's surprise, the grant was awarded. That was a mixed blessing for Arnold, however. The grant, along with teaching and her work as head of Social Sciences, made it nearly impossible to continue work on *Memory and the Brain*.

From the beginning, Arnold was frustrated by the failure of the college to prepare for the grant (it appears that no one was confident that the grant would actually come through) and by subsequent lack of administrative commitment and faculty interest once it was funded. Worse, the students who subsequently were recruited to participate in the study had no motivation to cooperate and were generally uninterested. Arnold remembered these years as the most difficult of her professional life, concluding that "I had worked harder in these three years than in any other three-year period of my career, and had less to show for it" (Arnold, n.d., p. 27). So, with much relief, Arnold retired at the conclusion of the project in 1975 and resumed full-time work on *Memory and the Brain*.

The University of South Alabama Medical School library gave Arnold access to the journals she needed, but she found that it was difficult to capture fully the rapidly expanding field of brain science that had begun to appear in the early 1970s. She reviewed an enormous range of theory and empirical work, working the findings into a volume aiming to relate the psychological operations involved in memory (perception, recall, recognition, and action) and to trace the brain structures and pathways that make these operations possible. In spring 1981 she at last finished the manuscript for *Memory and the Brain* and believed that the book would soon be published. As sometimes happens, the publisher's early enthusiasm was eclipsed by one unexplained delay after another, and it was 3 years before the book finally appeared in 1984. For some topics this might not unduly hamper the book's impact, but Arnold was writing on the cusp of great change in cognitive psychology and neuroscience, and the delay had serious implications for its impact.

Arnold's painstaking analysis of available data pertaining to emotion's place in interconnected brain circuits anticipated later scientists' acknowledgement of the relevance of emotion to the several forms of memory, especially autobiographical memory (Tassinary, Smith, & Bortfeld, in press). Her writing about memory was much influenced by her ideas concerning appraisal. She critiqued the dominant computational model view of memory as a series of information states, and argued instead that memory is better conceptualized in terms of interconnected dynamic processes. Tassinary et al. (in press) noted that Arnold's ideas about memory were ahead of her time in several significant ways, and her theorizing anticipated findings from research done in the past 25 years, research that was impossible before the introduction of the many brain-mapping techniques that have since been developed and are now used routinely.

CONCLUSION

In the late 1980s Arnold moved to Tucson, Arizona, to be near one of her daughters. She lived in her own home until she was in her late 90s and continued to publish, but at a slower pace. She became quite active in church activities. She was generous with her time, spending many hours visiting sick and elderly individuals, many of whom were quite a bit younger than she was. Arnold died peacefully in Tucson on October 2, 2002, 2 months before her 99th birthday.

Arnold's work, as influential as it was in stimulating appraisal theories of emotion, has faded into the background in recent years. Her contributions, like that of too many other foremothers in psychology, were on the verge of being overlooked and lost. Recent developments in appraisal theories of emotion, especially the growing emphasis on the multilevel nature of appraisal processes, however, have stimulated new interest in her work. The occasion of her centenary has also encouraged reassessment of her work and has revealed the many ways in which she was a pioneering theorist. The 2004 meeting of the International Society for Research on Emotions honored her contributions to emotions research and theory with a special symposium. A special issue of *Cognition and Emotion* (Shields & Kappas, in press) is devoted to an overview and examination of her work as it relates to contemporary research on motivation, appraisal, and the cognitive neuroscience of emotion. Other efforts, too, are being made to ensure that Arnold's legacy is recognized (Fields, 2004).

Arnold's life as a scientist, who also happened to be a woman, an immigrant, and a devout Catholic, further influenced the opportunities and barriers she encountered along the way. In considering Arnold's life and work, three themes stand out. A first theme is that it is impossible to consider Arnold's life without sensing her passion for research and writing and her commitment to grounding the psychology of emotion in brain processes. Her investment in the project never wavered.

A second theme concerns the connections and sometimes the conflicts between Arnold's identity as a hard-nosed scientist and a person of deep religious faith. One example, among many, is a decision to work within the context of Catholic higher education. In 1950, Arnold left Bryn Mawr, a college environment that she loved, to take a position at Barat College in Lake Forest, Illinois (an affiliated college of DePaul University since 2001), a low-prestige, underfunded Catholic college with poorly prepared students. She did so because she felt a sense of obligation to contribute to Catholic higher education. American society was experiencing a backlash against Catholics that created a level of hostility that had not been seen since the nomination of Al Smith, the first Catholic candidate for U.S. president, in 1928 (Gleason, 1995). To make matters worse, Catholic colleges were generally regarded by non-Catholic educators and many Catholic intellectuals as intellectually narrow and of poor quality (Gallin, 2000; Gleason, 1995).

A third theme is that it is impossible to tell Arnold's story without also telling the story of 20th-century psychology. Her career as a psychologist began with a fascination with Freud, weathered behaviorism, and anticipated the neuroscience turn in emotions research. Arnold's resistance to the prevailing paradigm may have been aided by the three people she credits with having the greatest influence on her career: her mentor as a student at the University of Toronto, Line, an important figure in the development of Canadian community psychology; her long-time collaborator Gasson, who had helped her think through the relevance of Thomas Aquinas's ideas on the nature of consciousness, knowledge, and emotion; and the personality theorist Gordon Allport, whom Arnold met while she was teaching a summer course at Harvard and with whom she corresponded over many years (Babarik, 1979; Cornelius, in press).

Perhaps the best way to end this chapter is with Arnold's own words. When I interviewed Arnold in Tucson, I asked what advice she would give colleagues who are beginning their careers in psychology today. Her response was prompt and vigorous: "Follow your attractions. Don't simply do what you think you *should* do. It's always the emotional attraction that will keep you persisting when things get rough."

REFERENCES

American Psychological Association. (2003). *2002–2003 faculty salaries survey.* Washington, DC: Author.

Arnold, M. B. (n.d.). *Autobiography.* Unpublished manuscript.

Arnold, M. B. (1944). Emotional factors in experimental neuroses. *Journal of Experimental Psychology, 34,* 257–281.

Arnold, M. B. (1945). Physiological differentiation of emotional states. *Psychological Review, 52,* 35–48.

Arnold, M. B. (1949). A demonstration analysis of the TAT in a clinical setting. *Journal of Abnormal and Social Psychology, 44,* 97–111.

Arnold, M. B. (1950). An excitatory theory of emotion. In M. L. Reymert (Ed.), *Feelings and emotions: The Mooseheart Symposium in cooperation with the University of Chicago* (pp. 11–33). New York: McGraw-Hill.

Arnold, M. B. (1960). *Emotion and personality (Volume I, Psychological aspects; Volume II, Neurological and physiological aspects).* New York: Columbia University Press

Arnold, M. B. (1962). *Story sequence analysis: A new method of measuring motivation and predicting achievement.* New York: Columbia University Press.

Arnold, M. B. (Ed.). (1970). *Feelings and emotions: The Loyola symposium.* Oxford, England: Academic Press.

Arnold, M. B. (1984). *Memory and the brain.* Hillsdale, NJ: Erlbaum.

Arnold, M. B., & Gasson, J. A. (1954). *The human person: An approach to an integral theory of personality.* Oxford, England: Ronald Press.

Babarik, P. (1979). The buried Canadian roots of community psychology. *Journal of Community Psychology, 7,* 362–367.

Beito, D. T. (2000). *From mutual aid to the welfare state: Fraternal societies and social services, 1890–1967.* Chapel Hill: University of North Carolina Press.

Candland, D. K. (Ed.). (1962). *Emotion: Bodily change, an enduring problem in psychology.* Princeton, NJ: Van Nostrand.

Cannon, W. B. (1927). *Bodily changes in pain, hunger, fear and rage* (2nd ed.). New York: D. Appleton.

Cornelius, R. (1996). *The science of emotion.* Upper Saddle River, NJ: Prentice Hall.

Cornelius, R. (in press). Madga Arnold's Thomistic theory of emotion, the self-ideal, and the moral dimension of appraisal. *Cognition and Emotion.*

de la Cour, L. (1987). The "other" side of psychology: Women psychologists in Toronto from 1920 to 1945. *Canadian Woman Studies, 8,* 44–46.

Duffy, E. (1941). An explanation of "emotional" phenomena without the use of the concept "emotion." *Journal of General Psychology, 25,* 283–293.

Fields, R. M. (2004). A life of science and spirituality: Magda B. Arnold (1903–2002). *Feminist Psychologist*, 11–12.

Gallin, A. (2000). *Negotiating identity: Catholic higher education since 1960*. Notre Dame, IN: University of Notre Dame.

Gasper, K., & Bramesfeld, K. D. (in press). Imparting wisdom: Madga Arnold's contributions to research on affect and motivation. *Cognition and Emotion*.

Gleason, P. (1995). *Contending with modernity: Catholic higher education in the twentieth century*. New York: Oxford University Press.

Kappas, A. (in press). Appraisals are direct, immediate, intuitive, and unwitting . . . and some are reflective. *Cognition and Emotion*.

Lyons, W. (1980). *Emotion*. Cambridge, England: Cambridge University Press.

Plutchik, R. (1962). *The emotions: Facts, theories and a new model*. New York: Random House.

Reisenzein, R. (in press). Arnold's theory of emotion in historical perspective. *Cognition and Emotion*.

Reymert, M. L. (1928). *Feelings and emotions: The Wittenberg symposium*. Worcester, MA: Clark University Press.

Reymert, M. L. (1950). *Feelings and emotions: The Mooseheart symposium in cooperation with the University of Chicago*. New York: McGraw-Hill.

Roseman, I. J., & Smith, C. A. (2001). Appraisal theory. Overview, assumptions, varieties, controversies. In K. R. Scherer, A. Schorr, & T. Johnstone (Eds.), *Appraisal processes in emotion: Theory, methods, research* (pp. 3–19). Oxford, England: Oxford University Press.

Schachter, S., & Singer, J. (1962). Cognitive, social and physiological determinants of emotional state. *Psychological Review, 69*, 370–399.

Sexton, P. (1976). *Women in education*. Bloomington, IN: Phi Delta Kappa.

Sherif, C. (1979). Bias in psychology. In J. A. Sherman & E. T. Beck (Eds.), *The prism of sex* (pp. 93–133). Madison: University of Wisconsin Press.

Shields, S. A. (1999a). A conversation with Magda Arnold. *Emotion Researcher, 13*(3), 3.

Shields, S. A. (1999b). Ethical issues for women's leadership in the university. In S. K. Majumdar, H. S. Pitkow, L. Bird, & E. W. Miller (Eds.), *Ethics in academia* (pp. 86–99). University Park: Pennsylvania Academy of Science.

Shields, S. A. (in press). Magda B. Arnold's life and work in context. *Cognition and Emotion*.

Shields, S. A., & Fields, R. (2003). Magda Arnold, 1903–2002. *American Psychologist, 58*, 403–404.

Shields, S. A., & Kappas, A. (in press). Special issue on Magda B. Arnold (1903–2002). *Cognition and Emotion*.

Solomon, B. M. (1985). *In the company of educated women: A history of women and higher education in America*. New Haven, CT: Yale University Press.

Stewart, A. J., & Shields, S. A. (2001). Gatekeepers as change agents: What are feminist psychologists doing in places like this? In D. L. Tolman & M. Brydon-Miller (Eds.), *Transforming psychology: Interpretive and participatory research methods* (pp. 304–318). New York: New York University Press.

Tassinary, L., Smith S., & Bortfeld, H. (in press). *Memory and the brain* (1984): A reappraisal. *Cognition and Emotion*.

Tomkins, S. S. (1962). *Affect, imagery, and consciousness* (4 volumes). New York: Springer.

Valian, V. (1998). *Why so slow? The advancement of women*. Cambridge, MA: MIT Press.

Wright, M. J. (1992). Women groundbreakers in Canadian psychology: World War II and its aftermath. *Canadian Psychology, 33*(2), 675–682.

Young, P. T. (1943). *Emotion in man and animal*. New York: Wiley.

Young, P. T. (1961). *Motivation and emotion*. New York: Wiley.

Nikolaas Tinbergen (Photo courtesy of Donald A. Dewsbury)

Chapter 15

Nikolaas Tinbergen:
Nobel-Prize-Winning Ethologist

Donald A. Dewsbury

Nikolaas Tinbergen was an ethologist, one of a group of European zoologists who shared a common interest in understanding the behavior of animals in relation to their natural environments. He thought of himself as a "curious naturalist," and spent much of his life "watching and wondering" about the causes of behavior in such species as stickleback fish, herring gulls, and digger wasps. Remarkably, because such awards for behavioral sciences were rare, in 1973 he shared with Konrad Lorenz and Karl von Frisch the Nobel prize for Physiology or Medicine (Dewsbury, 2003). Perhaps equally remarkable was the awarding of the American Psychological Association's (APA) Award for Distinguished Scientific Contributions to this nonpsychologist. Clearly, his work touched a wide audience. In this chapter, I portray the life, complexities, and work of this impressive man whose contributions to animal behavior studies were of such importance as to merit a Nobel prize, but who devoted the later years of his career to the study of problems in humans (Dewsbury, 1990; Hinde, 1990; Kruuk, 2003; Röell, 2000; N. Tinbergen, 1985).

THE LIFE OF AN ETHOLOGIST

Tinbergen was born in The Hague, the Netherlands, on April 15, 1907, the son of Dirk Cornelius, a language and history teacher in grammar schools, and of Jeanette (Van Eek) Tinbergen. Niko, as he was called, was the third of five children. Older brother Jan became a theoretical physicist who later turned to the field of economics, where he also won a Nobel prize in 1969. Young Tinbergen was not a diligent student; his lessons bored him. He loved nature and lived just an hour's walk from the shore. Thus, he spent much of his time collecting seashells, watching birds, studying fish, identifying plants, and camping.

It is important to understand the environment to which Tinbergen was exposed and in which Dutch ethology was to flourish (see Röell, 2000). Nature study in the Netherlands was well organized and popular among children of the day. School teachers J. P. Thijsse and F. Heimans produced a series of books based on nature walks that became quite popular. They and a colleague then published a magazine, *Living Nature* (*De levende natur*) and also wrote newspaper columns on the subject. A series of stickers portraying nature scenes was issued by a Dutch bisquit (cookie) manufacturer. The stickers came wrapped alongside the firm's product and could be pasted into albums issued each year. Children would collect and trade them much as American children collect baseball cards. As American children of the day, armed with bats and gloves, flocked to baseball fields, many Dutch youth, armed with bicycles, camping gear, cameras, and binoculars, went off to study nature. Several natural history associations for youth were organized. It was in these organizations "that the network was formed for future professional biologists, conservationists, and supporters" (Röell, 2000, p. 182).

Tinbergen read the books and magazines and collected the cookie stickers. He joined the Dutch Youth Association for Nature Study. His interest in nature developed in a supportive environment, as several of his teachers and other adult naturalists encouraged him. Even as a schoolboy, he gained insight into the functions of behavior, such as why hooded crows covered their caches of shellfish.

After graduation from high school, the budding naturalist spent a few months at the Vogelwarte Rossitten, a bird observatory in East Prussia that had developed the technique of bird banding. After his experiences at the observatory, Tinbergen decided on a career in biology, rather than photography, physical education, or farming, all of which he had considered earlier, and he entered the State University of Leiden. A gifted athlete, while at the university Tinbergen played on the Dutch national hockey team. Summers were spent in nature study at his parents' cottage in Hulshorst, near the Dutch coast. There he studied the behavior of wasps, and Tinbergen was amazed at how the simple process of marking the wasps turned them from anonymous insects into individuals whose particular lives he could follow. Eventually, in 1932, he completed his doctorate with a 32-page thesis on the ways in which wasps located their nests; it was the shortest (accepted) thesis on record at the university.

On graduation, Tinbergen married chemistry student Elizabeth (Lies) Rutten; the couple eventually had five children, two sons and three daughters. They joined a meteorological expedition to Greenland for their 14-month "honeymoon." The couple lived with Angmagssalik natives, studying the behavior of arctic foxes, guillemots, phalaropes, snow buntings, seals, sledge dogs, and the natives themselves. In 1933, Tinbergen accepted a faculty position back at the university in Leiden. He developed the study of his precious stickleback fish for a project in his laboratory course for undergraduates. He and his students also conducted field studies of homing in sand wasps, sexual behavior in Grayling butterflies, and the displays of hobbies (birds).

In 1936, Konrad Lorenz visited Leiden for a seminar, and the two men clicked immediately. It can be argued that the field of ethology was developed during the spring of 1937, when the Tinbergens spent time working and talking with Lorenz at the family home near Vienna. The two men complemented each other well, with Lorenz being the speculative and enthusiastic developer of theories and hypotheses and Tinbergen being the more critical man, striving to put speculations to empirical test. Lorenz had a love and gift for keeping captive animals; Tinbergen preferred the field. Lorenz was gifted with intuition. Like von Frisch, who influenced him and may have been a model for the use of experimental methods in nature, Tinbergen was gifted with the ability to conduct simple, yet seemingly incisive, experiments.

In 1937, Tinbergen made his first trip to the United States, where he met a number of American biologists and psychologists. He was critical of the broad generalizations some psychologists were making on the basis of limited observations of a few species observed in captivity.

When, in 1942 during World War II, Tinbergen and some colleagues protested the dismissal of three Jewish professors from the university, they were imprisoned in a Nazi hostage camp in the south of the Netherlands. The Germans threatened to kill prisoners in retaliation for sabotage efforts by the Dutch; several prisoners were in fact executed. Tinbergen used his time to continue writing, completing a draft of *Social Behaviour in Animals* (1953) and two children's books. Released from prison after 2 years, Tinbergen was named professor of experimental zoology at the same university and, with his students, resumed his studies of behavior in a variety of species.

In 1949, Tinbergen made a momentous decision to emigrate and accepted a lectureship at Oxford University, where he spent the rest of his academic career. Tinbergen explained his move as an effort to facilitate the spread of ethology in English-speaking countries, an essential step in its success. Kruuk (2003) suggested that additional factors included a growing disillusion with life in Holland, its politics, and its stifling regulations. Tinbergen's administrative and lecturing responsibilities were growing, and he was irritated by the Dutch bourgeoisie. Thus, the move was multidetermined.

In England, his pattern of conducting and supervising an extensive program of field studies continued, although he sometimes found it harder to get out into the field. He came to emphasize the study of shore birds, especially gulls. Tinbergen was happiest in the field studying behavior with his students, rather than remaining in an office as a supervisor. He loved the shore, on which he had been imprinted as a youth, and spent as much time as possible working there.

Tinbergen produced a steady flow of books that helped to bring ethology to a broad range of scientists in the English-speaking world. These included *The Study of Instinct* (1951), *Social Behaviour in Animals* (1953), *Curious Naturalists* (1958), and *The Herring Gull's World* (1961). A collection of some of his most important journal articles was published in the two-volume *The Animal in Its World* (1972a). Tinbergen was also a gifted artist, photographer, and filmmaker. His film portrayal of the life history of lesser-black-backed gulls, *Signals for Survival*, made with Hugh Falkus during the 1960s, was especially influential.

During the 1950s and 1960s, the European ethologists had increasing contacts with North American psychologists. Their systems were in conflict, as the Europeans emphasized the study of the evolution of behavior in a broad range of species in relation to the natural environment, whereas the psychologists stressed the development and immediate control of behavior studied under the controlled conditions of the laboratory. As a result of these interactions and the efforts of Tinbergen and other ethologists, along with such psychologists as Frank Beach and Daniel Lehrman, both sides softened their positions, with some ethologists coming to recognize the important role of the environment in the epigenetic development of behavior and some psychologists developing their views on the evolution of behavior that had been present, but not sufficiently emphasized, in the earlier comparative psychology (see also Beach, 1950). It was Tinbergen and the English-speaking psychologists who most facilitated this rapprochement, whereas the German-speaking ethologists remained more conservative in their views on the innateness of much behavior. A few American psychologists, such as T. C. Schneirla, remained unconvinced of the merits of the new ethology.

The unexpected Nobel prize was awarded to Lorenz, Tinbergen, and von Frisch in 1973. Tinbergen, modest as always, was amazed at how this led others to place him on a pedestal and treat him as somehow different from his fellow human beings. Among his other awards were the Jan Swammerdam Medal of the Netherlands and the Distinguished Scientific Contribution Award of the APA in 1987. He received honorary degrees from the universities of Edinburgh and Leicester. Tinbergen was a member of several academies, including the National Academy of Sciences of the United States.

Tinbergen died in Oxford on December 21, 1988. His students and colleagues published two books in his honor (Baerends, Beer, & Manning, 1975; Dawkins, Halliday, & Dawkins, 1991). In 1987, the Ethological Society of German-Speaking Countries initiated the Niko Tinbergen Prize to honor a scientist under age 35 for an outstanding publication in ethology.

Among the reasons for Tinbergen's influence were his sheer joy in conducting research in nature, his ability to convey that joy, and his brilliant writing style. At a time when psychologists were emphasizing the rigor of their laboratory experiments, Tinbergen's articles were punctuated with statements about the happy hours he spent studying animals and about his fascination with his work

(Dewsbury, 1997). These writings stimulated the next generation of animal behaviorists to seek out ethologists as role models (Dewsbury, 1995). His students admired his combination of enthusiasm, humility, perseverance, and rigor. He was a part of their research group rather than a paternalistic overseer. Tinbergen was a modest man dedicated to nature study. At the same time, however, he felt a great social responsibility and some guilt about spending so much time in pursuits that appeared to have little immediate effect on the human condition. He would try to remedy that during the last part of his career.

Tinbergen was human and thus imperfect. He could be excessively demanding on those around him. His strong work ethic may have imparted costs to both his family and his enjoyment of life. Beginning after the war and continuing through the rest of his life, Tinbergen was subject to periods of deep, dark depression. "He sought psychiatric help, on several occasions spending time in hospital, but the actual cause of his depressions was never identified" (Kruuk, 2003, p. 258). His physical and mental decline in the 1960s took a toll on his work. He was effective, however, in hiding these problems from his children and from those outside of his immediate circle. In his public persona, one still saw the buoyant personality of the curious naturalist. This was an honest presentation of self, but it appears to have been mixed with periods of considerably less buoyancy.

THE FOUR QUESTIONS

It can be argued that Tinbergen's early work was strictly descriptive and that it lacked a coherent interpretive framework (Röell, 2000). Later, he systematized his methodology. Among Tinbergen's most influential conceptions was his elucidation of the famous "four questions" that characterized ethological study and are now regarded as the foundation of the broad study of behavior (N. Tinbergen, 1951, 1963a). Paraphrasing Tinbergen, a complete understanding of a behavioral pattern requires information regarding the immediate causation, development, evolutionary history, and adaptive significance of the behavior.

However, as is sometimes forgotten, Tinbergen stressed that the first tasks in the study of behavior are observation and description. Answers to the four questions could be obtained only once a thorough understanding of the natural behavior of the animal has been developed. He criticized most psychologists for trying to conduct experiments before they were fully familiar with the behavior and animals under study. Tinbergen sought principles of generality, but they had to be built on a solid observational base. However, he was not naive, and realized that observation does not take place in a vacuum; completely unbiased observation is impossible. He noted that "when we observe, we are hypothesizing all the time" (in Cohen, 1977, p. 382) and "what is particularly worrying is to experience in oneself how strongly one's expectations, even one's non-rational moods, can colour and even distort what the senses report" (p. 325).

The first of the four sets of questions, which related to immediate causation, concerns events, both internal and external, occurring around the time of the behavior. This includes stimuli and other environmental events as well as such internal factors as neural and hormonal influences. Questions of development, the second category, concern longer term influences of genes and environment interacting with the organism as it matures. These two sets of questions have sometimes been grouped as "proximate" or "how" questions and have been prevalent in psychology. Less common have been questions sometimes grouped as "ultimate" or "why" questions. The evolutionary history of a behavioral pattern concerns the phylogenetic origins of the behavior. Thus, by studying closely related species one can find similarities and differences that suggest the evolutionary history of the behavior in a manner parallel to that possible with the study of the bones of related species. The fourth question concerns the adaptive significance, or function, of the behavioral pattern. Most behavioral patterns occur because, on average and over time, they have enhanced the total reproductive success, or fitness, of the individual that displayed them, and thus genes correlated with the behavior have been favored. The study of adaptive significance concerns the manner in which this seems to occur. Thus, for example, social dominance in male baboons may function by increasing access to females and the subsequent production of offspring. There is no implication that the animal understands these effects; rather, the behavior has been shaped by evolutionary forces. It is important that the four sets of questions be kept separate and that the answers provided are appropriate to the kind of question under consideration. Increased attention to all four sets of questions can lead to a more comprehensive psychology.

Tinbergen obviously constructed this system by building on the writings of others, but he delineated it so clearly that his system has had widespread influence throughout the study of animal behavior, including comparative psychology and evolutionary psychology. It can be found in article after article and textbook after textbook. It is perhaps surprising that with all of the research and other integrative articles that Tinbergen published, it is his 1963a "On Aims and Methods of Ethology" that has been the most frequently cited. *The Study of Instinct* (1951), which also included a version of this formulation, has been cited more than 1,400 times (according to *Expanded Science Citation Index*). Jensen (1997) wrote that "it is difficult to overstate the importance of Tinbergen's questions to the development of modern behavioral biology" (p. 292) and argued that "these questions provided an escape from Lorenzian dichotomous theory and dogmatism without reducing the importance of biological function and adaptiveness in understanding a behavior or the importance of evolution in producing adaptedness" (pp. 292–293).

TINBERGEN'S ETHOLOGY

Perhaps the most characteristic aspect of Tinbergen's work was his ability to conduct simple, but meaningful, experiments under natural conditions. His methods entailed detailed observations of the animals under study, the development of hypotheses about the causes of the behavior observed, and the conduct of straightforward experiments to test these hypotheses. In his thesis, for example, he observed his wasps' trips to and from their burrows, then altered the arrangements of objects around the burrows, and found that the wasps were using visual cues to locate the burrows—a study of immediate causation.

Tinbergen's program of research on the behavior of several species of gulls is a model of systematic study. He provided a precise description of the behavioral patterns involved in the mating, social interactions, parent–young interactions, and many other aspects of their behavior. Few details escaped his eye. He conducted often cited research on the role of the red spot on the bills of some species in directing the young to peck at the parent to be fed. He was interested in both the controlling stimuli and the function of these behavioral patterns. In a classic study of adaptive significance, Tinbergen and his associates noticed that after eggs hatch, parents generally remove the egg shells from the vicinity of the nest. They speculated that this might be because the white shell fragments might attract predators to the vicinity of their chicks. In a series of experiments conducted in the field, they varied the distance of egg shells from gull nests and found that, indeed, predation was increased in the presence of the shells (N. Tinbergen, 1963b). As was typical, he was also interested in the stimulus attributes that trigger the removal of the shells. A relatively simple series of experiments, conducted in the field, revealed the importance of this seemingly trivial behavior in facilitating reproductive success. In addition, his student Esther Cullen (1957) showed that this behavior was lacking in kittiwakes, a species of cliff-dwelling gull, where egg shell removal would provide little benefit. Many other behavioral patterns typical of beach-breeding gulls were altered for kittiwake life on cliffs. Thus, the comparative method and a systematically organized experimental program provided further insight into the lives of these animals.

Perhaps because Tinbergen's experiments in nature were so striking, it is sometimes forgotten that he was also an able laboratory scientist. Another set of classic studies, this time dealing with immediate causation, was conducted with sticklebacks in laboratory tanks. Tinbergen and his associates were able to describe the complete reproductive cycle from the establishment of territories by males through courtship, fertilization of the eggs, and the male's paternal behavior. Through the use of models of both males and females they tried to determine the most important features of the stimuli eliciting the behavior. For example, they reported that the red bellies of males were important in triggering territorial defense; the swollen bellies of gravid females were important in triggering court-ship (e.g., N. Tinbergen, 1952).

Lorenz and Tinbergen developed a theoretical system to explain the behavioral patterns they observed. They termed these *fixed action patterns* (FAPs), sequences of behavior that were thought to be the result of evolution by natural selection and to be innate. They suggested that these sequences were triggered by relatively simple stimuli in the environment, *releasers, sign stimuli* or *key stimuli*. The stimuli were thought to act on specific areas of the brain, the *innate releasing mechanisms*, to trigger, or release, the behavioral pattern. Each behavioral pattern was thought to have a source of motivation, but conflicting motivational systems could be activated under some conditions. These conflicting tendencies often led to ambivalent behavior, such as that when tendencies to attack and to withdraw would be activated when animals were in conflict at a territorial boundary. Under such circumstances, an animal could attack an innocent bystander, *redirected behavior*, or display an out-of-context behavioral pattern such as grooming, a *displacement activity*. Both Tinbergen and Adriaan Kortlandt (Kortlandt, 1940) developed independently hierarchical models to explain the structure of the behavior they observed. In his most important book, *The Study of Instinct* (1951), Tinbergen developed his hierarchical model of the organization of FAPs that ranged from individual motor units at the lowest levels to major instincts, such as reproduction, at the highest. It had considerable heuristic value but has now been discarded by most animal behaviorists. Tinbergen was a better theorist than he liked to claim, but it is his approach, his descriptions, his clever experiments, and his pivotal role in advancing ethology that live on.

It is perhaps unfair to evaluate Tinbergen's pioneering work according to the contemporary standards of the field. That said, however, some of his simple, clear experiments are now regarded as flawed (Kruuk, 2003). Because they were not conducted using double-blind procedures, it is likely that the observers' expectations may have influenced the results. Tinbergen failed to provide adequate quantification of his results. Some of his findings have not held up well when studied with more recent methods. Although male stickleback fishes do court gravid females with considerable alacrity, the red belly of the male is now thought to be less important in triggering attack than he believed. The role of experience in determining the effectiveness of certain configurational stimuli in eliciting gaping by nestling gulls so that the parent can feed them is greater than he suggested. There are similar problems in his conclusions that the same cardboard model moved overhead elicits different reactions in geese, depending on whether the direction of movement made it appear to be a goose or a hawk. A strength of his writing was its simplicity but, as he retold stories in his popular books, his "simplicity sometimes involved barely acceptable simplifications, arrived at by removing the 'ifs and buts' from individual studies" (Kruuk, 2003, p. 150; see also Dewsbury, 1998). However, these reevaluations are often the fate of the work of pioneers. Tinbergen developed the methods of experimenting on the immediate causation, development, evolutionary history, and adaptive significance of behavior in relation to the natural habitat. Those who followed in his footsteps improved on his methods and found some of the details of his results to be wanting. This illustrates the power of the approach and the role of self-correction in the scientific endeavor. Tinbergen appears to have fostered a critical skepticism in his students, and that encouraged a healthy reexamination of the specific phenomena that he reported.

TINBERGEN, THE HUMAN CONDITION, AND PSYCHOLOGY

Throughout his career, Tinbergen expressed concern about social issues and the role of ethological work for understanding human behavior. This may have been due, in part, to the guilt he felt as a man who grew up in a post-Victorian era that emphasized the importance of duty, however unpleasant, whereas he had spent so much of his life in endeavors that were pure joy (Hall, 1974). In his semi-autobiographical *Curious Naturalists* (1958), he wrote of his "little devil" who would challenge the value of his basic research and the ways in which he would answer himself regarding the value of his endeavors. It appears as though his little devil eventually won.

In the 1960s, Tinbergen and some colleagues worked, over substantial opposition, to establish a course in the human sciences at Oxford. This entwined Tinbergen in academic politics to a degree that he avoided during most of his career (Hinde, 1990). The course was designed to integrate knowledge from the biological, psychological, and social sciences. Later, he donated some of his Nobel prize money for the purchase of books for the course.

In several addresses, such as "On War and Peace in Animals and Man," his inaugural lecture as professor of animal behavior at Oxford (N. Tinbergen, 1968), his Croonian Lecture on "Functional Ethology and the Human Sciences" (N. Tinbergen, 1972b), and his Nobel address on "Ethology and Stress Diseases" (N. Tinbergen, 1974), he turned to the role of ethologists in improving the human condition. Some of his ideas had been expressed by others in the growing environmentalism of the time, but they took on special meaning when one considered their source.

Several authors of the day had written books in which they generalized findings from ethology to humans. Tinbergen was skeptical of such approaches, arguing that it is the methods of ethology, rather than the results, that could help in the understanding of human behavior. Nevertheless, he was greatly stimulated by the efforts in this regard of his former student, Desmond Morris, a prolific practitioner of this endeavor (e.g., Morris, 1967).

Tinbergen was interested not only in the similarities between human behavior and that of other species but in the differences as well. He stressed the use of the comparative method in understanding cultural, as well as biological, evolution. In addition, he tended to emphasize our ignorance about human behavior rather than our knowledge.

Tinbergen appreciated the reciprocal relationship between science and society. He understood that scientific developments, such as the popularity of behaviorism in a progressivist era, occur in the context of broad social trends. Yet he also thought that science should influence society. This could be accomplished in two ways: by making the environment more suitable for humans and by making humans better able to deal with their environments. Anticipating a common theme in recent evolutionary psychology, Tinbergen argued that much of human behavior evolved in an earlier era and is no longer appropriate for the new era as it has been shaped by humans. He wrote that "because both our behaviour and our environment have changed so much since the cultural evolution began to gather momentum, we are faced with a bewildering variety of anthropogenic modifications—one could say distortions—of environments and of behaviour systems" (N. Tinbergen, 1972b, p. 399). He saw several signs that the demands on human nature had exceeded the limits of phylogenetic adjustability. There was decreased mother–young interaction, and that disrupts the formation of close mother–young bonds. A second sign was the prevalence of early childhood autism, which he attributed to increased social stress.

In proposing to modify the environment, Tinbergen highlighted a return to a decreased population density and a move away from anonymous societies toward increased social contact in smaller in-groups. He was also concerned about the progressive depletion of resources and pollution of the environment.

In proposing modification of human behavior, Tinbergen noted that we needed to accomplish, through cultural evolution in a very short period of time, the kind of broad changes that had resulted from biological evolution over long time spans. Knowledge of behavioral mechanisms would be critical in accomplishing this task of bioengineering that would bring behavioral propensities back into synchrony with environmental demands. He proposed the transformation of educational practices so that exploratory learning in a social context, which had been suppressed in favor of a more regimented institutional form of education in the schools, would be replaced with "a return to a biologically more balanced form of education" (N. Tinbergen, 1972b, p. 406).

Tinbergen believed that humans have strong tendencies toward aggression but advocated the sublimation of aggression-related energies toward scientific research. He regarded scientific research, along with art and religion, as uniquely human ways of meeting nature, and maintained that if we are ultimately to succumb to environmental pressures, "we could at least go down with some dignity, by using our brain for one of its supreme tasks, by exploring to the end" (N. Tinbergen, 1968, p. 1418).

AUTISM

The research program that became the focus of the last part of Tinbergen's career was that conducted jointly with his wife Lies on early childhood autism (E. A. Tinbergen & N. Tinbergen, 1972; N. Tinbergen & E. A. Tinbergen, 1983). The Tinbergens emphasized the autistic child's withdrawal from the environment, failure to acquire speech, slow acquisition of various skills, preoccupation with a limited number of objects, persistent stereotyped movement patterns, and a high level of arousal in the electroencephalogram (EEG). They argued that ethological methods could be used in assessing the causes of these behavioral patterns. Believing that variations in behavior can be understood only in relation to what is more typical (i.e., comparative study), they began to study normal children, as well as autistic children, with an emphasis on nonverbal behavior—a topic amenable to ethological analysis. They concluded that even normal children sometimes show bouts of what appear to be autistic behavior. These passing attacks occur in situations of conflict between incompatible motivations, tendencies to explore and socialize versus fear and apprehension. The Tinbergens came to favor an environmental, rather than genetic, etiology, interpreting the autistic behavior as a reaction to environmental, particularly social, stress. They proposed an approach to therapy that would lead to a gradual improvement in social contact through operant conditioning, starting with low-level interactions based on touch and with minimal eye contact. The emphasis was on the reduction of anxiety to restore normal socialization.

The Tinbergens' approach has found little support in recent work. Strong genetic and organic influences on autism have been uncovered (e.g., Happé & Frith, 1996; LeCouteur, 1990). The results of tests of the Tinbergens' proposals have been disappointing (Richer & Richards, 1975; Wing & Ricks, 1976). The Tinbergens interpreted some of the criticism as reaction to their poaching on the territory of psychiatrists but agreed that, in their first formulations, they had underestimated the importance of genetic and organic factors (E. A. Tinbergen & N. Tinbergen, 1976). Kruuk (2003, p. 278) concluded that Tinbergen's "excursion into autism science did his reputation little good."

However, if anything has been learned from the conflict between ethologists and psychologists, it has been to remember the importance of gene–environment interaction in the development of behavior. Even behavioral patterns with strong genetic influences may have complex ontogenies. Thus, the demonstration of a genetic influence need not exclude the possibility of important environmental factors. There may yet prove to be a place for the kind of approach suggested by the Tinbergens.

CONCLUSION

It is a long way from the supposedly innate, or "environment-resistant," behavior of wasps and sticklebacks to environmental influences on the development of autism in human children. However, this illustrates the range of interests and concerns of Tinbergen and his openness to diverse explanations and interpretations.

The central aspect of Dutch ethology, as developed by Tinbergen and his associates, was its combination of nature study and experimentation. It was best characterized by its method. "The history of ethology, in a nutshell, consists of the 'discovery' of a new method which was applied for its own sake. The dynamics of ethology were governed by the means rather than the goal" (Röell, 2000, p. 186). This was personified in the work of one of its leaders, Niko Tinbergen.

The curious naturalist who spent so much of his life watching and wondering about animal behavior believed in the ethological method, tried to apply it wherever he could, and worked for the spread of this approach. He believed that it could be used for the betterment of humanity and tried to apply the ethological method in the service of improving the human condition. He saw the state of humanity as becoming increasingly divorced from its natural roots and sought ways to restore balance. Tinbergen was concerned that human culture was no longer in accord with its environment and evolved character; he suggested that we would do well to return to a more natural way of life (Röell, 2000). Still, recognizing reality, he tried to apply his methods to the world as it exists.

On balance, it is clear that Tinbergen had a complex personality. He was, at the same time, both self-effacing and demanding, ebullient and depressed, and an innovator of methods with a flawed methodology. The awarding of the Nobel prize provided a tangible indication that, on balance, he was successful. He was a true pioneer who influenced his many outstanding students and many more who read his charming books and articles or viewed his films.

His blemishes should not be permitted to obscure Tinbergen's many contributions. Along with Lorenz, he developed the field of ethology. He was its primary experimenter and its most effective ambassador. The colorful and expansive Lorenz cut a stronger profile for the broad public, but it was Tinbergen's calm approach and his openness to change that were especially effective in gaining respect for the ethological approach among scientists. It was Tinbergen who negotiated a productive alliance with English-speaking colleagues.

The APA awarded Tinbergen its Distinguished Scientific Contribution Award "For pioneering research on the behavior of animals, with profound implications for understanding the roots of human behavior and its development. His studies of social behavior led to fundamental insights concerning the evolutionary relationships between behavior and the ecology of animals" (APA, 1988).

Although he was not a psychologist, Tinbergen had great influence on both comparative psychology and the growing field of evolutionary psychology. Along with several psychologists (e.g., Beach, 1950), he helped to make comparative psychology more truly comparative. He was indeed an important pioneer in psychology.

REFERENCES

American Psychological Association. (1988). Citation for Distinguished Scientific Award: Niko Tinbergen. *American Psychologist, 43,* 228–229.

Baerends, G., Beer, C., & Manning, A. (Eds.). (1975). *Function and evolution in behaviour: Essays in honour of Professor Niko Tinbergen, F. R. S.* Oxford, England: Clarendon.

Beach, F. A. (1950). The snark was a boojum. *American Psychologist, 5,* 115–124.

Cohen, J. (1977). Niko Tinbergen. In D. Cohen (Ed.), *Psychologists on psychology* (pp. 316–331). New York: Taplinger.

Cullen, E. (1957). Adaptations in the kittiwake to cliff nesting. *Ibis, 99,* 275–302.

Dawkins, M. S., Halliday, T. R., & Dawkins, R. (1991). *The Tinbergen legacy.* London: Chapman & Hall.

Dewsbury, D. A. (1990). Nikolaas Tinbergen (1907–1988). *American Psychologist, 45,* 67–68.

Dewsbury, D. A. (1995). Americans in Europe: The role of travel in the spread of European ethology after World War II. *Animal Behaviour, 49,* 1649–1663.

Dewsbury, D. A. (1997). Rhetorical strategies in the presentation of ethology and comparative psychology in magazines after World War II. *Science in Context, 10,* 367–386.

Dewsbury, D. A. (1998). Robert Yerkes, sex research, and the problem of data simplification. *History of Psychology, 1,* 116–129.

Dewsbury, D. A. (2003). The 1973 Nobel Prize for Physiology or Medicine: Recognition for behavioral science? *American Psychologist, 58,* 747–752.

Hall, E. (1974, March). A conversation with Nobel prize winner Niko Tinbergen. *Psychology Today, 18*(3), 65–80.

Happé, F., & Frith, U. (1996). The neuropsychology of autism. *Brain, 119,* 1377–1400.

Hinde, R. A. (1990). Nikolaas Tinbergen 15 April 1907–21 December 1988. *Biographical Memoirs of Fellows of the Royal Society, 36,* 549–565.

Jensen, D. D. (1997). A metatheory and mantra for behavioral biology. *Contemporary Psychology, 42,* 292–293.

Kortlandt, A. (1940). Wech sel wirkung zwischen Instinkten. *Archives Néelandaises de Zoologie, 4,* 443–520.

Kruuk, H. (2003). *Niko's nature: The life of Niko Tinbergen and his science of animal behaviour.* Oxford, England: Oxford University Press.

LeCouteur, A. (1990). Autism: Current understanding and management. *British Journal of Hospital Medicine, 43,* 448–452.

Morris, D. (1967). *The naked ape: A zoologist's study of the human mind.* New York: McGraw-Hill.

Richer, J., & Richards, B. (1975). Reacting to autistic children: The danger of trying too hard. *British Journal of Psychiatry, 127,* 526–529.

Röell, R. (2000). *The world of instinct.* (M. Kofod, Trans.). Assen, the Netherlands: Van Gorcum. (Original work published 1996)

Tinbergen, E. A., & Tinbergen, N. (1972). Early childhood autism: An ethological approach. *Advances in Ethology, 10,* 1–53.

Tinbergen, E. A., & Tinbergen, N. (1976). The aetiology of childhood autism: A criticism of the Tinbergens' theory: A rejoinder. *Psychological Medicine, 6,* 545–549.

Tinbergen, N. (1951). *The study of instinct.* Oxford: Oxford University Press.

Tinbergen, N. (1952). The curious behavior of the stickleback. *Scientific American, 187,* 22–26.

Tinbergen, N. (1953). *Social behaviour in animals.* London: Methuen.

Tinbergen, N. (1958). *Curious naturalists.* New York: Basic Books.

Tinbergen, N. (1961). *The herring gull's world.* New York: Basic Books.

Tinbergen, N. (1963a). On aims and methods of ethology. *Zeitschrift für Tierpsychologie, 20,* 410–429.

Tinbergen, N. (1963b, August). The shell menace. *Natural History, 72*(7), 28–35.

Tinbergen, N. (1968). On war and peace in animals and men. *Science, 160,* 1411–1418.

Tinbergen, N. (1972a). *The animal in its world: Explorations of an ethologist 1932–1972* (2 vols.). Cambridge, MA: Harvard University Press.

Tinbergen, B. (1972b). Functional ethology and the human sciences. *Proceedings of the Royal Society of London, 182B,* 385–410.

Tinbergen, N. (1974). Ethology and stress diseases. *Science, 185,* 20–27.

Tinbergen, N. (1985). Watching and wondering. In D. A. Dewsbury (Ed.), *Leaders in the study of animal behavior* (pp. 431–463). Lewisburg, PA: Bucknell University Press.

Tinbergen, N., & Tinbergen, E. A. (1983). *"Autistic" children: New hope for a cure.* London: George Allen & Unwin.

Wing, L., & Ricks, D. M. (1976). The aetiology of childhood autism: A criticism of the Tinbergens' ethological theory. *Psychological Medicine, 6,* 533–543.

Abraham H. Maslow (Photos courtesy of the
Archives of the History of American Psychology,
University of Akron)

Chapter 16

Abraham H. Maslow: Reconnaissance for Eupsychia

Deborah J. Coon

Abraham H. Maslow (1908–1970), who died at the end of what may have been the most socially tumultuous decade of the 20th century, considered himself a reconnaissance man for a new, more human-centered science of psychology (Hoffman, 1999, p. 153). He dreamed of a science of psychology rooted in human values, a science that studies individuals who stand out as exemplars of humanity, those who are wise, creative, spontaneous, and generous. Such a science, he believed, could ultimately lead to a better world, a utopia of psychologically balanced people, which he dubbed *Eupsychia*.

Maslow helped found the "Third Force" of humanistic psychology, offering what many viewed as a needed alternative to the behaviorist and psychoanalytic schools. He urged psychologists to study and theorize about mentally healthy and successfully functioning people and not to focus narrowly on the abnormal or on mentally unhealthy people. He played the role of gadfly, needling his experimentalist colleagues for their devotion to quantitative and experimental methods. He urged them to abandon notions of value-free science and instead to orient their research toward issues of social change and world betterment. He did not change the mainstream of psychological science, but he helped create a clear alternative path within the broader discipline.

Although Maslow's influence within psychology was significant, it pales beside his impact on broader American culture—from styles of "enlightened management" in U.S. corporations to the language and ideals of the 1960s counterculture. His "motivational hierarchy" (to be discussed below) is taught in virtually every introductory psychology course and in many education and management courses as well. Maslow popularized phrases such as "self-actualization," "peak experience," and "synergy," once in vogue in the popular culture of the 1960s and 1970s. Works of his such as his "A Theory of Human Motivation" (1943), *Religions, Values, and Peak Experiences* (1964), *Eupsychian Management: A Journal* (1965), and *Toward a Psychology of Being* (1968/1998) were read both on and off college campuses for decades. Their influence extended from the heads of corporate America to the pioneers of the women's movement, campus revolutionaries, and the founders of the Esalen Institute in California, home of New Age psychology.

GROWING UP MASLOW

Born on April 1, 1908, in New York City, Maslow was the eldest in a family of seven children, one of whom died in infancy. Many of Maslow's childhood memories were unhappy. He remembered himself as a skinny, gangly child with too large a nose, continually subjected to anti-Semitism on the streets and in the schools of New York where he grew up. Family life was far from ideal. His father, who was more absent than present during much of his childhood, declared at a family gathering that Abraham was the ugliest kid he'd ever seen. His mother, at least according to his memory, berated him constantly. He recalled how, with unbelievable cruelty, she had smashed the skulls of two kittens Abraham brought home as a child. To his death, Maslow harbored a hatred for her that psychoanalysis did not touch (Hoffman, 1999, p. 8).

Given the problems of his immediate family, his extended family was especially important to Maslow. He credited the warmth and kindness of an uncle with keeping him sane while he was growing up. Also, at about the age of 9, Abraham developed a close friendship with his cousin, Will Maslow. Will was bright, athletic, and more confident than Abraham; through their relationship Abraham began to experience some of his happiest childhood memories. As neighbors and best friends, they attended the Boys High School in Manhattan, a prestigious public school that both boys found stimulating. A powerful memory for Maslow was reading the muckraking works of Upton Sinclair on the recommendation of one of his teachers. Maslow later recalled how Sinclair's exposés of working conditions in the meat-packing industry had stirred his moral and social conscience and given him a lifelong inclination toward socialism (Hoffman, 1999, p. 14).

When Maslow was 14, he met his first cousin Bertha Goodman, newly emigrated from Russia. He tutored her weekly in English, and through the course of his high school years their friendship grew into romance. Ultimately Abraham and Bertha married in December 1928 during Abraham's college years. Maslow credited Bertha with helping him gain confidence and overcome his shyness.

COLLEGE AND GRADUATE SCHOOL

Abraham first attended college at the City College of New York (CCNY). He transferred to Cornell for one semester (spring 1927), but ultimately grew homesick for Bertha and moved back to New York City. In all, Maslow's college years were relatively lackluster, and he was even on academic probation for a semester. However, he later recalled in his diaries a few significant and life-shaping influences of those years. He remembered reading William Graham Sumner's *Folkways* (1906), which, according to his account, affected him as dramatically as Sinclair's work had done earlier. Sumner's book was a wide-ranging discussion of customs and mores of various world cultures. More striking to Maslow than the cultural particulars was the overriding message of Sumner's book—that scientific reason was the crucial bulwark separating contemporary civilization from the superstitions and barbarities of its primitive past.

Maslow also recalled the importance of reading Carl Murchison's book, *Psychologies of 1925* (1928), during his sophomore year at CCNY. What particularly inspired him was the discussion of behaviorist John B. Watson's vision of psychology and its potential to change society. As a result, Maslow looked up Watson's work. He reminisced in his diary on May 19, 1962, about the powerful results of that earlier reading: "Wow! I remember reading it as a great peak-experience & turning point of my life. I read it at 42nd St. Library & then met Bertha &, in high excitement & exhilaration, danced down 5th Ave., jumping & shouting & gesturing, trying to explain to her what it meant" (Lowry, 1979, Vol. 1, p. 164). To Maslow's mind, behaviorism was a formative part of his background that he would not abjure even after he had moved away from it and founded humanistic psychology.

Excited by the suggestion that scientific psychology might be put to utopian ends, Maslow decided to finish his undergraduate training at the University of Wisconsin, where he would study biology, psychology, and philosophy. The University of Wisconsin was developing a reputation for its progressive ideals and high-quality education, the combination of which appealed to the young Maslow. He transferred there in the fall of 1928. That winter he went back to New York to marry Bertha, and returned with her to Wisconsin, where she became a student. For perhaps the first time in his life, he began to blossom academically, socially, and emotionally.

Maslow earned his baccalaureate and stayed at Wisconsin for graduate school, eventually earning his doctorate under primatologist Harry Harlow, who was just out of graduate school himself and new to the Wisconsin faculty in 1930. Maslow's dissertation explored the relationship between dominance and sexual behavior in nonhuman primates, using both naturalistic observations of primates at a zoo and experimental research in the laboratory. Having read, and been intrigued by, the writings of both Sigmund Freud and Alfred Adler, Maslow hoped to answer the question of whether the basis of motivation lay in the sex drive (as asserted by Freud) or in the drive for power and mastery (as asserted by Adler). What he found in nonhuman primates was a complex relationship between sex and power: Copulation was not used just for reproduction but was often used to assert and maintain social dominance. The drive toward power and mastery, it seemed, was more fundamental than the sex drive, at least in nonhuman primates.

While completing his dissertation, Maslow applied for postdoctoral funding from the National Research Council to continue his research under the direction of Robert M. Yerkes, the famous primatologist, at Yale's research station in Orange Park, Florida. Maslow saved a copy of his rejected research proposal and later wrote on it, "I was told some years later that I didn't get any grant or fellowships because of anti-Semitism" (quoted in Hoffman, 1999, p. 53).[1]

After having his postdoctoral fellowship application turned down, Maslow was disappointed, but plunged into completing his doctorate. He also began to publish the results of his primate research, with papers in the *Journal of Comparative Psychology*, the *Journal of Experimental Psychology*, and the *Journal of Genetic Psychology*. These included not only his dissertation work on sexual behavior and dominance but also research on food preferences and delayed reaction in nonhuman primates. All were based on thorough-going, rigorous experimental work; in later life, Maslow continued to take pride in this early experimental and observational research as demonstrating his foundation in scientific thinking and his abilities at it.

Although he would eventually become a leader in the humanistic revolt against dogmatic scientism, Maslow never lost his respect for well-designed experimental research. He wrote in his journal in March of 1964,

> I still feel the same love and admiration for objectivistic research. I have not repudiated it nor will I attack it as such. All that has happened is that I was forced to realize its limitation, its partial quality, its failure as a general & comprehensive philosophy of all psychology. . . . I learned that it was just one kind of tool, usable for certain purposes & not others, part of the armamentarium of the psychologist but not the whole of it. (Lowry, 1979, Vol. 1, p. 278)

When he completed his doctorate in 1932 and had failed to win a postdoctoral fellowship, Maslow began to look for a permanent teaching position. Everyone knew that American universities at the time were notoriously anti-Semitic. Colleagues and mentors urged Maslow to change his name to disguise his Jewish ancestry, but he refused. He was turned down from no fewer than 12 positions.

Although things looked bleak for his professional career, Maslow continued to write up his research results for publication and to prepare talks for conferences.

---

[1] For a keen analysis of anti-Semitism in the history of psychology during this period, see Andrew Winston (1996, 1998).

In spring of 1935 he prepared a paper for a symposium that was to be chaired by the eminent Edward L. Thorndike of Teacher's College, Columbia University. What Maslow did not know was that behind the scenes his friend, psychologist Gardner Murphy (also at Columbia), was lobbying Thorndike on his behalf, and Thorndike soon offered Maslow a year's postdoctoral fellowship to work with him at Columbia. Maslow's biographer writes that "Maslow did not know it until years later, but Murphy had nearly jeopardized his own academic position by pressing for the hiring of a Jew" (Hoffman, 1999, p. 64).

POSTDOCTORAL YEARS

The fellowship with Thorndike, one of the leading figures in the field of intelligence testing, turned out to be Maslow's ticket to success. What transpired when Maslow arrived at Columbia in the fall of 1935 is the stuff of legend. The story comes from Maslow's correspondence after many intervening years, so self-interest and the vagaries of memory are doubtlessly involved, but this is what he remembered, according to his biographer.

During Maslow's first few weeks at Columbia, he was required to submit to a battery of psychological tests. When he had completed them, the staff in charge simply told him that he had done a good job. Thorndike assigned Maslow his first research topic: Maslow was to determine the relative importance of heredity versus environment in causing various human behaviors. After briefly contemplating the research he might do to address the topic, Maslow found that his heart wasn't in it. So he did something almost unbelievably bold. He sat down and wrote a brief paper for Thorndike, explaining why, in his view, the topic was fundamentally flawed. Not surprisingly, Thorndike called Maslow to his office shortly after receiving the paper. As Maslow told it, he was uncertain what to expect, but knew that he had probably overstepped his position and might even be fired as a result (Hoffman, 1999, p. 67).

To Maslow's surprise, Thorndike did not berate him, but instead told him that according to the tests that he had taken, Maslow had an IQ of 195. Therefore, Thorndike continued, he was prepared to "support him for the rest of his life if he were unable to secure a permanent job." Thorndike told him that he did not like the research Maslow was doing on sex and dominance, but he was going to let Maslow continue doing his own research because if Thorndike did not stand behind his own intelligence tests, who would? In short, he said, "I'll assume that if I give you your head, it'll be the best for you and for me—and for the world" (Hoffman, 1999, p. 68).

For the next 2 years, Maslow enjoyed almost complete freedom to pursue his own research without constraints. He continued his studies of sexuality and dominance, but now began to study human subjects, chiefly women, pioneering in the field of sexology. As a pioneer, he had to develop his own research tools, devising a test of social dominance that he called the Social Personality Inventory and developing an intensive interview process for his research participants. In his research, he found that higher-dominance women (as opposed to lower- and middle-dominance women) were more casual and playful about sex, more wide-ranging and experimental in their sexual behaviors, and more open in talking about it. In a paper titled "Self-Esteem (Dominance-Feeling) and Sexuality in Women," published in the *Journal of Social Psychology* (1942), he summarized his research from these years and drew an important conclusion: Because domi-nant women were more willing to talk about their sexual experiences than less dominant women, any research that relied on volunteers would be biased toward dominant women. This would eventually become a contentious issue within sexology, with pioneer sexologist Alfred Kinsey relying on volunteers, and Maslow calling him to task for it (Hoffman, 1999, p. 156).

BROOKLYN COLLEGE YEARS

In the spring of 1937, Maslow was appointed to his first permanent academic position at Brooklyn College. It was a relatively new institution that catered primarily to a local population, a large proportion of whom were first-generation Americans. Importantly, Brooklyn College had no quota on hiring Jews, and therefore offered a haven of sorts for talented scholars of Jewish background.

New York in the 1930s was a vibrant intellectual environment for Maslow as he began his teaching career. New York City had recently become a haven for Jewish and socialist intellectuals fleeing Hitler's Germany. The New School for Social Research had opened its doors to the German émigrés, hiring a dozen faculty members in different fields, including the renowned Gestalt psychologist Max Wertheimer. On arriving in New York in 1937, Maslow quickly embraced Wertheimer as a role model and mentor. Witty, casual, and energetic, Wertheim-er's personal style was especially attractive to Maslow. In the next few years he also sought out and studied with Alfred Adler, Ruth Benedict, Erich Fromm, Karen Horney, Kurt Goldstein, and Kurt Koffka, among others. Evening salons provided stimulating companionship and fascinating discussions on psychological and philosophical issues, world politics, and social justice.

Teaching occupied much of Maslow's time and energy in the late 1930s. He felt a sympathetic bond with his Brooklyn College students, many of whom had similar backgrounds to his—lower-middle-class children of immigrants, with the brashness and rough edges that made for survival on the New York streets. Maslow devoted himself to being advisor, counselor, and mentor to them as he taught his psychology classes.

Inspired by Benedict and her views on the need for cross-fertilization among psychology, psychiatry, and anthropology, Maslow traveled to Canada for field research among the Blackfoot Indians in the summer of 1938. His summer among the Blackfoot had a few important effects. Maslow found that his personality tests for dominance were too "culture-bound"—they were designed for American culture and were inappropriate for use among the Blackfoot people. However, he believed that he saw the same range of personality types among the Blackfoot Indians as among other groups he had studied, and so decided that personality type is probably universal rather than specific to particular cultures. Finally, Maslow was struck by the Blackfoot tribe's view of wealth, which was in striking contrast to American society's and was much closer to a socialistic ideal that he found attractive. For the Blackfoot, wealth was not measured by money and property but by generosity. The wealthiest man in their eyes is one who has almost nothing because he has given it all away.

Sometime around 1940 and the beginning of World War II, Maslow decided to change his entire research program. He had been publishing his work on dominance and sexuality, and continued to publish in that field for a few more years. However, Maslow had an epiphany of sorts after watching a patriotic parade of veterans honoring the soldiers who were going off to fight in World War II.

> I had a vision of a peace table, with people sitting around it, talking about human nature and hatred and war and peace and brotherhood. I was too old to go into the army. It was at that moment that I realized that the rest of my life must be devoted to discovering a psychology for the peace table. That moment changed my whole life. (quoted in Hoffman, 1999, p. 137)

Modern society, it seemed to Maslow, was in too much danger for intellectuals to waste time on anything but working to save it. As he later reflected on it, it was at that moment that he decided he would dedicate himself to studying social psychology and abnormal psychology, trying to plumb the depths of human nature and to discover what brought out the best and worst in individuals and in human societies. A scholar might not choose to fight with guns, but he could fight with words and theories that could take root and change the world.

MASLOW SELF-ACTUALIZED

Maslow began to come into his own in the 1940s. With daughters born in 1938 and 1940, he had a young family, a stable job, stimulating friends and colleagues, and a passionate cause to embrace. Bertha accused him throughout life of a Messianic urge, and perhaps he did have one, but it gave him a new sense of mission and purpose that inspired some of his most famous work.

As far as any written record indicates, Maslow had begun to explore questions of human motivation in about 1938. He started with the assumption that people are fundamentally good. What, then, causes them to behave in mean and cruel ways? He wrote in an unpublished journal, "In a word, it is because they are not liked. The insecurity cycle—from this flows everything. . . . The person who behaves badly behaves so because of hurt, actual and expected, and lashes out in self-defense, as a cornered animal might" (quoted in Lowry, 1973, p. 17). Insecurity and low self-esteem, then, are the roots of harmful and hateful human behavior; conversely, people would behave well if given a secure foundation: "The fact is that people are good, if only their fundamental wishes are satisfied, their wishes for affection and security. Give people affection and security, and they will give affection and be secure in their feelings and behavior" (quoted in Lowry, 1973, p. 18).

Maslow's view of human nature as fundamentally good ran counter to the dominant psychological theories of his day. The behaviorist tradition in which he had been trained asserted that there is nothing fundamentally good or bad in humans; good or bad behavior develops as a result of environmental conditions in which an individual grew up. Psychoanalysis, the other reigning psychological theory, and one that Maslow studied and discussed with colleagues in New York, held that humans are driven by primitive instincts for self-preservation and sex (a sort of species-preservation instinct). Although not necessarily evil, these instincts did not fit prevailing concepts of virtue, either. When people appear to be behaving in "good" or noble ways, they are merely acting in ways that satisfy their own primitive instincts. Both dominant theories placed humans firmly within the amoral world of animals. In Maslow's 1938 journal entries he, too, was thinking in these terms: The insecure person "lashes out in self-defense, as a cornered animal might" (p. 17).

However, Maslow's thinking was evolving. In his first published venture away from the research path he had been following, Maslow coauthored a textbook of abnormal psychology in 1941 with Bela Mittelmann, a psychiatrist and Hungarian émigré whose evening salon Maslow often attended. Maslow had been teaching the subject at Brooklyn College for a number of years, and the book helped him consolidate his views. Maslow was increasingly thinking, talking, and writing about issues of human motivation and about the pathological in human nature. In 1941 and 1942 he published papers on deprivation and frustration, on self-esteem, on security–insecurity, on destructiveness, and on the personality characteristics of liberal leaders.

Asked in 1943 to give a talk on his developing theory of motivation, he wrote up his thoughts and published two articles. One of them was to become the paper that cemented his eminence as a psychologist. Maslow titled his paper "A Theory of Human Motivation," and published it in the prestigious *Psychological Review* in 1943. In it, he introduced his hierarchical theory of motivation and, as a crucial part of it, his concept of "self-actualization." The paper was bold and clear in its rejection of both behaviorist and psychoanalytic traditions in motivation theory. Writing that "the integrated wholeness of the organism must be one of the foundation stones of motivation theory," he aligned himself at the outset with the less popular Gestalt movement as against the psychoanalytic and behaviorist camps within psychology (Maslow, 1943, p. 370).

In case his divergence from the dominant camps was not obvious enough, he continued that motivation theory should be "human-centered rather than animal-centered," and that it should be "based upon goals rather than upon instigating drives or motivated behavior" (1943, p. 371). Most previous discussions of motivation (with the exception of Edward Chace Tolman, whose work Maslow cited) had talked about behaviors being motivated by hunger, thirst, and the sex drive. Maslow heretically declared that behavior is also, and more importantly, based on a *striving toward* various goals and purposes.

Maslow theorized that human needs are arranged in "hierarchies of pre-potency." That is, as soon as one type of need is met, another arises to take its place: "Man is a perpetually wanting animal" (1943, p. 373). Specifically, at the base of the hierarchy are the physiological needs: hunger, thirst, sexual drive. These he considered the most fundamental or "most pre-potent" because "A person who is lacking food, safety, love, and esteem would most probably hunger for food more strongly than for anything else" (1943, p. 373). Once the physiological needs are satisfied, the "safety needs," or needs for personal safety and well-being, arise as prime motivators. After these are the needs for love and affection, followed by the need for esteem, both self-esteem and the esteem of others.

Once all these needs are met, humans are free to pursue their highest need—the need for self-actualization. Maslow mentioned that the term had been coined by Gestalt psychologist Kurt Goldstein, but that Maslow was using it in a "more specific and limited fashion" to mean "the desire for self-fulfillment" or the tendency "to become everything that one is capable of becoming" (1943, p. 382). When our more basic needs are met, the desire to fulfill our potential becomes our chief goal and highest aspiration as human beings. Those who have all their needs fulfilled so that they are able to pursue their full potential and to self-actualize will exhibit "the fullest (and healthiest) creativeness" (1943, p. 383).

Once the lower needs are filled, they no longer have power as motivators, according to Maslow. "A basically satisfied person no longer has the needs for esteem, love, safety, etc." (1943, p. 393). Unfortunately, however, in the present state of society, people are often stuck trying to meet their most fundamental needs, so that "basically satisfied people are the exception" rather than the rule. One suspects that Maslow was thinking of his own experience when he wrote that many people spend their adult lives trying to overcome the insecurity and poor self-esteem that results when the basic needs are not met during childhood. He believed that debilitating neuroticism and more severe psychopathologies may result when children's basic physiological, safety, love, and esteem needs are not met.

Maslow viewed his theory as having two crucial differences from the leading theories of motivation. First, his theory started "with the human being rather than any lower and presumably 'simpler' animal," as the behaviorists did (1943, p. 392). Second, and perhaps more significant, in his view needs do not *drive* human behavior deterministically but needs are instead goals that humans strive to fulfill. Humans actively pursue the fulfillment of their needs, rather than being purely driven by them. This may seem to be a fine point, but it was clearly an important one to Maslow, who was trying to escape the deterministic worldview of both the behaviorists and the Freudians.

Maslow's paper only briefly discussed self-actualization, declaring it "a challenging problem for research" (1943, p. 383). Soon, however, he embraced it as a focus of his research and theorizing for the rest of his life. In May 1945, he began to keep a journal he called the "Good Human Being Notebook" (GHB), now published as an appendix to Richard Lowry's intellectual biography of Maslow (1973). Maslow had already been thinking about the issue for years. He later reminisced that he had been inspired by the example of two of his early teachers, Wertheimer and Benedict, to ask what made some people truly extraordinary—kind, wise, funny, talented, and successful (Maslow, 1971/1993, p. 40). In his GHB notebook, he began to work out his thoughts about how to study the topic "more formally and rigidly" (Lowry, 1973, p. 81).

A major problem confronting Maslow from the outset was that self-actualized people are very much in the eye of the beholder, so selecting people to study was not straightforward scientifically. Maslow tried to develop a rigorous and objective method of selecting students who could qualify as "good human beings," but he rapidly ran into difficulties. He picked out potential GHB's "just by looking at them in class," then looked up their scores on the objective Security/Insecurity test that he had given to all class members and submitted them to a lengthy Rorschach test and an hour-long interview. Recall that, according to his theory, one would expect self-actualizers, or GHBs, to be extremely secure people, because only if people are secure should they be capable of realizing their full potential. Unfortunately, Maslow found that many people he selected as good were not "secure" according to his test, and many people who scored as secure were far from his idea of self-actualizers.

Deciding that perhaps college students are too young to have had a chance to fulfill their potential, he turned toward mature adults, compiling a list of people whom he viewed as self-actualized, and then interviewing and corresponding with them. Here, too, he confronted a problem. Many of the people were reluctant to talk about themselves and had strong needs for privacy. In fact, Maslow would eventually decide that the need for privacy is one of the characteristics of the self-actualized person. This, too, made studying the self-actualized a challenging research topic.

The problem of whom to call self-actualized and how to conduct rigorous scientific research on such individuals dogged Maslow for the rest of his career. This is not to say that Maslow dropped the topic or ever gave up the hope that he might one day find a way to study it rigorously. It is just to say that he ultimately decided that he preferred suggestive and provocative theorizing, even if it was ultimately unprovable, over experimentation that was rigorous but uninteresting to him. Perhaps he took heart from something William James had written in his famous *The Principles of Psychology*: "At a certain stage in the development of every science a degree of vagueness is what best consists with fertility" (1890, Vol. 1, p. 6).

Indeed, it was around this same time that Maslow began keeping a notebook that he hoped would result in a magnum opus comparable to James's *Principles*. Just as James had advocated a science useful to humankind, so Maslow hoped for a psychology that would embrace human values and strive for social improvement. Although he never published his magnum opus, it leaked out in snatches over the years. For example, in a 1946 *Philosophy of Science* article titled, "Problem-Centering Versus Means-Centering in Science," Maslow echoed James when he criticized contemporary psychology for focusing too narrowly on rigorous methods when those methods excluded some of the most interesting problems about human nature. Also in this vein was his 1966 book, *The Psychology of Science: A Reconnaissance*, which tried to show the limitations of objective, impersonal science in dealing with human beings.

In the late 1940s, Maslow suffered a complete breakdown in health that led him to take a medical leave from Brooklyn College. At the time no one was able to diagnose his problem, although years later doctors realized that he had suffered a heart attack. Maslow's brothers provided him with an escape and opportunity. They owned and operated a cooperage, a new branch of which they had opened in a small town in California. They hired Maslow as manager, and he moved his own family to California in the spring of 1947. For the next 2 years, Maslow slowly recuperated and simultaneously gained experience as a salesman and manager. This was practical experience that he would later draw on when speaking to corporate managers and military leaders. As his health improved, Maslow made contacts at the University of California, Berkeley, and joined in seminars there with leading lights such as Edward Chace Tolman, David Krech, and Else Frenkel-Brunswik. He continued thinking and theorizing about the hierarchy of needs, and especially about self-actualized people. By the spring of 1949 he was healthy enough to move back to Brooklyn and resume his teaching duties in the fall.

In published papers, books, talks, and lectures over the next 25 years, Maslow theorized about the characteristics of self-actualized people and how society might provide the right set of conditions for more people to fulfill their true potential. His first major published exploration of it was in a 1950 article titled, "Self-Actualizing People: A Study of Psychological Health." In it, he examined historical figures as well as contemporaries that he believed could safely be called self-actualized: They presented no major psychological problems and they seemed to have achieved their full potential in their chosen fields. Among the common qualities of the self-actualized were that they had embraced causes outside themselves; and they were emotionally warm, humorous, creative, spontaneous, aesthetically sensitive, and unconventional.

For Maslow the self-actualizing person is not "an ordinary man with something added, but rather . . . the ordinary man with nothing taken away. The average man is a human being with dampened and inhibited powers" (Lowry, 1973, p. 91). In other words, self-actualizers are not some sort of super-persons. Every person at birth has tremendous potential if properly nurtured. We might not all become Wertheimers and Benedicts, but given the right conditions, we could all become fully ourselves.

MOVE TO BRANDEIS

Maslow's work on motivation increasingly brought him national attention. In the spring of 1951 he accepted a position as chair of the psychology department at Brandeis University in Boston. Brandeis was a new Jewish-sponsored, nonsectarian university; Maslow would have the chance to shape the psychology program however he liked. Maslow began his Brandeis career in the fall of 1951. But he never felt the camaraderie with his students there that he had had with his Brooklyn College students. Perhaps it was because fewer Brandeis students shared his background, or because his attention was increasingly drawn away from his teaching as he was getting better known. In any case, Maslow continually complained about his teaching responsibilities at Brandeis. One of his new responsibilities was training graduate students, and it is a role that Maslow later reflected was perhaps his greatest failure in life. Over the 20 years that he taught at Brandeis, many of his graduate students left him for other advisors. Hoffman reported that some of Maslow's former graduate students still complained bitterly about their experience with him years later (Hoffman, 1999, p. 202). From Maslow's point of view, most graduate students were not independent enough; from the students' point of view, he failed to give them appropriate guidance or to help them figure out meaningful ways to turn his theories into appropriate research topics.

In the course of the 1950s, Maslow's fame grew. He continued to focus much of his attention on studying self-actualizers, both historic and contemporary. One of his innovations of the mid-1950s was the notion of "peak experiences." Virtually all self-actualizers reported having these almost euphoric moments of intense emotional and cognitive experience accompanied by feelings of timelessness and transcendence. Maslow began to view peak experiences as one of the essential marks of the self-actualized, and he gathered whatever evidence of them he could find. When he wrote up his research about peak experiences for publication, however, the mainstream journals in psychology and psychiatry, including the *Psychological Review*, *American Psychologist*, and *Psychiatry*, all rejected it (Hoffman, 1999, p. 206). Maslow chose to deliver his manuscript as a keynote address at the American Psychological Association (APA), as the newly elected President of APA's Division 8, Society for Personality and Social Psychology. He eventually found a publication outlet for it in the *Journal of Genetic Psychology*, where he published it under the title, "Cognition of Being in the Peak Experiences" (1959). Later reprinted in *Toward a Psychology of Being*, it was a paper that he regarded as among his most important (Maslow, 1968/1998, p. 81).

In the address and paper, Maslow distilled the results of interviews and written reports from more than 200 individuals asked to describe their "happiest moments, ecstatic moments, moments of rapture" (Maslow, 1968/1998, p. 83). From their descriptions he drew up a list of "Being-values" or "B-values" that are typical of such states: wholeness, perfection, completion, justice, aliveness, richness, simplicity, beauty, goodness, uniqueness, effortlessness, playfulness, truth, and self-sufficiency. For Maslow, peak experiences are typical of self-actualizers, but others also have them. In fact, peak experiences are moments in which average (i.e., non–self-actualized) people temporarily achieve self-actualization. Maslow viewed this as an evolution of his concept of self-actualization. No longer was self-actualization a sort of elite state that could only happen to some; now it was a state or episode that "can, in theory, come at any time in life to any person" (1968/1998, p. 106). He hoped that this also made it more amenable to research because peak experiences could be found in virtually anyone and not just in a rare subsection of the general population.

Although Maslow publicly made the best of his paper's rejection from the mainstream journals in his profession, privately he was badly stung by the rebuff and never submitted articles to them again. He had hoped to lead psychology in a clarion charge toward human betterment, not to wander off on a mad Quixotic quest. Believing himself definitively outside the mainstream was jarring, so much so that a decade later, he was genuinely startled to find himself nominated and then elected as president of the APA in 1967. He confided in his journal on May 9, 1966, "Astonished by being nominated to presidency of APA. Apparently I've read the situations incorrectly, feeling out of things, alienated from the APA, rejected & rejecting" (Lowry, 1979, Vol. 2, p. 730).

If the mainstream of psychology seemed to reject him in the late 1950s, however, there was nonetheless a growing movement of psychologists and psychiatrists who also believed in Maslow's dream of a human-centered science with the goal of social justice and human betterment. In the next few years, Maslow became a driving force in founding the *Journal of Humanistic Psychology* (1961) and the American Association for Humanistic Psychology (1962). By starting their own scholarly journals and organizations, these kindred spirits guaranteed themselves a publication outlet and a forum for their work, and the humanistic psychologists became known as a "Third Force" or alternative to the dominant forces of behaviorism and psychoanalysis.

By the late 1950s, corporate and military leaders were also beginning to notice Maslow's work and to call on his expertise on creativity and on motivation. This was a period of intense U.S. competition with the Soviet Union, so American leaders were seeking to foster not only productivity but also the creativity that might lead to the next scientific or technological breakthrough. It was also a period of intense social conformity within the business world, so Maslow's message was all the more iconoclastic: Managers could not "simply mandate greater creativity" (Hoffman, 1999, p. 221). Rather, they had to nurture it by allowing "room for the unfettered individual" to grow and self-actualize. It is amusing to imagine the reaction of the roomful of U.S. Army engineers in 1957 when Maslow declared, "In the early stages of creativeness . . . you've got to be a bum, and you've got to be a bohemian, you've got to be crazy. . . . We'll have to find some way of permitting people to be individualistic in an organization" (Hoffman, 1999, p. 221).

Five years later, Maslow was offered an all-expenses-paid summer studying the inner workings of a company called Non-Linear Systems in La Jolla, California. The company's founder, Andy Kay, had been influenced by Maslow's work on motivation and creativity, and was proud of his own innovative, democratic management style; he invited Maslow to have a look. Maslow was so impressed with what he saw that he conducted extensive interviews with managers and workers, publishing his notes in an informal style as *Eupsychian Management: A Journal* (1965), which became an influential book espousing techniques of enlightened management.

While Maslow lectured and wrote about concrete ways of fostering creativity and self-actualization in the workplace and elsewhere, he also always thought in grander terms. For several years he had been team-teaching a course on utopias with historian Frank Manuel at Brandeis. In a radio address of 1960, Maslow voiced a thought experiment in which he imagined 1,000 self-actualized people stranded on an island. The society they created together would be a utopia, or as Maslow chose to call it, Eupsychia. It would have none of our present social ills such as theft and murder, and because its inhabitants were all self-actualizers, it would instead excel in all the most positive aspects of human experience. Creativity in the arts and sciences would flourish; generosity would be the norm; warmth, humor, and spontaneity would be *de rigeur*; women would have as much of an opportunity to flourish as men. Maslow believed such a society is possible if psychologists would apply themselves to figuring out how to foster self-actualization in everyone.

AMBIVALENT GURU OF THE COUNTERCULTURE

Early in the 1960s, psychologist Timothy Leary at Harvard University began to conduct laboratory research on the mental effects of drugs like psilocybin and LSD. Leary's findings seemed to suggest that certain drugs could induce states that were much like the peak experiences that Maslow described. Maslow, at nearby Brandeis, was intrigued. He became friends with Leary, and his daughter Ellen even worked as Leary's research assistant for a time. Although Maslow never fully condoned nor embraced the use of these pharmaceutical shortcuts to self-actualization, he continued to support Leary's right to conduct such research, even preparing to defend him before the APA's Ethics Committee, which was looking into Leary's practices, until the hearing was called off.

In 1968, Maslow collected a number of his most important essays and talks into a book called *Toward a Psychology of Being* (1968/1998). A popular book, it made its way from colleges into the broader counterculture, and the terms *peak experience* and *self-actualization* became part of the street vernacular of the 1960s. "Flower children" sought the rush of peak experiences through any means possible: meditation, sex, LSD, marijuana, peyote, and other drugs. Maslow was skeptical and sometimes scornful of what he perceived as this instant self-actualization. As he had told Leary early on, "It's too easy. . . . To have a peak experience, you have to sweat" (Hoffman, 1999, p. 246).

Maslow's work also had a powerful influence on the women's movement of the 1960s, through the work of Betty Friedan. Friedan had read about Maslow's motivational hierarchy and his concept of self-actualization, and had then met and talked with him. In her book, *The Feminine Mystique* (1963), she devoted a chapter to a discussion of Maslow's work. She urged that society's emphasis on femininity thwarted women's ability to fulfill their human potential, and, noting how few women were on the list of the self-actualized, used it as a call to arms for feminists (Herman, 1995, pp. 290–292).

Maslow was now writing and publishing in a number of arenas. In 1964, he published *Religions, Values, and Peak-Experiences*, a book that echoed James's *Varieties of Religious Experience* (1902) in showing mystical experiences as natural states of consciousness typical of religious prophets and mystical seers, rather than as supernatural occurrences. Ever restless intellectually, Maslow began to view spirituality and religiosity as the next frontier for psychology, and coined the term "transpersonal psychology" for the field that would focus on them.

Although the counterculture embraced his ideas, Maslow was markedly ambivalent about the attention. He spoke and wrote about how conformity and authoritarianism discourage self-actualization, but he grew impatient and scornful of the anticonformity and antiauthoritarian diatribes of the street. He complained in his journal about feeling misunderstood by the public. The following example from Hoffman's biography is indicative (Hoffman, 1999, pp. 272–276, 284, 293). Maslow was invited to hold a seminar at Esalen, a countercultural institute in California where humanistic psychology and eastern thought were explored and discussed. What took Maslow aback was how his work on self-actualization and peak experiences seemed to have been stripped of intellectual and academic rigor. Experience was lauded at the complete expense of reason. When Maslow attempted to hold an intellectual discussion, he was ridiculed by therapist Fritz Perls, who treated Maslow like an antiquated pedant and then rolled on the floor in an infantile display. Maslow was shocked by his treatment at Esalen, and wrote bitterly of the experience in his journal (Hoffman, 1999, pp. 272–276). He later returned to Esalen, exhorting them to value reason, duty, and responsibility and not just to indulge in raw experience for its own sake (Hoffman, 1999, p. 284). Although Maslow was frustrated by Esalen and its treatment of his ideas, he nonetheless continued to be good friends with Esalen's founder, Michael Murphy, returning there a number of times and even entertaining the idea of helping to found a version of it in the eastern United States (Hoffman, 1999, p. 293).

Increasing fame brought greater numbers of honors and invitations, which, although flattering, were increasingly exhausting to Maslow. In December 1967, he suffered a major heart attack and was hospitalized. It was then that doctors found scarring on his heart that indicated he had suffered a heart attack long ago, explaining his mysterious illness of the late 1940s. For the last 2 years of his life, Maslow believed he was living on borrowed time, with every moment precious. Eager to spend his last years writing, he accepted a fellowship from the Sage Administrative Corporation in Menlo Park, California, to research and write whatever he chose for up to 4 years. He took a sick leave from Brandeis and moved with Bertha to California, where he lived for 1½ years before he died of a massive heart attack on June 8, 1970, at the age of 62.

CONCLUSION

What does one make of this complex man's life? We do not need to probe deeply to imagine at least part of the basis for his motives and accomplishments. Is it merely coincidence that a homely child who felt unloved, misunderstood, and at times humiliated by his own parents grew up to stress the importance of love and esteem in human development and mental well-being? Or that a sensitive child who felt emotionally abused by his parents grew up to emphasize the importance of physical and emotional safety? Or that a brilliant child whose parents fell far short of his parental ideal grew up to seek those ideal parents elsewhere, found them in two beloved mentors, Wertheimer and Benedict, and then tried to develop a formula for replicating them and populating the world with their like? Yet, do we then see Maslow's life as merely a purging of his own emotional demons? Surely that would be to oversimplify. He read widely in many fields, noted social and political events and injustices, thought deeply, and tried to make sense of the whole through the filter of his own life experience.

Maslow's work struck a chord that resonated with many Americans. His writings were read and talked about not only by psychologists but by a broad spectrum of the American public, including college students, business leaders, military leaders, and hippies. His work has grown less familiar to the general public today, but his theory of motivation is still taught widely in psychology, education, and business. What is the source of Maslow's lasting appeal? Perhaps it is that his theory of motivation embodies deeply felt American democratic ideals expressed in psychological terms. It is hopeful and optimistic, even utopian in its dream of an eventual Eupsychia. Given the right set of psychological and social conditions, every person among us has the potential to become happy, fulfilled, creative, emotionally whole—in Maslow's terms, self-actualized. It is the American ethos of self-improvement taken to its ultimate psychological conclusion, and it unabashedly embraces our right to life, liberty, and the pursuit of happiness.

REFERENCES

Friedan, B. (1963). *The feminine mystique.* New York: Norton.

Herman, E. (1995). *The romance of American psychology: Political culture in the age of experts.* Berkeley: University of California Press.

Hoffman, E. (1999). *The right to be human: A biography of Abraham Maslow* (Rev. ed.). New York: McGraw-Hill.

James, W. (1890). *The principles of psychology* (Vols. 1–2). New York: Henry Holt.

James, W. (1902). *The varieties of religious experience: A study in human nature.* New York: Longmans, Green.

Lowry, R. J. (1973). *A. H. Maslow: An intellectual portrait.* Monterey, CA: Brooks/Cole.

Lowry, R. J. (1979). *The journals of A. H. Maslow* (Vols. 1–2). Monterey, CA: Brooks/Cole.

Maslow, A. H. (1942). Self-esteem (dominance-feeling) and sexuality in women. *Journal of Social Psychology, 16,* 259–294.

Maslow, A. H. (1943). A theory of human motivation. *Psychological Review, 50,* 370–396.

Maslow, A. H. (1946). Problem-centering vs. means-centering in science. *Philosophy of Science, 13,* 326–331.

Maslow, A. H. (1950). Self-actualizing people: A study of psychological health. *Personality symposia: Symposium #1 on Values* (pp. 11–34). New York: Grune & Stratton.

Maslow, A. H. (1959). Cognition of Being in the peak experiences. *Journal of Genetic Psychology, 94,* 43–66.

Maslow, A. H. (1964). *Religions, values, and peak experiences.* Columbus: Ohio State University Press.

Maslow, A. H. (1965). *Eupsychian management: A journal.* Homewood, IL: R. D. Irwin.

Maslow, A. H. (1966). *The psychology of science: A reconnaissance.* New York: Harper & Row.

Maslow, A. H. (1993). *The farther reaches of human nature.* New York: Penguin. (Original work published 1971)

Maslow, A. H. (1998). *Toward a psychology of being* (3rd ed.). New York: Wiley. (Original work published 1968)

Maslow, A. H., & Mittelman, B. (1941). *Principles of abnormal psychology: The dynamics of psychic illness.* New York: Harper.

Murchison, C. (1928). *Psychologies of 1925: Powell lectures in psychological theory.* Worcester, MA: Clark University Press.

Sumner, W. G. (1906). *Folkways: A study of the sociological importance of usages, manners, customs, mores, and morals.* Boston: Ginn.

Winston, A. (1996). "As his name indicates": R. S. Woodworth's letters of reference and employment for Jewish psychologists in the 1930s. *Journal of the History of the Behavioral Sciences, 32,* 30–43.

Winston, A. (1998). "The defects of his race": E. G. Boring and antisemitism in American psychology, 1923–1953. *History of Psychology, 1,* 27–51.

Kenneth B. Clark (Photo courtesy of the Library of Congress)

Chapter 17

Kenneth B. Clark: The Complexities of Activist Psychology

John P. Jackson Jr.

Perhaps best remembered for his important work as an expert consultant for the National Association for the Advancement of Colored People—Legal Defense and Education Fund's (NAACP–LDEF) campaign against segregated schooling in the 1950s, African American social psychologist Kenneth B. Clark (1914–2005) embodied the difficulties of combining social activism with social science. Clark's career can be read as a constant negotiation of a number of dichotomies. First, Clark attempted to weave together an objective, fact-free view of science with a view of science that recognized the value-laden assumptions that informed it. Second, although Clark is often viewed as one of the preeminent voices in the 20th century for racial integration (Hentoff, 1982; Meyers & Nidiry, 2004; Roberts, 1995), his views were informed by Black Nationalism and racial separatist thought (Phillips, 2000). Finally, Clark, although constantly working for racial justice in the United States, which had to be fueled by optimism that such work made a difference, often surrendered to a deep pessimism about the permanence of racism and the impossibility of its amelioration.

BACKGROUND AND TRAINING

Clark was born in the Panama Canal Zone in 1914, and moved to New York City with his mother when he was 7 years old. Clark's mother, like millions of other Black individuals in the 1920s, was a follower of Marcus Garvey, the flamboyant Black Nationalist who taught that racial integration was impossible and that the only real solution to racial friction was complete separation of the races, ideally by the creation of a homeland for Black people on the African continent. As an adult, Clark (1943) dismissed Garveyism as "grandiose racism and ethnocentrism among members of an oppressed minority group" (p. 420), however his exposure to Garvey's ideas as a child influenced the formation of Clark's thought. Garvey's rhetoric clearly laid out how Black individuals were damaged by the White oppressor, an idea that Clark would make central to his psychological work (Scott, 1997, pp. 96–97). In addition, although Clark would often be painted as the quintessential integrationist, his writing treated Black calls for racial separation respectfully, and used the insights of Black Nationalists to inform his own work.

After he graduated from high school, Clark enrolled in the premedical program at Howard University in Washington, DC, in 1932. As the leading Black university in the United States, Howard as an institution benefited in some ways from the rampant racial discrimination in the United States. Brilliant African American scholars who were denied faculty positions at prestigious White universities often ended up on Howard's faculty (Holloway, 2002, pp. 35–83). One such scholar was the chair of the psychology department, Francis Cecil Sumner, who had been trained at Clark University by G. Stanley Hall, one of the founders of American psychology. Under Sumner's direction, Howard's psychology department was a place of rigorous and disciplined study (Sawyer, 2000). After taking Sumner's psychology course Clark later recalled that he said to himself, "To hell with medical school. This is the discipline for me" (quoted in Hentoff, 1982, p. 45). He went on to receive his bachelor's and master's degrees in psychology at Howard, under Sumner's direction, and then moved to Columbia University where he studied with Otto Klineberg (1899–1992), who had done path-breaking work discrediting any link between race and intelligence (Klineberg, 1935; Richards, 1997).

Clark also convinced his fiancé to become a psychologist. Mamie Phipps was born in 1917 in Hot Springs, Arkansas. She enrolled at Howard University at age 16, where she met Clark. Because she was interested in the psychology of children, Kenneth suggested that Mamie continue Eugene and Ruth Horowitz's work on racial identity in children (Horowitz, 1936; Horowitz & Horowitz, 1938). The work became her master's thesis at Howard, and the articles she and Clark went on to publish became some of the best known psychological studies of the 20th century.

PROJECTIVE TESTS AND RACIAL IDENTITY

In the first set of studies the Clarks published, they were interested in when children became aware of their own racial identity (Clark & Clark, 1940). When asked to identify themselves among a number of drawings, they noted that the African American children with dark complexions reasonably associated themselves with the "colored boy," as did African American children with medium complexions. However, the Clarks argued,

> There would be ... a definite incompatibility if the majority of light [African American] children identified themselves with the drawings of the colored boy, hence the persistence of their identifications with the white boy. It is obvious that these children are not identifying on the basis of "race" because "race" is a social concept which they learn at a higher stage of development. They are however, definitely identifying on the basis of their own skin color which is to them a concrete reality. (Clark & Clark, 1940, p. 168)

In 1940, a grant from the Julius Rosenwald Fund allowed Mamie Clark to enter Columbia's PhD program in psychology and gather another round of data for a second series of articles (Cross, 1991). In these studies, the Clarks were expressly interested in racial self-preference—that is, did Black children wish to be White? These studies would be heavily influenced by Kurt Lewin's theories of Jewish self-hatred. Lewin argued that in a hierarchically arranged society, some groups were dominant and some subordinate. The inhibition against individuals moving out of a subordinate group into a dominant one set up a psychological tension within the individual and could result in Jews attempting to distance themselves from all things Jewish, a phenomenon Lewin argued could be viewed as Jewish self-hatred (Lewin, 1941).

The Clarks would refashion Lewin's theory to apply self-hatred in Black individuals (Cross, 1991, pp. 28–38). The subjects of the Clarks' study were 253 Black children, 134 of which were in segregated southern schools and 119 in integrated northern schools. The children were presented with two Black dolls and two White dolls. Except for color the dolls were identical in every other way. The children were asked a series of eight questions concerning the dolls. The first four questions were designed to reveal racial preferences—"Give me the doll that you like the best" or "Give me the nice doll." The second three were designed to discover racial identification—"Give me the doll that looks like a White child," "Give me the doll that looks like a colored child," and "Give me the doll that looks like a Negro child." The final question, "Give me the doll that looks like you," was to reveal self-identification" (Clark & Clark, 1947, p. 169). The Clarks wrote that "the majority of these Negro children prefer the *white* doll and reject the colored doll" (Clark & Clark, 1947, p. 175). Two thirds of the children consistently wanted to play with the White doll and claimed that it was the "nice" doll. A concomitant percentage rejected the Black doll. The Clarks wrote that, "The importance of these results for an understanding of the origin and development of racial concepts and attitudes in Negro children cannot be minimized. Of equal significance are their implications, in the light of the results of racial identification already presented, to racial mental hygiene" (Clark & Clark, 1947, p. 175).

In a similar study, wherein children were asked to use crayons to color in drawings of a leaf, an apple, an orange, a mouse, a boy, and a girl, the Clarks found that 48% of the children colored their boy or girl brown or black, 36% chose white or yellow, and 16% chose an "irrelevant color." The Clarks interpreted the rejection of the color brown as a "fundamental conflict at the very foundations of the ego structure. . . ." of the children tested (Clark & Clark, 1950, p. 330).

The Clarks' projective tests show how they were interested in enrolling their scientific expertise in the cause of social justice. They both never surrendered their belief that science and society were intertwined and that to be a good social scientist, one had to be a social activist. Such a view was commonly held among African American social scientists at the time (Holloway, 2002; Phillips, 2000).

SCIENCE AND SOCIETY

With the entry of the United States into World War II, many social scientists looked for ways to use their expertise to aid the war effort. A key problem faced by the United States concerned what was called "morale." Morale work aimed to keep the country united behind the war effort and infuse the country with a spirit of optimism during the hardships caused by the war. Many social scientists believed that reducing problems between minority and majority groups in American society was the key to building national unity for the war effort (Capshew, 1999, pp. 116–127; Herman, 1995, pp. 48–81). In one study of morale, Clark (1942) wrote that, "In a consideration of civilian morale, it is not only pertinent but imperative that one be concerned with the racial tensions of our American society and the dynamic force of those tensions upon the attitude and behavior of Negro and white Americans" (p. 228). To ensure that morale among Black people would be high, it was necessary for governmental action to begin to tear down the barriers of segregation and discrimination. Clark (1943) argued, "The Negro's morale today is not likely to be appreciably raised by concessions made within the framework of a rigid policy of racial segregation and discrimination" (p. 226)

Such work on civilian morale was imbued with a sense of urgency after the summer of 1943, when a series of race riots swept major cities in the United States, including Detroit, Los Angeles, and New York City. In his study of the New York riot, Clark argued that the key to a rioter's behavior was the social isolation brought about by racial prejudice, which in turn led to individuals who lack any sort of empathy for other individuals or respect for private property. Ultimately these warped personalities rejected all social authority, leading to rioting. Clark and Barker (1945) concluded that "the stability of the individual and the stability of the larger society are inextricably interrelated and therefore the socially accepted dehumanization of an individual or group must inevitably manifest itself in societal disturbances" (p. 147).

In 1942, during World War II, Clark joined the faculty of the City College of New York (CCNY), the first Black on that faculty. Mamie Clark, who had received her PhD in psychology from Columbia a few years after Kenneth, faced the double hurdle of being both Black and female. Unable to find employment befitting her training, she and Kenneth opened their own clinic, the Northside Center, to provide psychological services for Harlem's children (Lal, 2002; Markowitz & Rosner, 1996). At the center's dedication Mamie Clark explained that the center would concentrate on both the "standard problems" of school children as well as the "disturbing factor" of color consciousness that "added emotional disturbance" to the life of Harlem's children ("Dedication Is Held at Harlem Center," 1946, p. 9).

BROWN V. BOARD OF EDUCATION

While Mamie ran the Northside Center, Kenneth continued to produce scientific work that documented the effects of racial prejudice on individuals. One such work was a report Clark prepared for the 1950 Mid-Century White House Conference on Children and Youth (Kerr, 1995). In this report, Clark summarized three broad trends in prejudice research: how prejudice affects the personality of the minority group members, how prejudice affects the personality of those who hold the prejudice, and an analysis of various techniques to reduce prejudice. According to Clark's report, prejudice produced "subjective feelings of inferiority, low self-esteem, ambivalent attitudes toward his own group, but also either overt or indirect hostility against both whites and Negroes" (Witmer & Kotinsky, 1952, p. 145).

On the personality of the prejudiced person, Clark relied heavily on what was then the definitive treatment of the subject: *The Authoritarian Personality* (Adorno, Frenkel-Brunswik, Levinson, & Sanford, 1950), which held that that racial prejudice was tied to a host of other personality traits that made up the "authoritarian personality." By tying racial prejudice to a more general personality type, especially such an unfavorable one, the book portrayed racial prejudice as something beyond merely irrational; racial prejudice made someone a potential fascist. In the White House Conference paper, Clark described the authoritarian personality as "an emotionally, maladjusted individual who has achieved social adjustment by taking pleasure in obedience and subordination" (Witmer & Kotinsky, 1952, p. 148). Clark concluded that, "These prejudices [of the authoritarian personality] inhibit social progress, defined in humanistic terms; they are a manifestation of men's more primitive propensities to debase and harm his fellow human beings ... and they distort, constrict, humiliate, and, in extreme cases, destroy the personalities of the victims" (quoted in Witmer & Kotinsky, 1952, p. 153).

Clark would soon get the opportunity to apply his scientific expertise against racial discrimination to testify on the harms of racial discrimination in a lawsuit designed to eliminate the legal segregation of public schools. By 1951, when the NAACP–LDEF contacted Clark, they were approaching the culmination of two decades of litigation designed to eliminate segregation in public schools. For most of the 20th century, 17 states and the District of Columbia had "Jim Crow" laws that prohibited Black and White people from sharing public facilities and accommodations. The U.S. Supreme Court had ruled in 1896 that such laws were constitutional as long as the separate facilities were equal (*Plessy v. Ferguson*, 1896). Despite the legal fiction of "separate but equal," such facilities were seldom equal, and Black citizens endured inferior facilities throughout the American South (Morris, 1984, pp. 1–39). The inequity in the two separate school systems was particularly egregious, leading to stunted economic and social opportunities for southern Black individuals (Irons, 2002; Margo, 1990; Patterson, 2001). Because the NAACP viewed education as the key to racial advancement, the legal campaign against segregation began with an attack on segregated education and, in 1951, were poised for the final push of litigation that they hoped would completely eliminate segregated education (J. P. Jackson, 2001; Tushnet, 1987).

In February 1951, Robert Carter of the NAACP–LDEF visited Clark and told him that the NAACP–LDEF was searching for information on the harms of segregation to schoolchildren. Clark gave Carter a copy of his White House Conference manuscript. A few days later Carter called Clark and exclaimed that the manuscript was "perfect" for the NAACP–LDEF. Clark later recalled that Carter asked him to do three things for the NAACP–LDEF: "(1) be a witness in the [*Brown* litigation], (2) enlist other social scientists, as prestigious as possible to testify, and (3) work directly with the NAACP lawyers in going over the briefs as they deal with the social science material. And he wanted me to get started yesterday" (quoted in Kluger, 1975, p. 321).

Clark spent the next several years working closely with the NAACP–LDEF, coordinating their efforts with those in the social scientific community who joined the fight against segregation. Among those who joined the fight were most of the researchers who had been studying race prejudice since the 1930s: Floyd Allport, Gordon Allport, Isidor Chein, Kenneth Clark, Mamie Clark, Stuart Cook, Allison Davis, Else Frenkel-Brunswik, Daniel Katz, Otto Klineberg, David Krech, Alfred McClung Lee, Gardner Murphy, Theodore Newcomb, Robert Redfield, Ira De A. Reid, Arnold Rose, Gerhart Saenger, R. Nevitt Sanford, and M. Brewster Smith. The NAACP–LDEF litigation campaign began in four different states: South Carolina, Kansas, Delaware, and Virginia, with trials at which the social scientists brought their arguments against segregation.

There were three basic arguments that the social scientific community could make as expert witnesses for the NAACP–LDEF (J. P. Jackson, 2001). First, there were no differences between the races in terms of intelligence or ability to learn, an argument that was most famously associated with Otto Klineberg, Clark's dissertation advisor at Columbia.

Second, there was a group of arguments about psychological damage that flowed from segregation. Although the Clarks' projective tests would be the most readily recognizable form of the damage argument, there was also a theoretical underpinning that came from Lewin's theories of self-hatred in groups that supported it. Although they would not be asked by the NAACP–LDEF to prove that *legally segregated education* caused psychological damage, social scientists believed for a number of reasons that they could isolate just that variable, at least in theory, as the cause of damage.

Third, there was a group of arguments advanced by the social scientists during the trial that addressed problems of desegregation. Social scientists believed desegregation could be expected to proceed smoothly, even though the South might vehemently deny that desegregation would ever be possible. The force of the law, appeals to democracy, the nature of the prejudiced personality, the nature of contact between different groups—all of these things, the social scientists could argue, meant that desegregation would indeed be possible, even in the South.

By 1952, as they expected, the NAACP–LDEF lost these trials and turned to appeal the cases to the U.S. Supreme Court. Clark, together with his colleagues Chein and Cook, wrote a "Social Science Statement" that was an appendix for the NAACP–LDEF brief and signed by 32 prominent social scientists (Appendix to Brief by Appellants, 1952). The Social Science Statement made two arguments: first, segregation was psychologically damaging both to minority and majority group children; and second, that desegregation can proceed smoothly and without trouble if it is done quickly and firmly.

For the first argument, the Social Science Statement followed the arguments that were laid out in Clark's White House paper that he had prepared 2 years before. For support it relied on the Clarks' studies using projective tests, such as those conducted by Helen Trager (who had testified at the Kansas case) and Marion Radke. It also relied on the theoretical perspectives offered by Krech and Newcomb in their textbooks on social psychology. Beyond the social psychological literature, the Social Science Statement cited the sociological works of E. Franklin Frazier and Gunnar Myrdal on the pathology of Black culture. The section on psychological damage concluded by citing a survey of social scientists that had been conducted by Chein that showed that the viewpoints in the Social Science Statement were shared by a large majority of the social science community (Appendix to Brief by Appellants, 1952, pp. 3–11).

The second argument made by the Social Science Statement was that segregation could be accomplished easily if it were so ordered by the Court. The statement cited evidence that contact between the races could lessen racial friction. Relying heavily on studies of contact in housing and employment, as well as studies of the desegregation of the military, the statement argued that, although outbreaks of violence were often predicted, in fact, few actually ever occurred.[1] The statement concluded that the Court should order desegregation quickly, firmly, and unequivocally if racial tension was to be avoided (Appendix to Brief by Appellants, 1952).

Clark's hard work appeared to pay off on May 17, 1954, when the U.S. Supreme Court decided that "to separate them from others of similar age and qualifications solely because of their race generates a feeling of inferiority as to their status in the community that may affect their hearts and minds in a way unlikely to be undone. . . . Whatever may have been the state of psychological knowledge at the time of *Plessy v. Ferguson* this finding is amply supported by modern authority" (*Brown v. Board of Education,* 1954, p. 494). Clark's Midcentury Report was the first authority quoted by the Supreme Court in support of this contention, bringing his name in front of a national audience for the first time.

For Clark, his sudden prominence was a mixed blessing. On the one hand, it led to the publication of his first book, *Prejudice and Your Child* (1955), in which he laid out his arguments for the psychological damage wrought by discrimination. However, not all commentators appreciated Clark's stances toward social activism and social science. A central criticism was that Clark had misrepresented the doll tests, because in the original studies, the Clarks had found that children in northern cities had a slightly greater preference for the White doll than southern children. The critics argued that Clark could not possibly isolate the legal segregation of the American South as the causal factor of psychological damage in Black children. Most disturbing for Clark was that these charges were not originally raised by White Southerners who were eager to maintain segregation but from supporters of the decision who claimed that the immature social sciences could not provide a firm foundation for civil rights (Cahn, 1955). Eventually, however, the criticisms of Clark's use of the doll tests became a constant theme in the White South's defense of segregation until the Civil Rights Act of 1964 brought a permanent end to legalized segregation (J. P. Jackson, 2004).

In his defense of his role in *Brown*, Clark pointed out that he had never claimed that legal segregation was the only causal factor in psychological damage (J. P. Jackson, 2001). Clark maintained that discrimination was damaging wherever it occurred, and that meant that segregated education was damaging as well. Moreover, he urged that the critics of the social scientists' role in the *Brown* decision look beyond the doll tests and to the entire body of research that had been presented to the court. Clark (1963) wrote that criticism "of the 'flimsy' nature of the scientific evidence would have to be taken more seriously" if the critics "had examined the nearly sixty references which were used as the basis for the social science brief which was submitted to the United States Supreme Court" (p. 202). However, few heeded Clark's advice, especially as subsequent

---

[1] The following year, Clark would publish a massive study of all available research on desegregation that solidified this argument (Clark, 1953).

research on the use of projective tests and racial identity increasingly questioned the Clarks' methods and interpretations (Cross, 1991).

In the 1950s, Clark's own professional organization, the American Psychological Association (APA), simply ignored his efforts to make psychology relevant to the larger society (Benjamin & Crouse, 2002). Clark himself became a symbol in the growing civil rights movement, a role he had never sought and accepted only with some reluctance (Keppel, 2002). Writing to a friend in 1955, Clark confided that he was tired of talking about segregation and "would much prefer to escape into my first love of studying the effects of attitudes on memory," which was the topic of his PhD dissertation in 1940. Clark told his friend that, "Every now and then I am obsessed with the idea that it is a tragic waste of time . . . we have to spend so much [time] discussing a problem that should be so clear to reasonable men" (quoted in J. P. Jackson, 2001, p. 210).

THE COLLAPSE OF THE INTEGRATIONIST ETHIC

In the wake of the *Brown v. Board of Education* decision in 1954, Black people began demanding their rights as guaranteed by the U.S. Constitution. In the mid-1950s, Black people in several southern American cities boycotted bus systems, demanding seating on a nonsegregated basis. The most famous, the Montgomery bus boycott begun in 1955, lasted more than a year and thrust a young Baptist minister, Martin Luther King Jr., into the national spotlight, transforming him into the spokesperson for the civil rights movement. But the civil rights movement went far beyond King. In 1957, in Little Rock, Arkansas, nine Black high school students braved mobs of angry White protesters and attended the previously all-White Central High School. In 1960, a group of college students in Greensboro, North Carolina, quietly sat at a lunch counter, protesting the fact that it was still segregated, and setting off a wave of "sit-ins" at lunch counters all over the South. At the same time, Black and White "Freedom Riders" traveled on busses throughout the South, where local authorities refused to protect them, and in many cases encouraged local White citizens to attack them. In 1962, James Meredith, a Black man, attempted to enroll at the University of Mississippi, sparking a riot that left three dead and hundreds injured. Many in the United States recoiled in horror at the television images of White, southern police forces turning fire hoses and police dogs on peaceful marchers, many of them children, in places like Birmingham, Alabama (Branch, 1988; Morris, 1984).

The culmination of the civil rights movement was the 1964 Civil Rights Act, which finally solidified the constitutional guarantees promised in *Brown* (Klarman, 2004). But on the eve of this great victory a series of violent uprisings swept cities that never suffered under the segregation laws of the South. This unexpected violence led to new thinking about race relations. Much of the thinking about race since World War II seemed naive, confused, or just plain wrong

(W. A. Jackson, 1990). Scholars in the United States began describing race relations as "internal colonialism." As unwilling immigrants to the United States, Black individuals lived in colonies within the United States. Many American scholars began studying race relations from a new perspective that grew out of the anticolonial movement. The traditional colonial order was based on an inequitable distribution of power and wealth. The colony existed only to provide resources for the mother country, whether in the form of natural resources, agricultural products, or cheap labor. Activist Stokely Carmichael and political scientists Charles Hamilton, in their manifesto, *Black Power* (1967), argued that assimilation was dangerous because it would wipe out Black culture. "The fact is that integration, as traditionally articulated, would abolish the black community. The fact is that what must be abolished is not the black community, but the dependent colonial status that has been inflicted upon it" (p. 55). Being Black became a source of pride and strength, and the idea that Black people should somehow submerge their Black identity to join White culture became repellent to many (Pellar, 1991; Steinberg, 1995).

Clark, who had been one of the most visible proponents of racial integration, could have been left behind once the integrationist consensus collapsed in the mid-1960s, especially because Clark's career had been built around the idea that Black individuals had been psychologically damaged by racial oppression, an idea that became anathema in the new political times. However, whereas Clark's activities in the 1960s can be seen as a direct outgrowth of his work in *Brown*, he also adopted his arguments to take into account the new thinking about the proper relationship between the races in the United States. Clark was a friend with both the integrationist Martin Luther King Jr. and the Black Nationalist Malcolm X; he interviewed both men on public television (Clark, 1988). As someone who understood both positions, Clark could meld them into his own stance on racial oppression and Black identity in the 1960s (Keppel, 1995).

Clark was one of the first scholars to present race relations in the colonial metaphor in a book, and its origins was one of Clark's most public failures: the Harlem Youth Unlimited (HARYOU) project. HARYOU began in 1961 when the Clarks, representing the Northside Center's board, launched a social outreach program to bring job training, an arts and culture program, and a number of educational programs to Harlem. Clark wrote an ambitious prospective for a much bigger program as a way of joining the project to President Lyndon Johnson's War on Poverty (HARYOU, 1964). However, Clark lost control of the project when Rep. Adam Clayton Powell seized control of the federal funding and Clark was relegated to figurehead status (Keppel, 1995).

After resigning from HARYOU in 1964, Clark reworked the project's blueprint into his book *Dark Ghetto* (1965), in which Clark argued that the bare "*facts* of the ghetto are not necessarily synonymous with the *truth* of the ghetto" (1965, xxiii). Clark (1965) wrote, "To obtain the truth of Harlem one must *interpret* the facts" (p. xxiii). Clark vividly portrayed Harlem as a true internal colony of the White United States. White power structures had systematically looted the Black ghetto, profiting from its social isolation from the larger society. "When tumult arose in ghetto streets in the summer of 1964, most of the stores broken into and looted belonged to white men," Clark (1965) noted, "Many of these owners responded . . . with bewilderment and anger. . . . They did not realize that the residents were . . . bitter, as natives often feel toward the functionaries of a colonial power who, in the very act of service, keep the hated structure of oppression intact" (p. 28). Yet even while embracing the colonial metaphor of the Black Nationalists, Clark (1965) rejected what he called their "strategy of alienation," which he argued was the "most desperate" strategy because "those who follow it admit their total loss of confidence in the possibilities of democracy" (p. 221). The only real possibility, Clark (1965) maintained, was that "White and Negro must fight together. . . . Negroes will not break out of the barriers of the ghetto unless whites transcend the barriers of their own minds. . . . The poetic irony of American race relations is that the rejected Negro must somehow also find the strength to free the privileged white" (p. 240).

CONCLUSION

The 1970s brought professional recognition to Clark. He became the first African American president of the APA, received the APA's Gold Medal Award for his work, and was appointed to the New York Board of Regents (Keppel, 1995, p. 172). However, controversy continued to follow Clark as he struggled to balance his roles as scientist and activist. Throughout the 1950s and 1960s, Clark had maintained that social scientists' role in society was simply that of providing facts to democratic institutions. Clark (1960) wrote, "Whatever power social scientists have, is secondary and ancillary, derived through the sufferance or request of those who control the power in society. Social scientists do not establish policy or make definitive decisions on crucial social issues" (p. 2).

The increasingly bleak tone of Clark's writing in the 1960s reflected his increasing despair that he was losing the fight against the disease of racism. In 1968, after the assassination of his friend Martin Luther King Jr., he told an interviewer that he felt that, "The involvement in social action and social change that have dominated my life add up to one big failure. I fear the disease has metastasized" (quoted in Hall, 1968, p. 21).

Perhaps it was this despair that led Clark to abandon the idea that social scientists should only be fact providers to those in power. In his Presidential Address to the APA in 1971, Clark (1974) openly called for what he called the "psychotechnical intervention" by social scientists to repress people's antisocial behaviors and enhance good social behaviors. Clark argued that "with the mobilization of scientific personnel, financial resources, and research facilities, it is now possible—as it is imperative—to reduce human anxieties, tensions, hostilities, violence, cruelty, and the destructive power irrationalities which are the basis of wars" (p. 174). Clark's stark call for the use of drugs and behavior modification to control the populace was controversial, to say the least, but was perhaps fueled by Clark's deepening pessimism about the efficacy of traditional methods to bring about a racially just world. Into the 1980s, his despair grew even more palpable. In 1989 he could "look back and shudder at how naive we all were in our belief in the steady progress racial minorities would make through programs of litigation and education. . . . I am forced to recognize that my life has, in fact, been a series of glorious defeats" (Clark, 1993, p. 18).

Yet, many psychologists and social activists do not share Clark's assessment of his own career. African American psychologists, and many others, continue to look to Clark for inspiration. A recent volume celebrating his life and work concluded that Clark "has had the unique opportunity to shape a decisive turning point in American history, an honor justified by his wise vision of democracy and equality for all. But the page he helped open for us all remains to be written" (Philogéne, 2004, p. 16). When Clark passed away in 2005, his death made national headlines. The tragedy of Clark's life is that racism, oppression, and discrimination are still deeply imbedded in American society. The hope is that he pointed the way toward a solution to these deeply imbedded social problems.

REFERENCES

Adorno, T. W., Frenkel-Brunswick, E., Levinson, D., & Sanford, R. N. (1950). *The authoritarian personality*. New York: Harper & Row.

Appendix to Brief for Appellants: The Effects of Segregation and the Consequences of Desegregation—A Social Science Statement. (1952). In P. B. Kurland & G. Casper (Eds.), *Landmark briefs and arguments of the Supreme Court of the United States: Constitutional Law* (pp. 43–61). Arlington, VA: University Publications of America.

Benjamin, L. T., & Crouse, E. M. (2002). The American Psychological Association's response to *Brown v. Board of Education*. (1954). 347 U.S. 483.

Branch, T. (1988). *Parting the waters: America in the King years, 1954–1963*. New York: Simon & Schuster.

Cahn, E. (1955). Jurisprudence. *New York University Law Review, 30*, 150–169.

Capshew, J. H. (1999). *Psychology on the march: Science, practice, and professional identity in America, 1929–1969*. Cambridge, England: Cambridge University Press.

Carmichael, S., & Hamilton, C. V. (1967). *Black power: The politics of liberation in America*. New York: Random House.

Clark, K. B. (1942). Morale among Negroes. In G. Watson (Ed.), *Civilian morale: Second yearbook of the Society for the Psychological Study of Social Issues* (pp. 228–248). Boston: Houghton Mifflin.

Clark, K. B. (1943). Morale of the Negro on the home front: World Wars I and II. *Journal of Negro Education, 12*, 417–428.

Clark, K. B. (1953). Desegregation: An appraisal of the evidence. *Journal of Social Issues, 9*, 1–77.

Clark, K. B. (1955). *Prejudice and your child*. Boston: Beacon Press.

Clark, K. B. (1960). Desegregation: The role of the social sciences. *Teachers College Record, 62*, 1–17.

Clark, K. B. (1963). *Prejudice and your child*. (Rev. ed.) Boston: Beacon Press.

Clark, K. B. (1965). *Dark ghetto: Dilemmas of social power.* New York: Harper & Row.

Clark, K. B. (1974). *Pathos of power.* New York: Harper & Row.

Clark, K. B. (1988). *King, Malcolm, Baldwin: Three interviews with Kenneth B. Clark.* Middletown, CT: Wesleyan University Press.

Clark, K. B. (1993). Racial progress and retreat: A personal memoir. In H. Hill & J. E. Jones (Eds.), *Race in America: The struggle for equality* (pp. 3–18). Madison: University of Wisconsin Press.

Clark, K. B., & Clark, M. P. (1940). Skin color as a factor in racial identification of Negro preschool children. *Journal of Social Psychology, 11,* 159–169.

Clark, K. B., & Barker, J. (1945). The zoot effect in personality: A race riot participant. *Journal of Abnormal and Social Psychology, 40,* 143–147.

Clark, K. B., & Clark, M. P. (1947). Racial identification and preferences in Negro children. In T. M. Newcomb & E. L. Hartley (Eds.), *Readings in social psychology* (pp. 169–178). New York: Holt.

Clark, K. B., & Clark, M. P. (1950). Emotional factors in racial identification and preference in Negro children. *Journal of Negro Education, 19,* 341–350.

Cross, W. E. (1991). *Shades of black: Diversity in African-American identity.* Philadelphia: Temple University Press.

Dedication is held at Harlem Center. (1946, March 2). *New York Times,* p. 9.

Hall, M. H. (1968, June). A conversation with Kenneth B. Clark. *Psychology Today, 2,* 19–25.

Harlem Youth Unlimited Project. (1964). *Youth in the ghetto: A study of the consequences of powerlessness and a blueprint for change.* New York: Author.

Hentoff, N. (1982). The integrationist. *New Yorker, 58,* 37–73.

Herman, E. (1995). *The romance of psychology: Political culture in the age of experts.* Berkeley: University of California Press.

Holloway, J. S. (2002). *Confronting the veil: Abram Harris Jr., E. Franklin Frazier, and Ralph Bunche, 1919–1941.* Chapel Hill: University of North Carolina Press.

Horowitz, E. L. (1936). The development of attitude toward the Negro. *Archives of Psychology, 28,* 1–45.

Horowitz, E. L., & Horowitz, R. E. (1938). Development of social attitudes in children. *Sociometry, 1,* 301–338.

Irons, P. (2002). *Jim Crow's children: The broken promise of the Brown decision.* New York: Viking.

Jackson, J. P., Jr. (2001). *Social scientists for social justice: Making the case against segregation.* New York: New York University Press.

Jackson, J. P., Jr. (2004). The scientific attack on *Brown v. Board of Education,* 1954–1964. *American Psychologist, 59,* 530–537.

Jackson, W. A. (1990). *Gunnar Myrdal and America's conscience: Social engineering and racial liberalism, 1938–1987.* Chapel Hill: University of North Carolina Press.

Keppel, B. (1995). *The work of democracy: Ralph Bunche, Kenneth B. Clark, Lorraine Hansberry, and the cultural politics of race.* Cambridge, MA: Harvard University Press.

Keppel, B. (2002). Kenneth B. Clark in the patterns of American culture. *American Psychologist, 57,* 29–37.

Kerr, C. (1995). Race and the making of American liberalism, 1912–1965. *Dissertation Abstracts International,* A57/01, 417.

Klarman, M. J. (2004). *From Jim Crow to civil rights: The Supreme Court and the struggle for racial equality.* New York: Oxford University Press.

Klineberg, O. (1935). *Race differences.* New York: Harper.

Kluger, R. (1975). *Simple justice: The history of* Brown v. Board of Education *and Black America's struggle for equality.* New York: Vintage Books.

Lal, S. (2002). Giving children security: Mamie Phipps Clark and the racialization of child psychology. *American Psychology, 57,* 20–28.

Lewin, K. (1941). Self-hatred among Jews. *Contemporary Jewish Record, 4,* 219–232.

Margo, R. A. (1990). *Race and schooling in the south, 1880–1950: An economic history.* Chicago: University of Chicago Press.

Markowitz, G., & Rosner, D. (1996). *Children, race, and power: Kenneth and Mamie Clark's Northside Center.* Charlottesville: University Press of Virginia.

Meyers, M., & Nidiry, J. P. (2004). Kenneth Bancroft Clark: The uppity Negro integrationist. *Antioch Review, 62,* 265–274.

Morris, A. D. (1984). *The origins of the civil rights movement: Black communities organizing for change.* New York: Free Press.

Patterson, J. T. (2001). Brown v. Board of Education: *A civil rights milestone and its troubled legacy.* New York: Oxford University Press.

Pellar, G. (1991). Race against integration. *Tikkun, 6,* 54–66.

Phillips, L. (2000). Recontextualizing Kenneth B. Clark: An Afrocentric perspective on the paradoxical legacy of a model psychologist–activist. *History of Psychology, 3,* 142–167.

Philogéne, G. (2004). Introduction: Visions of democracy and equality. In G. Philogéne (Ed.), *Racial identity in context: The legacy of Kenneth B. Clark* (pp. 15–16). Washington, DC: American Psychological Association.

Plessy v. Ferguson. (1896). 183 U.S. 537.

Richards, G. (1997). *"Race," racism and psychology: Towards a reflexive history.* London: Routledge.

Roberts, S. (1995, May 7). An integrationist to this day: Believing all else has failed. *New York Times,* p. E7.

Sawyer, T. F. (2000). Francis Cecil Sumner: His views and influence on African American higher education. *History of Psychology, 3,* 122–141.

Scott, D. M. (1997). *Contempt and pity: Social policy and the image of the damaged Black psyche, 1880–1996.* Chapel Hill: University of North Carolina Press.

Steinberg, S. (1995). *Turning back: The retreat from racial justice in American thought and policy.* Boston: Beacon Press.

Tushnet, M. V. (1987). *The NAACP's legal strategy against segregated education, 1925–1950.* Chapel Hill: University of North Carolina Press.

Witmer, H. L., & Kotinsky, R. (Eds.). (1952). *Personality in the making: The fact-finding report of the Midcentury White House Conference on Children and Youth.* New York: Harper.

Index

Numbers in italics refer to listings in reference sections.